There are three ways to do things: the
right way, the wrong way, and my way.

Hay tres maneras de hacer las cosas:
la correcta, la incorrecta y la mía.

Esta edición está dedicada a mi padre, que llegó por primera vez a Ibiza en 1958 en una goleta vela cangreja de dos mástiles y 26 metros llamada "Tuluaq". En aquellos tiempos había pocos extranjeros y todos tenían algún apodo, el de mi papá era "George, el danés". Tenía amigos actores, escritores o artistas, entre ellos Jon Pertwee, Terry Thomas, Nina & Frederik van Pallandt, Denholm Elliot, Clifford Irving y Elmyr d'Hory, el gran falsificador. Todos eran renegados e Ibiza era su refugio. Mi padre conoció aquí a mi madre, "Bella", y vivía en la ciudad de Ibiza, en Sa Penya, hacía cerámica y tocaba la guitarra en las fiestas a las que iban todos. Eran tiempos idílicos antes de que el turismo de masas sumergiera la isla.

This Edition is dedicated to my dad who arrived in Ibiza in 1958, on a two-masted 84 ft Gaff Rigg schooner named "*Tuluaq*" (illustrated above). There were few foreigners in those days and all had nick-names. My dad was called "Danish George". Amongst his friends were artists, writers and actors such as Jon Pertwee, Terry Thomas, Nina & Frederik van Pallandt, Denholm Elliot, Clifford Irving and Elmyr d'Hory, the great art forger. They were all renegades of some sort and Ibiza was their refuge. My dad met my mum here, "Belle" and she lived in Sa Penya in Ibiza Town making pottery and playing Spanish guitar at every party she went to. They were idyllic times before mass tourism engulfed the island.

Published by Hjordis Fogelberg

First edition. 2014
Second edition (revised and enlarged) 2016

Concept by Hjordis Fogelberg
Written and created by Hjordis Fogelberg
hjordis@myibiza-guide.com

Written by Hjordis Fogelberg and most of text edited by Ruby Warrington
First Edition: Translated and edited by Sally Riera and María Jesús Zafra "Chus"
Second Edition changes: Translated by María Jesús Zafra "Chus"
Design and layout by Hjordis Fogelberg

ISBN: 978-84-608-7433-1

Printed in Spain at Jiménez Godoy S.A. Depósito Legal MU-764-2011

MY IBIZA

& Formentera 2017-18

by Hjordis Fogelberg

written with
heaps of love and, of course,
from my own point
of view...

escrito con mucho cariño
y desde mi punto de vista,
naturalmente...

AND SO...
THE ADVENTURE
BEGINS:

HOW TO USE THIS GUIDE BOOK

THIS GUIDE STARTS IN IBIZA TOWN, THEN GOES TO THE OUTSKIRTS OF TOWN, THEN CLOCKWISE AROUND THE ISLAND, INLAND AND ENDING WITH FORMENTERÁ

ESTA GUÍA EMPIEZA EN IBIZA CIUDAD, SIGUE HACIA LAS AFUERAS DE LA CIUDAD, LUEGO EN EL SENTIDO DEL RELOJ ALREDEDOR DE LA ISLA, EL INTERIOR Y TERMINANDO CON FORMENTERA

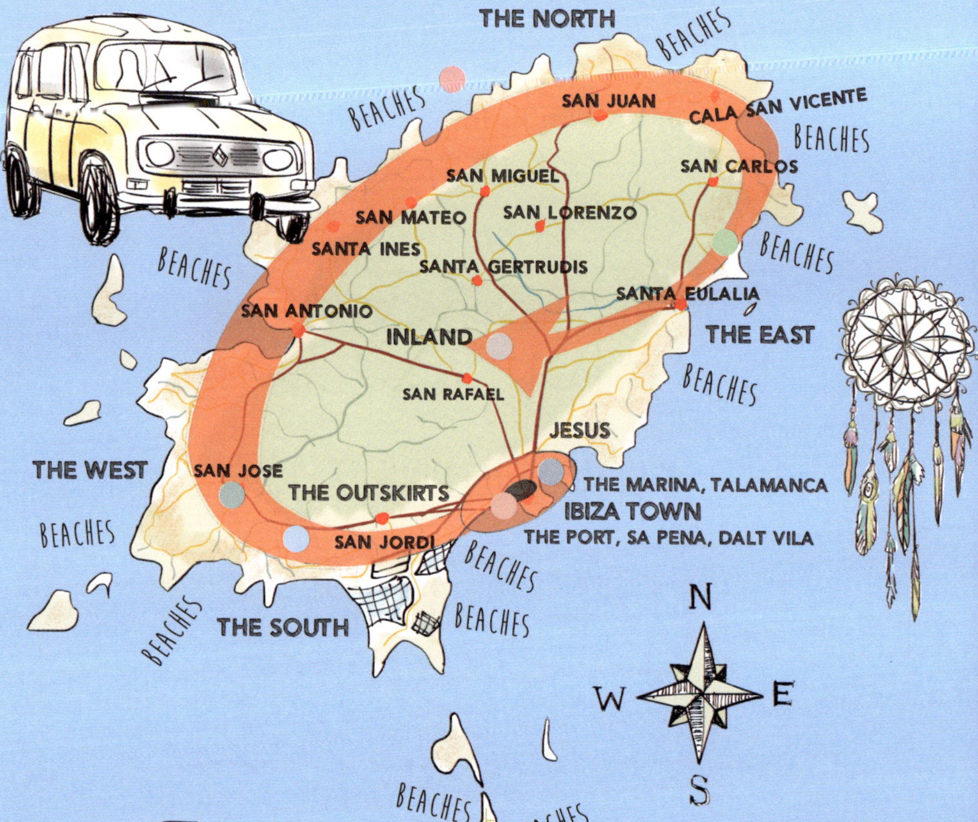

FORMENTERA

FORMENTERA STARTS IN LA SAVINA PORT, HEADING SOUTH AND ENDING UP WITH THE BEACHES

FORMENTERA EMPIEZA CON EL PUERTO DE LA SAVINA, DIRECCIÓN SUR Y ACABANDO CON LAS PLAYAS

CONTENTS

DISCOVER

CONTENIDOS

SPAIN´S FINEST GIN
orange peel
pimientos de padrón
ibiza sea salt
common juniper berries
lemon peel
cucumber
prickly pear
phoenician juniper
LAW
PREMIUM DRY GIN
handcrafted small batches
44%
70cl
HIGO CHUMBO • PIMIENTO DE PADRÓN • SEMILLAS DE CILANTRO
www.law-gin.com
100% MADE IN IBIZA
USING NATURAL BOTANICALS FROM THE ISLAND
"8 AWARDS IN INTERNATIONAL COMPETITIONS IN 2016"
"BEST GIN DISTILLERY OF SPAIN" (New York Spirits Competition)

A BIT ABOUT MYSELF AND THIS GUIDE

Three years ago I published the 1st Edition of this Guide Book. I had no idea what to expect, I thought I might get laughed at and I expected a lot of criticism. None of which happened. All I received back was kind and positive messages.
It was a wonderful feeling to be understood. I just wanted to do something different that I felt was missing on the island, a tool for new comers and residents. I was tired of the commercial side of the island, the mass advertising and club publicity everywhere (of which I was part, of course).
I never expected the positive reaction I received, and to this day I still feel so much appreciation from readers worldwide.

This edition is a revised, corrected and partly changed version of the first published in 2014. To my surprise, a lot has changed in the last two years, new places opening and others closing. I have done my best to be as accurate as possible.An index has been added and a few things that I felt were necessary after helpful feedback from my readers.
For those of you that did not purchase the first edition, here is the Forward from it, which explains who I am.

My parents arrived here with the first wave of hippies in the early 1960s and never left. For me, summer meant running around barefoot from May until September, my skin would turn a deep golden brown and my hair would bleach white in the sun. As kids, we spent hours catching crabs in the rock pools of our local beach cove, and feeding lizards at our suntrap house in Talamanca.

My teenage years coincided with the burgeoning party scene on the island, with the famous 'trance' parties. I would ride my beat-up old moped everywhere, down dusty tracks with my heels in my bag just in case there happened to be a fancy party somewhere...

I waitressed my summers away to pay for graphic design studies during the winter in the UK. By my late twenties I had created album covers for the music of Mike Oldfield and SNAP, before returning to Ibiza and setting up my own design agency, Blue Cactus, and starting on iconic club artwork for Manumission and Space.

The launch of *Pacha Magazine*, where I was cofounder and Art Director, turned into a landmark event in Ibiza publishing, starting a trend for club-sponsored magazines.

After the birth of my daughter 15 years ago, my priorities shifted and my needs changed, and I couldn't help noticing that the scope of the island's tourist community seemed to be narrowing.
Visitors to the island tend to become engulfed in the billboard and advertising culture, and miss out on so much of the alternative and exciting aspects on offer in Ibiza and Formentera.

The islands can be affordable, even in the era of beach butlers and private jets. It's a great place to go off the beaten track, and as an islander I know that some of the best bars or restaurants will never be advertised.

So this guide is a personal collection of recommendations gathered over the years through trial and error, offering an insight into a diverse island that is hard to explore fully in a short visit. I hope it helps you and is a useful discovery tool so you get the best out of your holiday in Ibiza and Formentera.

I would like to add that any mistakes are unintentional, and I appreciate good feedback for the next edition being sent to me at:

hjordis@myibiza-guide.com

ATZARÓ
beach cala nova
Arroces y Pescados
OPEN ALL YEAR
Fish & Paella
Atzaró Beach – Cala Nova Beach, Es Canar. Santa Eulália – Tel. +34 971 078 228 – www.atzaro.com

UN POCO SOBRE MÍ Y ESTA GUÍA

Hace ya trés años desde que publiqué la primera edición de esta Guía. No sabía qué esperar, tuve miedo, pensé que a lo mejor la gente se reiría de mí y estaba preparada para las críticas.
No pasó nada de eso. Sólo recibí reacciones y mensajes positivos.
Fue una sensación maravillosa saber que los lectores entendían lo que yo estaba haciendo. Quise hacer algo diferente, algo que faltaba en la isla, una herramienta para los recién llegados pero también para residentes. Estaba cansada del lado tan comercial de la isla, la publicidad masiva de discotecas en todas partes...
Nunca me esperé la reacción que recibí, y hasta el día de hoy siento mucho aprecio por parte de mis lectores.

Esta edición que tienes en tus manos es la versión revisada, corregida y en parte cambiada de la primera edición. Sorprendentemente muchas cosas han cambiado en dos años, han abierto nuevos sitios y otros han cerrado. He añadido un índice al final que era necesario y un par de cosas más después de los consejos tan útiles que me han mandado los lectores. Para aquellos que no compraron la primera edición, a continuación está la misma introducción que explica quién soy.

Mis padres llegaron a Ibiza con la primera ola de hippies, a principios de los años 60, y decidieron quedarse aquí a vivir. Yo me pasaba los veranos descalza, mi piel se doraba y mi pelo se desteñía por el sol. De niños, pasábamos horas cogiendo cangrejos en las rocas de una calita cercana y dando de comer a las lagartijas en nuestra casa en Talamanca.

Mi adolescencia coincidió con el boom de fiestas en la isla, con las raves en el campo y las after-parties. Solía ir a todas partes en mi mobilette destartalada, bajando por caminos de tierra con los tacones en el bolso por si había alguna fiesta chula por el camino.

Trabajé de camarera durante años para pagarme mis estudios de diseño gráfico en el Reino Unido en invierno. Rozando los treinta ya había creado carátulas de discos para Mike Oldfield y SNAP, antes de regresar a Ibiza y montar mi propia agencia de diseño "Blue Cactus", donde empecé a diseñar los legendarios carteles para Manumission y Space.
El lanzamiento de la Revista Pacha, de la que fui co-fundadora y Directora Artística, marcó un hito en las publicaciones de Ibiza y empezó la moda de revistas patrocinadas por discotecas que continúa hasta hoy.

Después del nacimiento de mi hija, hace 15 años, mis prioridades y necesidades cambiaron, me di cuenta que en la isla faltaban otras ofertas turísticas.
Los visitantes de la isla tienden a ser engullidos por una cultura de carteles y vallas publicitarias, y suelen perderse muchas de las emocionantes alternativas que ofrecen las islas.

Las islas pueden ser asequibles, incluso en esta era de mayordomos de playa y jets privados. Es un lugar magnífico para salir de la rutina, y como isleña sé que muchos de los mejores bares y restaurantes nunca se darán a conocer.

Así que esta guía es una colección personal de mis recomendaciones, recogidas a base de años de probar y conocer, ofreciendo una percepción de una isla diversa que es difícil de explorar plenamente en una visita corta. Espero que esta guía te ayude y que sea práctica para que puedas sacar el mejor partido a tus vacaciones en Ibiza y Formentera.

Me gustaría añadir que cualquier error en la guía no ha sido intencionado y apreciaría que me enviarais vuestros comentarios para futuro contenido a:

hjordis@myibiza-guide.com

DAY & DINNER
BEACHOUSE
PLAYA DEN BOSSA BEACH
beachouseibiza.com • info@beachouseibiza.com
T: +34 971 39 68 58

MY IBIZA AND FORMENTERA

BUCKET LIST

- [x] BUY A "MY IBIZA" GUIDE FOR A FRIEND
- [ ] TAKE A FERRY TO FORMENTERA FOR THE DAY (PG. 17)
- [ ] GO TO THE DRUMMING AT BENIRASS ON SUNDAYS (PG. 176)
- [ ] JUMP OVER FIRE AT THE SAN JUAN FESTIVAL IN JUNE (PG. 24)
- [ ] SPOT THE FLAMINGOES ON SALINAS SALT FLATS (PG. 121)
- [ ] TAPAS AT BAR COSTA IN SANTA GERTRUDIS (PG. 225)
- [ ] WALK DOWN TO ATLANTIS (PG. 131)
- [ ] LUNCH AND SWIM AT CALA ESCONDIDA (PG. 138)
- [ ] SUNSET AT HOSTAL LA TORRE (PG. 160)
- [ ] PAELLA AT CAN SALINAS (PG. 123)
- [ ] LAS DALIAS HIPPY MARKET (PG. 218)
- [ ] TASTE A GREEN BEAST COCKTAIL AT BAR 1805 (PG. 65)
- [ ] GO TP FORMENTERA AND RENT A MEHARI (PG. 256)

AIRPORT INFO/Aeropuerto de Ibiza: Tel: 913.211.000 - 902.404.704

GETTING HERE BY AIR
LLEGAR POR AIRE

Arriving at Ibiza airport, you feel the buzz as soon as you get off the plane. An array of all sorts stand at the arrival gate awaiting their loved ones, and there's always at least one barefoot man with dreadlocks holding up a name card reading "YOGA CAMP". My friend Ben Turner calls them "the great unwashed", but actually, they always have that golden, sun-kissed skin that glows. Time as you know it immediately slows down by at least 20%, and as you walk through to the taxi rank, chances are you're already being told the plans for the evening ahead, which usually involves a party or a BBQ at a villa somewhere on the island. It's what I call coming home.

Al llegar al aeropuerto de Ibiza sientes la agitación nada más bajarte del avión. Una variedad de personajes esperan a sus seres queridos en la puerta de llegadas, y siempre hay al menos un hippie con pies descalzos y rastas con una señal que dice "CAMPAMENTO DE YOGA". Mi amigo Ben Turner los llama "¡los grandes desaliñados!". Pero en realidad, siempre tienen ese brillo dorado en la piel.
El tiempo tal y como lo conoces inmediatamente se ralentiza un 20% y mientras esperas en la cola de los taxis, lo más probable es que ya tengas los planes hechos para esa misma noche, que normalmente incluyen una fiesta o barbacoa en una casa en algún rincón de la isla. Eso es lo que yo llamo llegar a casa.

THE AIRPORT * EL AEROPUERTO

Nearly 7km southwest of Ibiza town, 5,726,581 people flew into Ibiza in 2013. But I can still remember as a child waiting for friends to arrive at the little wooden gates of the old airport, now the VIP airport for private jets.

Casi a 7km al sur de Ibiza ciudad, 5.726.581 personas volaron a la isla en 2013. Pero todavía puedo recordar cuando esperaba a amigos que llegaban atravesando las pequeñas puertas de madera del viejo aeropuerto, que ahora es el aeropuerto VIP para los jets privados.

Flight information / Información vuelos: **Tel: 971.809.000**
Luggage / Equipaje: **Tel: 971.809.277**

AIRLINES * LÍNEAS AÉREAS

- **Iberia/Air Nostrum. Tel: 902.400.500 - iberia.com**
- **Air Europa Tel: 902.401.501 - aireuropa.com**
- **Vueling. Tel: 807.200.100 - vueling.com**
- **British Airways. Tel: 902 .111.333 - britishairways.com**
- **Air Berlin. Tel: 902.116.402 - airberlin.com**
- **Thomson Airways. Tel: 971.398.309 - thomsonfly.com**

PARKING * APARCAMIENTO

Parking at the airport costs roughly 0.02 euros a minute, around 14.50 euros per day. Loss of the ticket will set you back 72.50 euros.

El aparcamiento del aeropuerto cuesta unos 0,02 euros por minuto, unos 14,50 euros por día. Si pierdes el ticket tendrás que pagar 72,50 euros.

DISABLED ACCESS * ACCESO DISCAPACITADOS

The airport has easy access for disabled passengers, with 3 lifts, digital numbering in Braille, differentiated surfaces on all pavements throughout the premises and adapted telephones and toilets. In fact, all public toilets in the terminal have disabled facilities and the same goes for the new parking block for hired cars.

El aeropuerto tiene fácil acceso para pasajeros discapacitados, con 3 ascensores, numeración digital en Braille, superficies diferenciadas en todos los suelos de todas las distintas zonas y teléfonos y baños adaptados. De hecho, todos los baños públicos de la terminal tienen instalaciones para discapacitados, al igual que el bloque de aparcamiento de los coches de alquiler.

PRIVATE JET * JETS PRIVADOS

Ibiza airport now has three different private jet terminals (FBOs), which look after private jet travel 24 hours a day. Last year there were 7,734 private flights in and out of Ibiza.
London to Ibiza takes roughly 3 hours and Barcelona to Ibiza takes 1 hour.
Fancy splashing out? Here are a few of the jet aircraft charter agencies available on the island:

El aeropuerto de Ibiza ahora tiene tres terminales diferentes para jets privados, que se encargan de los vuelos privados las 24 horas. El año pasado aterrizaron unos 7.734 jets privados en Ibiza.
De Londres a Ibiza la duración estimada de vuelo es de 3 horas y de Barcelona a Ibiza una hora.
Éstas son algunas de las agencias en Ibiza:

Tel: 932.202.025 - ibizajetcharter.com
Tel: 971.317.967 - 608.684.925. ibizaviparea.net
Tel: 911.146.562 - privatefly.com
Tel: 608.959.256 - genieibiza.com

✱ TAXIS

The taxi rank just outside the entrance to the airport gets very busy in high summer, so I tell friends to pre-book from Radio Taxi de San José. A number worth saving - this taxi service is available 24-7 to take you across the island!.
They charge € 20 to €40 to travel between cities.
La parada de taxi a la salida al aeropuerto se llena en verano, así que dile a tus amigos que te vengan a buscar o reserva un taxi a través de Radio Taxi de San José. Un número que deberías guardarte, ya que el servicio de taxis está disponible todos los días las 24 horas. Cobran entre 20€ y 40€ el desplazamiento entre municipios.

Sms Taxis: txt Ibiza taxi - sms 60300
Taxi Aeropuerto: 971.395.481
Radio Taxi Ibiza Tel: 971.307.000 / 971.398.483
Radio Taxi San José Tel: 971.398.340
Taxi Parada Santa Eulalia Tel: 971.333.033
Radio Taxi Ibiza San Antonio
Tels: 971.343.764 / 971.340.074
Radio Taxi Formentera Tel: 971.322.342

BUSES ✱ AUTOBUSES

There are bus stops all over Ibiza and timetables vary monthly. There is a bus stop infront of the airport. Number 10 goes into Ibiza town every 20 minutes.
Hay autobuses por toda la isla. Desde el aeropuerto puedes tomar la Línea 10 hasta Ibiza centro que sale cada 20 minutos.

ibizabus.com soloibiza.com

GETTING HERE BY SEA
LLEGAR POR MAR

In close proximity to mainland Spain, there are plenty of opportunities to reach Ibiza by ferry, a good option if you're afraid of flying.
Regular ferries run between mainland Spain (Barcelona, Valencia and Dénia) and Ibiza, which means at least one ferry every day in the summer. The super fast boat will take you from Dénia to Ibiza in just about two hours and from Valencia to Ibiza in about three hours.
The journey from Barcelona is a longer, but it's generally overnight which means a chance to rest if you've driven from somewhere else in Europe. Baleària's new high-speed route also connects Barcelona and Ibiza in four hours.
Arriving by ferry brings you directly into the port of Ibiza or San Antonio. From here it's easy to grab a taxi or a bus to your final destination.

Al estar cerca de la península, hay muchas opciones para llegar a Ibiza en barco, una buena opción especialmente si te da miedo volar.
Hay ferries entre la península (Barcelona, Valencia y Denia) e Ibiza al menos una vez al día en verano. Los barcos súper rápidos de Denia a Ibiza sólo tardan dos horas y desde Valencia a Ibiza tres horas. El trayecto desde Barcelona es más largo pero generalmente es por la noche, lo que te da la oportunidad de descansar si has estado conduciendo desde algún punto de Europa.
La nueva ruta rápida de Baleària también conecta Barcelona e Ibiza en cuatro horas.
El ferry te trae directamente al puerto de Ibiza (Eivissa) o de San Antonio (Sant Antoni). Desde aquí es fácil coger un taxi o un autobús a tu destino final.

IBIZA <> FORMENTERA <> IBIZA

Formentera island is half an hour by ferry from the port of Ibiza, the terminal is on the left as you drive into Ibiza Town. There are a selection of companies at your disposal and ferries leave every half an hour throughout the summer.
La isla de Formentera se encuentra a media hora en ferry desde el puerto de Ibiza, que está a la izquierda justo cuando entras en Ibiza ciudad. Hay una selección de compañías a tu disposición y los ferries salen cada media hora durante todo el verano.

FERRY TERMINAL / ESTACIÓN MARÍTIMA IBIZA
Tels: 971.310.711 - 902.314.433

FERRY TERMINAL / ESTACIÓN MARÍTIMA
Formentera, Puerto de La Savina
Tel: 971.323.107

FERRY COMPANIES / COMPAÑÍAS DE FERRYS

- **Iscomar**
Tel: 902.119.128
iscomar.com
iscomarferrys.com

- **Acciona**
Trasmediterránea
Tels: 971.313.413 - 902.454.645
trasmediterranea.es

- **Baleària**
Tels: 971.314.005 - 902.160.180
balearia.com

- **Mediterránea Pitiusa**
Tel: 971.322.443
mediterraneapitiusa.com

- **Trasmapi FAST ferry**
Ibiza - Formentera - Ibiza
Tel: 971.314.486
trasmapi.com/umafisa

la belle ibiza
FRENCH KITCHEN

IMPORTANT NUMBERS
NÚMEROS IMPORTANTES

+34 BEFORE NUMBER WHEN RINGING FROM ABROAD.
+34 ANTES DEL NÚMERO CUANDO LLAMES DESDE EL EXTRANJERO.

EMERGENCIES / EMERGENCIA	112
FIREMEN / BOMBEROS	971.313.030

POLICE / POLICÍA	091
POLICÍA NACIONAL	971.398.831
LOCAL POLICE / POLÍCIA LOCAL	092
LP. SAN ANTONIO	971.340.830
LP. SANTA EULALIA	971.330.841
LP. SAN JOSE	971.800.261
LP. FORMENTERA	971.322.087

CIVIL GUARD / GUARDIA CIVIL

GC. IBIZA	971.301.100
GC. SAN ANTONIO	971.340.502
GC. SANTA EULALIA	971.330.227
GC. SAN JUAN	971.333.005
GC. IBIZA-EIVISSA	971.398.831
GC. FORMENTERA	971.322.022

CITIZENS ASSISTANCE OFFICE
OFICINA ATENCIÓN CIUDADANO 900.713.878

GESA ELECTRICAL (BREAKDOWNS)
GESA (AVERÍAS) 902.534.902

AMBULANCE / IBISALUD	061

HOSPITALS / CENTROS SANITARIOS

CLÍNICA DEL ROSARIO	971.301.916
HOSPITAL CAN MISSES	971.397.000
RED CROSS / CRUZ ROJA	971.390.303
HOSPITAL FORMENTERA	971.321.212

SERVICES / SERVICIOS

ROAD TEST (MOT)	971.195.906
INSPECCIÓN TÉCNICA(ITV)	971.195.906
WATER (BREAKDOWNS)	902.136.013
AQUALIA (AVERÍAS)	902.136.013

TOWN HALLS / AYUNTAMIENTOS

IBIZA / EIVISSA	971.397.500
SAN ANTONIO	971.340.111
SANTA EULALIA	971.332.800
SAN JOSÉ	971.800.125
SAN JUAN	971.333.003
FORMENTERA	971.321.087

ROAD ASSISTANCE	971 39 59 00
GRÚAS IBIZA	971 39 59 00

A BRIEF HISTORY OF IBIZA (Eivissa)

The Carthaginians discovered Ibiza in 654 B.C. and founded Ibiza Town, making this one of the earliest towns in Europe. These guys were merchants and traders, and Ibiza became an important trading centre due to the 'White Gold' – salt – they found here.

Ibiza also played an important role in Carthaginian culture as one of their largest burial ground and amongst their religious icons, the Goddess Tanit is perhaps most famous. She is the Mother of the Gods, the Goddess of the Earth and of fertility, and still a potent figurehead for Ibiza today.

The Romans came along in 123 B.C, and although Ibiza was not made part of their Empire, evidence of their occupation can still be seen by the gates at the entrance to Dalt Vila (the Old Town), where there are two copies of Roman statues, and in Santa Eulalia, where the old Roman bridge crosses the now mostly dried-up river at the entrance to the town.

The 5th to the 9th century A.D. was the time of the Goths and Visigoths in Europe, a dark age, about which there is little historical record. But then the Arabs arrived on Ibiza, and stayed for almost 500 years. Their influence can still be felt strongly in some of the houses, traditional costumes and musical instruments, and of course in the island dialect, 'Ibicenco'.

When the Catalans invaded on August 8th 1235, they tore down the Muslim mosque and built the present day Cathedral on its foundations. The villages of the island were renamed after Christian saints, and several churches were constructed. The medieval festival held every year on the second Friday in May gives you an idea of how they lived here almost a thousand years ago!
The Catalans' rule was also marked by marauding corsairs. In order to defend themselves, the villagers built churches with fortified walls, which often had cannons on their roofs.
Watchtowers lining the coast, some of which can still be seen today, were built a bit later. Originally, each of these towers was within sight of the next one and in the event of an invasion the guard would light a warning fire, which could be seen by the next in line, which in turn lit its own fire, and so on, until the entire island was aware of the danger.

And to this day, Ibiza continues to be taken over by people of many different cultures, who descend on the island each year. Of course, the locals have been used to this type of behaviour for thousands of years – only now they have found a way to capitalize on it!

UNA BREVE HISTORIA DE IBIZA (Eivissa)

Los cartagineses descubrieron Ibiza en 654 A.C. y fundaron Ibiza ciudad, convirtiéndola en una de las primeras ciudades de Europa. Esta civilización era de mercantes y comerciantes e Ibiza se convirtió en un importante centro de comercio debido al 'Oro Blanco', o sal, que encontraron aquí.

Ibiza también jugó un papel importante en la cultura cartaginesa como su cementerio más extenso, y entre sus iconos religiosos, la Diosa Tanit quizá sea la más famosa. Ella es la Madre de los Dioses, La Diosa de la Tierra y de la Fertilidad y hoy en día sigue siendo una figura relevante en Ibiza.

Los romanos llegaron en el año 123 A.C. y aunque Ibiza no formó parte de su Imperio, la evidencia de su ocupación todavía se aprecia en la puerta de entrada a Dalt Vila (el Casco Antiguo), donde hay dos ejemplares de estatuas romanas; y en Santa Eulalia, donde el viejo puente romano cruza el río seco a la entrada del pueblo.

Los siglos V y IX D.C. fueron la época de los godos y visigodos en Europa, la Edad Media, de la cual se cuenta con escasa documentación histórica. Pero entonces llegaron los árabes a Ibiza y permanecieron casi 500 años. Su influencia todavía puede apreciarse en algunas de las casas, trajes tradicionales e instrumentos musicales y por supuesto en el dialecto de la isla: el ibicenco.

Cuando los catalanes invadieron la isla el 8 de agosto de 1235, destruyeron la mezquita árabe y construyeron la catedral que existe hoy en día en sus cimientos. Los pueblos de la isla fueron rebautizados con nombres de santos cristianos y entonces se construyeron muchas de sus iglesias. El festival medieval que se celebra cada año el segundo viernes de mayo te da una idea de cómo vivían hace más de 1000 años.

El reino catalán se vio marcado por los saqueos de piratas. Para poder defenderse, los pueblerinos construyeron iglesias con muros extra-fortificados que a menudo tenían cañones en sus tejados.
Las torres de vigía que rodean la costa, algunas de ellas todavía pueden apreciarse hoy en día, fueron construidas un poco más tarde. Originalmente, cada una de estas torres estaba a la vista de la siguiente y en caso de invasión se encendía una hoguera como señal de alarma en la torre, que podía ser vista desde la siguiente, que a su vez encendía una hoguera y así hasta que la isla entera estuviera al tanto del peligro.

Ibiza continúa siendo invadida por gente de diferentes culturas hoy en día que descienden a la isla cada año. Por supuesto, la gente local está acostumbrada a este tipo de comportamiento desde hace miles de años, ¡aunque ahora han encontrado una forma de capitalizarlo!

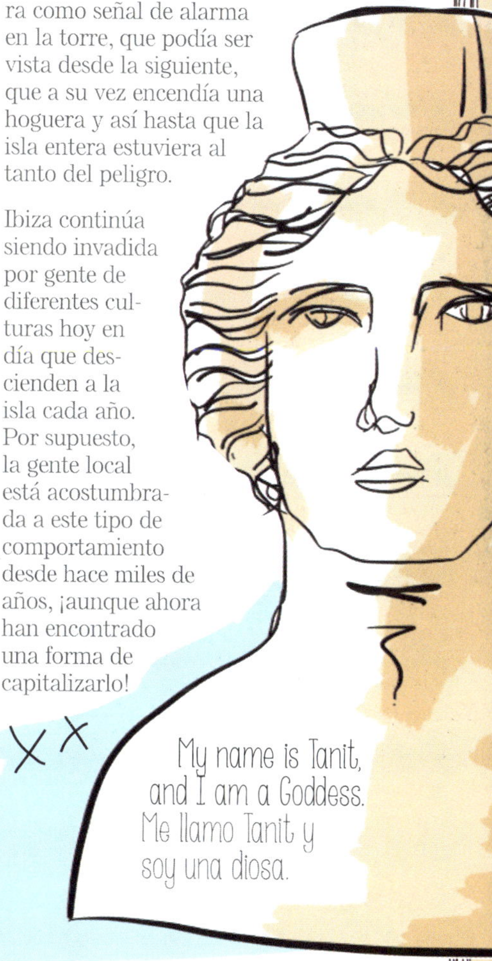

Essential Ibiza Is
The Ultimate Guide
From People That Live
And Breathe The Island.
• Most Comprehensive Island News Resource
• Information As It Happens
• VIP Club & Beach Club Tables
• Club & Boat Party Tickets
• Concierge
• Villa & Hotel Bookings
• Boat Charter
• Car Hire

essential
ibiza.com

AGENDA

For club info, check the posters that are up everywhere or go online at:
Para información sobre las discotecas, hay posters por toda la isla o mira online:

- pacha.com
- amnesia.es
- privilegeibiza.com
- lioibiza.com
- spaceibiza.com
- ibizarocks.com
- cocoon.net
- ushuaiaibiza.com
- thezooproject.com
- sankeysibiza.info
- dc10-ibiza.ibiza-clubs.net
- heartibiza.com

POPULAR PARTIES, EVENTS AND MARKETS ON IBIZA
FIESTAS POPULARES, EVENTOS Y MERCADILLOS

THINGS THAT ARE WORTH GOING TO + COSAS QUE MERECEN LA PENA HACER.

MAY-MAYO

- **Las Dalias: Hippy Market/Mercadillo:** Saturdays/sábados, 10-22hrs. lasdalias.es
- **Cala Llenya Market/Rastrillo Cala Llenya:** Sundays/domingos, 9-15hrs.
- **Sant Jordi Market/Mercadillo:** Saturdays/sábados, 9-22hrs.
- **Medieval Festival Ibiza:** Dalt Vila Ibiza. medieval-festival-ibiza.ibiza4all.org
- **International Music Summit (IMS) Finale Dalt Vila.** *internationalmusicsummit.com*
- **Circo Loco Opening Party at DC10.** End May/final mayo. *circolocoibiza.com*
- **Flower Power at Pacha.** Mondays/lunes. *flowerpowerpacha.com*
- **Ibiza Rocks Live Gigs.** Check line-ups at/ver bandas: *ibizarocks.com*
- **Mercat de Forada, Bar Can Tixedo, Buscastell, San Antonio:** Saturdays/sábados, 10hrs.

JUNE-JUNIO

- **Summer Solstice, San Juan/Noche de San Juan, San Juan.** 23-24.
- **Flower Power at Pacha.** Mondays/lunes. *flowerpowerpacha.com*
- **Ibiza Rocks Live Gigs.** Check line-ups at/ver bandas: *ibizarocks.com*
- **Las Dalias: Hippy Market/Mercadillo:** Saturdays/sábados, 10-22hrs. lasdalias.es
- **Cala Llenya Market/Rastrillo Cala Llenya:** Sundays/domingos, 9-15hrs.
- **Sant Jordi Market/Mercadillo:** Saturdays/sábados, 9-22hrs.
- **Las Dalias Wax Da Jam:** Wednesdays/miercoles. lasdalias.es
- **Namaste Las Dalias:** Wednesdays/miércoles. lasdalias.es
- **Mercat de Forada, Can Tixedo Bar, Buscastell.** Saturdays/sábados, 10hrs.
- **Drumming in Benirras Beach/Tambores en Benirras.** Sundays/domingos. 19-23:30hrs.

JULY-JULIO

- **Las Dalias: Hippy Market/Mercadillo:** Saturdays/sábados, 10-22hrs. lasdalias.es
- **Las Dalias Night Market:** Mondays + Tuesdays/lunes y martes. 19-01hrs. lasdalias.es
- **Cala Llenya Market/Rastrillo Cala Llenya:** Sundays/domingos, 9-15hrs.
- **Sant Jordi Market/Mercadillo:** Saturdays/sábados, 9-22hrs.
- **Namaste Las Dalias:** Wednesdays/miércoles. lasdalias.es
- **Atzaro Fashion Festival:** Yearly event in July/evento anual en Atzaro. atzaro.com
- **Ibiza Rocks Live Gigs.** Check line-ups at/ver bandas: *ibizarocks.com*
- **Flower Power at Pacha.** Mondays/lunes. *flowerpowerpacha.com*
- **Drumming in Benirras Beach/Tambores en Benirras.** Sundays/domingos. 19-23:30hrs
- **Mercat de Forada, Can Tixedo Bar, Buscastell.** Saturdays/sábados, 10hrs.

AUGUST-AGOSTO

- **Las Dalias: Hippy Market/Mercadillo:** Saturdays/sábados, 10-22hrs. lasdalias.es
- **Las Dalias Night Market:** Mondays + Tuesdays/lunes y martes. 19-01hrs. lasdalias.es
- **Cala Llenya Market/Rastrillo Cala Llenya:** Sundays/domingos, 9-15hrs.
- **Sant Jordi Market/Mercadillo:** Saturdays/sábados, 9-22hrs.
- **Namaste Las Dalias:** Wednesdays/Miercoles. lasdalias.es
- **Atzaro Art, Westbank Gallery & Montana Gallery.** Info: atzaro.com
- **Saint Ciriac Fiestas, Ibiza.** 8. Fireworks at midnight/Fuegos artificiales a medianoche.
- **St Bartholomew Fiestas, Sant Antoni.** 24. Traditional dancing, fireworks and a walk to the Holy Cave/Música tradicional, baile, fuegos artificiales y caminata a las cuevas.
- **Ibiza Rocks Live Gigs.** Check line-ups at/ver bandas: *ibizarocks.com*
- **Flower Power at Pacha.** Mondays/lunes. *flowerpowerpacha.com*
- **Drumming in Benirras Beach/Tambores en Benirras.** Sundays/domingos. 19-23:30hrs
- **Mercat de Forada, Can Tixedo Bar, Buscastell.** Saturdays/sábados, 10hrs.

SEPTEMBER-SEPTIEMBRE

- **Las Dalias: Hippy Market/Mercadillo:** Saturdays/sábados, 10-22hrs. lasdalias.es
- **Las Dalias Night Market:** Mondays + Tuesdays/lunes y martes. 19-01hrs. lasdalias.es
- **Cala Llenya Market/Rastrillo Cala Llenya:** Sundays/domingos, 9-15hrs.
- **Sant Jordi Market/Mercadillo:** Saturdays/sábados, 9h-22hrs.
- **Flower Power at Pacha.** Mondays/lunes. *flowerpowerpacha.com*
- **Namaste Las Dalias:** Wednesdays/miércoles. lasdalias.es
- **Drumming in Benirras Beach/Tambores en Benirras.** Sundays/domingos. 19-23:30hrs
- **Mercat de Forada, Can Tixedo Bar, Buscastell.** Saturdays/sábados, 10hrs.
- **Village Fest, San Miguel/Fiesta Patronal de Sant Miquel.** 29.

OCTOBER-OCTUBRE

- **Halloween.** bambuddha.com, ibizarockshouse.com, sankeysibiza.info, boutiquehostalsalinas.com
- **Las Dalias: Hippy Market/Mercadillo:** Saturdays/sábados, 10-22hrs. lasdalias.es
- **Las Dalias Night Market:** Mondays + Tuesdays/lunes y martes. 19-01hrs. lasdalias.es
- **Cala Llenya Market/Rastrillo Cala Llenya:** Sundays/domingos, 9-15hrs.
- **Mercat de Forada, Can Tixedo Bar, Buscastell.** Saturdays/sábados, 10hrs.
- **Sant Jordi Market/Mercadillo:** Saturdays/sábados, 9-22hrs.

NOVEMBER-NOVIEMBRE

- **Las Dalias: Hippy Market/Mercadillo:** Saturdays/sábados, 10-22hrs. lasdalias.es
- **Cala Llenya Market/Rastrillo Cala Llenya:** Sundays/domingos, 9-15hrs.
- **Mercat de Forada, Can Tixedo Bar, Buscastell.** Saturdays/sábados, 10hrs.
- **Sant Jordi Market/Mercadillo:** Saturdays/sábados, 9-22hrs.

DECEMBER-DICIEMBRE

- **Las Dalias: Christmas Hippy Market/Mercadillo de navidad:** lasdalias.es
- **Cala Llenya Market/Rastrillo Cala Llenya:** Sundays/domingos, 9-15hrs.
- **Mercat de Forada, Can Tixedo Bar, Buscastell.** Saturdays/sábados, 10hrs.
- **Sant Jordi Market/Mercadillo:** Saturdays/sábados, 9-22hrs.

JANUARY-ENERO

- **Las Dalias Hippie Market:** Every Saturday: lasdalias.es lasdalias.es
- **Cala Llenya Market/Rastrillo Cala Llenya:** Sundays/domingos, 9-15hrs.
- **Mercat de Forada, Can Tixedo Bar, Buscastell.** Saturdays/sábados, 10hrs.
- **Sant Jordi Market/Mercadillo:** Saturdays/sábados, 9-22hrs.

FEBUARY-FEBRERO

- **Pintxa, San Antonio**: Mid febuary - mid March/med febrero-med marzo. Tapas + caña.
- **Cala Llenya Market/Rastrillo Cala Llenya:** Sundays/domingos, 9-15hrs.
- **Mercat de Forada, Can Tixedo Bar, Buscastell.** Saturdays/sábados, 10hrs.
- **Sant Jordi Market/Mercadillo:** Saturdays/sábados, 9-22hrs.

MARCH-MARZO

- **Pintxa, San Antonio**: Mid febuary-mid March/med febrero-med marzo. Tapas + caña.
- **Easter Procession, Ibiza + Santa Eulalia**: End March/Final marzo.
- **Flower Power, Sant Josép:** Street party/fiesta en la calle.
- **Fira des Gerret, Santa Eularia.** 1st weekend in March/1er fin de semana en marzo.
- **Atzaro Spring Opening Party**: atzaro.es
- **Bambuddha Summer Opening Party**: bambuddha.com
- **Cala Llenya Market/Rastrillo Cala Llenya:** Sundays/domingos, 9-15hrs.
- **Mercat de Forada, Can Tixedo Bar, Buscastell.** Saturdays/sábados, 10hrs.
- **Sant Jordi Market/Mercadillo:** Saturdays/sábados, 9-22hrs.

TICKETS

I LOVE YOU TO THE MOON AND BACK

NEW — FULL

FULL MOON CALENDAR

Plenilunio

CALENDARIO LUNAR

2017

10 **MAY** MAYO
FLOWER FLORES

9 **JUNE** JUNIO
STRAWBERRY FRESA

9 **JULY** JULIO
THUNDER CIERVO

7 **AUGUST** AGOSTO
STURGEON ESTURIÓN

6 **SEPTEMBER** SEPTIEMBRE
HARVEST COSECHA

16 **OCTOBER** OCTUBRE
HUNTERS CAZADOR

14 **NOVEMBER** NOVIEMBRE
BEAVER CASTOR

14 **DECEMBER** DICIEMBRE
COLD FRÍA

SOLAR ECLIPSE 21 AUGUST

2018

2 **JANUARY** ENERO
WOLF LOBO

11 **FEBUARY** FEBRERO
SNOW NIEVE

2 **MARCH** MARZO
WORM GUSANO

30 **APRIL** ABRIL
PINK ROSADA

29 **MAY** MAYO
FLOWER FLORES

28 **JUNE** JUNIO
STRAWBERRY FRESA

27 **JULY** JULIO
THUNDER CIERVO

26 **AUGUST** AGOSTO
STURGEON ESTURIÓN

25 **SEPTEMBER** SEPTIEMBRE
HARVEST COSECHA

LUNAR ECLIPSE 31 JANUARY + 27 JULY

5 THINGS YOU SHOULD DO
5 COSAS QUE DEBERÍAS HACER CUANDO ESTÉS AQUÍ

1. Have breakfast at Croissant Show (p.58)
Desayunar en el Croissant Show

2. Shop your Boho Ibiza look at Ganesha (p.47)
Hacer compras Bohemias en Ganesha

3. Have tapas at Can Terra (p.40)
Ir de tapas a Can Terra

4. "Moules et frites" in Bar 1805 (p.65)
Mejillones y patatas fritas en Bar 1805

5. Walk up to Dalt Villa for a "Farm to Table" dinning experience at El Portalón (p.71)
Subir a Dalt Vila y cenar en El Portalón

IBIZA TOWN, DALT VILA, THE PORT & Sa Penya

Ibiza, Dalt Vila,
El Puerto y Sa Penya.

Gigglewater
"SUMMER STARTS HERE!"
PROSECCO D.O.C + FRIZZANTE SECCO
FRIZZANTE SECCO
Giggle Water
Secco
VINO BIANCO FRIZZANTE
GIGGLEWATER: 1920'S TERM FOR ALC BEVERAGE
1920'S TERM FOR ALC BEVERAGE
GIGGLEWATER
PROSECCO
D.O.C.
MADE IN ITALY
AVAILABLE FROM:
WWW.CHAMPAGNESOLUTIONS.ES
INFO@CHAMPAGNESOLUTIONS.ES
WWW.GIGGLEWATERWINES.COM

IBIZA TOWN CENTRE

EL CENTRO DE IBIZA CIUDAD

UNESCO World Heritage Site.
I feel so proud that my little island hosts a world-class marina, and sometimes it's easy to forget the history of Ibiza's ancient fishing quarter, 'La Penya'. But in fact the town centre remains architecturally true to its old self. The cobbled back streets offer a labyrinth of restaurants, local shops and boutiques, as does the walled Old Town within Dalt Vila. Over the years, I've spent countless nights drinking and catching up with friends before heading out to the clubs. But the views from the top of Dalt Vila make an equally lovely walk at dusk.

Patrimonio de la Humanidad por la UNESCO. Estoy orgullosa de que mi pequeña isla albergue esta marina de primera categoría; a veces es fácil olvidarse de la historia del antiguo puerto de pescadores de Ibiza, "Sa Penya". Pero de hecho, el centro de la ciudad preserva su arquitectura antigua. Las callejuelas empedradas te ofrecen un laberinto de restaurantes y tiendas, al igual que la ciudad amurallada de Dalt Vila. He pasado noches en el centro de copas antes de ir de discotecas. Pero al anochecer, las preciosas vistas desde lo alto de Dalt Vila te invitan a dar un bonito paseo.

C. DE CARLES III
C. DE PERE FRANCÉS
AV. IGNASI WALLIS
C. DE MADRID
C. DE FELIPE II
C. DE GASPAR PUIG
C. DE CARLOS V
AV. D'ISIDOR MACABICH
AV. BARTOMEU DE ROSELLÓ
C. VICENTE CUERVO
C. DE PERE DE PORTUGAL
C. DEL BISBE HUIX
C. JOAN D'AUSTRIA
C. DE CASSTELLA
C. DE CATALUNYA
AV. BARTOMEU VICENT RAMÓN
C. D'ARRAGÓ
PASSEIG VARA DE REY
C. DEL LLEÓ
AV. ESPANYA
C. CAYETANO SOLER
VÍA PÚNICA
C. JAUME 1
VÍA ROMANA
64
31
24
23
18
48
33
47
22
60
42
59
19
63
61
62
8
57
58
53
55
56
51
52
54

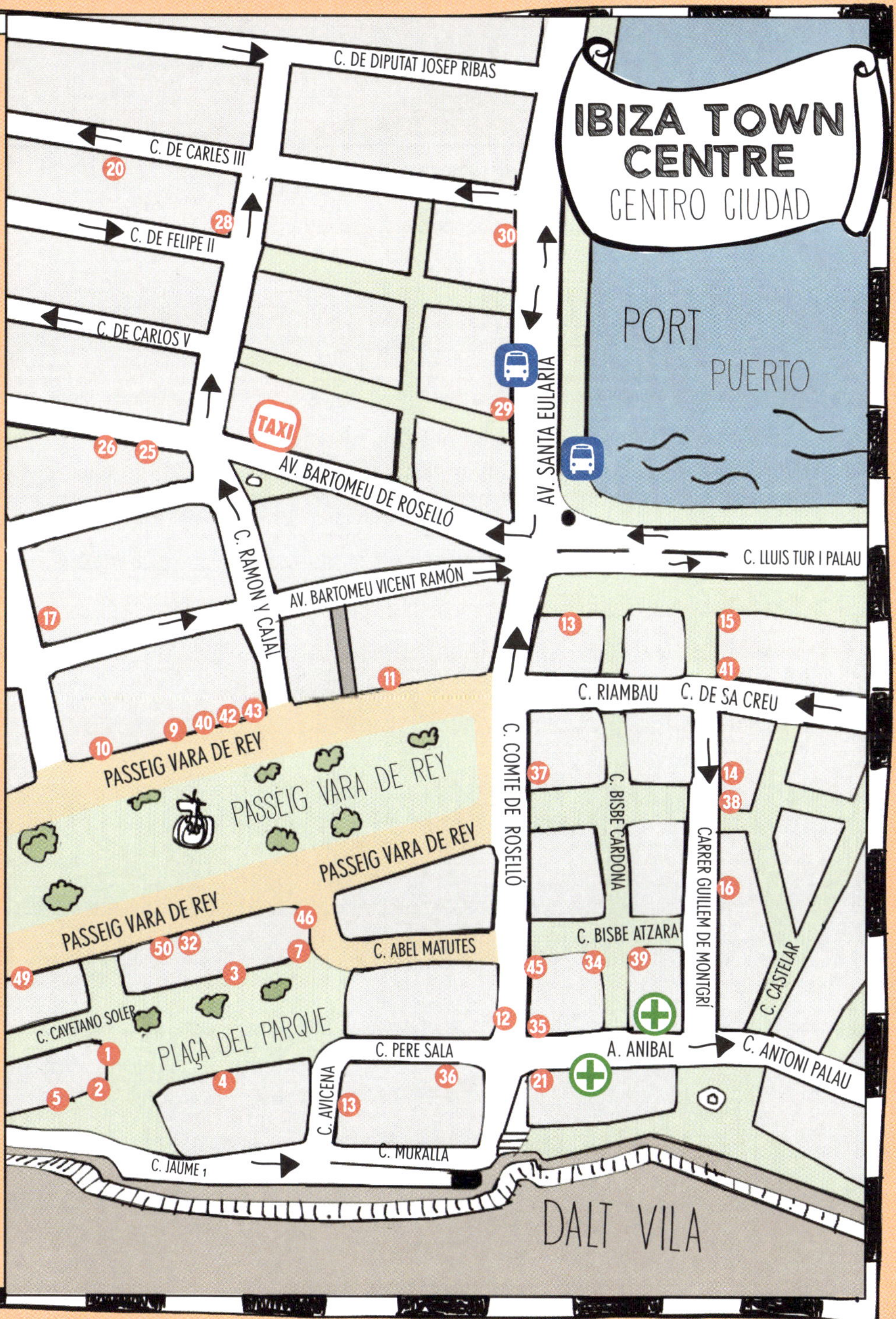
IBIZA TOWN CENTRE
CENTRO CIUDAD
PORT
PUERTO
C. DE DIPUTAT JOSEP RIBAS
C. DE CARLES III
C. DE FELIPE II
C. DE CARLOS V
TAXI
AV. BARTOMEU DE ROSELLÓ
AV. SANTA EULARIA
C. LLUIS TUR I PALAU
C. RAMON Y CAJAL
AV. BARTOMEU VICENT RAMÓN
C. RIAMBAU
C. DE SA CREU
C. COMTE DE ROSELLÓ
C. BISBE CARDONA
CARRER GUILLEM DE MONTGRÍ
C. CASTELAR
PASSEIG VARA DE REY
C. BISBE ATZARA
C. ABEL MATUTES
C. CAYETANO SOLER
PLAÇA DEL PARQUE
C. PERE SALA
A. ANIBAL
C. ANTONI PALAU
C. AVICENA
C. MURALLA
C. JAUME 1
DALT VILA
1
2
3
4
5
7
9
10
11
12
13
14
15
16
17
20
21
25
26
28
29
30
32
34
35
36
37
38
39
40
41
42
43
45
46
49
50

EAT, DRINK, SHOP AND SLEEP IN THE CENTRE...
...COME, BEBE, COMPRA Y DUERME EN EL CENTRO

1 Hostal Parque

Plaça del Parc, 4, Ibiza
Tel: 971.301.358.
hostalparque.com

A hostal and restaurant all in one that is in prime position on the Plaza del Parque. I often have bacon and eggs here on my way to work or order their Vitello Tonato for lunch.

Hostal y restaurante todo en uno y en un lugar privilegiado en la Plaza del Parque. A menudo desayuno huevos con beicon aquí de camino al trabajo o un Vitello Tonato al mediodía.

2 El Patio de Los Pasajeros

C/ de Jaume 1, Ibiza

This is a tiny urban tapas joint just off Plaza del Parque facing the old town walls, Great value and celebrity chef Sid Shanti recommends the breadcrumbed fried aubergine.

Un pequeño bar de tapas urbano muy animado al lado del Hostal Plaza del Parque. Buen precio y las tapas aquí están para morirse; Sid Shanti recomienda las berenjenas empanadas.

3 Café Madagascar

Plaça del Parc, 4, Ibiza
Tel: 971.555.555
ibizacafemada.com

Funnily enough even though this place has been here for years, I have only really started going in the last year. It's open late in the summer so it's the perfect place for a night cap and it's packed all day and night due to its relaxed island vibe. I've never tried the food though…

Curiosamente, y a pesar de que este lugar ha estado aquí durante años, sólo he empezado a ir aquí este último año. Está abierto hasta tarde en el verano, así que es el lugar perfecto para la última copa de la noche. Está lleno día y noche debido a su ambiente y buen servicio, aunque nunca he probado la comida...

4 Locals Only

Plaça del Parc, 5, Ibiza
Tel: 971.301.997
localsonlyibiza.com

Tito runs this fab restaurant serving delicious home cooked Italian mediterranean food. It is all absolutely yummy and they do a lunch menú for a set price. In the summer the terrace is a perfect place to sit and watch the world go by and of course the locals! Love it!

Tito dirige este fabuloso restaurante que sirve una comida casera italiana y mediterránea riquísima. Todo está delicioso y también tienen menú del día. En verano la terraza es un lugar perfecto para sentarte y ver el mundo pasar. ¡Me encanta!

5 Out of Time People

C/ Jaume, 2, Ibiza
Tel: 971.392.321

Great for when you need a vitamin fix, this café serves super-healthy raw food, vegan choices, salads and juices. Their little terrace facing the old town walls is

PARKING TIP
CONSEJOS PARKING

FREE PARKING AND A NICE BOAT RIDE

Ok, so drive to the end of Marina Botafoch and park your car near El Corso Hotel, or Talamanca beach area. The taxi boat is just in front of El Corso Hotel, costs a few euros and goes across to Ibiza town and back all day every 20 minutes, via Lío Club on the way.

APARCAR GRATIS Y TOMAR EL BARCO

Conduce hasta Marina Botafoch y aparca tu coche frente al Hotel El Corso, o por la zona de Talamanca. Luego coge el barquito que sale en frente del Hotel Corso. El barco cruza la bahía hasta la ciudad de Ibiza y de vuelta. Cuesta unos pocos euros y funciona todo el día cada 20 mins. Se para en Lío Club de camino.

1 h = 1 €

PARKING MACHINES METHOD:
Type in: numberplate + time.
PARQUÍMETRO: Matrícula + tiempo.
App: Elparking

lovely and they also have a great selection of books inside on spirituality.
Genial para cuando necesitas una dosis de comida cruda porque esta cafetería sirve comida sana, vegana, ensaladas y zumos. Su pequeña terraza encarada a las murallas antiguas es muy acogedora y tiene una magnífica selección de libros espirituales.

7 Herry's Bar

Plaça del Parque 2, Ibiza

My mum likes to sit here when she's in town. It's worthy of mention as it was the first bar to open on the square. It used to be a barber's shop.
Lovely to sit and watch the world go by from one of its little tables outside, and it is considered to be one of the less roudy of the places on this square.
A mi madre le gusta sentarse aquí cuando está en la ciudad. Es digno de mención ya que fue la primera cafetería que abrió en la plaza y antes fué una barbería.
Es muy agradable ver pasar el mundo desde una de sus mesitas afuera y es considerado como uno de los menos ruidosa de los que están en esta plaza.

8 La Bufalina

Passeig de Vara de Rey, 13, Ibiza
Tel: 971.302.894
labufalina.es

I eat here often because it's right next to my office and the people who run it are always nice and friendly, and such hard workers. Their pizzas are fantastic, and you can sit and watch the guy spinning the dough around. My favourite topping has to be the zucchini and ricotta cheese with rocket sprinkled over the top. They can be a bit slow if you order a freshly made pizza.
Como aquí a menudo ya que está junto a mi oficina y la gente que lo dirige es muy simpática, amable y muy trabajadora. Y sus pizzas también son fantásticas, y puedes sentarte y ver cómo el pizzero le da vueltas a la masa. Mi favorita es la de calabacín con queso ricotta y rúcula por encima. Pueden tardar bastante si pides una pizza fresca que no está en la barra.

9 Gelato Ibiza

Passeig de Vara de Rey, 12, Ibiza
Tel: 971.931.133

A lovely ice cream parlour facing the main square in town. They sell home-made high quality deliciousness although not cheap and they also do ice-creams in traditional pudding flavours such as the "Flao" that are eally worth trying!.
Una buena heladaría en la plaza central. Hacen helados italianos artesanales de alta calidad pero no son baratos. Tienen sabores locales como el del flaó (postre local), ¡que merece la pena probar!

10 Can Alfredo

Paseeig de Vara de Rey, 16, Ibiza
Tel: 971.311.274
canalfredo.com

Juanito Riera is the current owner of this restaurant, but everyone seems to call him Alfredo so I always thought that was his name. It is perfect for a lazy lunch or a cosy dinner inside. The rice and fish dishes are excellent. I like the "blind" paella which is basically a paella without all the bits and just the juicy flavourful rice. Check out the celebrities displayed on the walls.
Try the garlic prawns!

Juanito Riera es el dueño actual del restaurante, pero parece que todo el mundo le llama Alfredo, yo también pensaba que era su nombre. Los ibicencos recomiendan este restaurante, perfecto para una larga comida. Los platos de arroz y pescado son excelentes. Me gusta la Paella Ciega, una paella sólo con arroz, pero con todo su jugo, delicioso. Echa un vistazo en sus paredes a las celebridades que han estado. ¡Prueba las gambas al ajillo!

A BIT ABOUT MONUMENTS... UN POCO SOBRE MONUMENTOS....

THE VARA DE REY STATUE

LA ESTATUA DE VARA DE REY

In the centre of the recently pedestrianised square of Vara de Rey, stands the figure of General Joaquín Vara de Rey y Rubio, with his sword in hand. Born in the Castle of Ibiza he died heroically fighting in the battle of El Caney, against the American army during the War of Independence of Cuba in 1898. The monument was built with donations from the Spanish people as a thank you. King Alfonso XIII attended its inauguration in 1904. I stare out of my office windows at it daily. Children play around it, climb onto it and couples take selfies with it as a backdrop. As a monument in my Ibiza life, it's as solid to me as the man it depicts.

En el centro de la plaza principal de Vara de Rey se encuentra la figura del General Joaquín Vara de Rey y Rubio, con su espada en mano. Nacido en el Castillo de Ibiza, murió heroicamente luchando en la batalla de El Caney, contra la armada americana, durante la Guerra de La Independencia de Cuba en 1898. El monumento fue construido gracias a las donaciones del pueblo español como forma de agradecimiento. El rey Alfonso XIII asistió a su inauguración en 1.904. La contemplo desde la ventana de mi oficina y veo a los niños jugando a su alrededor, y algunos se atreven a escalarla. Las parejas se hacen fotos con la estatua de fondo. Es un monumento que forma parte de mi vida, fuerte como el hombre al que representa.

OH AND DID YOU KNOW? AH, ¿Y SABÍAS QUE?

In Ibiza port on C/ Andenes, stands an Obelisk, the only monument in the world dedicated to the corsairs.

En el puerto de Ibiza en la C/ Andenes, está el Obelisco, el único monumento en el mundo dedicado a los corsarios.

11 Teatro Pereyra

C/ del Comte de Rosselló, 3, Ibiza
Tel: 971.304.432
teatropereyra.com

I love this place for its anti-VIP rule! It's also one for live-music lovers. Set in a beautiful old building with high ceilings, that once had a cinema at the back, the red velvet curtains still remain, lending it a theatrical touch. It has been open since 1889.

Me encanta este sitio por sus reglas anti-VIP! Además es para los amantes de la música en directo. Situado en un edificio antiguo precioso con techos altos, donde antes además había un cine en la parte trasera, además las cortinas de terciopelo rojo continúan dándole un toque teatral. Lleva abierto desde 1889.

12 La Cava

Passeig de Vara de Rey, 4, Ibiza
Tel: 971.316.074
lacavaibiza.com

I often have breakfast here as they have a good affordable variety, but a glass of wine here after work and a tapa also works for me. Right on the main square of Vara de Rey, this modern place is very popular and the staff love topping up my wine! Open til late.

A menudo desayuno aquí porque tienen una seleccion buenissima, pero una copa de vino aquí después del trabajo también me valen, y ademas me pillo una tapita. Este moderno local es muy popular y a los camareros les encanta rellenarme la copa. Abierto hasta la noche.

13 Pastis

C/ Avicena, 2, Ibiza
Tel: 971.391.999
pastisibiza.com

On the little pedestrian street just next to the Plaza del Parque Square, this inside only Bistro-style restaurant is perfect for a romantic dinner. They do a great steak but they are rather pricey!

En una pequeña calle junto a la Plaza del Parque, este restaurante tipo bistro y solo zona interior es perfecto para una cena romántica. El chuletón es fantástico pero es un lugar caro.

14 Can Gourmet

C/ de Montgri, 18b, Ibiza
Tel: 611.395.994

It used to be an old basket, herbs and honey shop that I was sad to see go… However I think what has replaced it is really fun and has a façade that stands out with hams hanging from a green Mehari parked in front so you really can´t miss it!. A sandwich place using all the local hams and island produce. Go try!

Antes fue una tienda de cestas, hierbas y miel. Me quedé triste al ver que la cerraban. Pero lo que la ha reemplazado es muy divertido y su fachada destaca mucho en la calle, con jamones que cuelgan de un Mehari verde asi que lo veras al pasar. Es un lugar de bocatas que utiliza jamones y productos típicos de la isla. ¡Pruébalo!

15 Can Pou Bar
C/ Lluis Tur i Palau, 19, Ibiza
Tel: 971.310.875

Great food, great tapas, great location and residents get a discount. I grab a cold beer and sit outside on a lovely summer's evening after catching the boat across the bay and watch all the crazy party people go by.

Buena comida, buenas tapas, buena situación y los residentes tienen descuento. Suelo tomarme una caña fresca y sentarme fuera al anochecer en verano después de coger el barco.

16 Comidas Bar San Juan
C/ Montgri 8, Ibiza
Tel: 971.311.603

Cheap Mediterranean food in one of Ibiza Town's oldest restaurants. Open all year round and the queue always goes out the door. You'll always find a very varied and eclectic Ibiza crowd inside. Good food with no frills.

Bocados mediterráneos baratos en uno de los restaurantes más antiguos de Ibiza. Abierto todo el año y la cola sigue siendo igual de larga en invierno. Comida buena y sin florituras. ¡Además aquí verás gente de lo más variada de Ibiza!

17 Es Portal
C/ de Vicente Cuervo, 8, Ibiza

I love coming here for their "Menu del Día". Every day they serve a different dish and you get way more than you can eat. There's a list of dishes served outside the door and it gets really busy. My favourite is the "Cocido Madrileño" which is a meaty vegetable stew.

Me encanta venir aquí para comer su "Menú del día". Cada día sirven un plato diferente. Hay un listado de los platos que se sirven en la puerta y está lleno de gente. Mi plato favorito es el cocido madrileño.

18 Es Baladre
C/ de Vicente Cuervo, 19, Ibiza
Tel: 971.311.967

I often have lunch here during the week as they have a set menu for 11,50€ which includes a starter, a main and a pudding, plus a glass of wine!. They also are part of the florist next door which is ideal for plant purchases in town.

A menudo almuerzo aquí durante la semana, ya que tienen un menú del día fijo por € 11,50 que incluye un entrante, un plato principal y un postre, además de una copa de vino. También son parte de la floristería de al lado, que es ideal para comprartr una planta en la ciudad.

19 Savianda
C/ Bartolomé Vicente Ramón, 27
Tel: 971.314.719

This is a typically spanish restaurant. No frills but very inexpensive and good. I like to come here for the set meñu.

Restaurante típico español sin lujos, pero bueno y barato. A menudo voy allí para comer el "Menú del Día".

20 Sushi and Love
C/ Carles III, 19
Tel: 971.318.013

A great value for amazing quality Take Away Sushi Bar. They offer a delivery service as well in a 5km radius of Ibiza Town.
My daughter and I always order the 16 piece tray which is 10 euros.

Buena calidad- precio en este Bar de Take Away de Sushi. Ofrecen un servicio de entrega a domicilio también en un radio de 5 km de la ciudad de Ibiza.
Mi hija y yo siempre pedimos la bandeja de 16 piezas que cuesta 10 euros.

21 Pastelería Panadería Can Vadell (Bakery)
C/ d'Annibál, 13
Tel: 971.310.728

Can Vadell has been here for almost 90 years. It's where I order birthday cakes, buy quiches or grab a sandwich. Try their "Coca" red pepper pizza, and if you need fresh yeast for baking, they have a stash in the back fridge.

Can Vadell lleva aquí casi 90 años. Es donde pido los pasteles de cumpleaños, compro quiches o bocatas. Prueba su coca de pimientos rojos y si necesitas levadura fresca para repostería, siempre tienen en la nevera.

22 Es Tap Nou

C/ de Madrid, 18, Ibiza
Tel: 971.399.841
estapnou.es

Okay, this little place makes the best salads in town, and offers a different "juice of the day" each day. I wish there were more places were like this in town! I'm addicted to their gazpacho and always order the spinach and goats cheese salad with bacon and mango and a sprinkle of pistachios. Undisputedly the best value lunch in town and they have a vegetable stand alongside.

Vale, este pequeño establecimiento hace la mejor ensalada de la ciudad y ofrece un zumo del día diferente cada día. Ojalá hubiera más lugares como estos en Ibiza. Soy adicta a su gazpacho y siempre me pido la ensalada de espinacas con queso de cabra, beicon, mango y pistachos. Indiscutiblemente el almuerzo más bueno y barato de la ciudad.

23 Can Terra

Av. d'Ignasi Wallis, 14, Ibiza
Tel: 971.310.064

This busy basque tapa bar is so popular and you need to get here early if you want a table. You can also just get a spot on their list and wait to get seated. But I often just stand, pick and eat. Their tapas are great and there's a nice little garden-patio at the back for the smokers.

Este bar de tapas vasco es tan popular que es mejor llegar temprano porque es bastante difícil conseguir una mesa mas tarde, aunque yo suelo tomarme una copa y picar algo de pie. Sus tapas están riquísimas y hay un patio al fresco en la parte posterior para los fumadores.

24 Mar A Vila

Av. d'Ignasi Wallis, 16, Ibiza
Tel: 971.314.778
maravilaibiza.com

This is where a lot of people go when Can Terra next door is too busy but to be honest with you the tapas are just as good and some even better!

Aquí es donde un montón de gente va cuando Can Terra, al lado, está lleno, pero la realidad es que las tapas están igual de buenas y algunos incluso mejor.

25 El Zaguán

Av. de Bartomeu de Roselló, 15, Ibiza
Tel: 971.192.882

In Spain we call them "Montaditos" - little slices of French bread with a layer of deliciousness on top. Take a plate, choose your selection which is all displayed along the long bar and then they count your toothpicks when you go to pay at the end - no cheating! I love the crab mayonnaise or the roasted brie with jam, and the waiters also sail by with hot-out-of-the-kitchen choices. Wash it all down with a good house red.

Coge un plato, elige tus montaditos preferidos que verás en el muestrario de la barra y luego contarán tus palillos cuando vayas a pagar al final, ¡sin hacer trampas! Me encanta el montadito de mayonesa con cangrejo y el de brie caliente con mermelada. Y los camareros también se pasean con montaditos calientes recién salidos de la cocina. Acompáñalo todo con un buen vino de la casa.

26 Va Bene Disco Burger

Av. Bartomeu de Roselló, 14, Ibiza
Tel: 971.194.180

I am not usually a big fan of burgers, but here there's an assortment of extras meaning you can build your own, so I love them! Their French fries are extremely good, and they also serve fresh salads. Plus the service is fast, which I always find important when there are hungry kids in tow. The decor is of a 1950s American -style diner, and you won't

break the budget.
No me suelen gustar mucho las hamburguesas, pero aquí la variedad de extras significa que puedes hacer la tuya propia, y eso me encanta. Sus patatas fritas están buenísimas, además también sirven ensaladas frescas. El servicio es rápido, lo que me parece importante cuando llevas a niños hambrientos. La decoración es del estilo de los *diners* americanos de los años 50, y aquí tampoco te saldrás del presupuesto.

OPEN 24HRS!
¡ABIERTO LAS 24 HORAS!

27 Sal-lot

Av. d'Ignasi Wallis, 14, Ibiza

Whenever I have a late night out in town and get the munchies and want to sober up before driving home, this place is perfect and serves food all night. You will always find an interesting array of Ibiza workers, local police, post party people here grabbing a bite before bed.
I like their egg and bacon sandwich with chips.
Cada vez que se me hace tarde en la ciudad, tengo hambre y me quiero espabilar antes de conducir a casa, vengo a este lugar que sirve comida durante toda la noche. Siempre encontrarás una interesante variedad de trabajadores de Ibiza, policías locales, fiesteros y demás gente comiendo algo antes de acostarse.
Yo me pido siempre el sándwich de huevo y bacon con patatas fritas.

28 Bar Los Amigos

C/ de Felip II, s/n, Ibiza
Tel: 971.313.818

This is an old school spanish bar on the corner which makes the best omelette sandwich on the island. it is always full of locals having their morning coffee with a dash of their preferred spirit.
Un bar español en la esquina que ha estado aquí desde siempre. Hacen el mejor bocadillo de tortilla en la isla y siempre está lleno de residentes tomándose su café de la mañana con una pizca de alcohol preferido.

29 Bella Napoli

Av. Santa Eulària des Riu, 9, Ibiza
Tel: 971.310.105
bellanapolibiza.com

A classic Italian restaurant that serves good Italian food, which means lots of fresh pasta. Their pizzas are cooked in a fire oven and they also do grilled meats, but I always order the penne a la Bolognesa with an extra shake of Parmesan.
Este restaurante clásico sirve cocina italiana casera y muy auténtica, lo que significa mucha pasta fresca y pizzas hechas en su horno de leña. Además ofrecen carnes a la brasa, pero yo siempre me pido la penne a la boloñesa con extra de parmesano rayado.

30 La Tagliatella

Av. Santa Eulària des Riu, 15, Ibiza
Tel: 971.194.136
latagliatella.es

I was pleasently surprised when I ate here. They serve traditional Italian food and have a large terrace outside in the summer. The lasagna "Tagliatella" with meat, caramelised onions and dried nuts is luscious, and they do a great selection of calzones, risottos and salads.
Cuando comí aquí quedé gratamente sorprendida. Sirven cocina italiana tradicional y tienen una gran terraza fuera en verano. Me encanta la lasaña "Tagliatella" con carne, cebolla caramelizada y frutos secos. También tienen una gran selección de calzones, risottos y ensaladas.

31 Cositas Ricas

C/ de Pere Francès, 21, Ibiza
Tel: 871.518.806

Open every day, this little glass fronted place on the street has a great selection of yummy dishes which you can eat in or they also offer you the service of food delivery and take away. They do Catering and Events and also have a little Shop.
Este lugar en la calle tiene una gran selección de platos deliciosos y está abierto todos los días. Puedes comer allí mismo o también ofrecen el servicio de entrega a domicilio o take away. Hacen catering y eventos, además tienen una pequeña tienda.

FOOD TO TAKE AWAY IN IBIZA TOWN

THE SALAD
Pg. 40
ES TAP NOU
C/ de Madrid, 18, IBIZA
TEL: 971.399.841

THE ITALIAN
Pg. 41
BELLA NAPOLI
C/ de Sta Eulària, 9, IBIZA
TEL: 971.310.105

THE JAPANESE
Pg. 39
SUSHI & LOVE
C/ Carles III, 19, IBIZA
TEL: 971.318.013
+ DELIVERY

THE VIETNAMESE
Pg. 41
MISS SAIGON
Av. d'Espanya, 59, IBIZA
TEL: 871.021.769

THE ROAST CHICKEN

GALLO NEGRO
C/ San Cristofol, 26, IBIZA
TEL: 649.487.870

COMIDA PARA LLEVAR EN IBIZA CIUDAD

THE KEBAB

Pg. 95

KEBAB LA PAZ

C/ de les Balears, IBIZA

TEL: 971.190.951

THE THAI

IBIZA THAI

C/ Felipe II, 15, IBIZA

TEL: 664.343.434

THE HEALTHY

Pg. 97

EAT IS LIFE

Av. de la Pau, 1, IBIZA

TEL: 971.312.201

THE PIZZA

Pg. 36

LA BUFALINA

Passeig Vara de Rey, 13, IBIZA

TEL: 971.302.894

+ DELIVERY

THE BURGER

Pg. 95

202 HAMBURGER & DELICIOUS

C/ del Bisbe Abad y Lasierra, 34, IBIZA

TEL: 971.313.919

SLEEP, DORMIR...

32 Casa Huéspedes Vara de Rey

Passeig de Vara de Rey, 7, Ibiza
Tel: 971.301.376
hibiza.com

A few flights of stairs up and you reach this boho haven. With patterned ceramic floors, mosaics and driftwood mirrors, this hostal is run by lovely smiley Argentinians Lia and Luis who make it all possible. Rooms range from the super-cheap (single, shared bath) to a romantic en-suite double with four-poster bed. Stunning old sandstone walls for real Ibiza on a budget.

Hay que subir algunos peldaños para llegar a este paraíso bohemio con suelos de cerámica decorativa, mosaicos y espejos de madera. Este hostal está regentado por Lía y Luis que hacen que todo sea posible. Las habitaciones van desde la más barata (individual con baño compartido) a una doble romántica con baño en-suite y cama con dosel. Echa un vistazo a sus paredes de piedra de arenisca que dan el verdadero toque ibicenco a buen precio.

33 Hostal Juanita

C/ de Joan d' Austria, 17, Ibiza
Tel: 971.314.828
hostaljuanita.com

Located in the centre of Ibiza just a few minutes walk from Dalt Vila, this B&B has recently been completely renovated and decorated in true Ibiza style. The rooftop chill out is decked out with large futons and soft couches which makes it a great spot for relaxing after a hard day on the beach (!), or a cocktail before you start your night out. It can get a bit noisy, so maybe not for you if you've come to Ibiza to sleep…

Situado en el centro de Ibiza ciudad sólo a unos minutos de Dalt Vila, este hostal acaba de ser totalmente renovado y decorado al verdadero estilo ibicenco. El chill out de la azotea tiene grandes futones y suaves cojines que lo convierten en un buen lugar para relajarse después de un duro día de playa (¡!), o para un cóctel antes de empezar la noche de fiesta. Un poco ruidoso, así que no es buena idea si vienes a Ibiza a dormir…

SHOPPING...

34 Purnima

C/ del Bisbe Azara, 5, Ibiza
Tel: 971.302.772

This jewellery store is run by the lovely Alessandra and is full of delights, with tables piled high with bowls of beads and stones and walls draped with pretty necklaces. If you feel like making a friend a personalized necklace. Let them guide you.

Esta joyería regentada por Alessandra está llena de abalorios, con cuencos rebosantes de cuentas y piedras, y paredes revestidas de preciosos collares. Si te apetece hacerle un collar personalizado a un amigo. Deja que te guíen.

35 Majoral

C/ d'Aníbal, 8, Ibiza
Tel: 971.508.863
majoral.com

A jewelry shop full of stunning hand-made pieces all inspired from the island of Formentera, the Mediterranean and the nature. I love my brushed gold ring from the "Poseidonia" collection.

Una tienda de joyería repleta de impresionantes piezas hechas a mano e inspiradas de la isla de Formentera, el mediterráneo y la naturaleza. Me encanta mi anillo de oro cepillado de la colección "Poseidonia".

36 Ibiza Bagus

C/ de Pere Sala, 1, Ibiza
Tel: 971.301.373
ibizabagus.es

Eva, the owner, designs and produces most of her stunning pieces in Bali. I adore her fluo kaftans. She believes that you should dress how you feel but with taste. She's right!

Eva, la dueña, diseña y produce la mayor parte de sus impresionantes piezas en Bali. Me encantan sus kaftanes flourescentes. Ella cree que se debe vestir como se quiera, pero con gusto.

IB
-1994-
IBIZA BAGÚS
always summer
www.ibizabagus.es

37 Religion

C/ del Comte de Roselló, 14, Passeig de Vara de Rey, Ibiza
Tel: 626.392.720
religionclothing.com

At the end of the main square this store is an Ibiza first for East London hipster fave, and it's where I head as soon as my pay-check comes in! I can never have enough of their rock chick T-shirts, skinny jeans and slinky dresses, and the men's clothes are just too sexy!

Justo en pleno Vara de Rey, esta tienda es la primera para la marca favorita del este de Londres, y es donde voy en cuanto recibo mi sueldo. Me encantan sus camisetas rock-chic, pantalones ajustados y vestiditos, y la ropa de hombre también es muy sexy.

38 Vincente Ganesha

C/ de Guillem de Montgri, 14, Ibiza
Tel: 971.193.605

Vicente has created an Indian/Ibiza bazaar of colourful cotton tunics, which stands out on the street and lures you in. I stock up on a new pair of Indian sandals here at the start of every summer, and my favourite drip-dry beach dresses are all Vicente's own designs. Inside it's a vintage treasure trove and a favourite with all the visiting fashionistas.

Vicente ha creado un bazar indio/ibicenco de túnicas coloridas de algodón, que resalta en la calle y te atrae a su interior. Siempre me compro un par de sandalias indias a principio de cada verano, y mis vestidos de playa desteñidos favoritos son diseños del mismo Vicente. Dentro hay una cueva del tesoro vintage, un favorito de los fashionistas que visitan la isla.

39 ReVolver

C/ del Bisbe Azara, 1, Ibiza
Tel: 971.318.939
revolveribiza.com

When my wardrobe needs an injection of designer cool or a pair of extra special sunglasses, this is where I go. Located in the heart of Ibiza on the pedestrian street leading off from the central square, this place stocks Q by McQueen, Sass & Bide and more...

Cuando mi armario necesita una inyección de ropa de diseñadores o unas gafas extra especiales, es aquí donde vengo. Situado en el corazón de Ibiza en las calles peatonales que van hacia la plaza central, aquí encontrarás Q by McQueen, Sass & Bide y muchas marcas del mismo estilo.

40 Lovy Ibiza by The Sandal Shop

Passeig de Vara de Rey, 12, Ibiza
Tel: 971.317.602

If you're in the market for a glamorous and bohemian beautifully made "Ibiza It bag", this shop has a fab selection of leather totes and clutches, as well as cuffs, purses and belts.

Si estás buscando un bolso sofisticado y bohemio hecho en Ibiza esta tienda tiene una selección de bolsos de mano y bandoleras, además de gemelos, carteras y cinturones.

41 Can Vinyes

C/ de Sa Creu, 34, Ibiza

This little shop on the corner has been here all my life, and to be a true Ibiza beach bum, you have to buy a "cesta" – a typical Ibizan basket. The little old lady who serves you is very helpful and there are all different sizes to choose from. I love the smell of baskets in here.

Esta pequeña tienda de la esquina ha estado aquí desde que recuerdo, y para ser un verdadero amante de la playa tienes que comprarte una cesta típica aquí. La señora que te atiende es encantadora y tiene cestos en todos los tamaños. Me encanta el olor a cestas en el interior.

42 Mayurka

Passeig de Vara de Rey, 10, Ibiza
+ Avinguda d'Ignasi Wallis, 11
Tel: 971.398.362

THE designer store in Ibiza. My more fashion-conscious friends wait for the end of the season sales and then raid the rails for some great bargains. And there are two shops to choose from.

LA tienda de grandes diseñadores en Ibiza. Mis amigas más seguidoras de la moda esperan al final de la temporada y luego arrasan en rebajas para encontrar verdaderas gangas.
Y hay dos tiendas para elegir.

43 Angels

Passeig de Vara de Rey, 10, Ibiza
Tel: 971.310.775
angelsshopibiza.com

This shoe shop on the square has been here since I was a kid and is a must if you're in search of a pair of desert or cowboy boots. All affordable and good quality.
They stock Panama Jacks.

Esta tienda de zapatos en la plaza existe desde que soy niña. Tienes que venir a esta tienda si buscas un par de botas vaqueras, y todo realmente asequible y de buena calidad. También tienen botas Panama Jack.

45 Sombrereria Bonet

C/ del Comte de Rosselló, 6, Ibiza
Tel: 971.310.668

This shop first opened in 1916 and is run by the third generation of the original family Bonet. It's kept its vintage style and stocks every kind of hat you can imagine. Think cowboy hats, trilbies, panamas and more, so if like me you like to spend the summer shaded, this is where to look.

Fundada en 1916 y regentada ahora por la tercera generación de la familia Bonet. Vende sombreros cowboy, de fieltro, sombrero de panamá y mucho más… Si te gusta tener tu cara a la sombra, ven a echar un vistazo aquí.

46 Can Murenu

Passeig Vara de Rey, 5. Ibiza
Tel: 971.301.930

Owner Joan Murenu's has created a lovely nautical atmosphere, and sometimes you can catch him strumming his guitar inside. The shop is a catchall of Ibizan products, from books to liquors, sandals, traditional baskets, keyrings, gifts and lots of trivia. I adore the oversized shells.
He also sells hunting and fishing supplies.

La tienda de Juan Murenu tiene un aire muy náutico y a veces puedes encontrar a Juan tocando la guitarra. La tienda ofrece multitud de productos ibicencos, desde libros a licores, sandalias, llaveros, cestos, regalos y montones de objetos triviales. Aquí siempre encuentro algo bonito y me encantan las conchas gigantescas. También vende utensilios para la caza y la pesca.

47 Campos de Ibiza

C/.de Vicente Cuervo, 20, Ibiza
Tel: 971.806.886
camposdeibiza.com

Campos de Ibiza is a well known brand on the island since the 80s that sells perfumes, bath gels, moisturizers, essential oils, scented candles, air fresheners and a household range of towels. Since I was a kid I have loved the fragrances and remember being given a gift of a heavenly scent made of mandarines.

Campos de Ibiza es una conocida tienda en la isla desde principios de los años 80 que vende perfumes, geles y sales de baño, cremas hidratantes, aceites esenciales, velas perfumadas, ambientadores y una gama de toallas. Desde que era una niña me han gustado las fragancias y recuerdo un regalo que me dieron de una fragancia olor a mandarinas que era divina.

HANDY HARDWARE, TIENDA MUY ÚTIL

48 Ferretería Ibiza

C/ de Joan d'Austria, 17, Ibiza
Tel: 971.315.823

Need a drill, a saw, nails or an axe? A ladder or a hose-pipe? Or maybe you just want to get some keys cut? This hardware store has everything, and the guys inside are always really helpful.

¿Necesitas un taladro, una sierra, clavos o un hacha? ¿Una escalera o una manguera? ¿O quizá quieras hacer copias de unas llaves? Esta ferretería tiene de todo, y los chicos siempre son muy atentos.

HANDY SHOP * TIENDA ÚTIL

ARMERÍA BALANZAT

I love this shop that sells all kinds of sports gear, including fishing equipment, masks and snorkels, French Opinel knives which I love, torches and hiking gear..

Me encanta esta tienda que vende todo tipo de equipamiento deportivo, incluyendo utensilios de pesca, gafas y tubos de bucear, cuchillos, y todo para senderismo.

Passeig Vara de Rey, 17
Tel: 971.300.589

49 Ruta Ibiza

Passeig de Vara de Rey, 13, Ibiza
Tel: 625.902.179
rutaibiza.com

I love this colourful and original clothes store on the main square. If you want to dazzle and wear somcthing a bit quirky this shop has some great pieces. Items here range from ready to wear, beach and party so you need look no further!.

Me encanta esta tienda original de ropa y accesorios en la plaza principal de Ibiza. Si quieres deslumbrar y ponerte algo diferente esta tienda tiene prendas divertidas. Artículos de pret a porter, playa y de fiesta, asi que encontraras todo lo que necesites aqui.

50 Vadepelo

Passeig de Vara de Rey, 7, 2ª, Ibiza
Tel: 971.393.469

Paula cuts hair like a dream and has some great hair products to get your shine back if you've been baking your hair in the sun. The best for highlights and for hair extensions, she's also really affordable. Book in advance because she's popular!

Paula te corta el pelo como nadie y tiene productos para hacer que tu pelo luzca brillante si has estado quemándolo al sol. Es la mejor para mechas y para extensiones y además es muy asequible. Pide cita con antelación, ¡es muy popular!

ON VIA PUNICA STREET...
EN LA CALLE VIA PÚNICA...

51 Mathiss Ibiza

Via Púnica, 18, Ibiza
Tel: 971. 393.489
mathissibiza.com

I love this shop! It has everything you need for your hair, nails and skin. All the best products and brands as well as profesional equipment. They stock great shampoos as well.

¡Me encanta esta tienda! Tiene todo lo necesario para tu cabello, uñas y tu piel. Tiene los mejores productos y marcas, así como utensilios profesionales.

52 Cachirulo Balloon Shop

Via Punica, 11, Ibiza
Tel: 971. 391.846 - 666. 108.624
cachiruloysusamigos.com

Cachirulo is known by all the parents and kids on this island because he creates the best kiddie shows with the help of lots of balloons, music and fun games.
They will entertain your kids with disco dancing, foam parties and even a bouncy castle.
Pass by the shop or call and they will arrrange it all.

Cachirulo es conocido por todos los padres y niños de la isla ya que crea los espectáculos más divertidos para niños usando globos y juegos. Los entretiene con música, bailes, fiestas de espuma y hasta un castillo hinchable.
Pásate por la tienda o llama y se encargarán de todo.

53 Chill Café

Via Púnica, 49, Ibiza
Tel: 971.399.736

This Café serves a mean coffee and also has delicious vegetarian food. It's a great Little pitt stop if you are in the area and has free wifi.

Esta cafetería sirve un café buenísimo y también tiene deliciosa comida vegetariana. Es una gran parada si estás en la zona, además tiene wifi gratis.

54 Cerrafer

Via Púnica, 53, Ibiza
Tel: 971.307.520

This small establishment copies and cuts your car keys, security keys and installs and fixes locks.

Aquí puedes hacer copias de tus llaves del coche y de seguridad, además instalan y reparan cerraduras.

55 Natural

Via Púnica, 40, Ibiza
Tel: 971.302.075

A shop packed wall-to-wall with all the organic produce you can imagine.
Vitamin supplements, natural cosmetics, cereals, lots of gluten-free options and so on...I love the fruit bars when I get that "need-to-plough-on" feeling, and my energy tank is depleted.

Este establecimiento está lleno de todos los productos ecológicos que puedas imaginar. Suplementos vitamínicos, cosmética natural, cereales, montones de opciones sin gluten y más... Me encantan sus barritas de fruta cuando necesito cargar las pilas.

HOTEL, SHOPS AND MORE...
HOTEL, TIENDAS Y MÁS

56 Urban Spaces Hotel

Via Púnica, 32, Ibiza
Tel: 871.517.174

I absolutely love this boutique hotel in town.
All the walls are covered with street art and each room is done by a different street artist. The beds are also super comfy.

Me encanta este pequeño hotel. Las paredes están cubiertas de arte urbano y las suites están decoradas cada una por un artista diferente. Además sus camas son muy cómodas.

57 Moms & Babies

Av. d'Espanya, 17, Ibiza
Tel: 971.307.766
momsandbabies.es

Moms & Babies was created by two couples, who were good friends and also new parents, having realised there were certain things they couldn't find on the island for their kids. Here they offer help and understanding as well as a pleasant environment for parents, relatives and friends to shop. Top quality products and gift vouchers.
It's also a photo studio.

Moms & Babies fue creado por dos parejas de buenos amigos, y también padres. Se dieron cuenta como padres que había cosas que no podían encontrar en la isla. Padres, familiares y amigos encuentran un entorno amable y ayuda para hacer la compra perfecta. Productos de calidad y vales regalo. Y también tienen un estudio de fotografía aquí.

58 Delta Disco

Av. d'Espanya, 7, Ibiza
Tel: 971.306.721
discosdeltaibiza.com

I bought my first ever vinyl here...think it was Supertramp's "Crime of The Century" or something by The Cure. These guys still have the best selection of music and it's a favourite with resident DJs.
They also sell trainers, clothes and souvenirs.

Compré mi primer vinilo aquí... creo que fue "Crime of the century" de Supertramp o algo de The Cure. Siguen teniendo la mejor selección de música y es la tienda favorita de los DJs residentes.
También venden deportivas, ropa y souvenirs.

59 Don Kroquet

C/ de Catalunya, 10, Ibiza
Tel: 661.628.996

My boyfriend told me about this place. I just love "Croquetas" which are typical in Spain and are like a potato bechamel fishcake... Here they have all sorts or fillings and are freshly made. They have a take away service and sell gourmet Basque products.

Mi novio me enseñó este delicioso lugar.
Me encantan las croquetas, y aquí tienen de todos los gustos y recién hechas. Ofrecen comida casera para llevar y venden productos gourmet del País Vasco.

SID SHANTI
INTRODUCES HIS NEW IBIZA CHILLI SAUCES

Sid Shanti, leading Ibiza Chef, caterer and author of the best selling lifestyle cookery book "Glorious Ibiza Food" is producing the first authentic Ibiza Chili Sauce on the island. Growing some of the hottest chilis in the world using all island ingredients. Ideal for bbq's or to take home to remind you of lazy days in the Balearic sun.

Sid Shanti, Chef líder en Ibiza y autor del libro de cocina de estilo de vida "Gloriosa Ibiza Food" está cultivando los chiles más calientes del mundo con todos los ingredientes de la isla y produciendo sus novedosos salsas de chili de Ibiza. Son ideales para barbacoas o para llevartelos casa y así tendrás un recuerdo de días bajo el sol balear.

C/ Abad i La Sierra, Ibiza town
Tel: 971.578.518
sidshanti.com

ON THE EDGE OF THE CENTRE...
SALIENDO UN POCO DEL CENTRO...

IT'S TEA TIME!

60 Petit Salon de Té "Queriendo-Te"

C/ d'Antoni Guasch Juan, 2, Ibiza
Tel: 971. 307.102

A little tea shop full of tea gorgeousness. Make an appontment and before you shop, sit and enjoy a delicious cup of whatever blend you prefer as there are teas from all around the globe on offer in here. Don't forget to ask for a slice of home made cake from his counter. Felix, the owner is a unique carácter, so go see for yourself.

Una pequeña tienda de té, llena de mezclas divinas. Haz una cita y antes de comprar, siéntate y disfruta de una deliciosa taza de la variedad que prefieras ya que aquí hay tés de todo el mundo y no te olvides de pedir un trozo de pastel casero. Félix, el propietario es un personaje único, así que compruébalo por ti mismo.

61 El Rápido

C/ Aragón, 69, Ibiza
Tel: 971.391.037 - 971.305.856
M: 647.802.148
elrapido.es

A fantastic little shop just heading out of town that repairs those worn-down dancing heels. They also specialize in mending buckles, zippers and orthopedic shoes. They cut keys as well and have an emergency locksmiths service for you 24 hours a day.

Una magnífica tienda donde reparan esos tacones desgastados por el baile. También se especializan en reparar hebillas, cremalleras y zapatos ortopédicos. Copian llaves además de tener servicio de cerrajero las 24 horas del día.

62 Katia Knitting Shop

C/ del Bisbe Abad y Lasierra, 5, Ibiza

If you're into knitting, which my mum and I both are, then you'll love this little shop which stocks all the wools you could possibly imagine. The ladies in here are really helpful and will help you find what you need, if you speak Spanish that is...

Si te gusta hacer punto, como a mi madre y a mí, te encantará esta pequeña tienda que vende todas las lanas imaginables. Las señoras aquí son muy atentas y te ayudarán a encontrar lo que necesites.

63 La Cucaña

C/ d'Aragó, 107, Ibiza
Tel: 971.303.880

The best shop in town to buy dressing-up stuff. Halloween, carnaval, Flower Power, this shop has it all. They have make-up, masks, wigs, costumes, just about everthing you need and great little outfits for kids as well.

De las mejores tiendas en la ciudad para comprar disfraces para Halloween, carnaval o "Flower Power".
Esta tienda lo tiene todo. También venden maquillaje, máscaras, pelucas y disfraces geniales para niños también.

64 The Barber Ibiza

c/ Menorca, 8, Ibiza
Tel: 971.312.877

This is the kind of Hair place you enter knowing you are going to come out looking edgier. They are beard and afro pros and all the customers look like they are from the land of cool. They take their time cutting, so be patient.

Ésta es el tipo de peluquería en el que entras sabiendo que vas a salir más guay. Son especialistas en cortes de barba y afro, y todos los clientes parecen sacados de una película supercool. Se toman su tiempo cortando así que ten paciencia.

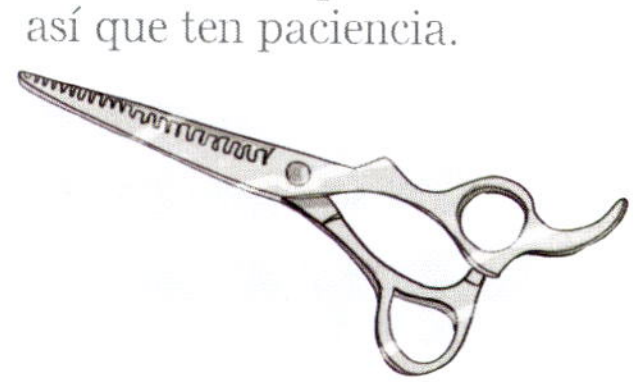

AROUND THE OLD MARKET, THE PORT + SA PENYA
ALREDEDOR DEL MERCADO VIEJO, EL PUERTO Y SA PEÑA

There's a quaint square at the foot of the historic Dalt Vila ramparts where you can shop for groceries, buy a vintage dress, have a tattoo and after all that, stop for a glass of wine or coffee all in one morning or afternoon.
There's a great little place in the market building where I always buy a tuna-and-olive sandwich with a spicy pepper thrown in and I also like meeting friends at the Croissant Show Café or at Bistrot Le Jardin. It's a busy square in the summer and bustling with life until late at night.
If you walk a bit away from it and on to the walking streets at the back, you'll reach a narrow maze of streets and rows of little white houses called Sa Penya, where once, the local fishing community lived. These days it's where you'll find the liveliest bar scene in town, a selection of shops, hippie stalls and some great little eateries, and some well hidden in the back. These cobbled streets are lovely to walk along with the family, but be warned - the volume cranks up later in the evening.
If you wonder too far up you'll find yourself in gypsy-land.
Not the most picturesque!

Puedes comprar fruta y verdura, comprar un vestido vintage, hacerte un tatuaje y luego pararte para una copa, todo en una misma mañana o tarde en esta pequeña plaza al pie de la entrada a la histórica Dalt Vila.
Hay un pequeño puesto en el mercado mismo donde a menudo compro un bocadillo de atún con guindilla y también me gusta quedar con amigos en el Croissant Show o en Bistrot Le Jardin. Es una plaza muy concurrida en verano y llena de vida hasta muy tarde.
Si te alejas caminando un poco de aquí llegarás a un entresijo de calles estrechas con sus hileras de casitas blancas que es la zona de Sa Penya, que fue antiguamente donde vivía la comunidad local de pescadores. Hoy en día, es donde encontrarás una zona de bares más animada de la ciudad además de un mercadillo hippy, tiendas y buenos restaurantes, algunos muy escondidos por detrás.
Estas calles adoquinadas son preciosas para caminar junto con la familia, pero os advierto que se calienta y sube el volumen bastante por la noche.Si subes aún más, llegarás a lo alto donde viven los gitanos. No tan recomendable...

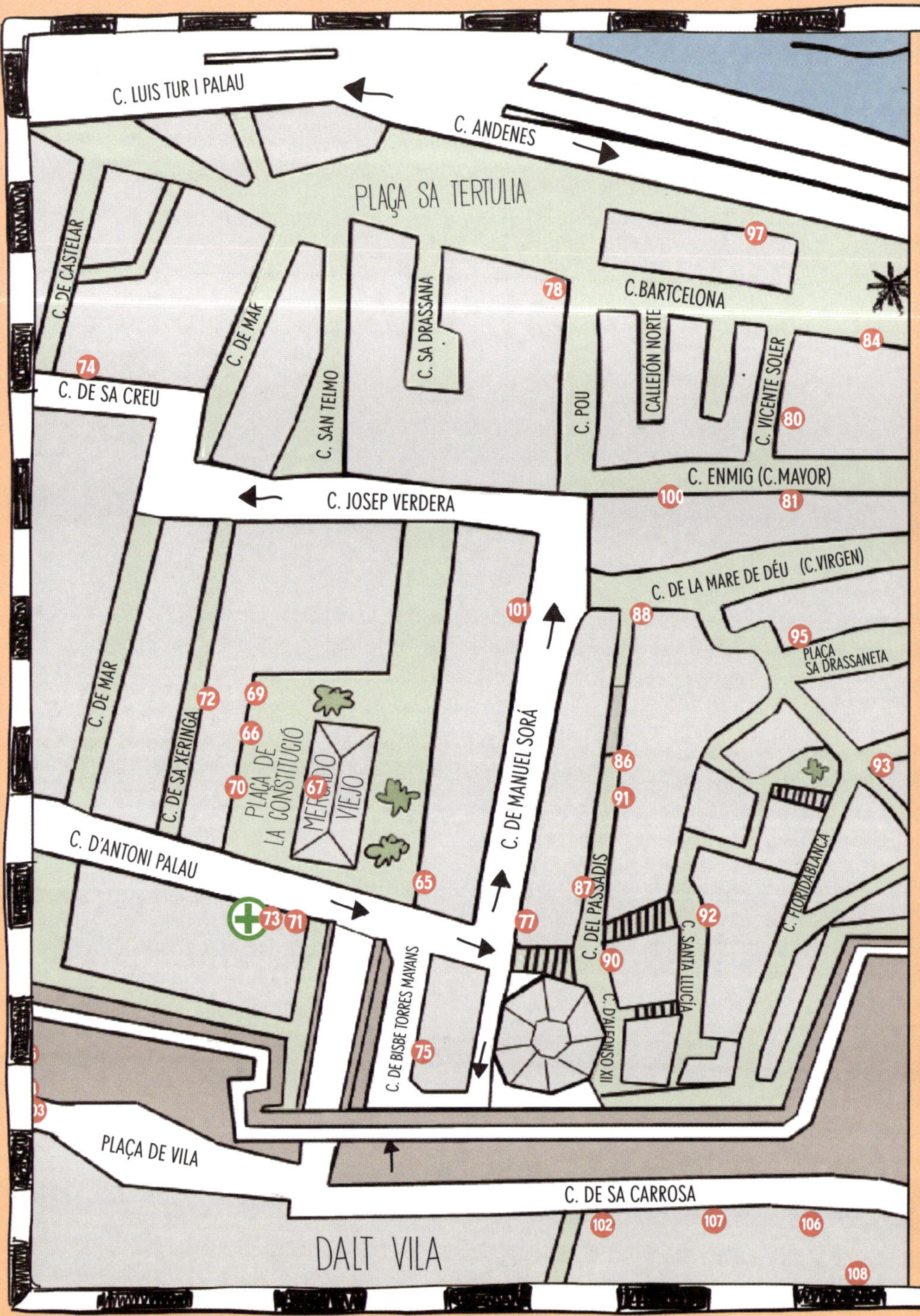
C. LUIS TUR I PALAU
C. ANDENES
PLAÇA SA TERTULIA
97
78
C.BARTCELONA
84
C. DE CASTELAR
C. DE MAR
C. SA DRASSANA
CALLEJÓN NORTE
C. VICENTE SOLER
74
C. DE SA CREU
80
C. SAN TELMO
C. POU
C. ENMIG (C.MAYOR)
100
81
C. JOSEP VERDERA
C. DE LA MARE DE DÉU (C.VIRGEN)
101
88
95
PLAÇA SA DRASSANETA
C. DE MAR
72
69
66
C. DE SA XERINGA
PLAÇA DE LA CONSTITUCIÓ
MERCADO VIEJO
67
70
C. DE MANUEL SORÁ
86
91
93
C. D'ANTONI PALAU
65
87
C. DEL PASSADÍS
C. FLORIDABLANCA
73
71
77
92
C. SANTA LLUCÍA
90
C. D'ALFONSO XII
C. DE BISBE TORRES MAYANS
75
PLAÇA DE VILA
C. DE SA CARROSA
102
107
106
DALT VILA
108

PORT
PUERTO
C. ANDENES
C. CIPRIANO GARIJO
83
85
PLAÇA SA RIBA
79
C. ENMIG (C.MAYOR)
94
82
99
96
C. DE LA MARE DE DÉU (C.VIRGEN)
98
C. FOSC
C. MIRANDA
SA PENYA
C. RETIR
C. ALT
C. VISTA ALEGRE
C. SA PEDRERA
DALT VILA
IBIZA PORT, SA PENYA & DALT VILA
PUERTO, SA PENYA Y DALT VILA

EAT, DRINK,...
COME Y BEBER...

65 Croissant Show

Plaça de la Constitució, Ibiza (Mercado Viejo)
Tel: 971.317.665
croissant-show-ibiza.com

Owned by Andre, an island character who stands out a mile with his curly French moustache, this is a lovely place to sit in the morning sun with your first coffee of the day. They have a large display of delicious fresh baked pastries, and my favourite here is the brie and tomato toasted baguette which I often have for brunch. You also often catch the after party crowd here for breakfast on no sleep!

Propiedad de Andre, un personaje de la isla que destaca a kilómetros por su bigote rizado a lo francés, éste es un lugar encantador para sentarse por la mañana con tu primer café del día. Tienen una gran variedad de hojaldres y mi plato favorito es la baguete con tomate y brie. Aquí puedes ver a la gente desayunando después de la fiesta.

66 Bistrot El Jardín

Plaça de la Constitució, 11, Ibiza (Mercado Viejo)
Tel: 669.606.565)

I call it Fred's Bistrot because it is actually! It is such a lovely spot on the old market square and their salmon bagels with cream cheese are the best I've ever tried in town. I also love the Cesar Salad here and their homemade Foie Gras. They do a light fluffy version of a cheese cake for pud which is a must.

Yo lo llamo el bistrot de Fred porque lo es. Un lugar encantador en la plaza del mercado viejo que tiene unos bagels de salmón con crema de queso que son de las mejores que he probado en el centro. También me encanta la ensalada César de aquí y su Foie casero. Además no debeís iros sin probar su postre de pastel de queso.

67 Bio Lunch

Plaça de la Constitució, Ibiza (Mercado Viejo)

A delicious and colourful selection of organic pastries, quiches and tarts all homemade by Javier and served up by Nicolás using their own fresh fruit and veg. These meals are perfect to take-away on a paper plate or to eat immediately perched on one of the three small tables in the delightful surroundings of the fruit and veggy market.

Una selección deliciosa y colorida de empanadas, quiches y tartas caseras y ecológicas elaboradas por Javier y servidas por Nicolás utilizando sus propias frutas y verduras frescas. Estas comidas son perfectas para llevar en un plato de papel o comer inmediatamente sentado en una de sus tres pequeñas mesas con el mercado de fruta y verdura como telón de fondo.

69 Inkadelic

Plaça de la Constitució 10, Ibiza (Mercado Viejo)
Tel: 676.168.122
inkadelictattooing.com

My lovely but slightly scary (not really) friend Neil Ahern runs this dark and sexy establishment – and when I say dark, I mean it's filled with skulls and baby somethings in formaldehyde! Neil has been tattooing Ibiza's bodies beautiful for over 20 years, so he´s the man to go to - but he wont smile much if you ask for a butterfly or a Pacha Cherry! Supermodels (Kate, Naomi and Linda), designers and a long list of DJs have all been inked here.

Mi amigo Neil Ahern, encantador y ligeramente aterrador (es broma), dirige este oscuro y atractivo local, y cuando digo oscuro, ¡me refiero a que está lleno de calaveras y otras cosas extrañas en formol! Neil lleva embelleciendo los cuerpos de Ibiza con tatuajes desde hace más de 20 años, si quieres un tatuaje, él es el hombre perfecto, ¡pero no esperes una sonrisa si le pides que te tatúe unas Cerezas Pacha! Supermodelos (Kate, Naomi y Linda), diseñadores y una larga lista de DJs se han tatuado aquí.

SHOPPING,...

70 Ho-La-La Vintage

Plaça de la Constitució 12, Ibiza (Mercado Viejo)
Tel: 971.316.537
holala-ibiza.com

Open since 1978, you can`t miss this colourful vintage store on the market square, and I always have to stop tojust make sure there's not a cute dress for me...I love the tie dyed slip dresses...

Abierto desde 1978, no puedes pasar por alto esta tienda vintage de gran colorido en la zona del mercado viejo. Yo siempre me paro para ver si hay algun vestido vintage para mí... y los vestidos lenceros desteñidos me chiflan...

71 Piratas de Ibiza

C/. d'Antoni Palau, Ibiza
piratas-de-ibiza.com

A funky pirate shop at the corner of the ramp up to Dalt Vila. Perfect if you want a Ibiza Pirate T Shirt. I bought a couple for a friend of mines kids as I think they are super cute. They sell women and mens clothes and accessories.

Una tienda de ropa pirata en la esquina de la rampa que sube a Dalt Vila. Es ideal si quieres una camiseta pirata de Ibiza. Compré un par para los hijos de una amiga y les encantó. Se vende ropa para chicas y chicos, y además tienen accesorios.

72 Mercería Luis Valero Sala

C/ de Sa Xeringa, 8, Ibiza
Tel: 971.310.187

This authentic little Spanish haberdashery has been here all my life and I can remember my mum buying me the cool badges that still decorate the windows of this place. We even used to buy our fresh cow`s milk from the shop in front, that my mum would bring home to boil. Some places in town really bring back old memories, and its lovely when they've stayed exactly as they were. Now I come here to buy my daughter hair bands, and always stock up on pins and needles. Their button collection is pretty fantastic!

Esta pequeña mercería lleva aquí toda mi vida y recuerdo que mi madre me compraba chapas que todavía decoran las ventanas de este local. Solíamos comprar leche de vaca fresca de la tienda de enfrente, que mi madre traía después a casa para hervirla. Algunos sitios de la ciudad realmente me traen viejos recuerdos, y me encanta cuando se conservan igual. Ahora vengo aquí para comprar las gomas de pelo para mi hija, y siempre me llevo agujas y alfileres.

73 Farmacia Juan Tur Viñas

C/. d'Antoni Palau, 1, Ibiza
Tel: 971.310.015

A great pharmacy on what us locals calls "The pharmacy street" as there are a few on this street. This one is just before the ramp up to the cathedral. They specialise in Natural products, orthopaedic products and homeopathic medicine.

Una gran farmacia en lo que nosotros los lugareños llamamos "la calle de las farmacias" porque hay más de una en esta calle. Ésta está justo antes de la rampa a la catedral. Son especialistas en productos naturales, productos de ortopedia y medicina homeopática.

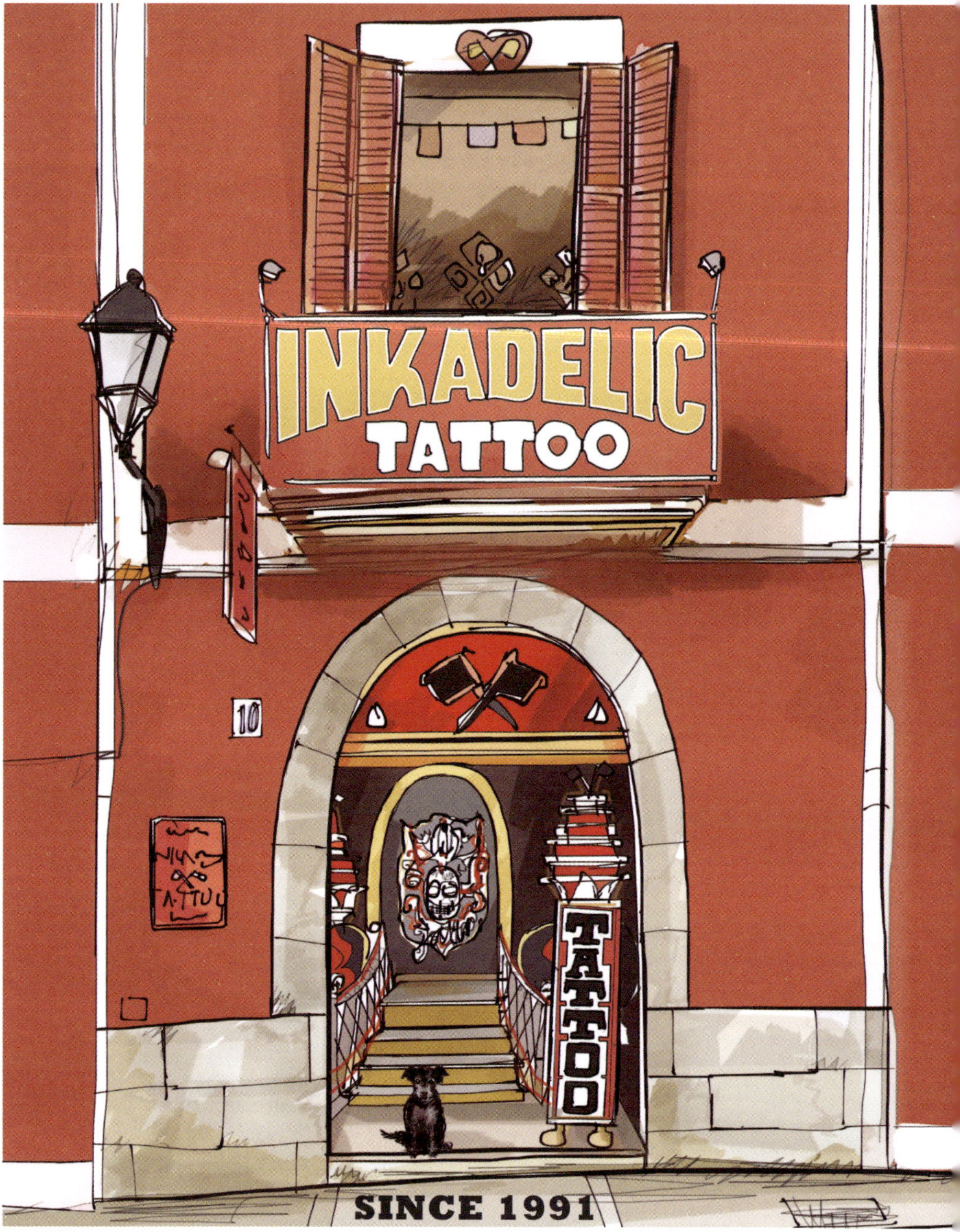
INKADELIC
TATTOO
10
TATTOO
SINCE 1991

SHOPPING...

74 La Boutik

C/. de Sa Creu, 12, Ibiza
Tel: 971.199.740

A colourful, bohemian shop on the little street past the San Telmo Church as you drive away from the Old Market square. Here you can find divine dresses, shirts, and accessories. I love their colourful embroidered tops.

Ésta es una pequeña tienda colorida y bohemia en la calle sinuosa después de la iglesia de San Telmo cuando conduces desde la plaza del Mercado Viejo. Aquí puede encontrar vestidos divinos, camisas y accesorios. Sus tops bordados de colores son divinos.

TAPAS...

75 La Bodega

C/ Bisbe Torres Mayans, 2, Ibiza
Tel: 971.192.740

I come here when I'm spending an evening in town with friends and kids and feel like an easy, affordable dinner. La Bodega is famous for its tapas. It has an unbeatable location beneath the old cathedral walls and the ramp to Dalt Vila.
There's also a great cocktail bar. For the best seat, book a street table on the pavement in advance.

Suelo venir aquí cuando vengo a la ciudad por la noche con familia y me apetece ir a un sitio agradable y asequible para cenar. La Bodega es famosa por sus tapas. Está situada en un lugar privilegiado bajo las viejas murallas de la catedral y la rampa que sube a Dalt Vila. Además de la carta, hay un bar de cócteles. Si quieres la mejor mesa, resérvala en la terraza con antelación.

77 Bar Maravillas

C/ de Manuel Sorà, 6, Ibiza
Tel: 634.234.543

This little bar sits at the foot of Sa Penya, at the back of the old market square. It's a busy spot and great for people watching in the evening til late or if you prefer in the morning for coffee.

Este pequeño bar se encuentra al pie de Sa Penya, detrás de la plaza del mercado viejo.
Es un lugar muy concurrido y genial para ver la gente pasar por la noche, o si prefieres, por la mañana para tomarte un café.

ICE CREAM... HELADOS

78 Los Valencianos

Plaça Antoni Riquer, Ibiza

I completely forgot to put this ice cream parlour in last year and it was the first ice cream parlour on the island. It has ben here ever since I was a kid and in the summer apart from ice creams, In the heat of the summer I take a walk along the port and stop here to get a take away "Limon Granizado" which is a lemon juice with crushed ice. Another fave of mine is the "Horchata", one of Spain's most loved summer drinks made of Tiger nut juice and crushed ice. It's a milky nut heaven that I have been enjoying since I was a little girl!

Me olvidé por completo de poner esta heladería en la guía del año pasado y fue la primera en abrir de Ibiza hace años. En verano, aparte de los helados, cuando pega el sol y entra la sed, me doy un paseo por el puerto a tomarme un limón granizado o una horchata de chufa, una de las bebidas de verano más conocidas en España que llevo disfrutando desde que soy muy niña.

79 Thai'd Up

Plaza de Sa Riba, Ibiza
Tel: 971.191.668

Lee runs this quaint little place right at the end of the port, and the food is ridiculously good. It's a lovely walk along the harbour and the view is breathtaking. While I normally go for their medium spicy green curry, they're also famous

for their Phad Thai. The cocktails are also amazing and I always find it hard to leave.

Lee regenta este local justo al final del puerto, y la comida aquí es deliciosa. Me encanta el paseo hasta aquí y la vista es preciosa. Aunque suelo pedirme su curry verde no demasiado picante, también es famoso por su Phad Thai. Los cócteles están riquísimos y siempre me cuesta marcharme.

80 Los Pasajeros Puerto

C/ Vicente Soler, 6, 1º, Ibiza
Tel: 653.350.961

An islanders secret. Tucked away down a side street you will see a staircase that leads up to this bustling little first- floor restaurant. You can't book a so you'll just have to queue on the stairs but it's worth it for the pre-party atmosphere and delicious (and cheap) home cooking. I love the grilled spinach starter and the leg of lamb for main.

Un verdadero secreto de los ibicencos y trabajadores. Escondido en una callejuela donde verás una escalera que sube a este pequeño y concurrido restaurante. No puedes reservar así que todos hacen cola en las escaleras pero merece la pena para una atmósfera de pre-fiesta y buena comida casera. Me encanta el primero de espinacas y la pierna de cordero con puré de patatas.

81 Restaurante Pinocho

C/ d'Enmig, 18, Ibiza
Tel: 971.310.176

An classic in the port and us long term islanders are fond of this old school pizzeria. A great place to perch up in the street at one of its outdoor tables and soak up the atmosphere, all whilst enjoying great pizzas and pastas.

Un clásico en el puerto y nosotros los isleños le tenemos mucho aprecio a esta vieja pizzería. Es un lugar perfecto para sentarte en una de sus mesas en la calle y empaparte del ambiente, todo mientras saboreas una pizza o la pasta.

82 El Rincón del Puerto

C/ Enmig, 50, Ibiza
Tel: 971.314.665
rincondelpuertoibiza.com

I had not been here for a while and then had dinner with friends this winter and

we had a great meal. My friends ordered the Pasta Parmesan which is placed in a semi hollowed-out huge Parmesan cheese and then mixed around until it is covered with Parmesan. I had some yummy Ravioli with pumpkin.

No había cenado aquí en bastante tiempo y este invierno cené con amigos en y tuvimos una cena maravillosa. Mis amigos pidieron la famosa Pasta Parmesano, que se elabora colocando la pasta cocida dentro de un queso parmesano enorme medio vaciado y se mezcla allí todo hasta que queda cubierto de queso. Yo pedí unos raviolis con calabacín. Riquísimo todo.

83 El Pirata

C/ Cipriano Garijo, 10, Ibiza
Puerto de Ibiza
Tel: 971.192.630

Hungry late at night? This is where the residents, workers and late night hungry gang grab a pizza fix during their break or before they go on out. Once you try you always return…

Si te entra el hambre tarde por la noche, aquí es donde los residentes, trabajadores de la isla y gente con hambre tardía van y compran un trozo de pizza durante su descanso o antes de seguir la fiesta. Una vez que pruebes volverás una y otra vez…

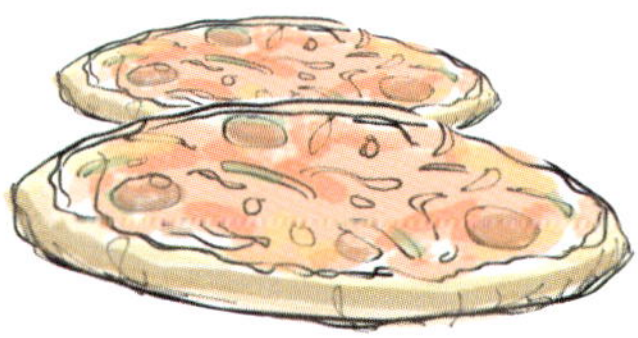

DRINKS… COPITAS…

84 White Buddha

C/ Cipriano Garijo, Ibiza
Tel: 625.529.406
whitebuddhaibiza.com

Some of my single-ish girlfriends from London make this is their first stop before heading out into the clubs. They say the bar staff are cute, and everyone's up for a good time.

Amigas mías más o menos solteras que llegan de vacaciones tienen este bar como su primera parada antes de ir a la discoteca. Dicen que los camareros son muy monos y siempre están muy animados aquí.

85 The Rock Bar

C/ Cipriano Garijo, Ibiza
Tel: 971.310.129

This place run by bubbly Bev is a classic amongst the Ibiza Brit pack and, as I only discovered last year, some pretty amazing cocktails are created here. If you want to find out what's on the clubbing agenda this is the place to pop into, and I always bump into everyone, as it's a walk-through crowd.

Este sitio es un clásico entre los británicos de Ibiza, sólo el año pasado descubrí que algunos de los mejores cócteles se crean aquí. Si quieres encontrar lo que está en la agenda de discotecas éste es el mejor sitio, y siempre me encuentro con algún conocido, ya que es un sitio de paso.

86 Las Libertinas

C/ Ses Pasadis, 10, Ibiza
Tel: 648.169.535

A little Lesbian Music Bar run by two straight girls. The waitresses are really nice and friendly. It has a great little vibe inside with colourful strobe lights and is lots of fun. I've heard that they serve a great strawberry daiquiri.

Un bar musical de lesbianas, ...pero dirigida por chicas heterosexuales. Las camareras son súper amables y simpáticas.
Dentro tiene lucecitas de colores y la verdad es que es muy divertido.
Además he oído que sirven unos daiquiris de fresa riquíssimos.

THE NAKED WINE BAR

An exciting new place that sells artisan made, organic, biodynamic wines from Spain and France. It's the only Wine Bar in Ibiza to specialise in such wines. The owners run it with passion. Wholesale and take-away.
Un nuevo concepto de bar que vende vinos artesanales españoles y franceses orgánicos y biodinámicos. Es la única vinoteca de Ibiza que se especializa en este tipo de vinos. Los propietarios lo gestionan con pasión. Venta al por mayor también.

Placa de Sa Riba, 10
Tel: 971.316.125 - 651889.099

87 La Tana

C/ del Passadis, 3, Sa Penya, Ibiza
Tel: 630.258.984

Friends of mine say that owner Leo is a true Italian culinary artist, so if it's authentic homemade Italian food you're after, this is definitely a winner. Nestled in the backstreets on Carrer d' Enmig this trattoria serves delicious antipasti, home made pasta and typical Italian puddings. It appeals to quite the party bunch, so come here to get the lowdown on the evening's after-parties while you sip their home-made limoncello.
Amigos me cuentan que el propietario Leo es un verdadero artista culinario italiano, así que si buscas auténtica comida italiana, este parece ser el ganador. Enclavado en las callejuelas traseras del C/ d'Enmig, esta pequeña trattoria sirve antipasti delicioso, pasta casera y postres típicos italianos. Atrae a los fiesteros, así que ven aquí para enterarte de las after-parties mientras te tomas su limoncello casero.

88 Osteria Il Gatto e La Volpe

C/ del Passadis, 28, Sa Penya, Ibiza
Tel: 871.700.738

This place is always really busy as it is a great little walk-by Italian restaurant on the street and just at the foot of the Carrer de La Mare de Deu (C/Virgen) with tables outside so you can people watch. They do cheap tapas and classic italian dishes and the draft beer is under four euros, making it a good choice for anyone on a Budget.
Éste es un restaurante Italiano que siempre está lleno, a lo mejor porque está en plena calle peatonal y justo al pie del Carrer de la Mare de Deu (C/. de la Virgen) con mesas en la calle. Hacen tapas a buen precio y platos italianos clásicos y la caña cuesta menos de cuatro euros, un buen sitio si tu presupuesto es ajustado.

90 Dôme

C / d'Alfons XII, 5, Sa Penya, Ibiza
Tel: 971.317.456

This is where all the parade lot stop for a drink or two. It has a large terrace with live DJs, and is the meeting point for many celebrities. I saw Kate Moss here once and she was just another pretty face in the crowd.

Aquí es donde la gente de los desfiles se para a tomar una copa o dos. Tiene una gran terraza con DJs pinchando en directo, y también es el punto de reunión de muchas celebridades y modelos. Una vez vi a Kate Moss aquí y era simplemente otra cara bonita entre la multitud, así que es magnífico para perderse y bajar la guardia.

91 Paradise lost

C/ del passidis, 14, Sa Penya,
Tel: 627589205
paradiselostibiza.com

Rum bar and den of iniquity. Ideal for lounging on Chesterfield's, sprawling on a chaise longue or basking on the terrace. Jimmy (James) mixes you a perfect cocktail, mine being the "Rosita Mala"
The choice of beers here is enough to tempt anyone into this quirky garden of Eden.

Bar de ron y antro. Ideal para tumbarte en el Chesterfield, sentarte en los sillones o sentarte en la terraza. Jimmy (James) te mezclará un cóctel. La mía es la "Rosita Mala".La gran selección de cervezas es suficiente para tentar a cualquier persona a pasarse por este jardín del Edén tan peculiar.

92 Bar 1805 (Bistro)

C/ Santa Lucía, 7, Sa Penya, Ibiza
Tel: 651.625.972
Bar1805ibiza.com

One of my favourite restaurants on Ibiza, for the atmosphere as much as the food. Famous for their Moules et frites (tip: save the fries til last and tip them into the leftover sauce from the moules), and they make a wicked Croque Monsieur. Owner Charles is a champion mixologist and his cocktails are superb – house speciality is an absinthe cocktail known as "The Green Beast".

Uno de mis restaurantes favoritos en Ibiza, tanto por su atmósfera como por su comida. Famosos por sus moules et frites (consejo: guarda las patatas para remojarlas al final en la salsa de mejillones), y también preparan un riquísimo Croque Monsieur. El propietario Charles es un campeón en mixología y sus cócteles son excelentes, la especialidad de la casa es El Cóctel de absenta llamado "Green Beast".

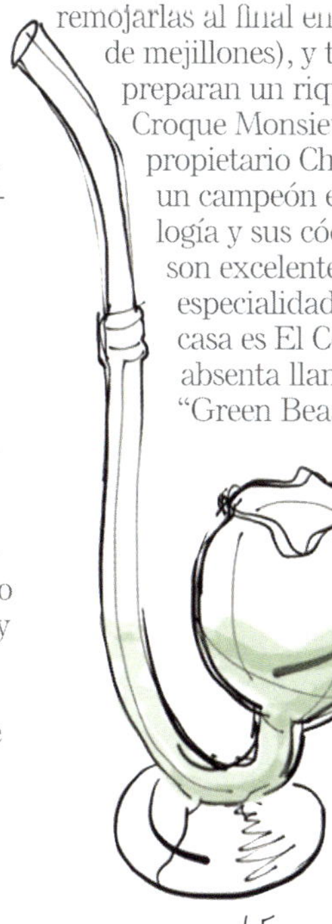

THE COCKTAIL
EL CÓCTEL

by Charles Vexenat (Bar 1805)

HOW TO MAKE A GREEN BEAST (For 4 people):
Grab any bowl big enough and fill it with;
1 cup of Pernod absinthe
1 cup of fresh lime juice
1 cup of sucre cane syrup
4 cups of still water
1 Dutch cucumber chopped in slices
1 bag of ice cubes
Stir it up well & enjoy

CÓMO PREPARAR UN GREEN BEAST (para 4 personas):
Coge un cuenco grande y llénalo con:
1 vaso de Pernod Absinthe
1 vaso de zumo de lima fesca
1 vaso de sirope de azúcar
4 vasos de agua
1 pepino cortado en rodajas
1 bolsa de hielo
Mezclar todo y disfrutar

93 Taller de Sa Penya

C/ Alt, 7, Sa Penya, Ibiza
Tel: 971.312.190
borisbuono.com

Tucked away in the maze of cobbled streets, lies the culinary dining concept that is Taller De Sa Penya, presented by chef Boris Buono. Innovative and surprising with each dish produced in Ibiza, all paired with fine hand-picked wines to enhance your dining experience. Reservations only.

Escondido en el laberinto de calles empedradas, se encuentra este concepto culinario innovador que es el Taller de Sa Penya, por el chef Boris Buono. Cada plato es creado en Ibiza y combinando con vinos escogidos para mejorar su experiencia. Reservar con antelación.

94 Il Pavone

C/ d'Enmig, 22, Sa Penya, Ibiza
Tel: 971.315.555

When it comes to Italian cuisine, these guys know how to do it right. If you can't get a seat on the little terrace, try to nab the balcony. You have to sample the pasta alla Siciliana and the tiramisu. Celebrities, or those just lying low use the side entrance.

Cuando se trata de cocina italiana, estos chicos sí que saben cómo hacerlo. Si no encuentras sitio en su pequeña terraza, busca sitio en su pequeño balcón donde tienes que probar la pasta a la siciliana y el tiramisú. Celebridades, VIPs o aquellos que vayan de incógnito prefieren utilizar su entrada lateral.

95 Sushiya Aoyama

Plaça de sa Drassaneta, 13, Sa Penya, Ibiza
Tel: 627.861.566

Located in a sweet little square at the back of Calle de la Virgen, the restaurant serves some of the best sushi on the island. The fish is always fresh and the rice perfectly cooked and seasoned, thanks to the Japanese chef who is a real sushi master.

Situado en una placita detrás de la calle de la Virgen, aquí el sushi está elaborado de forma simple, pero definitivamente es de los mejores de la isla. El pescado es siempre fresco y el arroz ha sido cocinado y sazonado a la perfección gracias a su chef japonés, que es un verdadero maestro.

96 Sunrise

C/ de La Mare de Déu, 44, (C/ de La Virgen) Sa Penya
Tel: 677.489.827

I ended up here once on a fun night bar crawling with a few girlfriends – and little did we know that it's Ibiza's only "official" lesbian bar. Anyway, it was hilarious in here and the bar tender was definitely male and super cute! Mixed crowds are always welcome, and with swings for barstools hanging at the bar, you're guaranteed hours of fun.

Acabé aquí en una noche divertida yendo de bar en bar con dos amigas, y es el único bar "oficial" de lesbianas en la isla. De todas formas, fue muy divertido y el camarero era definitivamente hombre y muy guapo. Aquí todos, hombres y mujeres, son bienvenidos y los columpios colgando en el bar, en vez de los clásicos taburetes, garantizan infinitas horas de diversión.

SLEEP, EAT & DRINK,... DORMIR, COMER Y BEBER

97 Hostal La Marina

C/ Barcelona, 7, Puerto
Tel: 971.310.172
hostal-lamarina.com

This hostal with its gorgeous blue facade sits facing the sea and is fab. Be warned that the soundproofing is not great in the rooms so try and get one at the top and overlooking the harbour which is stunning to thus avoid the noise that travels up from all the bars.

Este hostal y su preciosa fachada azul está en pleno centro del puerto de Ibiza. Muy asequible, pero la insonorización en las habitaciones no es buena, así que mejor reserva una habitación con vistas al mar para así evitar el ruido que sube de los bares.

98 La Dama d'Eivissa

C/ de sa crue, 20
Tel: 971.310.771.
ladamadeibiza.com

Located just down from Dalt Vila and the old port, past the front door you'll find a private guest house that's friendly and discrete. Each room has a sink, hair dryer, magnifying mirror, bathrobe, TV, safety box and vintage fan, and there's Wifi access in bedrooms and on the roof terrace. Shared showers and toilets though! But it's cheap – prices range from 40 to 155 euros in high season.

Situado justo a los pies de Dalt Vila y el puerto, pasada la puerta principal y te encontrarás con una casa de huéspedes privada que es cordial y discreta. Cada habitación tiene un lavabo, secador, espejo de aumento, albornoz, TV, caja fuerte y ventilador vintage, y hay acceso a WiFi en las habitaciones y la azotea. ¡Aunque las duchas y los baños son compartidos! Pero es barato - los precios van de 40 a 155 euros en temporada alta.

99 La Virgen

C/ de La Mare de Déu, 75,
(C/ de La Virgen) Sa Penya
Tel: 665.594.705

My first date with Charles Vexenat from Bar 1805 landed up here. I was petrified and he kept ordering more rum and cokes.
It was special and as a result I am rather fond of this little music bar at the end of the street.

Mi primera cita con Charles Vexenat del Bar 1805 acabó aquí. Yo muy tímida y él no paraba de pedir más cubatas. Fue muy especial y por eso soy bastante aficionada a este pequeño bar músical al final de la calle.

SHOPPING IN THE AREA ...DE COMPRAS POR AQUI

100 La Casita Ibicenca

C/ d'Enmig, 8, Sa Penya, Ibiza
Tel: 619.471.436

If you want to buy some gifts to take back home to friends and family, here you will find everything Ibiza related.
The shop is at the start of the street that runs parallel to the sea on the port.
It is such a sweet shop and full of Ibiza products.

Si quieres comprar algunos regalos para llevar a casa a la familia o amigos, aquí encontrarás todo relacionado con Ibiza. La tienda está al principio de la calle que corre paralela al mar e el puerto. Es una tienda muy dulce y llena de productos tipicos de la isla.

101 Le Studio

VINTAGE

C/ de Manuel Sora, 25,
Tel: 658.216.746
lestudioibiza.com

This is a heavenly Vintage and second-hand Clothing Shop. It stocks a really original choice. Some pieces are expensive and actually vintage designer and others much more affordable. The shop is on two floors with a little balcony.

Se trata de una tienda preciosa de ropa Vintage y de segunda mano. Tienen una selección de lo más original. Algunas piezas son de marca y más caras y otras mucho más asequibles. La tienda es bohemia y en dos plantas con un pequeño balcóncito.

TAKE YOUR CAMERA! ¡LLÉVATE LA CÁMARA!

VISITING DALT VILA SUBIENDO A DALT VILA

A city inside a fortress, this landmark is visible from many kilometres away and has become a sort of emblem for Ibiza. It was originally built to defend the island from the pillaging of pirates, and today is classed as a UNESCO World Heritage Site. It's actually one of the only completely preserved Renaissance citadels in Europe.
It's a lovely walk up through the arches and tunnels, past limestone walls and along cobbled streets. On your way up you'll come across all sorts of shops, galleries and restaurants, as well as palatial homes, hotels, the Cathedral, the impressive City Hall, the Castle and churches. Ladies beware: don't attempt the walk in heels or flats with no grip; I for one have slipped over many a time on the sloping cobbled streets.

Una ciudad dentro de una fortaleza que se ha convertido en un emblema de Ibiza. Fue construido originalmente para defender la isla de los ataques piratas y en el presente está clasificado por la UNESCO como Patrimonio Histórico de la Humanidad. De hecho es una de las pocas fortalezas completamente preservadas renacentista en Europa. Es una delicia poder pasear a través de sus arcos y túneles, cruzando muros de piedra caliza y por las calles empedradas. En tu paseo hacia la cima te cruzarás en tu camino con tiendas, galerías y restaurantes, además de casas palaciegas, hoteles, la Catedral, el impresionante ayuntamiento, el castillo e iglesias. Chicas, por favor tened cuidado: si intentáis subir en tacones o zapatos de suela deslizante; más de una vez me he resbalado en sus empinadas calles.

EAT & DRINK...
COMER Y BEBER...

102 El Portalón Eivissa

Plaça dels Desemparats,1 Dalt Vila
Tels: 871.110.925
elportalonibiza.com

On the ground floor of a gorgeous restored historic Palacio with a shady terrace overlooking the street that leads you up to the Old Cathedral. This place radiates pure Ibiza Vintage Chic. The food is Mediterranean influenced farm to table. Using locally sourced ingredients from the owners farm, Can Riero Organics, and influenced by "Eivissa" the Ibiza Cook Book by my dear friend and author, Anne Sijmonsbergen working alongside Executive Chef, Filippo Alberi . Treat yourself and taste Ibiza at its best.

En la planta baja de un precioso palacio antiguo restaurado, con terrazas a la sombra de cara a la calle que te lleva hasta la antigua catedral de Ibiza.
Este sitio iradia un estilo Vintage Chic.
La comida es de estilo Mediterráneos utilizando infgredientes locales de la granja de los dueños, "Can Riero Organics" y influenciado por el libro de cocina "Eivissa" de mi querida amiga y autora, Anne Sijmonsbergen que se ha juntado a trabajar junto al Chef Ejecutivo, Filippo Alberi.
Disfrute de los sabores de Ibiza en su mejor momento.

103 La Dispensa

C/ la Santa Creu, 10, Dalt Vila
Tel: 971.124.365

You will find this pretty restaurant on a quaint little street up in the Old Town. I love to sit out under the stars with a Bellini before ordering. The food is a mix of tapas and Itailan specialities. They have a kids menú, vegetarian options and some great aperitifs.

Encontrarás este simpático restaurante en una pintoresca calle en el casco antiguo. Me encanta sentarme bajo las estrellas con un Bellini antes de pedir mi comida. Aquí sirven una mezcla de tapas y especialidades italianas. Además tienen aperitivos, cócteles, un menú para niños, platos vegetarianos y postres deliciosos.

104 La Oliva

C/ la Santa Creu, Dalt Vila, Ibiza
Tel: 971.305.752

I love this Provencal family -run restaurant in Dalt Vila. The tables are set out on the sloping narrow cobbled street, and their food is consistantly good every year. You can sit and watch people walk past as well as the occassional street performer. Oh, and the goats cheese pastry starter is heavenly

Me encanta este restaurante provenzal regentado por una familia en Dalt Vila. Las mesas están fuera, en la calle empedrada, y la comida nunca me decepciona. Puedes ver la gente pasar además de algun animador de calle. Por cierto, el entrante de pastel de queso de cabra esta riquísimo.

105 S'Escalinata

C/ Portal Nou, 10, Dalt Vila, Ibiza
Tel: 653.371.356
sescalinata.es

This Little spot is up in the old town by La Plaza de Sol at some steps (thus the name) which are laid out with colourful cushions, so you can sit outside on them, which I just love. It's a youngish crowd that come here and they serve tapas, sandwiches and salads all day. Perfect for a pit stop during a walk.

Este lugar está en el casco antiguo de Ibiza y es conocido por sus escalones con cojines coloridos para sentarte fuera, algo que me encanta. La clientela es más bien joven y colorida. Sirven tapas, sandwiches y ensaladas durante todo el día. Es perfecto para una parada si estás de caminata por la zona.

EL PORTALON
EIVISSA
MODERN
MEDITERRANEAN
CUISINE
ORGANIC FARM
TO TABLE
COCKTAILS
& BAR

ISIDORO MACABICH STATUE / ESTATUA. **Sa Carrossa, Dalt Vila.**

Placed as a statement to his importance in the culture of Ibiza. A man who devoted his life to church activities but also a writer, poet, archaeologist and teacher. His most important work were the 4 volumes of the History of Ibiza, published in 1966.

Una estatua que declara su importancia en la cultura de Ibiza. Un hombre que dedicó su vida a actividades de la iglesia, y también escritor, poeta, arqueólogo y profesor. Su obra más importante fueron los 4 volúmenes de la Historia de Ibiza, publicado en 1966.

HOTELS... HOTELES...

106 El Mirador

Plaça d'Espanya, 4, Dalt Vila
Tel: 971.303.045
hotelmiradoribiza.com

A beautiful renovated villa halfway up the old town with marbled floors and high ceilings and a swimming pool that make it a five star Relais Chateux hotel. It's a lovely walk up and sits in a small cobbled square near a church. Chauffeur service straight from the airport.

Una casa señorial en lo alto de Dalt Vila, con sus suelos de mármol, techos altos y piscina lo convierten en un Relais Chateux de cinco estrellas esencial.
Es un precioso paseo desde el centro en una placita al lado de la iglesia. Servicio de chófer directamente del aeropuerto.

107 La Ventana

C/ de sa Carrossa, 13, Dalt Vila, Ibiza
Tel: 971.390.857
laventanaibiza.com

An Ibicencan town house hotel painted in pale yellow with perfect windows and shutters and set in the middle of the history-soaked Dalt Vila. Furnished with incredibly comfortable four-poster beds, art and grainy antique mirrors, it's a perfect choice for couples. Friends say that the view from the rooftop chill out is not to be missed.

Un hotel boutique clásicamente ibicenco pintado de amarillo pastel con ventanas y persianas perfectas que está en pleno centro de Dalt Vila, empapándose de la historia del casco antiguo. Amueblado con camas con dosel, obras de arte y antiguos espejos. Una elección perfecta para parejas, y me cuentan que la vista desde su azotea es sobrecogedora.

108 Torre del Canónigo

C/ Mayor, 8, Dalt Vila, Ibiza
Tel: 971.303.884
latorredelcanonigo.com

I always feel like I'm entering a castle when I come here. The hotel is set within a 14th century tower in Dalt Vila, and gives panoramic views over Ibiza Town bay. They've installed a stunning stone pool in the terraced area, as well as a garden and restaurant where you can enjoy your summer evenings. Each room is unique and breakfast is served until 2pm which means you can hit the snooze button.

Cuando entro aquí siempre tengo la sensación de estar en un palacio. El hotel está en una torre del siglo XIV en Dalt Vila, con vistas sobre la ciudad. Con una piscina de piedra magnífica en su terraza, además de un jardín y restaurante donde puedes disfrutar de las noches de verano. Cada habitación es única. El desayuno se sirve hasta las 14.00, lo que significa que puedes apretar el botón y "seguir durmiendo".

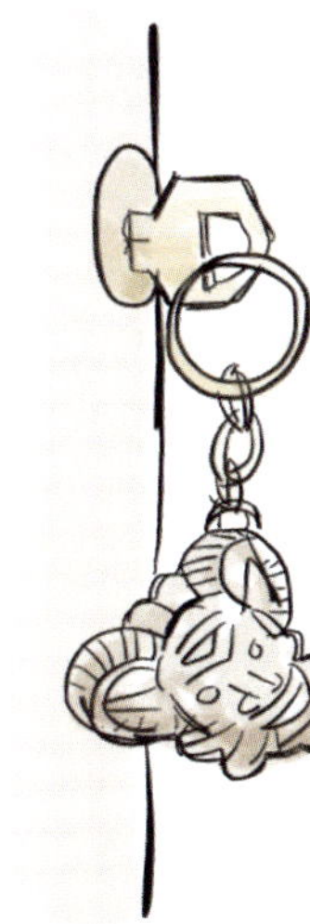

5 THINGS YOU SHOULD DO
5 COSAS QUE DEBERÍAS HACER CUANDO ESTÉS AQUÍ

1. Have an evening stroll along Talamanca beach
Da un paseo por la playa de Talamanca al atardecer

2. Have a super healthy lunch at Passion (p. 77)
Tómate un almuerzo saludable en Passion

3. Enjoy a drink and view from Sa Calma (p. 80)
Disfruta de un aperitivo y la vista desde Sa Calma

4. Mexican food and mezcal at Deseo (p. 87)
Comida mejicana y Mezcal en Deseo

5. Have a dance at Pacha Nightclub
Baila en la discoteca Pacha

The Marina, Talamanca Jesús & the Outskirts

La Marina, Talamanca, Jesús y las afueras

AROUND THE MARINA + BOTAFOCH EL PASEO Y MARINA BOTAFOCH

Marina Botafoch sits across the bay facing Ibiza Town, and is like a mini-village of boaty people and shops. Mixed in with a few little tapa spots, restaurants and some lively bars, easy parking and stunning views in the evening, it's no wonder it's becoming more popular each summer.

Marina Botafoch se sitúa al otro lado de la bahía mirando hacia Ibiza ciudad y es como una pequeña aldea de gente y tiendas náuticas. Mezclado con restaurantes, locales de tapas y bares, es fácil aparcar aquí y las vistas por la noche son impresionantes, con todo esto no me sorprende que cada verano se haga más popular.

EAT & DRINK... COMER Y BEBER...

Restaurante Club Náutico Ibiza

Av. de Santa Eulària des Riu, 1006
Marina Ibiza
Tel: 971.314.023

As you start walking from Ibiza Town, this restaurant is attached to the side of the first Yacht Club you will pass. My dad used to love it here. He'd sit on the terrace with a beer looking at the view of the boats and remeniscing… I don't think he ever quite got over selling his schooner "Tuluaq" which can still be found photographed on old postcards of Ibiza in the 60's. The restaurant serves typical Ibicenco food including great seafood dishes and they offer clients a set day menú for about 12 euros, as well as a separate menú if you fancy something specific. I always have the seafood soup which is on the menú.
You won't be disappointed.

A medida que comienzas a

caminar desde el centro de Ibiza es de los primeros clubs náuticos que pasarás.
A mi padre le encantaba este lugar; se sentaba en la terraza con una cerveza mirando los barcos y recordando sus tiempos como marinero. Creo que nunca superó la venta de su velero, que todavía puede verse en fotografías y postales antiguas de la Ibiza de los 60. El restaurante sirve comida típica ibicenca incluyendo riquísimos platos de pescado y marisco. Ofrecen a los clientes un menú del día por unos 12 euros, además de otro menú por si te apetece algo específico. Yo siempre pido la sopa de pescado.

Passion Restaurant

Passeig Juan Carles I, 23,
Edificio Mediteraneo
Tel: 971.305.130
passion-ibiza.com

Gorgeous Lana has created this amazing health bar and café on the Marina strip, where she serves juices and superfoods, the best salads, gourmet burgers, wraps, pasta and, of course, her famous homemade cakes and desserts. She also offers detox programmes made to measure. Don't miss the new Passion Juicery at the back of Passion on C/ Gregal, 9.
La bella Lana ha creado este restaurante-cafetería en el paseo marítimo, donde sirve zumos y superalimentos, las mejores ensaladas, hamburguesas gourmet, rollitos, pasta y, por supuesto, sus famosos pasteles y postres caseros. También ofrece programas de desintoxicación personalizados. No te pierdas el nuevo Passion Juicery, detrás de Passion en la Calle Gregal, 9.

A Son de Mar

C/ Ponent, 118,
Port Deportivo Marina Botafoch
Tel: 971.313.151
restauranteasondemar.com

A gorgeous spot on the marina offering Mediterranean cuisine with a bit of all cultures added in the mix and classic rice dishes like Paella or Fideua.
Try the Gourmet burger, Nebraskan Steak or the fresh pasta. Open all day.
Un precioso lugar en el puerto deportivo de Botafoch. Ofrecen una cocina mediterránea con una mezcla de culturas, además de platos típicos de la isla como la paella o la fideuá. Prueba la hamburguesa Gourmet, el entrecot de Nebraska o la pasta fresca. Abierto todo el día.

Cafe Sidney

Port Deportivo Marina Botafoch
Tel: 871.112.521
cafesidney.com

A great Cafe that has been here for years despite closing for a few years to then open again due to popular demand. They offer breakfasts, brunches, lunches and dinners as well as views of the boats and Ibiza town. Open all day everyday.
Un café que ha estado aquí durante años a pesar de cerrar durante unos años para luego abrir otra vez debido a demanda popular. Ofrecen desayunos, almuerzos y cenas, así como vistas de los barcos y Dalt Vila.
Abierto todos los días.

Los Pasajeros de Botafoch

Marina Botafoch
Tel: 971.317.828

This is a great little super-relaxed restaurant that has quickly become one of my absolute budget favourites – it's always great value and always delicious, plus they do take-away.
Este restaurante rápidamente se ha convertido en uno de mis favoritos cuando no quiero gastar mucho, el precio es siempre bueno y todo está delicioso, además preparan comida para llevar.

Il Giardinetto

Passeig de Joan Carles I
Marina Botafoch
Tel: 971.314.929

I've been going here for years as I love Italian food, and this place does one of my favourite dishes – a raw artichoke salad. It sounds weird but it's healthy and delicious, even if it does make you feel a bit like a horse chewing!
Their homemade pasta Bolognaise is also exceptional.
Hace años que vengo aquí porque me encanta la cocina italiana, y este restaurante prepara uno de mis platos favoritos, ensalada de alcachofas crudas. Suena raro, pero es sano y delicioso, aunque te parezca que estés masticando como un caballo. Sus pasta boloñesa está riquísima.

passion
JUICERY
100%
COLD PRESSED

Bar Barlovento

Port Deportivo Marina Botafoch
Tel: 971.317.717

In all the years I've lived in Ibiza, this old-school tapas bar has not changed much, despite being located right in the middle of all the new restaurants. I love the "bocarones en vinagre", which are small fish marinated in vinegar and garlic, knocked back with a cold beer. It's good value and has a fab view from their little terrace.

En todos los años que llevo viviendo en Ibiza, éste es un clásico bar de tapas que no ha cambiado nada. Nosotros siempre nos pedimos los boquerones en vinagre. Todo aquí está a buen precio y tiene magníficas vistas desde su pequeña terraza.

Sushi Point

Marina Botafoch, Local 205
Tel: 971.318.153
sushipointibiza.com

This is an Asiatic mediterranean fusion restaurant that turns into a kind of club after midnight. They serve great cocktails and have a long line-up of DJs that play all year round. In the Winter it becomes the residents weekend hang-out.

Este restaurante de fusión asiática-mediterránea se convierte en un pequeño club después de medianoche. Sirven unos cócteles excelentes y tienen una larga lista de DJs pinchando todo el año. Los fines de semana de invierno se convierte en el lugar más popular entre los residentes.

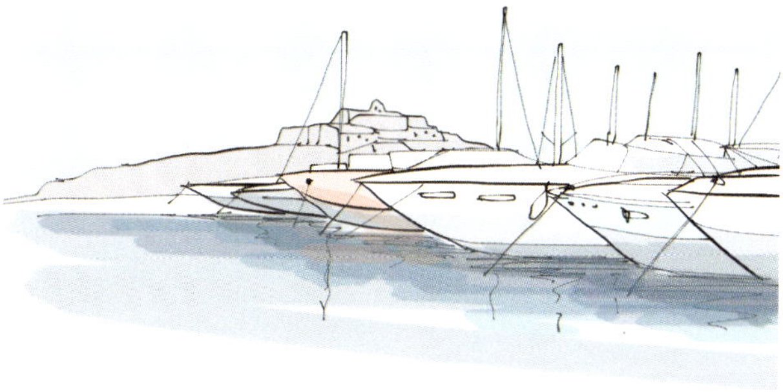

La Terrasse Botafoch

Marina Botafoch, Local 114
Tel: 971.316.654

Boasting an incredible view over the marina, this little french restaurant is such a great spot for breakfast, lunch and dinner.
They have a lunch menu that changes each week and serve dishes like salmon Tartare, Cod Brandade and Oysters. They also have delicious deserts. It is really worth trying.

Con una increíble vista a la marina, este pequeño restaurante francés es el lugar ideal para desayunar, almuerzar y cenar. Tienen un menú del día que cambia cada semana y sirven platos como Tartar de Salmon, Brandada de Bacalao y Ostras. Ademas tienen deliciosos postres. Realmente vale la pena probar.

Just Fish Ibiza

Marina Botafoch, Local 105b
Tel: 971.508.761

My friend Melchior from Nagai Restaurant, recommended this seafood bar for my guide. He explained that they have fresh fish from the market, presented on a huge frozen tray from where you choose what you want. Lobsters, prawns, mussels, squid, bream, etc... and then gets cooked for you on the spot. Open for Lunch and dinner.

Mi amigo Melchor del restaurante Nagai me recomendó este bar de mariscos para esta guía. Me explicó que tienen pescado fresco del mercado, presentado en una bandeja congelada de la que puedes eligir lo que quieres. Langostas, gambas, mejillones, calamar, dorada,...y te lo cocinan en el acto. Abierto almuerzo y cena.

Temakinho Ibiza

Marina Botafoch, Local 113
Tel: 971.199.944

With great views over the port and a tasteful decor, this place fuses Japanese cooking with Brazilian along with the rhythms of Samba and Bossa Nova in the background. They do great Sushi too.

Con preciosas vistas sobre el puerto y una decoración de buen gusto, éste fusiona la cocina japonesa con la brasileña junto con los ritmos de Samba y Bossa Nova en el fondo. Hacen Sushi también.

Box 7

Passeig Joan Carles I, 39
Tel. 971.199.880
box7ibiza.com

Located just before the little roundabout at the end of the Marina strip. This place does lovely breakfasts, a great roast beef sandwich, salmon sandwich, as well as a selection of fresh fruit, juices and pastries. Also worth knowing that they offer a catering and take-away service.

Justo antes de la pequeña rotonda del paseo de la marina, aquí saben preparar buenos desayunos y también un magnífico bocadillo de ternera o salmón, además de una selección de zumos de fruta fresca y vegetales, especialidades caseras y hojaldres. Además es bueno saber que tienen servicio de catering y comida para llevar.

Trattoria del Mar

Port Deportivo Marina Botafoch
Tel: 971.193.934
trattoriadelmaribiza.com

The international 'jet set' dine al fresco at this contemporary waterfront hotspot, which is one of the only places in the Marina that's open all year round. Fine Italian cuisine and an unbeatable location with a gorgeous wooden wraparound terrace makes for a winning combination.

La jet set internacional cena al aire libre en este local contemporáneo frente al mar, uno de los pocos sitios en Marina que está abierto todo el año. Cocina italiana sofisticada y una situación privilegiada con una preciosa terraza de madera, una combinación ganadora.

Sa Calma

Marina Ibiza
Tel: 971.595.595

This waterfront spot in Marina Botafoch is perfect for a coffee, breakfast, lunch and dinner, with Lío club behind you, the super-yachts to your left and Dalt Vila (straight ahead), a prime location. The view of Ibiza town at night is a glistening array of lights reflected in the sea.

Este local en primera línea de Marina Botafoch es perfecto para desayunar, almorzar o tomar un aperitivo. Todo a la vez que disfrutas con los yates a tu izquierda y Dalt Vila justo enfrente. Realmente bién ubicado y la vista de noche del casco antiguo reflejado en el mar es inmejorable.

Sa Nansa

Av. 8 d'Agost, 27
Tel: 971.318.750
restaurantesanansa.com

A typical Ibizan restaurant that won't disappoint you. Specializing in seafood and Mediterranean cuisine and they make the best paella and rice dishes. Not to mention a good wine list to go with your meal.

Un restaurante típico ibicenco que no te decepcionará porque de verdad saben cocinar pescado, marisco y cocina mediterránea. Además hacen de las mejores paellas y arroces, y tienen una carta de vinos muy buenos para acompañar tu comida.

Prince Bakery

Paseo Juan Carlos I, Local 3
Tel: 871.718.361

This boutique bakery Café sits in the middle of the Pacha nightlife overflow and is perfect to satisfy your post clubbing appetite. They have homemade bread and italian Panini. The best bit is that they are open from 6 am until 11:30 pm

Esta panadería y cafetería pequeña se encuentra en el centro de la movida nocturna de la zona de Pacha y es perfecto para satisfacer tu apetito después de la fiesta. Tienen pan casero y panini italiano. Y lo mejor es que están abiertos desde las 6 de la mañana hasta las 23:30.

Keeper

Paseo Juan Carlos I, s/n
Tel: 971.310.509
keeperibiza.com

This pre-Pacha spot has been a favourite with locals since the 80s. As they say - the magic nights of Ibiza, always start in Keeper... These days it's mainly frequented by the sailing crowd, as well as those who like to hit the dance floor earlier than 3am!

Este local pre-Pacha es el favorito de los españoles desde los 80. Como dicen: las noches de magia en Ibiza, siempre empiezan en Keeper... Hoy en día lo frecuentan principalmente los navegantes, además de aquellos a los que les gusta lanzarse a la pista antes de las 03:00.

THE LARGE HAND SCULPTURE

A monument by the sculptor Andreu Moreno, which pays tribute to the Ibizan hound or "podenco."

LA GRAN ESCULTURA DE LA MANO

Un monumento del escultor Andreu Moreno, que rinde tributo al perro ibicenco o "podenco".

SLEEP... DORMIR...

Ocean Drive

Playa de Talamanca, Marina Botafoch
Tel: 971.318.112

Inspired by the architecture of South Beach and Miami, its impressive facade looms at the end of the Ma rina strip. Here breakfast is served until 4pm.
Open all year round.

Inspirado en la arquitectura de South Beach y Miami. Su impresionante fachada ilumina el final del paseo marítimo. Aquí se sirve el desayuno hasta las 16:00. Abierto todo el año.

Hotel Argos

Playa de Talamanca
Tel: 971.312.162
hotelargos-ibiza.com

This four star hotel was recently refurbished and has and indoor and an outdoor pool, a gym and offers its clients a beach service as well. It is located directly on the beach with stunning sea views. Talamanca Beach is a family beach that has a selection of restaurants and offers water activities to everyone.

Este hotel de cuatro estrellas ha sido recientemente reformado y dispone de una piscina cubierta y otra aire libre y un gimnasio y ademas ofrece a sus clientes servicio de playa. Está situado directamente en la playa con preciosas vistas al mar. La playa de Talamanca es una playa familiar que tiene una selección de restaurantes y actividades deportivas.

Ibiza Gran Hotel

Paseo Juan Carlos I
Tel: 971.806.806

What can I say, just go check it out and if you can afford it, stay at least a night in this impressive place!
A five-star establishment that is home to Cipriani's buzzing Ibiza Downtown restaurant and the only casino in Ibiza.
If you really want to splash out go for the Vanity Fair Suite on the top floor, where your private terrace comes complete with a Jacuzzi and heated pool and stunning views of the old town.

Qué puedo decir, ve a echar un vistazo y si puedes permitírtelo, ¡hospédate al menos una noche! Este establecimiento de cinco estrellas alberga al restaurante Downtown Ibiza de Cipriani y al único casino de Ibiza. Si quieres derrochar, entonces decídete por la Suite Vanity Fair en la última planta, donde tu propia terraza privada se completa con jacuzzi y piscina climatizada.

El Hotel

Paseo Juan Carlos I
Tel: 971.806.806

This is the perfect hotel if you want to be at the heart of the action. Just a few steps away from Pacha nightclub, Lío and the marina. There's always a lot going on here with exhibitions, and events so don't expect to get a lot of sleep!

Este es el hotel perfecto si quieres estar en plena acción. A unos pasos de la discoteca Pacha, Lío y la Marina. Siempre hay muchos eventos aquí con exposiciones, desfiles... ¡no esperes dormir mucho!

TALAMANCA BEACH PLAYA DE TALAMANCA

This idyllic bay is an ocean (literally) of calm just a few minutes drive, or a pleasant half an hour walk from the centre of town. With a selection of nice restaurants and places to stay, the beach itself is also delightful with a long wooden boardwalk that's perfect for an early morning run.

Esta idílica bahía es verdaderamente un mar de calma a tan sólo unos minutos en coche del centro de la ciudad o a un paseo de media hora. Acoge una selección de restaurantes y alojamientos, y la misma playa también es una delicia con un largo paseo de madera perfecto para hacer jogging por las mañanas.

EAT... COMER

Bar Flotante

C/ de Talamanca, Talamanca
Tel: 971.190.466

I love my bacon and eggs with a side order of chips here. They also do a great omelette which my daughter loves. This basic bar sits literally on the sea edge, thus its name, "the floating bar," which is meant to suggest that when the storms come in the bar could almost be washed away.

Me encantan los huevos con beicon que sirven aquí con una ración de patatas fritas a parte. También hacen una tortilla muy buena. Este bar está pegado al mar, de ahí su nombre, que además sugiere que cuando se acercan las tormentas el bar podría acabar inundado.

Hostal Talamanca

C/ de Talamanca, Talamanca
Tel: 971.312.463
hostaltalamanca.com

This is a restaurant as well as a Hostal. Sleep and eat by the beach, and affordably in this simple but sweet hostal that ticks both boxes. Room prices range from just 35 euros. There's also free wi-fi, and the restaurant serves delicious seafood and every friday there's fresh sardines and live music.

Si quieres alojarte y dormir junto a la playa por un buen precio, este hostal simple pero simpático es perfecto. Los precios de las habitaciones van desde los 35 euros. También hay wi-fi gratuito y un restaurante muy bonito con terraza en la playa y vistas al mar.

The Harbour Club

C/ de Talamanca, Talamanca
Tel: 971.193.380
theharbourclub.com

Located in the middle of the beach, think fine wining & dining where they serve seafood, steaks and sushi, it certainly isn't cheap but the high quality of the food makes it good value for money and the views are heavenly. If your are feeling flush get a day bed for the day.

Imagínate una elegante cena de pescado y marisco, entrecotes o sushi, con unas vistas espectaculares al mar. No es un lugar barato pero la calidad de su cocina hace una buena relación calidad-precio. Si quieres de verdad disfrutar, píllate una hamaca durante el día...

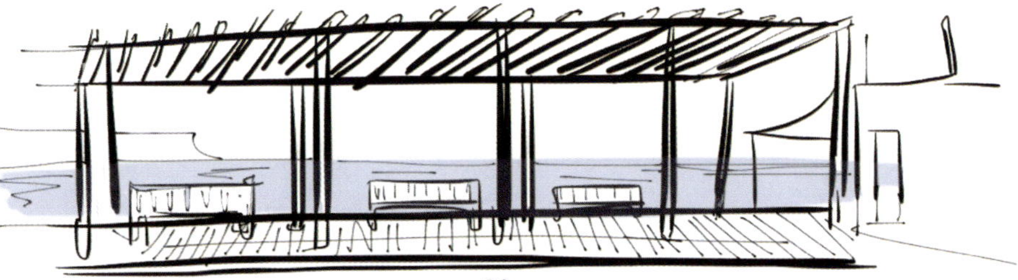

Restaurante Bellamar

C/ de Talamanca, Talamanca
Tel: 971.191.335

A small beach spot where you can enjoy a meal with your toes in the sand. You can walk from the Talamanca beach parking along the wooden promenade, and the owners are very laid back which makes it great for kids. Really good value and amazing views. Un chiringuito donde puedes hundir los pies en la arena mientras disfrutas de tu comida. Puedes pasear desde el parking de Talamanca por el paseo de madera, y los propietarios son gente relajada, lo que hace que sea un lugar magnífico para los niños. Buen precio e increíbles vistas.

El Pulpo Restaurante

C/ de Talamanca, Talamanca
Tel: 971.191.530

Bang on the beach and famous for their "bullit", a traditional stew made with different varieties of fish. They also have a barbecue, and in the evening offer grilled meats. Dining with your feet in the sand and an uninterrupted sea view. What more could you ask for?
En medio de la playa, muy conocido por su "Bullit", el guiso de pescado tradicional elaborado con diferentes variedades de pescado. También tienen una barbacoa, y por la noche ofrecen carnes a la parrilla. Aquí puedes comer con los pies en la arena y una vista al mar espectacular. ¿Qué más se puede pedir?

Talamanca Club

C/ de Ses Feixes, Talamanca
Tel: 971.313.574

A great place to go with a large group and the kids. They go and horse about on the beach and we all sit back, relax and enjoy the Italian menu of fresh pastas, pizzas, fish and grilled meats. I always order the prawn and courgette pasta, which has a creamy sauce and is always cooked al dente. Open all year for lunch and dinner. Service can be really slow.
Uno de nuestros favoritos en verano ya que es perfecto para venir en grupo y con los niños. Los niños se van a jugar por la playa y nosotros disfrutamos de una deliciosa carta italiana con pastas frescas, pizzas, carnes y pescado a la brasa. Suelo pedirme la pasta de gamas y calabacín, que tiene una salsa suave y cremosa y siempre está al dente. Abierto todo el año, mediodía y noche. El servicio puede ser un poco lento.

The Fish Shack

C/ Calandria, Sa Punta, Talamanca

My mum's absolute favourite and actually she gave it its name years ago...although it's also known as "4 Latas".
To find it walk past Sa Punta restaurant...keep going...and there it is. They serve the simplest dishes here. The fish is freshly caught that morning and the lamb chops are incredible, all served with a potato and tomato salad. Desserts and coffee are all local too. You can't book in advance unless you physically go there and reserve, which is classic old-school Ibiza! I like to grab a table and then go for a quick dip off the rocks right before eating.
"4 Latas", es el favorito de mi madre, venimos mucho en verano. Para encontrarlo pasa el restaurante Sa Punta y sigue caminando. Un local sencillo donde sirven platos simples y delisiosos.

El pescado fresco del día y las chuletas de cordero están riquísimas, todo servido con ensalada de patatas y tomate. Los postres y el café también son típicos de Ibiza. No puedes reservar a menos que vengas físicamente, ¡a la vieja usanza! Pero lo que más me gusta es coger una mesa y antes de sentarme a comer, pegarme un baño rápido antes.

La Bodega Talamanca

C/ Ses Figueres, 18, Talamanca
Tel: 672.494.847
labodegaibiza.es

The 'sister' restaurant of La Bodega in Ibiza has settled here in a really nice location, with a shady terrace overlooking the bay of Talamanca and extremely pretty in the evenings. Known for its large choice of delicious tapas, good wines and great cocktails.

El restaurante hermano de La Bodega en Ibiza está situado en una zona muy bonita con una terraza sombreada y vistas a la bahía de Talamanca que es precioso para pasar una velada. Muy conocido por su larga carta de deliciosas tapas, vinos y cócteles.

Sa Punta

C/ Calandria, Sa Punta
Tel: 971.193.424

Possibly one of the prime locations in the bay, this classy restaurant has a large roof terrace with a great view of Ibiza town. With daybeds for all-evening lounging and a chilled out soundtrack, it's the perfect place to watch the sunset after a day on the beach or a stunning location for a wedding, just ask our translator Sally.

Posiblemente tiene una de las situaciones más privilegiadas de la bahía, este elegante restaurante tiene una enorme terraza en su azotea con magníficas vistas a Ibiza ciudad. Con tumbonas para relajarse durante la noche y una banda sonora de chill out, es el lugar perfecto para contemplar la puesta de sol después de un día en la playa o un lugar magnífico para celebrar una boda, pregúntaselo a nuestra traductora Sally.

Bar Restaurante Alegría

C/ de Talamanca, Talamanca
Tel: 971.313.574

A little shack, right beside Hostal Talamanca that buzzes from early evening onwards as locals descend to drink sangria and listen to the Spanish guitarists who rock up most nights of the week. They have a big outdoor barbecue and a terrace which gets the

sunlight most of the day. A lovely Spanish lady prepares meat on the grill outside, and apart from this they serve up fresh fish and other seafood - all fresh that day. Open all year for lunch and dinner, and inside there's a funky old bar with a few small tables.
Este chiringuito, justo al lado del Hostal Talamanca, se llena desde primera hora de la tarde en adelante con gente de Ibiza que desciende en masa para beber sangría y escuchar guitarra española en directo casi todas las noches de la semana. Tienen una gran parrilla al aire libre y una bonita terraza a la que le da el sol casi todo el día. Una encantadora señora prepara carne a la parrilla en la terraza, también sirven pescado y marisco, fresco del mismo día. Abierto todo el año para el almuerzo y cena. Dentro hay una barra vieja y divertida con unas pocas mesas pequeñas.

...SLEEP... DORMIR

Lux Isla
C/ Josep Pla, 1, Talamanca
Tel: 971.313.469
luxisla.com

This peaceful hotel is set back a bit from Talamanca bay, and is as popular in the winter as it is in the summer. It's affordable and clean. And I've heard that it's a great little weekend spot as it's walking distance from everything you need. You can hit the beach right outside and hire a windsurfer for the day or simply lounge on the sand.
Este hotel está situado en las calles traseras de la bahía de Talamanca, es un hotel muy asequible y limpio. He oído que es un alojamiento perfecto para el fin de semana y está a un paso de todo lo que necesitas, puedes cruzar a la playa que está justo al otro lado de la calle y alquilar una tabla de windsurf por el día o simplemente relajarte en la arena.

Hotel Simbad
C/ Ses Figueres, 22, Talamanca
Tel: 971.311.862
hotelsimbad.es

This place has been here forever - I remember staring up at it from the beach as a child. Perfectly placed on Talamanca's promenade and beach, it really has magnificent views of the Mediterranean and Dalt Vila. Inside you'll find a spa and heated pool, waterfall, sauna, Jacuzzi, and even a fully equipped gym.
Este hotel lleva aquí toda mi vida, recuerdo contemplarlo desde la playa cuando era pequeña. Al estar perfectamente situado junto al paseo de Talamanca y la playa, realmente presume de unas vistas magníficas del Mediterráneo y Dalt Vila. Dentro encontrarás un spa y una piscina climatizada, cascada, sauna, jacuzzi e incluso un gimnasio totalmente equipado.

Destino Pacha Ibiza Resort
C/ Pettirojo, 18 Cap Martinet
Tel: 971.317.411
destinoibiza.com

This luxury Resort sits perched up on the cliffs with sensational views of Dalt Vila across the dense blue bay of Talamanca. The pool area is very sophisticated with daybeds and Jacuzzis set around a gorgeous solarium.
The restaurant serves all sorts, but I think the sushi is outstanding here. Be prepared to spend!
Este complejo goza de unas vistas a Dalt Vila y la bahía azul de Talamanca sensacionales. La zona de la piscina es muy sofisticada, con grandes tumbonas y jacuzzis alrededor de un extenso solarium. El restaurante sirve todo tipo de comida, y el sushi aquí es realmente excepcional. ¡Prepárate para gastar!

"click" JESÚS VILLAGE EL PUEBLO DE JESÚS

This growing village suburb is about ten minutes northeast of Ibiza town and is a short drive to Talamanca beach. Surrounded by residential streets and hills with pine forests. Jesús has a cosmopolitan air, thanks to a good selection of upmarket restaurants, shops, and even a gym.
In the center sits its main feature, the parish church, with it's painted arches which dates back to the 1400s with an impressive altarpiece within. The face of the Virgin Mary engraved on this rare masterpiece is considered to be one of the most beautiful pieces of medieval iconography in the Balearics.

Este pequeño pueblo a diez minutos al norte de Ibiza ciudad está cerca de la playa de Talamanca, y rodeado de una zona residencial y montañas de bosques de pino. Jesús tiene un aire cosmopolita, gracias a una buena selección de restaurantes, tiendas e incluso un gimnasio. En el centro se sitúa su monumento principal, la iglesia gótica, que data de 1400 y fue reconstruida un siglo después con un altar impresionante. El rostro de la Virgen María grabado en este monumento histórico ha sido considerado como una de las piezas más bonitas de la iconografía medieval en España.

EAT AND ENJOY...
COMER Y DISFRUTAR

Bon Lloc

Ctra. a Cala Llonga, Jesús
Tel: 971.311.813

Bon Lloc is located directly on the roadside facing the church, with screaming scooters, trucks and cars tearing past. But it's worth stopping off for the great Ibicencan tapas, and extensive lunch and dinner menus. They do a good paella on Sundays, and the waiters are always lovely as they serve you on the wraparound terrace. A great spot to watch the world go by.

Bon Lloc está situado justo al lado de la carretera frente a la iglesia, con motos, camiones y coches estridentes pasando siempre a toda prisa. Pero merece la pena pararse aquí para probar sus magníficas tapas ibicencas y una extensa carta tanto para comer como para cenar. Hacen una paella fabulosa los domingos y los camareros son encantadores mientras te sirven en su envolvente terraza.
Un lugar magnífico para ver el mundo pasar.

Canadian

C/ des Cap Martinet, 8, Jesús
Tel: 971.194.881
canadiancoffeeculture.co

At the famous Jesus junction at the side of the church sits the island's answer to Starbucks.
I love the healthy snacks and juices with supplements of your choice that make a really healthy start to the day. But if you are a coffee buff then the espresso here is considered one of the best on the island, and they have really nice cakes too!

En el famoso cruce de Jesús frente a la iglesia, se asienta la respuesta de Ibiza a Starbucks.
Me encantan los aperitivos y zumos sanos con suplementos de tu elección que hacen que empieces el día de forma sana. Pero si eres adicto al café entonces el café solo aquí es considerado uno de los mejores de la isla y además tienen muy buena repostería.

La Vinería

C/ des Cap Martinet, 3, Jesús
Tel: 971.191.827
lavineriaibiza.com

I love good Italian food, and that's exactly what you get here – not surprising that my first visit was with an Italian friend. The anti-pasti is particularly good, especially the mussels with white wine sauce or the gratinéd aubergine with mozzarella and parmesan. They also do a great day menu.

Me encanta la comida italiana, y eso es exactamente lo que encontrarás aquí, creo que mi primera visita fue con un amigo italiano. El anti pasti es especialmente bueno, sobre todo los mejillones con salsa de vino blanco o la berenjena gratinada con mozzarella y parmesano.
Aquí también sirven un menú del día magnífico.

El Deseo Jesús

C/ des Cap Martinet, 7, Jesús
Tel: 971.194.635
eldeseoibiza.com

A great mexican restaurant beside the church in Jesús. They serve really good Mexican specialties, and Tex-Mex along with a tapa bar. The decor is cosy and cute and it is always packed with residents and locals. I love their ceviche and the burritos with Chilli con carne in it. They are also a Mezcaleria with a Cocktail and Juice bar. We can't seem to go here without getting offered mezcal shots by the guy at the bar. Oh and they do a great breakfast here and the Tequila is optional of course!!

Un restaurante mexicano buenísimo al lado de la iglesia en Jesús. Sirven especialidades mexicanas, Tex-Mex, y tapas. Me encanta el ceviche que hacen y el burrito de chilli con carne. También son una Mezcalería con un bar de cócteles y zumos. Siempre que vamos nos invitan a chupitos de Mezcal al final. También hacen unos desayunos riquísimos, ¡y la Tequila es opcional claro!

Ascua
C/ Faisán, 8, Jesús
Tel: 971.194.881
ascua.es

This place comes highly recommended by my friend the musician Lenny Ibizarre. The name "Ascua" refers to the embers of their wood oven and grill, where all is created. On entering you will see a huge blackboard that changes daily depending on what's fresh, and they also have exquisite tapas and an extensive wine list.

Mi amigo Lenny Ibizarre recomienda este sitio encarecidamente. Su nombre "Ascua" se refiere a las brasas de su horno y parrilla de leña, donde se prepara todo. Al entrar verás una enorme pizarra que cambia diariamente dependiendo de lo que tengan fresco y además tienen tapas exquisitas y una carta de vinos muy asequible.

Carpe Diem
C/ des Cap Martinet, 54, Jesús
Tel: 971.314.520

I go here for the pizzas because they make them in a proper Pizza oven, but if someone wants to share the T-bone steak for two it's also a favourite. My daughter always orders the spaghetti bolognaise, and licks the plate clean! The interior is cosy and out the back is a sweet chill-out garden. They advertise takeaway and delivery service, but it's worth checking if they go outside a 10km radius.

Vengo aquí para saborear las pizzas que hacen en el horno, pero si alguien quiere compartir el chuletón para dos también es uno de mis grandes favoritos. Mi hija siempre pide espagueti boloñesa y lame el plato hasta que está limpio. Su interior es acogedor y en la parte trasera hay un jardín chill out muy dulce. Anuncian servicio para entrega a domicilio, pero merece la pena averiguar si se salen de un radio de 10km.

Marc's Restaurante
Ctra. Cala Llonga Km 0,6, Jesús
Tel: 971.316.245
restaurante-marcs-ibiza.com

You'll find this place as you leave Jésus, headed north on the road to Cala Llonga. Tastefully decorated, it has a really good reputation and while I haven't been for years, friends say it's amazing. With a pretty garden at the back and a cosy atmosphere, it generally draws a chic crowd.

Encontrarás este restaurante a la salida de Jesús, en dirección al norte por la carretera a Cala Llonga. Decorado con gusto, tiene muy buena reputación y aunque hace años que no voy, mis amigos dicen que es increíble. Con un bonito jardín atrás y una atmósfera acogedora, generalmente atrae a una clientela chic.

FOOD TO GO... COMIDA PARA LLEVAR

Rita Savor
C/ des Cap Martinet, Edificio Balcón de Jesús II
Tel: 971.190.305

I swing by here often on Saturday morning to grab fresh croissants for breakfast with friends. Their homemade quiches and pies are a great to take away for dinner later and the lemon meringue pie is divine.

Suelo pasarme por aquí los sábados por la mañana para comprar croissants frescos para desayunar con mis amigos. Sus quiches y hojaldres caseros son deliciosos y la tarta de limón y merengue es divina.

BUTCHER AND MORE... CARNICERO Y MÁS...

Carnicería JR Can Español
C/ des Cap Martinet s/n, Jesús
Tel: 971.300.269

When I go past this place I chuckle at the logo that must scare away all vegetarians. They stock meat and cold cuts, but also local products (vegetables, bio organic eggs, baskets,...) and a great selection of delicatessen and wine.

Cuando paso por delante de esta tienda su logotipo ensangrentado me hacer reír ya que debe de ahuyentar a vegetarianos. Esta carnicería no sólo vende carne y fiambres, también productos locales (verduras, huevos payeses, cestas, sombreros…) y una gran selección de las mejores marcas de delicatesen y vino.

Kodo

C/ des Cap Martinet, esq C/ Llinquer
Tel: 971.193.319
kodoibiza.com

A fairly new addition to the little village. The name means heartbeat in japanese. They serve a variety of delicious modern style Japanese dishes including Ramen which I adore.

Un restaurante relativamente nuevo en el pueblo. El nombre significa corazón en japonés. Sirven una variedad de platos japoneses con toques modernos ademas de Ramen que es de mis platos favoritos.

THE SUPERMARKET + NEWS AGENTS
SUPERMERCADO Y PAPELERÍA

Comestibles + Papeleria Can Pascual

Ctra. Cala Llonga, Jesús
Tel: 971.310.528
can-pascual.com

Everyone in a 10km radius's favourite little supermarket. They seem to sell virtually everything you could possibly need, as well as fresh bread and plenty of organic produce. The shop has a newsagent stuck to the side, so its great for buying the Sunday morning papers after a shop on sunday.

El supermercado favorito de todo aquel que vive a un radio de 10km. Parece que venden virtualmente de todo lo que podrías necesitar, además de pan fresco y montones de productos ecológicos. La tienda tiene una papelería anexa, así que es perfecta para hacer la compra los domingos por la mañana seguido de la compra de los periódicos.

Ferreteria Clapés Guasch

HARDWARE STORE

Local 3, Jesús
Tel: 971.313.276

I love a hardware store and think it's important to know which towns or villages have a good one. This has everything from paint, brushes and broomsticks to nails and anti-fly curtains. A very practical treasure trove!

Me gustan las ferreterías y pienso que es importante conocer qué pueblos o municipios tienen una buena. Aquí hay de todo, desde pintura, cepillos y escobas hasta clavos y cortinas anti moscas. ¡Una cueva del tesoro muy práctica!

THE VETERINARY

Clínica Veterinaria Jesús

C/ Faisán, 4, Jesús
Tel: 971.312.929
Emergency Tel: 649.984.777

This little vet is located in a small house at the back of Jesús village and to get here you go down the side of Bon Lloch Restaurante on Carrer Faisan and then turn right. The people who run it are always very helpful, and stock cat and dog food as well as flea repellants and also medicines.

Esta pequeña clínica está situada en una casita detrás del pueblo de Jesús, bajando por el lateral de Bon Loch por la Calle Faisán, y tomando la primera calle a la derecha. La gente que la regenta es encantadora. Además venden comida de gatos y perros y también medicinas.

JESÚS > TALAMANCA...

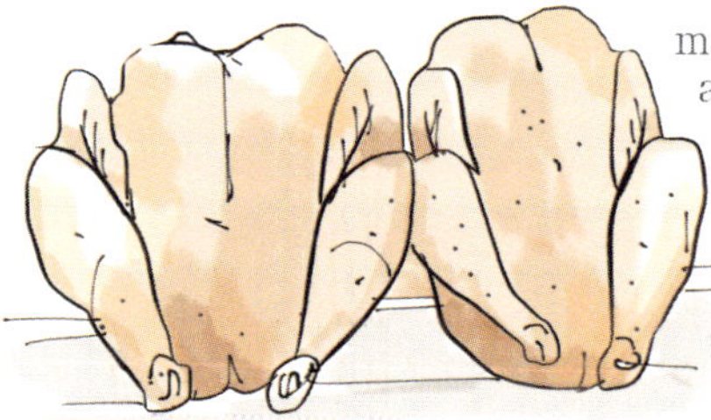

Ses Torres

C/ de Jesús > Cap Martinet
Tel: 971.318.932

I lived in the vicinity of Talamanca for many years, and this little roadside eatery became a handy stop off to grab a takeaway on the way to the beach, usually the potato omelette or even better their rotisserie chickens which are the best on the island. If you're eating in, it has a shaded little beer garden and generally football on the TV inside.

Yo viví en la zona de Talamanca durante muchos años y este pequeño restaurante en la carretera era muy útil cuando quería comida para llevar, normalmente me pido tortilla de patata o incluso pollo a l'ast, que es el mejor de la isla. Si prefieres sentarte a comer, tiene un pequeño jardín a la sombra y fútbol en la tele de dentro.

S'ESTANYOL BEACH – PLAYA DE S'ESTANYOL

When I was little, we had a Renault 4 that my dad had taken the side and back doors off, and we would drive here every afternoon with our dog running behind. The beach hasn't changed since then, and the dusty track is pure Ibiza to me. It's not a sandy beach, more a seaweedy one, but if you get here early you can grab a fisherman's hut and set up camp for the day. No Phone reception either!

De pequeña teníamos un Renault 4 al que mi padre le había quitado todas las puertas e íbamos aquí todas las tardes, con nuestro perro corriendo detrás. Esta playa no ha cambiado nada desde entonces, y para mí el camino polvoriento es parte de la Ibiza auténtica. No es una playa de arena, más bien es de algas, pero si llegas pronto puedes colocarte bajo una caseta y pasar el día.

Cala Bonita

Cala de S'Estanyol. Tel: 605.450.592

This beach restaurant opened last year. The food is delicious and so are the cocktails. Rumour has it that it is a bit of a game-changer.

Este chiringuito abrió el año pasado y la comida es fresca y deliciosa y los cócteles riquissimos. Corre el rumor de que es una novedad culinaria.

SES FEIXES

A marshland between Jesus, Talamanca and Ibiza town where a mixture of fresh and salt waters are home to a wide variety of flora and fauna.
When I was little I would cycle here with my brothers and play for hours catching little fish to put in our pond at home.
The feixas road was the original old road from Ibiza to Talamanca.
It is said that in the past the Arabs established a unique system of irrigation here based on capillary watering. The channels were small plots of land called "feixes." These channels were connected with other underground channels by circulating water, and with the use of gates they could regulate the level of the water in the channels and feixes. The entrance to each feixa or plot was through a characteristic arch called a "portal feixa", which you can still see although many arches have now collapsed and some look like they are literally "walking away" due to the moving marshland.

TO FIND THIS SPOT: DRIVE TOWARDS PACHA FROM TALAMANCA AND TURN RIGHT BEFORE THE BUILDINGS START AND TAKE THE DIRT TRACK.

Un terreno apantanado entre Jesús, Talamanca e Ibiza ciudad donde una mezcla de agua fresca y salada acoge a una gran variedad de flora y fauna.
Cuando era niña solía ir en bicicleta por aquí con mis hermanos a jugar por los pantanos, cogiendo peces para nuestro estanque en casa.
El camino de Ses Feixes era el antiguo camino que iba de Ibiza a Talamanca y dicen que antiguamente los árabes establecieron un sistema único de irrigación basado en el riego capilar. Los canales eran pequeños terrenos llamados feixes. Estos se conectaban con otros canales subterráneos por donde circulaba el agua, y con el uso de contrapuertas se regulaba el nivel de agua en los canales y feixes. La entrada a cada feixa o terreno era a través de un arco característico llamado portal feixa, que aún se pueden ver aunque muchos de estos arcos ya se han derrumbado y algunos parecen estar andando debido al movimiento de las tierras en los pantanales.

PARA ENCONTRAR ESTE LUGAR: CONDUCE HACIA PACHA DESDE TALAMANCA Y GIRA A LA DERECHA JUSTO ANTES DE LOS EDIFICIOS, POR UN CAMINO DE TIERRA.

PUIG D'EN VALLS AND AROUND LA ZONA DE PUIG D'EN VALLS

Puig d'en Valls is kind of no man's land for tourists and travellers, you'll forever feel like you're driving past it. But there are actually a couple of really noteworthy spots to check out.
To get there you drive out of Ibiza heading to San Antonio. Just after the first roundabout take the slip road on the right, signposted Puig d'en Valls. You will pass the Bfit Gym, brush the left side of the large electricity plant and pass under a bridge.

Puig d'en Valls es una especie de tierra de nadie para turistas y viajeros, siempre te sentirás de paso. Pero hay un par de sitios que merece la pena probar. Para llegar hasta aquí sales de Ibiza en dirección a San Antonio. Justo después de la primera rotonda toma la vía de acceso a la derecha, señalizado Puig d'en Valls. Pasarás el gimnasio Bfit, por la izquierda de la gran central eléctrica y debajo de un puente.

...EAT COMER

Es Cami Vell

C/ Vicente Marí Mayans, s/n
Puig d'en Valls, Ibiza
Tel: 971.316.665

I often grab lunch here with my daughter, who loves the Canelones. This restaurant is always rammed with locals and workers on a lunch break because they offer a three-course day meñu for under 12 euros. I normally have the fresh cheese salad, followed by the oven baked leg of lamb when I am extra peckish and take the bone home to my dog.

A menudo como aquí con mi hija, a quien le encantan los canelones. Siempre está repleto de gente local y ofrecen un menú de tres platos por menos de 12 euros. Cuando tengo hambre suelo pedir la ensalada de queso fresco y de segundo la pierna de cordero al horno y me llevo el hueso a casa para mi perro.

Oli Tapas

C/ Mar Mediterràni, 34, Puig d'en Valls
Tel: 971.315.951

Located right behind Decathalon (described further on), it's set within a restored little farm house, and is all about exposed stone walls and wood. The locals love it, and mums and dads drop by for a snack before they pick up the kids from the school nearby. There's also a small playground at the front.

Situado detrás de Decathlon (descrito en el texto siguiente), está ubicado en una finca restaurada con paredes de piedra y madera expuesta. A la gente del barrio le encanta, y las madres y padres vienen a tomarse un aperitivo antes o después de recoger a los niños del colegio. Además hay un pequeño parque enfrente para los niños.

SHOPS... TIENDAS

Box 3

Poligono Sa Blanca Dona Sector 1, Nave 3 - Puig d'en Valls, Ibiza
Tel: 971.199.731
box3ibiza.com

My dearest friends run this architects office and Interior Design Showroom. They have impeccable taste along with a lot of experience on this island. Their bathrooms and kitchens are to die for.

Mis amigos más queridos llevan esta Oficina de Arquitectura y Diseño de Interiores. Tienen un gusto impecable, junto con una gran cantidad de experiencia en esta isla.
Los cuartos de baño y cocinas son para morirse.

Decathlon

Finca Sa Olivera, 3, Puig d'en Valls
Tel: 971.318.088
decathlon.es

This is a big warehouse-style sports shop, where you can get everything you need from masks and snorkels to tents, ski and hiking gear. There are also footballs and skateboards for the kids, and it's really affordable. Open until 10 pm!

Unos grandes almacenes de deporte donde puedes encontrar todo lo que necesites, desde gafas y tubos de buceo a tiendas de campaña y ropa para la escalada y esqui. También hay pelotas de fútbol y monopatines para los niños, y todo a muy buen precio. Abren hasta las 22 horas.

THE HARDWARE STORE... ...LA FERRETERÍA

Fita

Av. de Sant Joan de Labritja, 25-33
Tel: 971.313.062
fitaibicentro.com

You can't miss this place as you drive into Ibiza town; it's on the main road with a huge grafiti painted on its façade. I love a rummage around a good hardware store, and this one has everything you need from TVs to blenders, coffee makers, pots and pans, light fittings, tools, drills, nails, garden stuff, paints…the list is endless.

No puedes pasar este sitio por alto cuando conduces hacia Ibiza ciudad, tienen un mural de grafiti pintado en su fachada. Me encanta pasearme por los pasillos de una buena tienda de bricolaje y ésta tiene todo lo que necesitas desde televisores a batidoras, cafeteras, ollas y sartenes, apliques de luz, herramientas, clavos, taladros, jardinería, pinturas… la lista es interminable.

FITNESS...

BFit Ibiza Sports Club

C/ Metge Domingo Nicolau Balançat, 4, Ibiza
Tel: 971.806.885
bfitibiza.com

I am not a fan of gyms – we're surrounded by beaches and stunning countryside, so the idea of running on a treadmill inside seems sad! However there's a good selection of group classes here, the most popular being the spinning. They have a good weights areaand they stick a DJ on the decks in the afternoon. Childcare facilities are another bonus here.

No soy fan de los gimnasios, estamos rodeados de playas y campos, ¡así que la idea de correr en una máquina me parece rara! Hay una gran variedad de clases en grupo, una zona de pesas y por las tardes pincha un DJ.

AROUND THE NEW MARKET + OUTSKIRTS
POR EL MERCADO NUEVO Y LOS ALREDEDORES

Drive or walk out of town on the Avenida Isidoro Macabich and you'll come to an area left of waiting buses with a large indoor food market that's open until 2pm, Monday to Saturday. It's well worth a visit, especially the little bars along the side where you can enjoy a real Ibizan tapa on their little terrace. Fried kidneys with parsley never tasted better. The area around here gets overlooked, but there are a few places in the vicinity and on the way that really deserve a mention.

Conduce o anda hacia las afueras por la Avenida Isidoro Macabich y te encontrarás a la izquierda de la parada de autobús con un gran mercado cubierto que está abierto hasta las 14.00 de lunes a sábado y merece la pena visitarlos bares, donde puedes degustar tapas en sus terracitas. ¡Riñones fritos con perejil nunca supieron mejor! Muchos pasan por alto esta zona de la ciudad pero hay sitios por aquí mientras estás de camino que me gustaría mencionar.

SHOP AND EAT
COMPRAR Y COMER

Kebab La Paz

C/ de Balears - C/ Agapit Llobet

I have to admit that I go here twice a week for the best kebabs I've ever found. They have a huge salad bar so you can fill your wrap, then choose to add chicken, beef or falafel with a choice of sauces, from spicy hot pepper to garlic tahini. They're only €4,50 and you can eat them in or take away.

Tengo que admitir que vengo aquí dos veces a la semana para el mejor kebab que haya probado nunca. Tienen una barra de ensaladas para llenar tu wrap, luego elige entre pollo, ternera o falafel con una selección de salsas desde muy picantes a tahini con ajo. Sólo cuestan 4,50 euros y puedes comértelos allí o pedirlos para llevar.

202 Hamburger & Delicious

C/del Bisbe Abad y Lasierra, 34, Tel: 971.313.919

I am not a big fan of burgers but this place happens to make the most amazing ones and veggie burgers too apart from salads and nachos. The meat is prepared to perfection and all the ingredients are fresh. The chips are homemade and despite the location being a bit ugly they have created the cutest spot with vintage and recycled furniture. Just love it.

No soy fan de las hamburguesas, pero en este lugar las hacen de miedo, además tienen hamburguesas vegetarianas, nachos y ensaladas. La carne se cocina a la perfección y todos los ingredientes son muy frescos. Las patatas fritas son caseras y a pesar de que la ubicación es un poco triste, han creado un lugar de lo más bonito con muebles vintage y reciclados.

Me encanta.

Charlotte Cafe-Ibiza

C/ de Canaries, 36, Ibiza
Tel: 971.315.405
charlotteibiza.com

At the back of Ibiza in the new side of town is this funky Café slash Bar. Tasteful interior and a good choice of bar mixes. This modern spot has become a busy little hang out for the locals.

Este moderno bar-cafetería se encuentra en la zona nueva de Ibiza. Cuenta con un interior decorado con buen gusto y una gran selección de bebidas en la barra. Este lugar se ha convertido en un punto de encuentro para los residentes.

Eat is Life

Av. la Pau, Ibiza,
Tel: 971.312.201
eatislife.es

This is a freshly home cooked health food restaurant that is a super delicious option if you can't face cooking and want to eat healthy. It has a very laid back atmosphere and sits directly by the roundabout on the outskirts of town. Very popular with the residents and a great option to dash in for some pre-school pick-up lunch.

Un restaurante de comida casera, recién hecha y sanísima y una deliciosa opción si no te apetece cocinar y quieres comer a lo sano. Se encuentra directamente pegada a la rotonda de Can Misses a las afueras de la ciudad. Y tiene una atmósfera muy relajada y por eso también es muy frecuentado por los isleños. Una buena opción para almorzar antes de recoger a los niños del cole o para llevarte comida a casa.

Miss Saigon

Av. d'Espanya, 59, Ibiza
Tel: 871.021.769

This is my new favourite place for lunch or dinner. An affordable little Vietnamese, run by a lovely couple.
I can´t get enough of their Chicken Pho soup, Vietnamese Rolls and Nems. Everything here is delicious. You can take away as well.

Este es mi nuevo lugar favorito para comer o cenar. Un restaurante vietnamita muy asequible, dirigido por una pareja encantadora. Me vuelve loca su sopa Pho de pollo, sus rollitos vietnamitas y los Nems. Aquí todo está delicioso. Puedes pedir para llevar también.

Wash and Drink

Av. d'Espanya, 53, Ibiza
Tel. 971.306.379

I love the concept of a place, where you can do your laundry and have a drink while you wait in their little bar next door. It's a short walk from the centre so it´s handy for those without washing machines.

Me encanta el concepto de este lugar, puedes hacer la colada y tomar una copa mientras esperas. Está a un paseo del centro, así que super práctico para los que no tienen lavadora.

ESCAPE THE ORDINARY.

Bar Astro

C/ Portinatx, 1, Av. Sant Josep
Tel: 971.302.338

A simple restaurant on the main road as you leave Ibiza towards San José. Its minimal décor might make you wonder whether it is worth it but I can tell you it s packed with locals at lunchtime and serves great food. They do a 11 euro menu at lunch.

Un restaurante en la carretera al salir de Ibiza en dirección San José. A la hora del almuerzo está lleno porque sirven buena comida a precios bajos. Tienen un menú del día por 11 euros.

Bicicletas Juan Ferrer

C/ d'Atzarò, 14, Casas Baratas
Tel: 971.391.401
bicicletasjferrer.com

Juan opened this shop over 20 years ago and his love of cycling is evident. It's by far the best place to buy top-of-the-range road bikes, mountain bikes and BMX's for the kids, and he also sells cycling clothes and accessories. Juan is also your man if you need your bike repaired.

Juan abrió esta tienda hace más de 20 años y su pasión por el ciclismo es evidente. Es el mejor sitio, con diferencia, para comprarte una bicicleta de primera marca, un mountain bike y BMX para niños, y también vende ropa y accesorios de ciclismo. Juan, realmente es un genio a la hora de arreglar tu bicicleta.

THE PAINT SHOPS
TIENDAS DE PINTURAS

Pinturas Martínez

C/ d'Atzarò, 15,
Tel: 971.301.081
martinezpinturas.com

Take right at the little gas station after you leave Ibiza town in direction San Jose. Then drive up a bit and its on the corner. Here they stock the best for everything decoration and paint related. Here you can buy the top brands of paints, tools, fixtures, flooring and decoration materia.

Al salir de Ibiza por la carretera en dirección San José, giras en la pequeña gasolinera y sigues hasta que lo verás en la esquina. De los mejores establecimientos para todo lo relacionado con la decoración y pintura. Aquí encontras tambien herramientas, moquetas, accesorios y decoración.

Pinturas Rubio

Riu Guadiana, 17,
Carretera San José
Tel: 971. 303.683
pinturasrubio.es

On the left after the second round-a-bout as you head towards San José. These guys stock a wide range of products which are ideal for painters, decorators and for that bit of DIY at home.

Después de la segunda rotonda dirección a San José. Tienen una increíble gama de productos, ideales para pintores, decoradores y por si quieres hacer un poco de bricolaje. Encontraras pigmentos al fondo.

IMAGE + SOUND
IMAGEN Y SONIDO

CONFORT

The best place to buy a TV, Washing Machine, Fridge or any kitchen appliances. With years of experience in the appliance sector, Comfort brings together three distribution companies in the electrical and electronics sector selling appliances and consumer electronics at the best prices.

El mejor lugar para comprar un televisor, una lavadora, un frigorífico o cualquier producto de cocina.

Con años de experiencia en el sector de electrodomésticos, Confort reúne a tres empresas de distribución del sector de venta de electrodomésticos a los mejores precios.

Av. Sant Josep de sa Talaia,18, Ibiza
Tel: 971.306.831
confort-electro.com

JUST AS YOU LEAVE IBIZA TOWN..
JUSTO A LA SALIDA DE IBIZA CENTRO...

FUN FOR KIDS AND FAMILY
DIVERSIÓN PARA LOS NIÑOS Y LA FAMILIA

Cinema Complex * Multicines

C/ es Cubells, Ibiza
Tel: 971.315.211
aficine.es/cines/ficha_ibiza.php

This is a great cinema complex just on the outskirts of Ibiza, but sadly most films shown are dubbed into Spanish. Sometimes they show English language films with Spanish subtitles, which are listed as VO (versión original). Listings marked "Anem al cine" are movies shown in the original language with subtitles, and shown on Wednesdays and Thursdays - call the cinema or pass by and grab a program to be sure. Before you settle in, there's a little bar with ice-creams, drinks and popcorn.

Estos multicines justo a las afueras de Ibiza ciudad son magníficos, aunque la mayoría de las películas han sido dobladas al español. A veces muestran películas en versión original con subtítulos en español (VO). Estas películas son parte del ciclo "Anem al Cine" y se emiten los miércoles y jueves, llama al cine o pasa a coger una programación para asegurarte.
Antes de coger asiento, hay una pequeña tienda que vende helados, bebidas y palomitas.

Vila Parc Bowling

C/ es Cubells, 32, Ibiza
Tel: 971.199.540
bowlingvilaparc.com

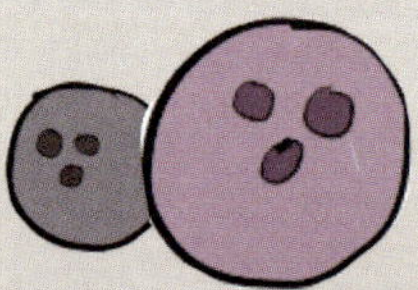

My daughter and I have spent many a happy Saturday at this great little leisure centre, which offers all the fun of bowling as well as a heap of other games for the kids. You can host birthday parties here or just come for a game with the whole family. There's a café serving basic food and drinks, and it opens at 5pm every day except Monday.

Mi hija y yo hemos pasado muchos sábados felices en este pequeño centro de ocio, que ofrece toda la diversión de la bolera además de montones de juegos para niños. Puedes celebrar fiestas de cumpleaños o simplemente venir a jugar una partida con la familia. Hay una cafetería que sirve cocina básica y bebidas y abre a partir de las 17:00 cada día, excepto lunes.

FIGUERETES + AROUND FIGUERETES Y LOS ALREDEDORES

Ibiza's urban beach. Stuck to the southwestern side of town, it is surrounded by hotels and cafés and has a really nice promenade lined with palm trees. In the summer there's a night market along the beach front and there's a great little vibe going on. Also with disabled access to the beach.

La playa urbana de Ibiza. Situada en la parte suroeste de Ibiza y rodeada de hoteles y cafeterías, tiene un paseo amplio y bonito alineado con palmeras. En verano hay un mercadillo por la noche junto a la playa y un ambiente muy bonito. Aquí hay acceso a la playa para minusválidos.

Restaurante Soleado

Passeig Ses Pitiusas, s/n, Figueretas
Tel: 971.394.811
soleadoibiza.com

A sweet couple own this romantic sea front spot in Figueretas. They serve food with a french touch all market fresh and great cocktails that you can enjoy on the top terrace.

Una pareja muy simpática regenta este lugar romántico frente al mar en Figueretas. Sirven comida con un toque francés y todo fresco directo del mercado. En la terraza superior puedes disfrutar de sus excelentes cócteles.

All Café Bistro

Passeig Ses Pitiusas, 28
Figueretes
Tel: 971. 301.925

I love this Restaurant/café for breakfast and its great when you fancy and a sea view. Good service and a varied choice of breakfasts ranging from continental to english. They are open all day until late and are known for their delicious seafood dishes.

Me encanta este restaurante-cafetería con buenas vistas para ir a desayunar. Buen servicio y una variada selección de desayunos, desde el continental al inglés. Abren todo el día hasta tarde y son conocidos por sus deliciosos platos de mariscos.

Casa 13 Piadina

C/ Periodista Francesc Escanellas, 13, Figueretes
Tel: 971.306.154

Charles Vexenat from Bar 1805 took me here last summer for a hangover breakfast and it has now become a firm favourite of mine. It's the sweetest spot in the área, and Alessia the owner has a smile that always lights up my day and from the little porch you even have a bit of a sea view. It's the cutest!

Charles Vexenat del Bar 1805 en Ibiza me trajo aquí el verano pasado para desayunar y quitarme la resaca; desde entonces se ha convertido en uno de mis sitios favoritos. Es el lugar más dulce de la zona y la sonrisa de la propietaria, Alessia siempre me alegra el día, además desde su pequeño porche puedes incluso ver el mar. ¡Es de lo más!

Retro Gusto

C/ del País Basc, 6, Figueretes

The awesome full English breakfasts here comes highly recommended by my friend Charles from Bar 1805, so its gotta be good because he knows his stuff! A sweet, colourful little spot in the not so colourful Figueretas.

Mi amigo Charles del Bar 1805 me ha recomendado su magnífico desayuno inglés, así que tiene que ser bueno porque él sí que es un sibarita. Un pequeño y colorido local en la no tan colorida Figueretas.

The Boo

Av. Pedro Matutes Noguera, 43, Figueretes
Tel: 661.690.434

This restaurant slash Bar is on a rather dull Street but worth a visit as the back patio is such a nice surprise. They've used that old crate Wood vibe for their furniture that I love. Their burgers are huge and they do salads and starters as well. Small appetites abstain!

Este bar-restaurante está en una calle bastante aburrida pero vale la pena visitarlo ya que el patio trasero sorprende positivamente. Me encanta la madera de palets que han utilizado para los muebles. Sus hamburguesas son enormes y también hacen ensaladas y entrantes. Abstenerse apetitos pequeños.

Rickyzza Osteria Pizzeria

Carrer del Músic Fermí Marí, 5 Figueretes
Tel: 971.303.132

I am not a big Pizza fan but when they are light and crispy I LOVE them. Here they really know how to make them well. They also have a delicious selection of home-made pastas and great wines. You can find them just behind Lidl Supermarket.

No soy gran fan de la Pizza pero cuando aqui son ligeros y crujientes y me encantan. También tienen una deliciosa selección de pasta caseras y buena carta de vinos. Se encuentra justo detrás del supermercado Lidl.

GO TO SLEEP ALREADY!
¡A LA CAMA YA!

Hostal Pitiusa

C/ de Galicia, 29, Figueretes
Tel: 971.301.905
hostalpitiusa.com

A small, affordable little hostel that I've been told is really good value for money, and the owners are lovely. Its squeaky clean and just steps away from the beach. The owners are really friendly and helpful, and all the rooms are large, have a TV, fan and terrace. Yey!

Un pequeño hostal muy asequible que me han dicho que está muy bien, y los propietarios son amables y cordiales. Está muy limpio y a unos pasos de la playa. Las habitaciones son grandes y tienen TV, ventilador y terraza. ¡Yuhu!

Hotel Cenit

Archiduque Luis Salvador, s/n Los Molinos, Figueretes
Tel: 971.30.40.93
hotelcenit.com

My boyfriend took me here as well!! We went one afternoon to have a gin tonic at the pool terrace.
He told me about the views but I never expected them to be so amazing. It is like being on top of the world. You can see all the way to Formentera. The hotel is reasonably priced but not great if you have a car and need to park. It is very popular with men and men if you know what I mean.

¡Sí, mi novio también me trajo aquí! Fuimos una tarde para tomarnos un gin-tonic en la terraza del bar de la piscina. Me dijo que tenía unas vistas impresionantes, pero nunca hubiera imaginado que fueran tan increíbles. Es como estar en la cima del mundo, además puedes ver hasta Formentera.
El hotel no es caro, pero complicado si tienes que aparcar. Es muy popular entre los hombres, no sé si me entendéis.

Es Vivé

C/ de Carles Roman Ferrer, Figueretes
Tel: 971.301.902

A Miami-style hotel with its well known façade that has an all-day party vibe around the pool, and late-night bar inside. The rooms aren't big, but most of your time will be spent down at the pool, which is a real meeting place for guests. I know several girls who've met their future husbands here! The bar does a killer strawberry daiquiri, which I recommend.

Un magnífico hotel al estilo de Miami con su fachada única, un ambiente de fiesta alrededor de la piscina, y un bar abierto hasta tarde. Las habitaciones no son muy grandes, pero la mayor parte del tiempo estarás abajo junto a la piscina, que es un verdadero punto de reunión para los huéspedes. Conozco varias chicas que han conocido a sus futuros maridos aquí. El bar prepara un delicioso daiquiri de fresa que os recomiendo.

THE CACTUS BESIDE EVERY FINCA IN IBIZA

It is said that these cactus's were planted beside the house to use as a toilet before toilets existed. The red fruit is sweet and edible and the trunks are still used for making shoes.

LA CHUMBERA AL LADO DE CADA FINCA

Se dice que se plantaron al lado de la casa para utilizar como un inodoro antes de que éstos existieron. La fruta roja es dulce y comestible, y los troncos se usan para hilos.

5 THINGS YOU SHOULD DO

5 COSAS QUE DEBERÍAS HACER CUANDO ESTÉS AQUÍ

---

1. Breakfast by the sea at Jockey Club (p122)
Desayuno en la playa en el Jockey Club

2. Heavenly Brunch at Vinyl Burger (p.115)
Un brunch inolvidable en Vinyl Burger

3. Cocktail and dinner for sunset at Coricancha (p.119)
Coctel y cena viendo la puesta de sol en Coricancha

4. Visit Cala D'Hort and enjoy the view of Es Vedrá (p.132)
Visita Cala D'Hort y disfruta de la vista a Es Vedrà

5. Seafood lunch at Es Boldadó (p.132)
Comida de pescados y mariscos en Es Boldadó

THE SOUTH Villages & beaches

El sur, sus pueblos, y playas

THE SOUTH: THE VILLAGES + THEIR BEACHES
EL SUR, LOS PUEBLOS Y SUS PLAYAS

The southern coast of Ibiza is often the most popular with tourists. It's easy to get to, and the beaches have calm seas, long stretches of sand and views across to Formentera island. The largest sand dunes are found here and there are some world class restaurants dotted along the largest beaches. Hotels, restaurants and shops are also plentiful in the cluster of towns in the South.

La costa sur de Ibiza suele ser muy popular entre los turistas. Es de fácil acceso y las playas tienen aguas tranquilas, largos tramos de arena y vistas a la isla de Formentera. Aquí puedes encontrar las dunas de arena más grandes y también hay restaurantes famosos esparcidos a lo largo de estas grandes playas. Hay montones de hoteles, restaurantes y tiendas en este conjunto de pueblos del sur.

Playa d'en Bossa

One of Ibiza's longest and whitest beaches on the southwestern coast, now famous for its raucous tenant Ushuaïa, with its infamous daytime parties. It's a shame about the high-rises that have built up over the years, but right at the far end you can still find a few peaceful dunes.

Una de las playas más largas y blancas al suroeste de Ibiza que es ahora famosa por su ruidoso vecino, Ushuaïa, y sus famosas fiestas alrededor de la piscina. Es una lástima que se construyeran edificios tan altos aquí, pero al final hacia la derecha todavía puedes disfrutar de sus dunas.

EAT + DRINK...
COMER Y BEBER...

Forty Fives Bistro Bar

Carrer de La Punta,
Playa d'en Bossa
forty-fives.com

This is a Brit Bistro facing the sea that serves all your favourites if you are feeling homesick for the UK. Open all year and on Sundays they do huge portions of roast with all the trimmings and puddings or fish and chips if you prefer. Live sports on the TV inside for those of you that want to eat by the TV.

Un bistro británico frente al mar que sirve toda tu comida favorita si tienes nostalgia de Gran Bretaña. Abierto todo el año y los domingos hacen enormes porciones de "Sunday Roast" con todos los adornos y puddings, o también "Fish and Chips" si lo prefieres. Dentro dejan la tele puesta con los deportes en directo para aquellos que quieren comer viendo la tele.

Beachouse
C/ de Platja d'en Bossa, 2
Playa den Bossa
Tel: 971 39 68 58
beachouseibiza.com

This is my favourite on Playa den Bossa. The layout is stunning and when you are here you feel so spoilt.
The food is fantástic, offering you a healthy spin on italian and mediterranean cuisine. Theres a juice bar and a cocktail bar and a divine little shop at the back selling heavenly tunics, swimwear and this guidebook as well!.
They host parties with live DJ's all summer so check their website for updates.
It's the perfect spot for a big birthday lunch, a wedding party or a business lunch. It's also very romantic...

Este es mi favorito en Playa den Bossa. El diseño interior del chiringuito es precioso y cuando estás aquí te sientes mimado.
La comida es fantástica, te ofrecen un giro saludable a la cocina italiana y mediterránea. Hay un bar de zumos y cócteles y una pequeña tienda en el fondo que vende túnicas, trajes de baño y esta guía también.
Ellos organizan fiestas con Djs en vivo durante todo el verano así que comprueba su sitio web para las actualizaciones.
Es el lugar perfecto para una cena de cumpleaños grande, un almuerzo de gallina o una fiesta de boda.
Es de lo más romántico...

Lips Reartes Ibiza
Porreres, 1, Playa d'en Bossa
Tel: 971.300.415
restaurantebeachclubibizalipsreartes.es

I'm not a big fan of fancy beach bars, I'm more of a surf shack kinda girl but it is really pleasant here. I've only eaten here twice but both times it was an absolutely delicious experience.
They do a menú for lunch which showcases some of the food they have on offer.
It's kid friendly in the daytime and often hosts a party at sundown.

No soy una gran fan de los chiringuitos de playa con madera blanca, soy más chica de choza, pero estar aquí es muy agradable.
Solamente he comido aquí dos veces y las dos fueron experiencias muy ricas. Hacen un menú del mediodía que muestra parte de lo que tienen en la carta.
Es un lugar genial para los niños durante el día y a menudo organizan fiestas para la puesta del sol.

Clandestino
C/ Pablo Picasso, 22
Playa den Bossa
Tel: 653.374.095 - 658.329.319

In a little house at the back of Playa d'en Bossa, there's no view but it's all about the vibe. Fresh for 2017 is an extensive menu of raciones, tapas and pinchos.
Pier Paulo, co owner, makes the best, freshest cocktails as well as a wicked Bloody Mary, and his partner Pedro makes the guests laugh and feel at ease. A great local, non pretentious hang-out.
I highly recommend it!

Ubicada en una casita en las calles traseras de Playa d'en Bossa, sin vistas pero con un ambiente genial.
Este año re-abren con una carta extensa de raciones, tapas y pinchos. Pier Paulo, copropietario, hace los mejores cocteles incluyendo un riquissimo Bloody Mary, y su socio Pedro hace reír y sentirse a gusto a los invitados. Un local no pretencioso. ¡Os lo recomiendo!

Passion

Edificio Bossamar
C/ de Platja d'en Bossa
Tel: 971.305.130

Lana Love has created an undisputed top health restaurant here on this touristy strip- and right in the middle of the crazy Bossa strip! Offering a wealth of raw, vegan, vegetarian and gluten-free options, as well as a varied selection of juices and smoothies, I love her pumpkin, feta, broccoli and rocket salad and when I am extra-starving I have her not-so-healthy full English breakfast that comes with sausages, bacon, hash browns and baked beans! Only open in summer.

Lana Love ha creado este restaurante indisputablemente saludable en Ibiza y en plena locura de la zona de Playa d'en Bossa. Ofreciendo platos veganos, vegetarianos y sin gluten, además de una gran selección de zumos y batidos. Me encanta su ensalada de calabaza, feta, brócoli y rúcula, pero cuando de verdad tengo hambre me planto aquí y pido su desayuno inglés que viene con habas, huevos, bacon, salchichas, tostada y todos los extras. Solo está abierto en verano.

...SLEEP...A BIT
DORMIR...UN POCO

Santos Ibiza Coast Suites

C/ Bruc, 3 - Playa d'en Bossa
Tel: 971.301.023
santosibizacoastsuites.com

Located directly on the beach with direct access to the sand, Santos is luxurious, fun and youthful. It has an arty decor, turquoise touches throughout and a rock 'n' roll vibe. All the suites are named after saints, there's an onsite club, amazing views of the Med and a large pool area with day beds and loungers.

Situado en la playa con acceso directo a la arena, Santos reúne todo lo bueno de la tradición ibicenca y lo pasa por un filtro de lujo relajado. Ofrece una experiencia hipermoderna de boho-chic, decoración vanguardista con toques vintage, actitud rock & roll y un poco de magia. Todas las suites reciben el nombre de santos, hay un club dentro, increíbles vistas al Mediterráneo y una gran zona de piscina con tumbonas y hamacas.

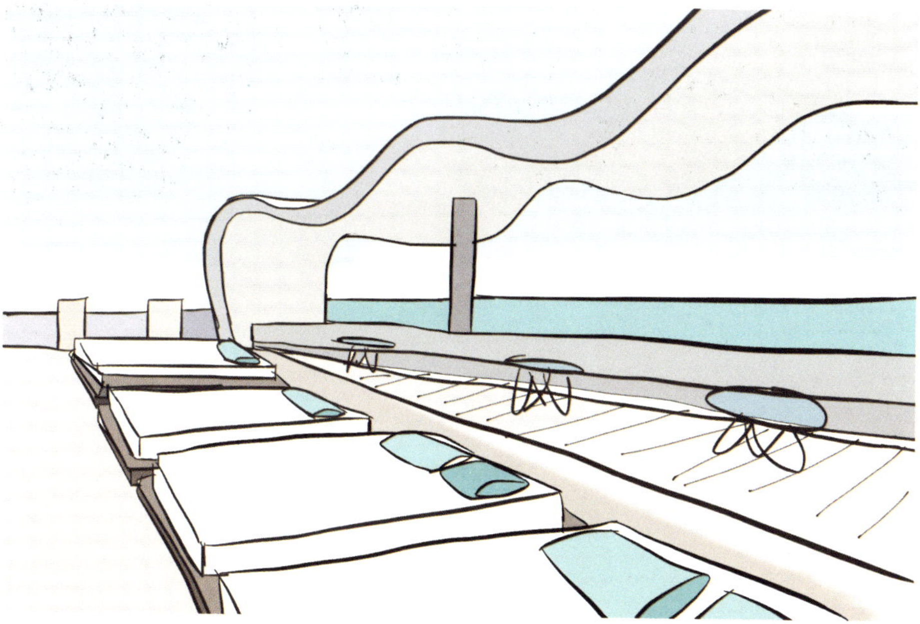

Santos Dorado Suites

C/ Bruc, 3 - Playa d'en Bossa
Tel: 971.393.268
santosibizacoastsuites.com

Santos Dorado Suites are the continuation of the project of Santos Ibiza. The suites are all based on gold records and have names like "Love me Tender" Elvis Presley song and so on. They are spacious and full of special details; Marshall equipment, your own bar, a king size bed and stunning sea views.

Santos Dorado Suites es la continuación del proyecto Santos Ibiza. Las suites, son discos de oro y reciben nombres como "Love me Tender", la canción de Elvis Presley. Son espaciosas y con muchos detalles; equipamiento Marshall, barra donde empezar la aventura ibicenca, camas kingsize donde reposar lo bailado y un salón con vistas al mar.

Tropicana Coast Suites

Deessa Tanit, 10/12
Playa d'en Bossa
Tel: 971.393.268
tropicanaibizacoastsuites.com

Just 200 meters from Playa d'en Bossa beach, the Tropicana Coast Suites styling has been inspired by the freshness and elegance of the Art Deco hotels in Miami, with a contemporary, fresh, festive and colorful Ibiza style. The decor plus its excellent service make it one of the best rated hotels on the island.

A sólo 200 metros de Playa d'en Bossa, el Tropicana Coast Suites se inspira en la frescura y elegancia de los hoteles Art Decó de Miami, consiguiendo un estilo personal y contemporáneo muy relacionado con el espíritu festivo y colorista de Ibiza. La decoración y un trato exquisito lo hacen uno de los hoteles mejor valorados de la isla.

Hotel Garbi

C/de la Murtra, 5, Playa d'en Bossa
Tel: 971.300.007
hotelgarbi-ibiza.com

This place is colorfully lit with fluorescent pink against black-and-white furnishings for a very futuristic look. Rooms are simple but elegantly done, and face either the sea or the large pool and sun-deck area. The restaurant overlooks the sea and there's also a spa and on site nightclub. I have girlfriends that keep coming back.

Un hotel con luces fluorescentes rosas contrastando con un mobiliario blanco y negro para un aspecto futurista. Las habitaciones no son amplias pero han sido elegantemente decoradas, y con vistas al mar o hacia la enorme piscina. El restaurante esta en la playa y también hay un spa y una discoteca.

Es Cavallet

Wilder and wavier than Salinas, this beautiful beach backed with rambling dunes has views of Ibiza town and Formentera. On a calm day the sea is outstanding, but it can get quite seaweedy when the winds are up.

Más salvaje y oleada que Salinas, esta preciosa playa con dunas tiene vistas a Ibiza y Formentera. En los días de calma el mar está impresionante, pero puede haber bastantes algas cuando se levanta el viento.

SHOPPING... DE COMPRAS...

Boheme Shop

Parking, Es Cavallet
Tel: 871.395.839

OK, if you've come straight from the airport, you park, hand over your keys (they have valet parking), head to the shop in the car park, choose a sarong, beach basket, bikini, hat and some sun screen, and you're ready to hit the sand!

Si vienes directo del aeropuerto puedes aparcar aquí, darle las llaves al aparcacoches, dirigirte directamente a la tienda en el parking a comprar un pareo, un cesto de playa, un sombrero y crema solar, ¡y estarás listo para la playa!

EATING + DRINKING... COMER Y BEBER...

El Chiringuito

Es Cavallet
Tel: 971.395.485
elchiringuitoibiza.com

Unbeatable for its white-washed, shady dining areas at the back, everyone should experience this place at least once. The seafood is superb and lunches always lead into the evening.

As you arrive you will be drawn into their little shop, which sells gorgeous kaftans and jewellery as well as lots of other fabulous stuff.

Incomparable por su zona de comedor blanca y sombreada, todos deberían probar este restaurante aunque sólo fuera una vez. El marisco está delicioso y las comidas aquí siempre acaban con sobremesas hasta tarde.

Cuando llegues te atraerá su pequeña tienda, con preciosas túnicas, joyería y aceites nutritivos, además de otros artículos fabulosos.

La Escollera

Es Cavallet
Tel: 971.396.572
laescolleraibiza.com

My friend Danny, who I worked alongside years ago in the Ibiza club scene, runs this famous restaurant. It has stunning views over the deep bluc to Formentera, chic Balinese inspired decor and bougan-villeas around the tables. Not to be missed. Try the grilled sardines or the T-bone steak. It's open all winter too.

Mi amigo Danny, con quien trabajé durante años en la noche de Ibiza, regenta este famoso restaurante. Con impresionantes vistas a Formentera, decoración balinesa muy chic y buganvillas rodeando las mesas, no debes perderte este sitio. Prueba las sardinas a la parrilla o el chuletón. Está abierto todo el invierno.

SAN JORGE TOWN EL PUEBLO DE SANT JORDI

This residential suburb near the airport has a few restaurants and bars and some shops It's also a must if you like your buildings, as the majestic 15th-century church is the best preserved of the four oldest on the island. It's surrounded by a gorgeous courtyard with flowers and palm trees and next door you'll find the charming village cemetery.

Este pueblo residencial cerca del aeropuerto tiene algunos restaurantes y bares y está bien para comprar. Debes visitarlo si te gustan los edificios antiguos, ya que la majestuosa iglesia del siglo XV es la mejor preservada de las cuatro en la isla. Rodeado de un precioso patio con flores y palmeras, a su lado encontrarás el pintoresco cementerio del pueblo.

...EAT + ENJOY COMER Y DISFRUTAR...

Vinyl Burger

Ctra. del Aeropuerto 31, Sant Jordi
Tel: 971.395.935
vinylburgeribiza.com

The tastiest possible comfort food comes courtesy of Larry from Barcelona and Pablo from Ibiza. They do a variety of gourmet burgers and the Mozzarella de Búfala salad is amazing, as their USP is high-quality local produce. A DJ also spins old-school vinyl every night. Their 'broken eggs on sautéed potatoes with baby chorizo' and a Bloody Mary is the most delicious and effective way to cure a hangover!

La comida más sabrosa viene de la mano de Larry de Barcelona y Pablo de Ibiza. Hacen las mejores patatas fritas caseras de la isla y una variedad de hamburguesas y la ensalada de mozzarela es total, mientras que su argumento de venta es la gran calidad de sus productos locales. Un DJ también pincha vinilos antiguos cada noche. Sus huevos rotos con patatas y chorizo están riquísimos y es la forma más eficaz de curar una resaca.

The church here was built back in the 15th century for the people who worked collecting salt at the lagoons and cultivating the fields.

La Iglesia fue edificada en el XVV para las personas que trabajaban recogiendo la sal en los estanques y cultivando los campos.

Rasca Lobos

Av. Vicente Serra, 25.
Sant Jordi
Tel: 971.395.860

A great Gastro Bar at the back of San Jordi village in a sweet overgrown terrace. Here you will always find delicious home-made food on the menu. They do a full english breakfast as well as juices and are also famous for their deserts so don't leave without trying one.

Una gran bar de tapas y restaurante en el pueblo de Sant Jordi con un agradable jardín donde siempre encontrarás una deliciosa comida casera en su menú. Además hacen un desayuno inglés completo, además de zumos y también son famosos por sus postres, así que no os vayáis sin probarlos.

ORGANIC BLISS...

S'Hortet Verd

C/ dels Pirineus, 11, San Jordi
Tel: 971.308.030
shortetverd.info

This is a handy organic supermarket and café that sells all your health pantry needs, a wide selection of bio fruit and veg and also offers breakfasts, fresh juices, and a selection of yummy vegetarian meals. There's a playground for the kids and wifi for you, as well as holistic medical advice and even massage.

Este supermercado ecológico y cafetería vende todos los productos ecológicos que puedas necesitar, una gran selección de fruta y verdura orgánica, además ofrece desayunos, zumos naturales y una selección de comida vegetariana. Hay un parque para niños, Wifi y ofrecen masajes y consejos médicos holísticos.

Pinzimonio

Carrer de Montblanc, 23,
Sant Jordi
Tel: 971.932.971

This cute place with colourful chairs and wooden decor sits at the back of Vinyl Burger and is such a worthwhile spot. Perfect for breakfast, lunch or dinner and they serve great home-made food, organic pizzas, salads, juices, smoothies and vegan food as well.

Este lugar con sillas de colores está úbicada detrás de Vinyl Burger y es perfecto para un buen desayuno, una comida o una cena. Sirven comida casera, pizzas orgánicas, ensaladas, zumos, batidos y comida vegana.

FLEA MARKET
MERCADILLO
SAN JORGE / SANT JORDI

Every time I come here I think, "where do all these people come from?" And it's busier in the winter! It's really more of a vast hippy car-boot sale than a flea market, so put a few hours aside to visit. Get here early to grab the best bits, but if you want the real bargains wait until the end.

Siempre que vengo aquí pienso, "¿de dónde sale toda esta gente?". ¡Y en invierno está aún más abarrotado! Es más un mercadillo hippie que un rastro, así que reserva un buen par de horas si quieres visitar este lugar. Ven pronto para hacerte con los mejores artículos, pero si quieres gangas espérate hasta el final.

Carretera Aeropuerto, San Jordi.
Tel: 971.396.669
Saturdays/sábados: 7-14h

Ferretería FSJ St Jordi

Ctra. Aeropuerto Km 3, 9
Tel: 971.395.646

A one stop shop for household essentials like mosquito net kits, painting paraphernalia, and basic bathroom and kitchenware, they also do key-cutting here. Run by Josefa and her daughter Lina, you'll find all that can be expected from a regular DIY shop, but with a female touch.

Una tienda para todos los esenciales domésticos como mosquiteras, pintura y toda su parafernalia, básicos para el baño y la cocina, y también hacen copias de llaves. Regentado por Josefa y su hija Lina, encontrarás todo lo que esperas de una tienda de bricolaje habitual pero con un cierto toque femenino.

Tabac St Jordi

Ctra. Aeropuerto 61 B, Sant Jordi
Tel: 971.396.589

A well stocked tabacco shop, and good to know if you're heading to the airport as it's on the same road if you come off at the Sant Jordi exit. They also sell postcards, stamps and educational children's toys for those last-minute gifts. Stationary fetishists beware, as it's a veritable treasure trove.

Este estanco está bien abastecido, es bueno saberlo si estás de camino al aeropuerto, ya que está en la misma carretera en la salida a Sant Jordi. Además venden postales, sellos y juguetes educativos para regalos de último minuto. Los fetichistas de la papelería estáis advertidos, es una verdadera cueva del tesoro.

ICE CREAM, ICE CREAM...

Heladería St Jordi

Ctra Aeropuerto, Edificio Las Olas
Tel: 971.599.566

An ice-cream parlour that's also much more! Owners Luca and Elise are lovely, while Luca trained at the famous University of Flavours in Italy. All their ice-creams are made daily on the premises and contain zero chemicals and dyes, while vegans will be happy that all the fruit flavours are made with soya instead of cows milk. The fabulous jazz you often hear is courtesy of Elise's musician father.

Una heladería y mucho más. Los propietarios Luca y Elise son encantadores, y Luca estudió en la a Universidad de los Sabores en Italia. Todos sus helados están hechos cada día en el mismo establecimiento y no contienen químicos o colorantes, y los veganos estarán contentos ya que todos los helados de frutas están hechos con leche de soja y no de vaca. El jazz fabuloso que a veces escuchas aquí es del padre de Elise, que es músico.

SAN FRANCISCO VILLAGE EL PUEBLO DE SANT FRANCESC

The little church of Sant Francesc de s'Estany is located within the Nature Reserve of Ses Salines. It was built in the eighteenth century to serve the salt workers. This tiny drive-through village centres around the church, a very simple building next to the salt flats, with a stone shield on the façade and a small forecourt.

Esta pequeña iglesia de San Francesc de S'Estany está situada dentro del Parque Natural de Ses Salines. Fue construida en el siglo XVIII para servir a los trabajadores de las salineras. Este pueblecito se centra alrededor de la iglesia, un edificio simple, pegado a las salineras con un escudo de piedra en su pared y un pequeño patio.

San Francisco Bar

Ctra. de Ses Salines, Km 2.5, San Francisco
Tel: 971.940.174

Cecilia and Martín, a fun-loving Argentinian couple, own this cute restaurant with palm trees and flowers everywhere. The menu is a mix of international fare and a welcome break from the prices in the area Home-made raviolis, Mexican quesadillas, and finely roasted pink beef served with toasted tomato bread are their best sellers along with generous burgers and to-die-for home-made deserts.

Cecilia y Martín, una simpática pareja argentina son propietarios de este coqueto restaurante con palmeras y flores alrededor. En la carta predominan las especias condimentando una mezcla internacional de platos. Un respiro a los precios de la zona. Raviolis caseros, quesadillas mexicanas y ternera asada servida sobre pan tostado con tomate son sus especialidades junto a sus hamburguesas y ricos postres caseros.

Coricancha

Ctra. de Ses Salines, Km 2.7, San Francisco
Tel: 971.074.226
coricanchaibiza.com

This Nikkei restaurant opened last year at this stuning spot. The food is an original mix of Japanese and Peruvian with really delicious choices and a great Ceviche which I always order alongside an incredible cocktial from the bar downstairs. Book the Sunset view table upstairs and come before 9 pm to enjoy watching the sun sink down over the salt flats. Pricey but worth it.

Este restaurante Nikkei abrió el año pasado en este lugar magico. La comida es una mezcla original de japonés y peruano con opciones realmente deliciosos. Me encanta el Ceviche y me lo pido con un coctel increíble de la barra de abajo. Reservate la mesa con la puesta de sol de arriba y llega antes de 21:00 para disfrutar viendo el sol hundirse en las Salinas. Carito pero vale la pena.

The Sculpture La escultura

"click"

Beside the church is a striking bronze sculpture by Pedro Hormigo, a tribute to the hardiness of the workers who extracted salt and carried it on their shoulders in the late 17th century.

Junto a la iglesia está la llamativa escultura de bronce de Pedro Hormigo, un tributo al sufrimiento de los trabajadores que extraían la sal y la cargaban a sus espaldas a finales del siglo XVII.

Cap d'es Falco

This strip of pebbles between the sea and the salt flats gets the sunset every evening in a glorious explosion of colours. If you're on a budget, bring your own bottle of bubbly and enjoy the sundown here otherwise grab a spot at the gorgeous Experimental Beach.

Desde este largo tramo de guijarros entre el mar y las salineras puedes ver la puesta de sol cada tarde en una gloriosa explosión de colores. Si tienes poco presupuesto, llévate tu propia botella de cava y disfruta de la puesta, por el contrario reserva una mesa en el Restaurante Experimental Beach.

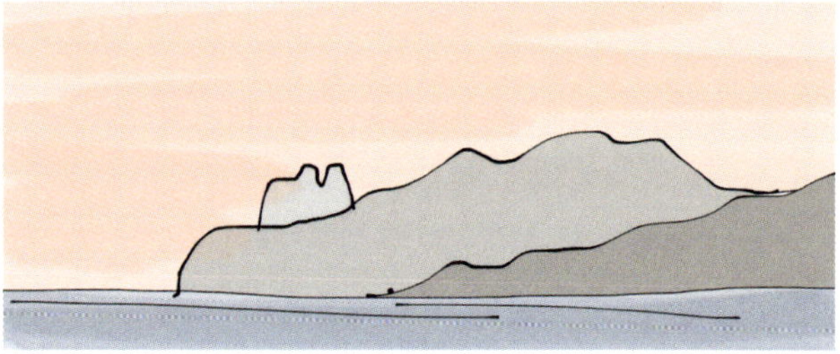

Experimental Beach

Playa d'es Codolar, Las Salinas
Tel: 664.331.269

The chic bohemian terrace overlooking the sea and sunset is simply a-mazing. I do feel like I'm repeating myself at times when I go on about the sunsets, but here they really are out of this world. The restaurant serves quality French-based cuisine and great cocktails, all with the view and the music it's worth every penny.

La terraza chic y bohemia con vistas al mar y a la puesta de sol es simplemente alucinante. A veces siento que me estoy repitiendo cuando hablo de las increíbles puestas de sol en Ibiza, pero aquí realmente son algo fuera de este mundo. El restaurante sirve cocina francesa de cálidad y cocteles que junto con la vista y la música valen cada céntimo.

NATURE * NATURALEZA

FLAMINGOES
FLAMENCOS

As you drive to Experimental Beach, look to your right and see if you can spot any wild Flamingoes. They come here to feed every summer.

Mientras conduces a Experimental Beach, mira a tu derecha y si tienes suerte verás flamencos salvajes. Vienen aqui cada verano.

ON IBIZA....
WHEN
THE SUN
GOES DOWN
THE SOUND
GOES UP

Las Salinas

Ibiza's most famous beach, Salinas, stretches far... and is edged with low-lying woods and dunes. It transforms into a series of little rocky coves before reaching the old watchtower at the far end.. It's a lovely walk in the winter, and the beach is absolutely heaving in the summer due to its selection of beach restaurants.

Salinas es la playa más famosa de Ibiza, se extiende larga distancia y está flanqueada por pequeños bosques y dunas. La playa se transforma en pequeñas calitas a medida que vas acercándote a la torre de vigía. El paseo hasta la torre es precioso en invierno y por supuesto, la playa está a tope en verano debido a su selección de restaurantes.

Jockey Club

Playa de Las Salinas
Tel: 971.395.788
jockeyclubibiza.com

The Jockey Club family are very close to my heart, and I've spent many a weekend here enjoying their company and food.
If you want to treat yourself, get a lounger and settle in for the day with the DJ playing deep house in the background, fresh fruit smoothies and cocktails and an amazing all-day menu. Don't forget to take a peek at the little shop before you leave: their polo shirts and beach towels with their logo on are Ibiza classics.

Le tengo mucho cariño a la familia del Jockey Club y he pasado muchos fines de semana aquí disfrutando de su compañía y su comida. Si quieres darte un capricho, reserva una hamaca y quédate todo el día disfrutando del sonido deep house sonando desde la cabina del DJ. Tienen batidos y cócteles de fruta fresca y una carta deliciosa todo el día. No te olvides de echar un vistazo en su tienda antes de irte, los polos y las toallas con su logo son clásicos de Ibiza.

Sa Trinxa

Playa de Las Salinas
Tel: 637.826.183
satrinxa.com

A total old school classic, I go here when I want to spend the whole day at the beach, but not necessarily on it. At the very end of Salinas beach, it's a bit of a walk but worth every step. Take a mask and snorkle, because the sea-life here is mental, fish are very friendly and the water translucent. And all with Jon Sa Trinxa's signature Balearic tunes in the background. Bring some extra cash for the boutique, which manages to nail all the trends each summer.

Un clásico de siempre, vengo aquí cuando quiero pasar el día en la playa, pero no necesariamente en la arena. Situado al final de la playa de Salinas, hay que caminar un poco pero merece la pena cada paso. Llévate unas gafas y tubo de bucear, porque la vida marina aquí es alucinante, los peces son muy chulos y el agua es translúcida. Y todo con los temas baleáricos característicos de Jon Sa Trinxa de fondo. Trae dinero extra para la boutique, que consigue acertar con las tendencias de cada temporada.

...SHOPPING... DE COMPRAS...

Echo A Mano

Ctra. Sa Canal, Las Salinas
Tel: 971.932.032
hostalsalinas.com

At the entrance to the parking area of Salinas is Argentinian Edu 's leather workshop. He's had this place for over 20 years and is a top leather craftsman. You can find original handmade leather handbags, belts and many other accessories with that hippy touch. He also takes orders and creates personalized client.

En la entrada al aparcamiento de Salinas está el taller y tienda de cuero del artesano argentino Edu. Este talentoso artesano del cuero lleva aquí más de 20 años. Puedes encontrar bolsos originales, cinturones y muchos otros accesorios con un toque hippy. También trabaja por encargo, por si estás en la isla más de unos días.

Super Can Pep Tixedó

Ctra. de Las Salinas
supercanpeptixedo.com

This unprepossessing supermarket near the exit to Es Cavallet is a gem. Stop en route to the beach for home made sandwiches, Argentinian pasties - or even a lilo! They tend to be quite busy so be prepared to wait your turn at the till.

Este deslucido supermercado cerca de la salida de Es Cavallet es una joya. Párate de camino a la playa para un buen bocadillo, empanadas argentinas, ¡y hasta una colchoneta! Suele estar lleno así que prepárate a esperar tu turno en la caja.

...SLEEP...A BIT DORMIR... UN POCO

Boutique Hostal Salinas

Ctra. Sa Canal, Las Salinas
Tel: 971.308.899
hostalsalinas.com

This place is a popular spot for locals and regular visitors. The owners and long-time island residents Duesi, Anita and David have done an amazing job and if I was coming for a fun, beachy holiday I would certainly stay here. Just a three-minute walk over the dunes to Salinas beach, they do good value, yummy food and the laid-back, party atmosphere means it's perfect for après-beach sessions on the terrace.

Este hostal es famoso entre los lugareños y los visitantes habituales. Los propietarios y viejos residentes de la isla, Duesi, Anita y David han hecho un trabajo increíble con este sitio. Si viniera para unas vacaciones de playa, me hospedaría aquí seguro. A tan sólo tres minutos a pie de la playa cruzando las dunas de Salinas, aquí hacen comida deliciosa a buen precio y su ambiente de fiesta relajada lo convierten en un lugar perfecto para una sesión después de la playa.

...EAT & ENJOY COMER Y DISFRUTAR...

Can Salinas

Ctra. de Las Salinas, Km3.7
Tel: 971.396.563

As you drive to Salinas or Es Cavallet Beach you will spot this little farmhouse just near the road. Manel is the king of the Fideua (noodle paella), as the sign for this place suggests! A great pitstop before a lazy afternoon at the beach.

En la carretera a Salinas o Es Cavallet verás esta pequeña finca cerca de la carretera. Manel es el rey de la fideuà, como sugiere el cartel de este sitio. Perfecto para comer después de una tarde larga en la playa.

...PAST THE AIRPORT...TOWARDS CALA JONDAL

PASADO EL AEROPUERTO...DE CAMINO A CALA JONDAL...

La Ponderosa

Carretera del Aeropuerto, km 7
Tel: 673.453.940

On the roundabout just before the airport is this great spanish Bar. They do good ham and cheese toasted sándwiches, in spain we call them Bikinis. I like their omelette sandwich the most. It's perfect to stop for a quick beer before catching your flight if you can't face the airport lounge food. There's also a set menu here daily. Rumour has it that in the summer on some evenings they have flamenco dancing…

En este bar pegado a la rotonda, justo antes del aeropuerto, hacen riquísimos sándwiches mixtos. A mi me gusta el bocadillo de tortilla. Realmente perfecto para tomarte una cerveza rápida antes de coger un vuelo si no soportas la comida de las salas del aeropuerto. Tambien hacen un menu del d'ia diario. Corre el rumor de que a veces en verano hay baile flamenco por las noches.

Restaurante Sa Caleta

Playa d'es Bol Nou, Sa Caleta
Tel: 971.187.095

Go right around the little roundabout as you leave the airport and follow the stunning coastal road. Restaurante Sa Caleta has a little pebble beach in front with red cliffs, and, open all year, their fish and rice dishes are to die for. Nearby you'll find the remains of the first Phoenician settlement on the island. I myself like to dive in for a quick swim before I sit down to an array of seafood starters followed by a fideua (noodle paella). And they're open until 1am!

Gira alrededor de la pequeña rotonda al salir del aeropuerto y conduce junto a la costa oeste por un tramo precioso. El restaurante Sa Caleta está bien señalizado y se refugia entre dos acantilados de tierra rojiza, con una pequeña calita de piedras en frente. Está abierto todo el año. Sus platos de pescado y arroz están de muerte. Cerca encontrarás unas ruinas arqueológicas que son los restos del primer asentamiento fenicio de la isla. A mí me encanta pegarme un baño en el mar seguido de una selección de entrantes y una fideuà.

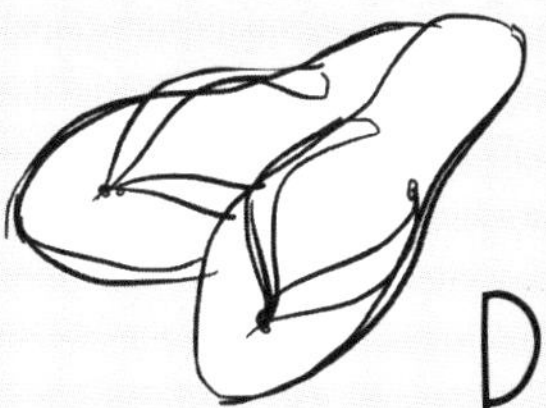

FIND YOUR PERFECT BEACH...

ENCUENTRA TU PLAYA PERFECTA...

* The Local/Swim-Before-Work beach: TALAMANCA (p.82)
  La playa local de los trabajadores de Ibiza
* The Touristy/Family/Clubby beach: PLAYA D'EN BOSSA (p.108)
  La playa de turistas, familias y fiesta
* The Fashionable/Partly Nudist beach: ES CAVALLET (p.114)
  La fashion y con algo de nudismo
* The Cool/Family/Sporty/Busy Ibiza beach: SALINAS (p..122)
  La playa cool, familiar, deportiva y muy llena
* The Rocky/Celebrity/Cool beach: CALA JONDAL (p..127)
  La playa cool de rocas y famosos
* The Magical/Western beach: CALA D'HORT (p.132)
  La playa mágica del oeste
* The Islanders/Hippie/Sunset beach: BENIRRAS (p.176)
  La playa de los isleños, hippies y de la puesta de sol
* The Surfers/Family beach: CALA NOVA (.p.197)
  La playa surfera y de familiias

..SUPERMARKET + CAFÉ
SUPER Y CAFETERÍA

Rincon de Es Codolar

Ctra. Sa Caleta, Es Codolar
Tel: 971.396.011

A handy little supermarket, selling everything you need to stock up that fridge and useful for a beach picnic. They have freshly made sandwiches, pastries and they make coffee, smoothies and fresh juices as well, so it's also perfect for breakfast on the little terrace outside.

Un supermercado súper práctico que vende de todo lo que necesitas para abastecer ese frigorifico y muy útil para picnic de playa. Hacen bocadillos frescos, y tienen pasteles y además hacen cafés, batidos y zumos naturales, así que también es perfecto para desayunar aquí en su terracita de afuera.

SLEEP... DORMIR

Cosmos Grand Hostal

Ctra. Sa Caleta, Es Codolar
Tel: 971.308.077 - 646.062.595
cosmosibiza.com

A spacious hotel and restaurant with a nice shady garden area, a covered terrace, bar and restaurant and a pool table which I love!!!
The Hotel has 6 double rooms and free wi-fi for its clients, its close to the beach of Es Codolar and just 5 minutes from the airport.
I think it even won an award a few years ago.

Un espacioso hotel y restaurante con jardín sombreado terraza cubierta, bar y restaurante y una mesa de billar que me chifla!!!
El hotel tiene 6 habitaciones dobles y wifi gratuito para sus clientes, está cerca de la playa de Es Codolar y a 5 minutos del aeropuerto.

Es Raco

Ctra Sa Caleta, Es Codolar
Tel: 971.591.541
esraco.eu

Hungry kids in the car after a long day at the beach? This is a great placc to stop and grab a pizza or pasta dish. I've heard that their Ravioli are good. and they also have grilled meat and a choice of seafood. There's have live music on Sundays and Mojitos in the funky garden outside with colourful bean bags and plants.

¿Niños hambrientos en el coche después de la playa? Pués este es el mejor lugar para parar y tomaros un plato de pasta o una pizza. He oído que los raviolis son ricos, la carne al grill y su selección de mariscos. Tienen música en vivo los domingos y la zona del jardín es muy acojedor con asientos de colores.

Cala Jondal

This beach gives you a choice of pebbles or sand. There are a few chiringuitos to choose from, all with a mixed clientele - some more low-key than others, some for the party crowd and others for the foodies. Take your pick and enjoy the view as the yachts roll in.

Esta playa te da a elegir entre cantos rodados y arena. Hay varios chiringuitos para elegir, todos con una clientela mezclada, algunos más relajados que otros, algunos más fiesteros y otros más gastronómicos. Escoge y disfruta de las vistas y de los yates anclar aquí uno tras otro.

Tropicana

Cala Jondal
Tel: 971.187.520
tropicanaibiza.com

At the far right of Cala Jondal beach you can sit under the shade of the pines and order endless jugs of Sangria. Try the fried baby squid and after lunch have an amazing massage. There's also a fab little boutique where it's hard not to spend.

En el extremo derecho de Cala Jondal puedes sentarte a la sombra de los pinos y pedir infinitas jarras de sangría. Pídete los chipirones fritos y luego date un increíble masaje. También tienen una boutique donde es difícil no comprarse algo.

Es Savina

Cala Jondal
Tel: 971.802.766 - 674.404.645

Lovely Susie from Yoga Retreats recommends this little place, and she's so right! It sits between the more pricey restaurants on Cala Jondal, with a small terrace shaded by juniper trees and actually has better access to the sea. The delicious Mediterranean menu is excellent value, and for those who are just in the market for a cold beer, cocktail or glass of chilled wine it has its own little beach bar called Joy. Grab a sunbed on the sandy area out front and enjoy the book you brought, along with the sea breeze washing over you.

La encantadora Susie de Yoga Retreats recomienda este pequeño establecimiento y tiene toda la razón. Se sitúa entre los restaurantes más caros de Cala Jondal, con una pequeña terraza cobijada por la sombra de las sabinas y lo que es más, tiene mejor acceso al mar. Su deliciosa carta mediterránea está muy bien de precio y para aquellos que simplemente quieran una cerveza fresca, un cóctel o una copa de vino tiene su propio bar en la playa llamado Joy. Reserva tu hamaca en la arena y disfruta de un libro y de la refrescante brisa marina.

Yemanja

Cala Jondal
Tel: 971.187.481
yemanjaibiza.com

This amazing beach restaurant just changed hands but the owner, who also owns its swishy neighbour Blue Marlin, swears it will remain the same as ever. Open all year round, they serve delicious fresh fish and amazing seafood starters and are known for their Champagne sangria. I also love the refreshing gazpacho here, which they serve in a glass adorned with edible greens.

Este magnífico restaurante de playa acaba de cambiar de dueño, ahora es propiedad del también dueño del lujoso Blue Marlin, aunque jura que lo dejará igual. Abierto todo el año, sirven delicioso pescado fresco y magníficos primeros de marisco y su sangría de cava es legendaria. También me encanta el refrescante gazpacho, que lo sirven en una copa adornada con verduras.

Blue Marlin

Cala Jondal
Tel: 971.410.117
bluemarlinibiza.com

A stunning location and good music right on the beach is how it all started years ago - a free party beneath the stars. But it's since become a mojito-champagne-bikini fest, and now your zone on the sand will cost! If you want to dance your arse off with the oligarchs, spend and be seen spending this is the place to be.

Todo empezó hace unos años con una situación privilegiada y buena música en plena playa, con una fiesta gratuita bajo las estrellas. Pero desde que se ha controcito de arena ahora tiene precio! Si quieres bailar con los oligarcas, gastar y que la gente te vea derrochando, éste es tu sitio.

Es Xarcú

Es Porroig
Tel: 971.187.867

This place is strictly for when I am feeling like a seafood treat, because it is not cheap - despite the fact it's a simple shack. The king prawns or the salt-baked sea bass are the dishes to try, and it's also a lovely remind er of the old days as you sit and enjoy the simplicity of this stony little bay.

Este sitio es estrictamente para cuando quiero darme el capricho de una buena comida de marisco, porque, ¡no es nada barato para ser que probar las gambas rojas o la lubina salvaje a la sal, un simple chiringuito! Tienes y además me recuerda a los viejos tiempos cuando te sientas y disfrutas de la sencillez de esta pequeña calita de cantos rodados.

Ses Boques

Playa de Ses Boques, Es Cubells
Tel: 606.081.570

Joan and his wife Lourdes opened this little rustic beach bar in the late 1970s. Sitting at the edge of a secluded cove when you drive down from the church of Es Cubells, they do incredibly tasty no-frills cuisine served at little wooden tables in the shade of a pine forest by the sea. Go for the lobster stew.

Juan y su mujer Lourdes abrieron este pequeño chiringuito a finales de los 70. En una calita aislada bajando por el camino junto a la iglesia de Es Cubells, sirven cocina sencilla y sabrosa en pequeñas mesas de madera a la sombra de los pinos junto al mar. Prueba la caldereta de langosta.

Es Torrent

Cala de Es Torrent, Es Porroig
Tel: 971.802.160

Owner Xico created this heavenly restaurant years ago facing the sea in a hidden rocky, cove. The food is top quality and known by residents as an exclusive fish restaurant. Make sure you choose your fish, and thus avoid being billed way over. It is expensive here!

Hace años, Xico abrió este restaurante frente al mar en una calita casi oculta. La comida es de alta cálidad y conocido por los residentes como un restaurante exclusivo de pescado. Asegúrate de elegir el pescado personalmente, y asi evitar una cuenta que no esperabas.

Es Cubells

This tiny village is located south of Sant Josep and has two restaurants, a grocery store and a lovely little square. The church sits high on the cliffs, with spectacular views over the sea - a real wedding hot spot.
Well worth the drive.
Este pequeño pueblo está al sur de San José y tiene dos restaurantes, una tienda de comestibles y una placita ideal. La iglesia es impresionante y se asienta sobre los acantilados con unas vistas espectaculares sobre el mar, convirtiéndola en un lugar perfecto para una boda.

The Church of Es Cubells was built in 1864 by Carmelite monk Francesc Palau, who spent long periods of his life on the rock of Es Vedrà. It sits high up on the cliffs, with spectacular views out to sea.
La Iglesia de Es Cubells fue construida en 1864 por el monje carmelita Francesc Paau que pasó largos periodos de su vida en la roca de Es Vedrà. Está encaramada en lo alto del acantilado, con unas vistas espectaculares al mar.

Bar Restaurante Llumbi

Es Cubells
Tel: 971.802.128

My friend Marita loves this little restaurant and understandably so. Sitting on the edge of the cliff next to the church, it has the most impressive views across the island, and the food is good and very reasonably priced.
A mi amiga Marita le encanta este pequeño restaurante y entiendo muy bien por qué. Enclavado al filo de un acantilado junto a la iglesia, tiene las vistas más impresionantes de la isla, la comida es buena y a muy buen precio.

Mo

Ctra. de Es Cubells, km 5,5
Cala de Bou
Tel: 971.802.150
restaurantemoibiza.com

My friend Mo (really) told me about this place. She said it was divine and set in a an old finca, tastefully decorated that serves Italian food, as well as delicious meat and fish dishes. And to top it has a view of Formentera from the chill out area by a pool
Mi amiga Mo me habló de este lugar. Lo describió como una vieja finca idealmente decorada que sirve comida italiana, carne y pescado. Y además tiene vistas a Formentera desde su zona chill-out junto a la piscina.

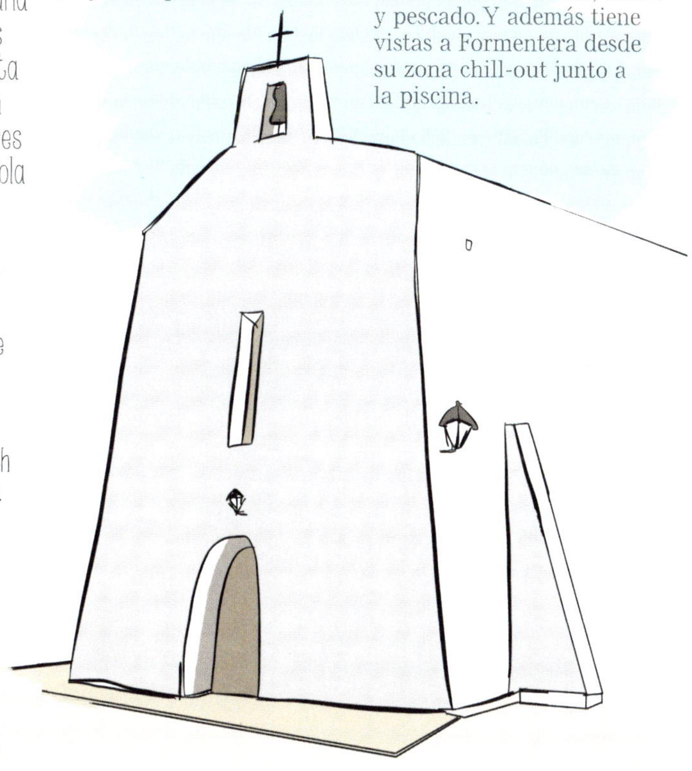

Km5

Ctra. Ibiza > San José
Tel: 971.396.349
km5-lounge.com

I'm always saying this, but oh! how we enjoyed this place years ago when it was smaller and emptier and infused with that effortless Ibiza chic. It actually started as a little bar-slash-disco, and has since become one of the island's most celebrated restaurants – and still a great place for meeting people. Sip your vodka lemon in the beautiful gardens and chat into the night, and if the parking here is a dusty affair – all part of the experience!

Siempre digo esto, ¡pero cómo solíamos divertirnos en este sitio hace unos años cuando era mucho más pequeño, menos concurrido e infundía ese toque chic desenfadado de Ibiza! Empezó como un pequeño bar con una pista de baile y desde entonces se ha convertido en uno de los restaurantes más afamados de la isla, aunque sigue siendo un sitio magnífico para reunirse con los amigos. Tómate una copa en su jardín y acabarás charlando toda la noche, y sí, el aparcamiento aquí es polvoriento, pero forma parte de la experiencia.

CAN BELLOTERA...

La Gourmandise

Ctra. San José > San Jordi
Tel: 627.681.930

This place is in an area of Can Bellotera and Sa Carroca, a few kilometres from Ibiza town on the San José road. It's a French patisserie where you can stop off for a breakfast, or grab a pastry, some cupcakes, a salad or tart to take away.

A unos kilómetros de Ibiza ciudad en la carretera a San José está Can Bellotera y Sa Carroca donde se encuentra esta pastelería francesa donde puedes pararte a desayunar o comprar una empanada, ensaladas o tartas para llevar.

Vino & Co

Ctra. San José > San Jordi
Tel: 971.305.324
vinoyco.com

High quality wine wholesalers. A family run shop done with incredible taste.

Mayoristas de vinos de alta cálidad. Una tienda familiar hecha con un gusto impecable.

Ostería La Taverna

Ctra. San José, km 1 > San Jordi
Tel: 971.303.221

My friends Mo and Jacob told me about this little spot. They always go here for lunch after selling at the San Jordi market. They serve up a cheap menu for lunch and its always packed.

Mis amigos Mo y Jacob me hablaron de este lugar. Siempre van aquí para almorzar después de vender en el mercadillo de San Jordi. Tienen un menú del dia y sus mesitas afuera siempre están llenas.

Cas Costas

Ctra. San José, km 3
Tel: 971.308.755
cascostasibiza.com

Cas Costas is a relativelty new place that offers you a delicious choice of traditional ibizan breakfasts, lunches or dinners on a delightful terrace. They have a grill and are good for large groups.

Cas Costas es un restaurante bastante nuevo que te ofrece desayunos, almuerzos y cenas elaboradas con productos Ibicencos que podrás disfrutar sentado en su amplia y bonita terraza exterior.

Atlantis

If you're feeling adventurous, and fit, drive towards Cala d'Hort and turn left before the road starts to go downhill, to reach the tower "des Savinar". To the left of the tower is a path that leads steeply down the hill to the sea. The walk down takes about 20 minutes and you will find a stunning quarry area at the edge of the sea with cut-out and rectangular pools in the stone, rocks were cut and transported by sea to build the cathedral of Ibiza. There's a small cave here where ancient stonemasons took refuge years ago and is now home occasionally to hippies who call this place "Atlantis", supposedly influenced by the magic island of Es Vedrà next door.

Si tienes espíritu aventurero y estás en buena forma, conduce hacia Cala d'Hort y gira a la izquierda antes de que la carretera empiece a bajar, para alcanzar la Torre d'es Savinar. A la izquierda de la torre hay un camino empinado que baja hasta el mar. La bajada es a pie y se tarda 20 minutos.

Cuando llegues encontrarás una increíble cantera al filo del mar con rocas esculpidas y piscinas rectangulares, las piedras fueron cortada aqui para ser utilizadas en la construcción de la catedral de Ibiza. Es un paisaje alucinante. También hay una pequeña cueva donde los antiguos mamposteros se refugiaban y que ahora en ocasiones sirve de hogar para hippies, quienes empezaron a llamarlo "Atlantis" bajo la supuesta influencia de la mágica isla de Es Vedrà.

Cala d 'Hort

For islanders this is kind a magical beach, mainly because the islets of Es Vedrà and Es Vedranell rise out of the water just in front. It's a busy beach as has great restaurants and heavenly turquoise waters so it's definitely snorkeling territory.
I like to dive off the rocks by the fishermen's huts on the left. There are a few good restaurants and a great little boutique in the middle.
Para nosotros, los isleños, es una especie de playa mágica, principalmente porque los islotes de Es Vedrà y Es Vedranell se levantan sobre el mar justo enfrente. Es una playa muy concurrida por sus restaurantes y sus aguas turquesas, y asi territorio para snorkel.
Me gusta sumergirme desde las rocas junto a las casetas de pescadores. Hay tres restaurantes muy buenos y una pequeña boutique muy coqueta en medio.

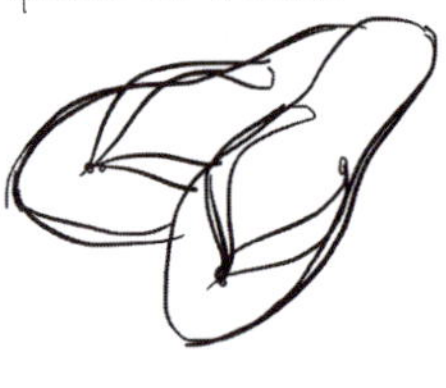

El Carmen

Cala d'Hort
Tel: 971.187.449

My friends love coming here in the summer.
The restaurant does a particularly tasty paella, and you can eat while enjoying the dramatic sea views.
And, you can also watch the kids on the beach from the terrace. Try the steamed mussels as a starter!
A mis amigos les encanta venir aquí en verano porque preparan una paella muy sabrosa, y mientras comes puedes disfrutar de sus vistas al mar y además controlar a los niños en la playa desde la terraza. ¡Los mejillones al vapor también están muy ricos!

Ca Na Vergara

Cala d'Hort
Tel: 971.935.036

This traditional Ibicencan restaurant is a bit of a classic with many islanders, it has the stunning backdrop of the sea and the islands of Es Vedrà and Es Vedranell. Owned and run by the Vergera family, it serves really good traditional rice, fish and meat dishes.
Este restaurante tradicional ibicenco es una especie de clásico para muchos isleños, con el mar y las islas de Es Vedrà y Es Vedranell como telón de fondo. Propiedad de la familia Vergara, sirve platos ricos y tradicionales de arroz, carne y pescado.

Es Boldadó

Camí de Cala d'Hort, s/n
Cala d'Hort
Tel: 626.494.537
restauranteboldado.net

I have not been for a few years but I know it remains the same. Here they specialize in seafood here and I suggest the red prawns and the fried squid as a starter. I've heard the "Espardenyes al ajillo", sea cucumbers are delicious although I can't quite imagine it. They are also famous for their Paellas here. I like the "ciega" best as it's free of all the bits. Book in advance as it is always busy and try to get a table by the windows so you can gaze at Es Vedra.
Turn right before you get down to the beach and drive a bit until you see a stone marking a dirt track on the left.
Aquí se especializan en mariscos y os recomiendo las gambas rojas y los calamares fritos como aperitivo, pero dice la gente que hay que probar las " Espardenyes al ajillo ". También tiene fama por sus ricas paellas. A mí me gusta la Paella ciega. Reserve con antelación, ya que está siempre lleno y tratar de conseguir una mesa por las ventanas para poder ver bien la isla de Es Vedra.
Gira a la derecha antes de llegar a la playa y conduce un poco hasta que veas una piedra marcando un camino a la izquierda.

Es Vedrà Island La isla de Es Vedra

This uninhabited island in the south west of Ibiza 2.5km out from Cala d'Hort beach, reminds me of that 1970s sci-fi film "Close Encounters of the Third Kind."
Last year the wild goats on it were removed leaving just falcons and blue lizards. The legends abound, and it's said to be the third most magnetic spot on Earth, a semi-dormant volcano and the home of the legendary Sirens, the mermaids who lured Odysseus from his ship in Homer's 'Odyssey'. It's hard to decipher fact from fiction, but what is known is that the Phoenicians worshipped this small island as the birthplace of their goddess, Tanit, patron saint of fertility and a strong symbol of Ibiza to this day, and that it was home to an exiled Carmelite monk in 1855.
As for spotting any actual UFOs? The tower that faces Vedrà just before Cala D'hort is the perfect spot to wait for them to make contact, as some people believe there's a secret UFO base under the sea and that Es Vedrà is the gateway!
...Meanwhile, some of my friends have actually witnessed powerful visions near here, (but who knows what they were drinking, or eating!) so among us islanders it certainly lives up to its reputation as a truly mystical place.

Este islote deshabitada al suroeste de Ibiza y a unos 2,5km de la playa de Cala d'Hort siempre me recuerda a la película de ciencia ficción "Encuentros en la tercera fase". El año pasado se retiraron las cabras montesas dejando sólo halcones y lagartijas azules. Las leyendas abundan, y se dice que es el tercer punto más magnético de la Tierra, un volcán inactivo y el hogar de las sirenas legendarias, que atrajeron a Odiseo desde su barco en la Odisea de Homero.
Como podeis ver, es difícil separar la verdad de la ficción.
Lo que sí se sabe es que los fenicios adoraban la isla como lugar de nacimiento de su diosa Tanit, la patrona de la fertilidad y símbolo de Ibiza hasta hoy, y que un monje carmelita estuvo exiliado aquí en 1855.
¿En cuanto al avistamiento de OVNIs? La torre frente a Es Vedrà, justo antes de llegar a Cala D'Hort, es un lugar perfecto para esperar a que hagan contacto ya que mucha gente cree que hay una base de OVNIs secreta bajo el mar aquí y que Es Vedrà es su portal.
Sin embargo, algunos amigos míos han sido testigos de visiones muy fuertes cerca de aquí (¡¡pero quién sabe lo que habían bebido o comido!!), así que entre nosotros los isleños ciertamente está a la altura de su reputación como lugar verdaderamente místico...

♡ 5 THINGS YOU SHOULD DO

5 COSAS QUE DEBERÍAS HACER CUANDO ESTÉS AQUÍ

---

1. Lunch + swim at Cala Escondida (p.146)
Almuerzo y baño en Cala Escondida

2. Hippy Market + aperitif at Kumharas (p.148)
Aperitivo y mercadillo en Kumharas

3. Tapas at Destino (p.139)
Tapas en Destino

4. Sunset at Hostal La Torre (p.160)
Puesta de sol en Hostal La Torre

5. Tortilla at Can Cosmi, Santa Inés (p.163
Tortilla en Can Cosmi, Santa Agnés

THE WEST
San José, San Agustín, the Beaches, & San Antonio

El Oeste, Sant Josep,
Sant Agustí, las playas,
y Sant Antoni

SAN JOSÉ SANT JOSEP DE SA TALAIA

What feels like a drive-through village has a surprisingly good little selection of eateries and shops along its central road and every year it grows and grows. It's also the last village before you turn off the main road to some of the loveliest western beaches, so it's perfect for a pre-beach breakfast or a post-beach dinner.

Te sorprendería ver la cantidad de restaurantes y tiendas que tiene este pequeño pueblo a lo largo de su carretera central y sigue creciendo. Además es el último pueblo antes de girar hacia las playas más bonitas del oeste, siendo perfecto para pararse a desayunar antes de la playa o parar a cenar después.

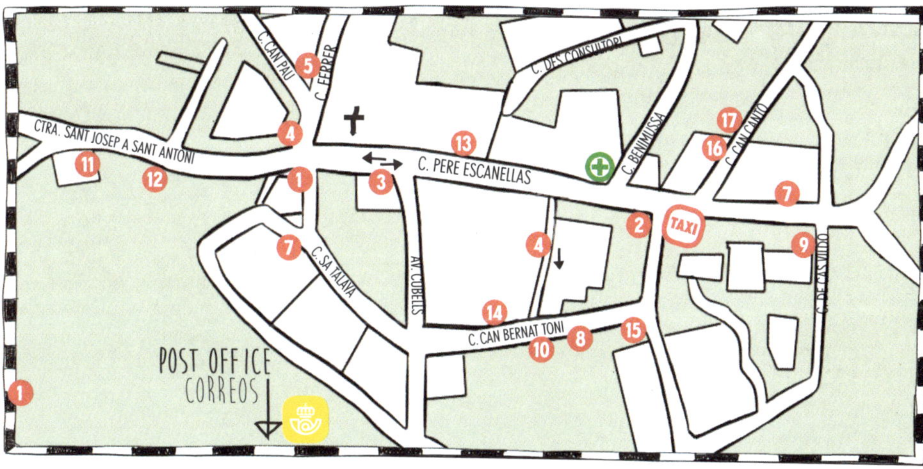

...EAT & DRINK
COMER Y BEBER...

1 Bar Ca'n Bernat Vinya
C/ de Pere Escanelles, San José
Tel: 971.800.703

An old-fashioned village cafe that has barely changed in decades, with little tables that sit in the shade in the orchard opposite. Always popular with local older men, who sit around with their berets on playing cards. Plus they do a great sandwiches!

Una antigua cafetería que no ha cambiado en décadas, con sus mesitas a la sombra en el huerto de enfrente. Es popular entre los señores locales, que con sus boinas puestas juegan a las cartas. ¡Preparan unos bocatas riquísimos!

2 La Movida Café
C/ de Pere Escanelles, San José
Tel: 971.800.002

This place is next to the church and always full of village locals. They do Mediterranean food and are also known for their delicious burgers. It's a nice place for a relaxed dinner, and also very affordable considering the quality of the food.

Esta cafetería junto a la iglesia siempre está llena de gente del pueblo. Preparan cocina mediterránea y también son conocidos por sus hamburguesas. Un lugar bonito para una cena relajada, además es muy asequible considerando la calidad de la comida.

3 Racó Verd
Ctra.Port d'es Torrent, San José. Tel: 971.341.407

The lovely owners Claire and Sam have created a

little gem with this place. Admittedly I don't get here often because I am an Easterner. Try their classic tapas and awesome Mexican plate, while you can have breakfast or lunch in the garden at the back. There's live music four times a week with Bossa Nova/Brazilian night on Tuesday, Rock and Blues on Thursday, unplugged Fridays and flamenco on Saturday. You will find it opposite San José church on the road. Oh, and here stands one of San José's oldest olive trees!

Los encantadores propietarios, Claire y Sam, han creado una pequeña joya en este local. Debo admitir que no vengo muy a menudo porque vivo al este de la isla. Prueba sus tapas clásicas y sus deliciosos platos mexicanos, también puedes desayunar o comer en el jardín de atrás. Hay música en directo cuatro veces a la semana con noche de Bossa Nova los martes, Rock y Blues los jueves, acústico viernes y flamenco los sábados. Encuéntralo frente a la iglesia de San José en la carretera. Ah, ¡y aquí encontrarás los olivos más ancestrales de San José!

4 Es Galliner

C/ de l'Ajuntament, 2, San José
Tel: 971.803.554

"The hen coop"- allegedly and originally named on account of how noisy and popular it can be. But actually this is a little haven of taste, style and great service. Owned by local lady Pepa, this is a family-run restaurant that satisfies both local tastes and international ones. They offer butter croissants for breaky but this gem of a restaurant is really worth visiting for their fantastic value set menus at lunch. Classic Spanish spiced up with savvy extras such as grilled veg with honey, stuffed potatoes, and salads. Standard Spanish tapas available as well.

El Gallinero, supuesta y originalmente nombrado por lo ruidoso y popular que puede ser. Pero de hecho es un paraíso de sabores y estilo y con un servicio muy bueno. Propiedad de Pepa, es un restaurante familiar que satisface a los paladares locales e internacionales. Ofrecen desayunos, pero este restaurante merece una visita por sus fantásticos menús del día. Cocina clásica española con extras especiales como verduras a la parrilla con miel, patatas rellenas y ensaladas. Tienen las clásicas tapas española

5 Passion

C/ de Pere Escanelles, San José
Tel: 971.801.085
passion-ibiza.com/san-jose

Lana's latest addition to her list of healthy restaurants that she has all over the island.
Located in a prime spot on a corner beside the church, here she has yet again created a stunning light and open space with spanich tiles and wood.
Her food is as always delicious, her juices and smoothies amazing and her cakes divine as well.

La última adición de Lana a su lista de restaurantes saludables que tiene por toda la isla. En una posición muy privilegiada en la esquina junto a la iglesia, aquí ella ha creado una vez más un espacio abierto y luminado azulejos hidraulicos y madera.
Su comida es deliciosa como siempre, sus jugos y batidos increíbles y sus pasteles divinos.

6 Café Can Llorenç

C/ Can Pou, 2, San José
Tel: 971.801.601

A sweet little town house in the centre of San José, serving superb tapas and little stacked sandwiches. Every Sunday they also do a homemade, thick chocolate drink with "churros" (batter sticks sprinkled with sugar) - a true old school Ibiza classic.
Una encantadora finca urbana en el centro de San José, que sirve tapas sabrosísimas y pequeños sándwiches. Cada domingo preparan el tradicional chocolate con churros, un viejo clásico aquí en Ibiza.

7 Destino

Plaza de la Iglesia, San José
Tel: 971.800.703

Asian and Moroccan tapas served on a cosy terrace with little Hispanic arches facing the church of San José. There's no menu here, so just check the counter indoors and choose.
My favourites are the tajine, the lentils with cumin and the Thai dishes.
Tapas de inspiración asiática y marroquí en una acogedora terraza con pequeños arcos hispánicos mirando hacia la iglesia de San José. Aquí no hay carta, así que mira en la barra dentro y haz tu elección. Mis favoritas son Tajine, las lentejas con comino y los platos tailandeses.

8 Pizzico di Pepe

C/ Can Bernat Toni, 10
Tel: 971.801.139

A Café slash Restaurant that has carpaccio, vitello tonato, provolone, pizza, lasaña, gnocchi, spaghetti, milanesa...it just has all Italian on the menu. Perfect for a post beach meal when the hunger kicks in.
Un Café-Restaurante que ofrece para comer carpaccio, vitello tonato, provolone, pizza, lasaña, gnochi, espagueti, milanesa... Un menú todo de productos italianos. Perfecto para una comida después de la playa cuando hay hambre.

9 No Te Olvides De Acordarte

C/ de Cas Vildo, San José
Tel: 678.962.434

A latin american Restaurant that opened recently serving Uruguayan influenced food, pies, sandwiches, salads, pizzas and breakfasts. They are open til late in the summer.
Un restaurante latinoamericano que abrió recientemente. Sirve comida con influencias uruguayas, empanadas, chivitos, ensaladas, pizzas y desayunos. En verano abren hasta tarde.

10 La Focacheria

C/ Bernat Toni, 10
San José
Tel: 971.801.130

Just behind the Town Hall car park is this fairly new little place that has a fresh vibe and serves all sorts of Focachas, the typical Genovès Focacha, with melted cheese too and more... They do take away as well.
Justo detrás del aparcamiento del ayuntamiento está este pequeño lugar con un ambiente fresco que sirve todo tipo de focachas: la típica genovesa, o con queso fundido... También tienen servicio para llevar.

11 Es Vergé

Ctra. Sant Josep Cruce Cala Vadella
Tel: 971.800.041
esverge.com

In a little red town house on the side of the road as you leave San José going towards San Antonio. This affordable little restaurant is a favourite among island reisdents. The pizzas are all made in a traditional pizza oven using fresh Ibizan produce. They also do fajitas and kebabs, and the outdoor terrace is buzzing in the high season with the post-beach posse.
Closed Mondays.
En una pequeña casa roja en la carretera justo a la salida de Sant Josep para San Antonio. Un restaurante realmente asequible que es un favorito entre residentes. de la isla. Las pizzas están hechas en un horno tradicional y utilizando productos frescos de la isla. También hacen fajitas y kebabs y la terraza está siempre a rebosar en temporada alta por las tardes. Cerrado los lunes.

12 Can Limo

Ctra. S.José, km 5,
Tel: 971 .800.550
canlimoibiza.com

A Peruvian fusion Tapa Bar and restaurant on the road as you leave San Jose village. It has great views of

San Antonio bay and you can enjoy a cocktail or two from its little Chill out.
Una bar de tapas-restaurante de fusión peruana en la carretera al salir del pueblo de San José. Tiene excelentes vistas a la bahía de San Antonio y puedes disfrutar de un buen cóctel desde su chill-out.

SHOPPING...

13 El Palio

C/ de Pere Escanellas, 32
San José
Tel: 971.800.047

A shop on the main street full of gorgeous decorative objects, furniture and art. Perfect for gifts.
Una tienda en la calle principal, llena de objetos decorativos, muebles y arte. Perfecto para regalos

14 Aurobelle

C/ Bernad Toniet, 5, San José
Tel: 971.800.920
aurobelle.com

A colourful den of delights selling beautiful dresses, tops, shoes and accessories. The sister store of Aurobelle in Santa Gertrudis which I visit often. It's perfect for finding a special gift and I love their sarongs which are a summer must.
Una tienda colorida llena de preciosos vestidos, tops, zapatos y accesorios. Es la tienda hermana de Aurobelle en Santa Gertrudis a la cual visito con frecuencia. Perfecto para encontrar un regalo o detalle especial para regalar. Me encantan sus pareos que son lo más para el verano.

15 Silk Ibiza

C/ Bernat Toniet, 12, San José
Tel: 971.801.698
silkibiza.es

I've had amazing feedback regarding this shop on the main street. So if you've just bought a house and need furniture, cushions, bed linen, or some extra design pieces, get over here and have a look.
He oído muchas cosas buenas sobre esta tienda. Si acabas de comprar una casa y necesita muebles, cojines, ropa de cama, o necesitas algunas piezas de diseño, ven a echar un vistazo.

16 Pescadería Oliver

C/ de Can Cantó, 3, San José
Tel: 971.800.420

Valeriano Iglesias started as a young man selling fish out of a van in the square, blowing a seashell to call his clients. He now owns this fishmonger, which always has the freshest catch of the day. Working alongside his sister Asunción, he sells to most of the restaurants in the area.
Valeriano Iglesias empezó de joven a vender pescado de una furgoneta en la plaza, haciendo sonar una caracola para llamar a sus clientes. Ahora es el propietario de esta pescadería. Trabaja con su hermana Asunción y abastecen a la mayoría de restaurantes de la zona.

17 Carnisseria Can Toni

C/ de Can Cantó, 3, San José
Tel: 971.800.707

Toni Ribas works with farmers on the island to ensure you get the best meat. Try his home-made "Sobrasada", an Ibicencan pepper sausage.
He is open all year.
Toni Ribas trabaja con granjeros de la isla para asegurar que siempre tiene la mejor carne. Prueba su sobrasada casera y las salchichas con pimiento de Ibiza. Abierto todo el año.

...SLEEP & RELAX
DORMIR Y RELAJARSE...

Calador Resort

C/ Cala Carbo S/N, San José
Tel: 971.808.424 - 656.912.495
caladoribiza.com

A recently reformed family run Resort facing the magical island of Es Vedra. All the apartments and studios have terraces with sea views, come with a small but well-equipped kitchenette as well as WIFI and share a large pool.
The restaurant offers Mediterranean specialties a selection of Spanish wines and cocktails at the bar as well as delicious breakfasts. They also offer this beautiful setting for events.
Un acogedor y familiar complejo frente a la isla mágica de Es Vedrá. Todos sus apartamentos y estudios disponen de terrazas con vistas al mar, una cocina pequeña y bien equipada, así como WIFI y compartan todos una piscina.
El restaurante ofrece especialidades mediterráneas, vinos españoles y cócteles en el bar, así como

deliciosos desayunos. También ofrecen su entorno para eventos.

Les Jardins de Palerm

Can Pujol d'en Cardona, San José. Tel: 971.800.318
jardinsdepalerm.com

Aclose friend of mine always stayed here and I loved visiting him. He even went on to build a house inspired by the place! It is basically a luxury finca in the hills surrounded by beautiful gardens, and even though it feels super secluded it's only a short walk from the centre of San José village which is handy, so it's just really quite perfect.

Un buen amigo siempre se hospedaba aquí y me encantaba visitarle. Incluso se construyó una casa inspirada en este hotel. Es básicamente una finca de lujo en las montañas rodeado de jardines preciosos y aunque te sientas muy aislado, está a un paseo del centro del pueblo de San José. Así que es simplemente perfecto.

Can Xuxu

Es Porroig, San José
Tel: 971.187.867

This beautifully restored boutique hotel in the hills near Cala Tarida has dark wood interiors and four poster beds that remind me so much of Bali. The pool is surrounded by tropical palms and there's a fabulous terrace where you can sip your cocktail and enjoy stunning sunset views.

Este hotel que ha sido bellamente restaurado en las colinas junto a Cala Tarida tiene madera oscura en su interior y camas de cuatro postes que me recuerdan mucho a Bali. La piscina está rodeada de palmeras y hay una terraza fabulosa donde puedes tomarte un cóctel y disfrutar de las vistas a la puesta de sol.

Ses Pitreras

C/ Valladolid, 1-3, San Agustín
Tel: 971.345.000
sespitreras.com

If you're into great architecture and design then this place ticks all the boxes. A contemporary space that has preserved the original Ibiza spirit. Only seven rooms each one completely unique. I love the wood decking at the pool, and thank heavens for the yummy room service.

Si te va la arquitectura y el diseño entonces este lugar es perfecto para ti. Un espacio contemporáneo que ha preservado el espíritu original de Ibiza.Sólo tiene siete habitaciones, cada una completamente única. Me encanta el entarimado de madera junto a la piscina y su servicio de habitaciones es realmente delicioso.

THE ROAD TO SAN JOSÉ...
LA CARRETERA A SAN JOSÉ

Chimi Churri

Ctra. Cala Conta, San José
Tel: 971 80 42 15
esverge.com

Love this place! A German/Argentinian steak house with top quality grilled meats, home-made burgers and schnitzel, and extremely generous portions. They also do an amazing variety of beers and the staff are always warm and friendly. You can really stuff yourself for under 20 euros! Closed Tuesdays.

¡Me encanta este sitio! Un asador alemán-argentino con carnes a la parrilla, hamburguesas caseras y schnitzel, las raciones son muy generosas. También tienen una gran variedad de cervezas y el servicio siempre es cordial y simpático. ¡Puedes salir rodando de aquí por menos de 20 euros!
Cerrado los martes.

Bar Stop

Crta. Cala Conta + Cala Tarida
Tel: 971.346.985

Bar Stop sits at the junction between Cala Tarida and Cala Conta and is one of those popular places for the locals in the area. It's always busy and always loud and they have a pool table.
It's a perfect stop for a quick coffee or drink, and they serve up typical Mediterranean home-made food and have a cheap day menu as well as tapas.
Live music on the weekends and open all year except over the Christmas period.

Bar Stop está en el cruce entre Cala Tarida y Cala Conta y es un punto de encuentro para la gente local de la zona. Siempre lleno, siempre ruidoso, y tienen una mesa de billares. Una parada clásica para un café o una copa, sirven cocina casera mediterránea y tienen menú del día además de aperitivos, tapas y hamburguesas. Música en vivo los fines de semana y abierto todo el año excepto durante la Navidad.

Falsonueve

C/. Sant Josep km 11,5, San José
Tel: 971.800.111
falsonueve.com

This is a traditional Italian Restaurant which is in the countryside just before you reach San Jose village. I found it by chance and mainly because I like the name. They do Neapolitan Pizzas, barbeque meat and in the summer there's a live band playing.

Restaurante tradicional italiano en el campo, justo antes de llegar al pueblo de San José. Lo encontré por casualidad y porque me gustaba el nombre. Hacen pizzas napolitanas, carnes a la barbacoa y en verano hay una banda tocando en directo. Un buen lugar para ir con la familia.

Botiga Can Jordi

Ctra. Ibiza >San José
Tel: 971.800.182

I love the simplicity of this place. It is more than a century old and has a supermarket, a basket shop, a post office, a bar, an art gallery… and they also do live music! Known to some as the 'Can Jordi Blues Station,' famous international musicians have been known to turn up for impromptu jam sessions.

Me encanta este lugar, más bien por su simpleza. Tiene más de un siglo y es a la vez supermercado, tienda de cestos, correos, bar y galería de arte… ¡y tienen música en directo! Conocido por muchos como 'Can Jordi Blues Station', músicos de fama internacional se han presentado y han hecho sesiones de música improvisadas.

Can Domingo

Ctra. Ibiza >San José, Km. 9.8
Tel: 971.800.184
candomingoibiza.com

A heavenly Italian restaurant perfect for a romantic dinner under the stars in its candle lit garden. Their menu is mouth-watering and they have a large selection of wines as well as a legendary home baked bread. Go try!

Un restaurante italiano exquisito y perfecto para una cena romántica bajo las estrellas en su jardín. Su menú es un sueño para tu paladar y tienen una gran selección de vinos, así como un pan horneado casero que es legendario.

…ROADSIDE SHOPPPING
TIENDA EN LA CARRETERA

Ibiza-Warehouse

Ctra. Ibiza >San José, Km 5
ibiza-warehouse.com

Lovely dutch Carole created this unique interior design store in a sweet town house on the roadside as a result of her love for vintage and 2nd hand markets worldwide and on Ibiza. Here you will find a unique selection of hand picked objects. She also sells her own handmade brand of leather bags and bracelets called the "fig tree-label".

La holandesa Carole creó esta tienda unica de diseño interior en una finca preciosa a pie de la carretera como resultado de su pasión por el vintage y los mercadillos de 2º mano en todo el mundo. y Ibiza. Aquí encontrarás una selección única además de su propia marca artesanal de bolsos de cuero y pulseras llamadas "fig tree-label"

SAN AGUSTÍN VILLAGE EL PUEBLO DE SANT AGUSTI

I call it the forgotten village of Ibiza. Tiny and pretty as a picture, follow the narrow lane that gently winds up from the main road to a square where the impressive 200-year-old whitewashed church stands proudly. A few little bars, a gallery and a simple local shop pretty much sums up the village, but this is the real, unadulterated rural Ibiza. I love it, and so will you!

Yo lo llamo el pueblo olvidado de Ibiza. Tan pequeño y bonito como una postal, para llegar sigue el estrecho camino que sube la colina desde la carretera principal llegando a una plaza donde se encuentra la imponente iglesia encalada de 200 años de antigüedad. Unos bares pequeños, una galería y una tienda local conforman el pueblo; ésta es la verdadera Ibiza. ¡Os encantará!

Can Berri Vell

Plaza Major, San Agustín
Tel: 971.344.321

Find this romantic little restaurant at the very top of the village, facing the church in the square. Located in the courtyard of a seventeenth century house, this is the perfect place to come with your lover for a candlelit meal for two.

Encuentra este restaurante pequeño y romántico en lo alto del pueblo, frente a la iglesia en la plaza. Situado en el patio de una casa del siglo XVII, es el lugar perfecto para venir con tu amante para una cena para dos a la luz de las velas.

Village Shop / Tienda

Plaza Mayor, San Agustín

This dark little shop remains completely unchanged since I used to run in as a kid to get pipas (salted roasted sunflower seeds). The family who run it also have the bar next door. Here they still add up pencil on a piece of paper.

Esta tienda pequeña y oscura permanece totalmente inalterada desde que solía correr a ella de niña para comprar pipas. La familia que la regenta también tiene el bar de al lado. Siguen haciendo la cuenta con papel y lápiz.

THE CHURCH OF SAN AGUSTÍN is simple and very beautiful with its typiclly white washed walls, a single arbor and side chapels that were added in the mid nineteenth century. With its stunning location out in the campo perched up on the hill it's really worth a visit. One of my best friends got married here and it was a idillic day, however they did get divorced later...!

LA IGLESIA DE SANT AGUSTÍ es simple y muy bonita con sus típicas paredes encaladas, y una planta sencilla con capillas a los lados que se añadieron a mediados del siglo XIX. Su situación en el campo en lo alto de la colina hace que merezca la pena visitarla. Uno de mis amigos se casó aquí, ¡aunque se divorció después...

BEACHES IN THE WEST PLAYAS EN EL OESTE

I personally think that the west of the island has some of Ibiza's most unusual and beautiful beaches and coves.
Cala Tarida, Cala Conta, Cala Molí, Cala Vadella, Cala Codolar, Cala Carbó and Cala d'Hort are all on the same strip on the western side of the island. They all have beach restaurants, white sand and crystal-clear waters. Ideal for snorkelling and spending a perfect day.

Creo que el oeste de la isla presume de las playas y calas más inusuales y bonitas de Ibiza.
Cala Tarida, Cala Conta, Cala Molí, Cala Vadella, Cala Codolar, Cala Carbó y Cala d'Hort están todas en el mismo tramo oeste de la costa. Todas tienen chiringuitos, arena blanca y aguas cristalinas. Perfectas para hacer snorkel y para pasar el día.

Cala Tarida

This beach was stunning years ago, before mass tourism took over. Its white sand and crystal-clear waters are shallow for quite a distance, and it has a nice selection of beach restaurants. It's also quite unique in that a little islet sits close to the beach in the middle of the bay.
Esta playa era preciosa hace años, antes de que fuera ocupada por el turismo en masa. Es una playa de arenas blancas y aguas cristalinas y poco profundas. Además tiene una buena selección de restaurantes. También es única porque tiene un pequeño islote cerca de la playa justo en medio de la bahía.

Chiringuito Cala Tarida

San José
Tel: 971.090.160
chiringuitocalatarida.com

This is a really gorgeous spot on the beach of Cala Tarida. Low key décor with driftwood here and there and lovely shady spots. Sadly it's a busy beach but sitting up here is a pleasure. The food is mediterranean influence and tapas as well as juices and cocktails.
It is also a nice spot for a birthday bash.
Un lugar hermoso en la playa de Cala Tarida. Tiene una decoración sencilla usando maderas blanqueadas y con espacios de sombra. Lamentablemente es una playa muy concurrida pero es un verdadero placer sentarse aquí. La comida es de influencia mediterránea y sirven tapas, zumos y cócteles. También es un buen lugar para celebrar una fiesta de cumpleaños.

Ses Eufabies

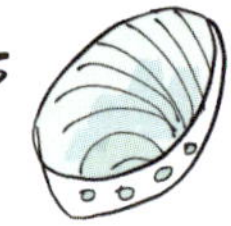

Cala Tarida, San José
Tel: 971.806.328
eufabies.com

Built in the fifties when there was nothing but sea and sand, I love the rustic look of this place.
My friend Carolina recommends the angler fish and the grilled sardines, and it's all very reasonable.
Try and reserve the little table outside on the edge of the rock, which they always set with a candle.
So romantic!
Construido en los cincuenta cuando no había nada más que mar y arena, me encanta el aspecto rústico de este sitio. Mi amiga Carolina recomienda el rape y las sardinas a la parrilla, y sus precios son muy razonables. Intenta reservar la pequeña mesa que siempre preparan con una velita junto a las rocas.
¡Tan romántico!

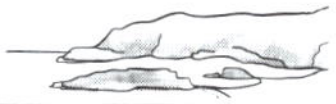

Aisea Terraza-Bar

Hotel Club Cala Tarida
Cala Tarida, San José
Tel: 971.806.167
aiseaibiza.com

This is a new little beach place that's been really nicely done, with recycled wood and a simple outdoor terrace. They serve mainly tapas and seem to have a bit of live music going on in the afternoons.
My proofreader loves their selection of mojitos.

Éste es un chiringuito nuevo que ha sido muy bien reformado, con madera reciclada y una terraza muy simple. Sirven principalmente tapas y parece que tienen música en directo por las tardes.

Cala Vadella

Not the easiest beach to reach, but it's worth the effort. An unsung hero of the sunset-viewing spot, soget here before sundown to watch the sun drop into the sea framed perfectly by mountains on either side. There's also a diving school here.

No es una playa de fácil acceso, ¡pero merece la pena el esfuerzo! Un lugar olvidado para la puesta de sol, llega antes del anochecer para ver cómo el sol se hunde en el mar con un marco perfecto de montañas a ambos lados. También hay una escuela de buceo aquí.

Cana Sofia

C/ Castelldefels, 10 , Cala Vedella
Tel: 971.808.273
canasofia.com

I missed out this great restaurant in the last edition but only because of human error and not at all intentional. The food is traditional mediterranean but with a creative twist using island products all the way. They are really profesional and have a superb catering service and host private events.
Theres a cocktail bar and the views of the sun setting into the sea are unmissable.

Me olvidé de incluir este restaurante en la primera edición de esta guía, pero sólo por puro error humano. La comida es tradicional mediterránea con toques muy creativos, utilizando productos de la isla. Son muy profesionales y tienen un servicio de catering excelente, además hacen eventos privados. Tienen un bar de cócteles y las vistas de la puesta de sol en el mar son espectaculares.

María Luisa

Cala Vadella, San José
Tel: 971.808.012.

A highly rated Sunday special according to friends, I've never been but its reputation is good. They say the seafood paella and fish here are superb and it's perfect for a lazy family day at the beach.

Dicen mis amigos que éste es un lugar perfecto para pasar un domingo, y aunque yo nunca he estado, he oído que aquí la paella y el pescado son deliciosos. y es perfecto para un día de playa relajado con la familia.

Can Jaume Beach Bar

C/ Castelldefels, 5, Cala Vadella,
Tel: 971.808.127
canjaume.com

If you are in the area, this place is not to be missed. Everything on the menu is delish and not too expensive, and it's set back away from any wind so perfect for a long chilled-out lunch. Also a top sunset viewing spot.

¡Si estás en la zona no debes perderte este sitio! Todo en la carta está delicioso y no es demasiado caro, y está protegido del viento así que es perfecto para una comida relajada. Además es un lugar perfecto para la puesta de sol.

Cala Moli

Not as sandy as its neighbours and primarily made of pebbles, be sure to wear suitable footwear to enter the water. It's well worth it once you're in as this is a great spot for snorkelling. There's a bar at the beach with a pool.

No tan arenosa como sus playas vecinas, predominan los guijarros, así que asegúrate de llevar calzado adecuado para entrar en el agua. Merece la pena una vez que estás dentro ya que es un lugar magnífico para hacer snorkel. Hay un bar con piscina en la playa.

Cala Codolar

One of those little Ibiza surprises with clear water and not as busy as its neighbours. A lovely option in the middle of summer when everywhere is heaving. Perfect for a snorkel by the cliffs. There's a little shack on the beach so you can grab a bite.

Una de esas pequeñas sorpresas que guarda Ibiza. Con aguas turquesas y no tan concurrida como sus playas vecinas es una buena opción en medio del verano cuando todo esta abarrotada. Perfecto para hacer snorkel. Y hay un pequeño chiringuito en la playa para picar algo.

MY IBIZA

ECO BEACH SHACK
CHIRINGUITO ECO
CALA ESCONDIDA

A tiny ecological Beach Shack that I love. Walk down the sandy cliff to the left of Sunset Ashram. Enjoy the peace!.

Un pequeño kiosko ecológica que me chifla. Camina a la izquierda de Sunset Ashram por el acantilado de arena. Disfruta.

Cala Conta (Cala Comte)

I love this corner of the island. There's a wildness to the long sand-swept approach, and on the beach the sand is bleached white and the pine trees are twisted by the wind. As far as I'm concerned it's also by far the best place to watch the sunse. You can also choose to swim at the beach or walk around to one of the little coves for a naked dive.

Me encanta este tramo de roca erosionada en la isla, tiene algo de salvaje, y en la playa la arena es blanca y los pinos han sido retorcidos por el viento. Para mí, éste es el mejor sitio para contemplar la puesta de sol en Ibiza. Puedes elegir entre un baño en la playa o acercarte a una de las calitas para sumergirte en el agua desnudo.

Sunset Ashram

Cala Conta, San José
Tel: 661.347.222

This stunning restaurant was created by Manel Aragonés, who really has the most beautiful eyes on the planet! It sits perched on a little headland at Cala Conta Beach. Islanders

flock here in the late afternoon for sunset dining so it gets pretty booked up. The shop at the front is great for a little tunic or an extra sarong, and when the sun dips you will understand how it got its fame.
Este magnífico establecimiento fue fundado por Manel Aragonés, que tiene los ojos más bonitos del planeta. Está encaramado sobre una punta en la playa de Cala Conta. Los isleños vienen aquí por la tarde y se llena en temporada alta. La tienda en frente es perfecta para comprar una túnica o un pareo, y cuando se ponga el sol entenderás su fama.

S'Illa Des Bosc

Cala Conta, San José
Tel: 971.806.161
silladesbosc.com

I love Sunset Ashram next door but this restaurant serves delicious seafood and is really popular with the locals, always a good sign. Book a table and then go for a dip at Cala Conta or take a dive into the clear waters of Cala Contita to the right.
Me encanta Sunset Ashram pero al lado está este restaurante que sirve deliciosos platos de pescado y marisco y es muy popular entre la gente de aquí, lo que siempre es buena señal. Reserva una mesa y luego vete a dar un baño en la playa de Cala Conta o sumérgete en las aguas cristalinas de Cala Contita a la derecha.

Cala Bassa

This beach is so beautiful in winter, but sadly gets very full in the summer. There are a few restaurants, none of them cheap, too many loungers and a regular boat service from San Antonio. I recommend a visit at the end of the day or very early in the morning, but avoid the masses over the weekend...and take a picnic!
Esta playa extensa es tan bonita en invierno, pero es una pena en verano porque está abarrotada. Hay varios restaurantes, y ninguno es barato, demasiadas tumbonas y un servicio de barco frecuente a San Antonio. Recomiendo visitarla al final del día o muy pronto por la mañana, pero evita las masas durante el verano... ¡y llévate un picnic!

Cala Carbo

A lovely little cove with a white sandy beach that is very popular with families and has two great little seafood restaurants. If you swim to the exit of the creek you can watch the sunset from the sea.
Una divina cala con arenas blancas que es muy popular entre familias y tiene dos magníficos restaurantes de pescado. Si nadas a la salida de la cala puedes ver la puesta de sol desde el mar.

Can Vicente

Cala Carbó, San José
Tel: 971.808.155

Owner Vincente fell in love with this little cove as a kid and years later, in 1981, decided to open a restaurant here. With the help of his wife Ana, they've created a delightful place serving top-notch paellas and fish.
I recommend the Avocado Mexican Style and any of the rice dishes. All equally good!
Vicente se enamoró de esta pequeña cala cuando era niño y años después, en 1981, decidió abrir este restaurante. Con la ayuda de su mujer Ana han creado un lugar precioso con una bonita terraza donde sirven una riquísima paella y pescado. Recomiendo el Aguacate a la Mexicana o cualquiera de los platos de paella. ¡Todo rico!

PORT D'ES TORRENT

The name means "mouth of a stream", but this popular tourist beach is surrounded by way too many shops and hotels for my liking. It gets packed in the summer, and the maze of streets can be confusing if you've never been here before. Despite this there are a couple of really worthwhile places to visit. To get here from Sant Josep you turn left off the roundabout before San Antonio, then just border the bay and go right at the next roundabout.

El nombre significa "puerto del torrente", pero esta playa turística tan popular está rodeada de demasiadas tiendas y hoteles para mi gusto. Se llena en verano y el entresijo de calles colindantes puede ser confuso si no has estado aquí antes. A pesar de esto, hay un par de lugares que merece la pena visitar. Para llegar aquí desde San José gira a la izquierda por la rotonda antes de San Antonio, luego bordea la bahía y ve a la derecha en la próxima rotonda.

...EAT & DRINK / COMER Y BEBER...

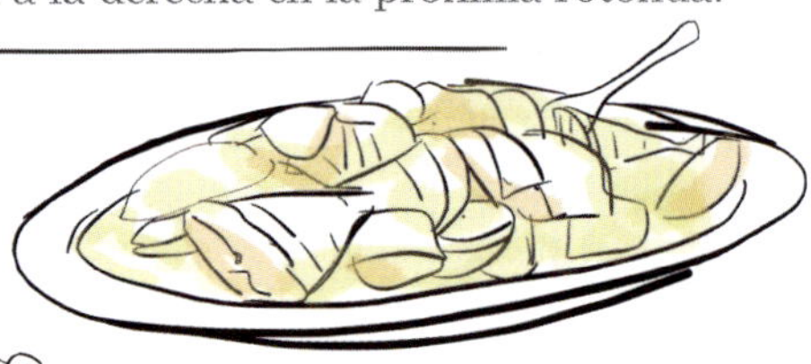

1 C'an Pujol

C/ des Caló, Port d'es Torrent
Tel: 971.341.407

Love fish? Well this is the best place for it! My brother Thor and his girlfriend Karyn love it too and it's been a fave for years. Sitting at the far southern end of San Antonio Bay with a lovely sea view, it is arguably the best seafood restaurant on Ibiza and mainly because if owner Lluc Torres does not find good fresh fish at the market that day he won't open! Their Alioli is the best and you must try the "all i pebre" which means garlic and pepper and "the bullit de peix" which is a fish stew for a main. Their rice dishes are another of their specialities. In fact it's all good!

¿Te gusta el pescado? Pues éste es el mejor restaurante para ello. A mi hermano Thor y a su novia Karyn les encanta. Está al sur, al otro extremo de la Bahía de San Antonio, con una magnífica vista al mar. Es indiscutiblemente el mejor restaurante de pescado de la isla, especialmente por la simple razón de que si su propietario Lluc Torres no encuentra buen pescado fresco en el mercado ese día, ¡no abre! El Alioli aquí es increíble y hay que probar el "all i pebre" o el "bullit de peix" de segundo. Sus platos de arroz son otra de sus especialidades. ¡La verdad es que todo está bueno!

2 Kumharas

C/ de Lugo, 2,
Port d'es Torrent
Tel: 971.85.740
kumharas.org

This place is everything a sunset bar should be. It is very unpretentious and with that original Ibiza trance vibe about it. There's a little hippy market, comfy sofas, cushions everywhere, and of course a magnificent sunset. It can be a bit hard to find, but

just follow the road along the coast from San Antonio headed south west through Port des Torrent (see map) and keep your eyes open for the sign. With its stone tower it also stands out along the San Antonio bay. The menu is mainly vegetarian with a couple of meat choices.
Este local es todo lo que un bar orientado a la puesta de sol debería ser, ya que es un sitio modesto y con un ambiente trance. Además de su buen ambiente, hay un pequeño mercadillo, sofás cómodos, cojines por todas partes y por supuesto una puesta de sol magnífica. Puede ser un poco difícil de encontrar, pero sigue la carretera junto a la costa de San Antonio en dirección sur, cruza Port d'es Torrent (ver mapa) y mantén los ojos abiertos para no pasar de largo su señal. Su torre de piedra hace que resalte en la bahía. Su carta es principalmente vegetariana con un par de platos de carne.

3 The Olive Tree

C/ Cantabria 40,
Port d'es Torrent
Tel: 971.340.907

This cosy gastro-restaurant in a renovated pub is located south of the bay in the area of Port d'es Torrent (see map) and very popular with island residents. The Sunday roast is a firm favourite on the island and it's the perfect meeting place for a good catch-up over a home-cooked meal, with the footie on in the background. They're open all week and the prices are very reasonable and with large portions. They also serve a wide selection of draught beers, including Guinness!
Este acogedor restaurante en un pub renovado está situado al sur de la bahía en la zona de Port d'es Torrent (ver mapa) y rápidamente se está haciendo muy popular entre los residentes. Los asados en domingo son un firme favorito en la isla y es el lugar de encuentro ideal para una comida casera, con fútbol de fondo. Abren toda la semana y los precios son muy asequibles. También sirven una gran selección de cervezas en caña, ¡incluyendo Guiness!

4 Relish Ibiza

C/ d'es Caló, Port d'es Torrent
Tel: 971.808.809
relishibiza.com

Everyone who stumbles on this little restaurant in San Antonio bay seems to end up coming back! I've heard reports that the slow-cooked leg of lamb is really tasty, and the pasta carbonara too. They also do a killer Sunday roast.
Todo aquel que prueba este pequeño restaurante en la bahía de San Antonio parece volver una y otra vez. Me ha llegado información de que la pierna de cordero asada lentamente al horno es realmente buena, y la pasta carbonara también. Hacen un asado los domingos para morirse.

5 Pom

Av. San Agustí, 73/75,
Cala de Bou
Tel: 971.078.182

A delicious choice if you are in the mood for a good Thai meal with that home cooked feel. The place is nicely styled and in the summer you can dine outside around the pool. The shop is worth a visit as well.
Una deliciosa opción si te gusta la comida tailandesa pero con ese toque casero. El lugar está decorado con mucho estilo y en verano puedes cenar al aire libre alrededor de la piscina. También merece la pena pasarse por la tienda.

SAN ANTONIO, THE WEST OF THE ISLAND

SANT ANTONI, EL OESTE DE LA ISLA

Located west of the island and boasting some of the best sunsets on the island, San Antonio was once the most beautiful bay in Ibiza. These days it's more famous for its raucous West End and for being a tourist trap, but the surrounding coastline still hosts some of the wildest and beautiful scenery in Ibiza.

Situado al oeste de la isla y presumiendo de las mejores puestas de sol de la isla, San Antonio antiguamente era la bahía más bonita de Ibiza. Hoy en día es más famosa por su ruidoso West End y por ser una trampa para turistas, pero la costa que lo rodea sigue albergando algunos de los paisajes más salvajes y hermosos de Ibiza.

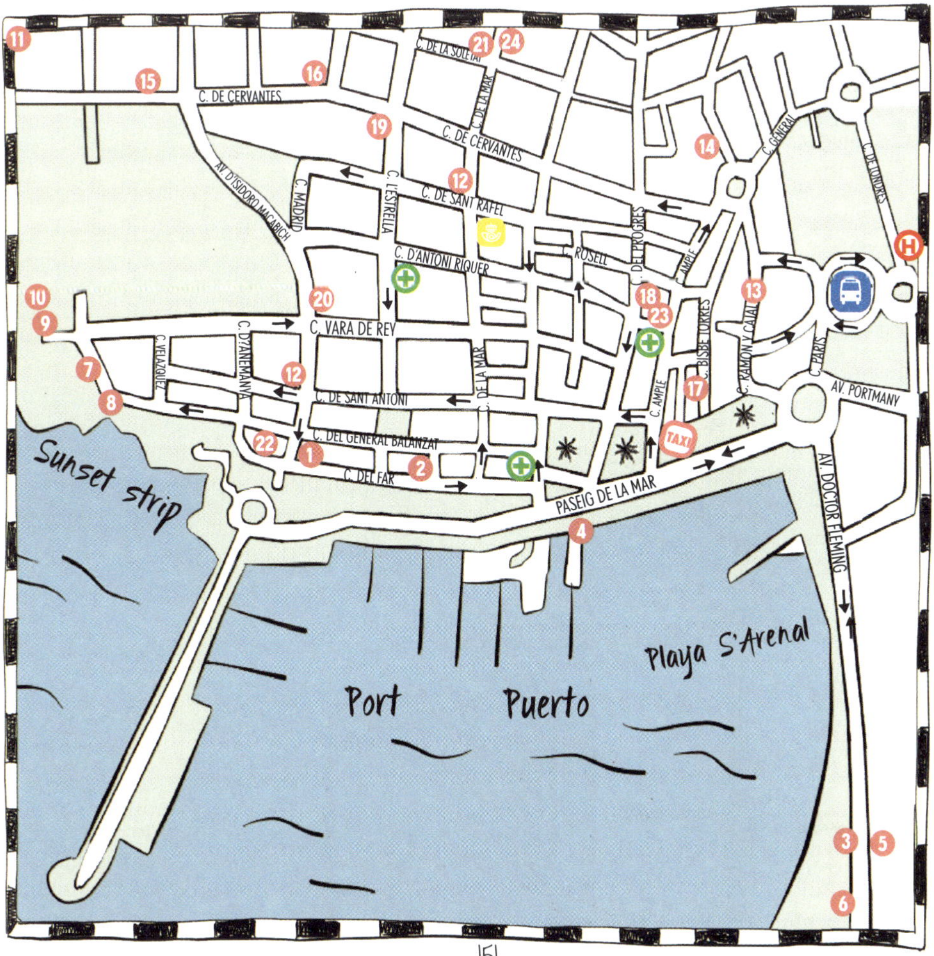

S'ARENAL BEACH AND THE MARINA
LA PLAYA DE S'ARENAL Y LA MARINA

This beach extends South until Port d'es Torrent and is perfect for those who don't want to drive anywhere. I'm not entirely sure how clean the sea is in high season due to all the boats but it looks okay to me! This urban stretch of sand is busy all day and also tons of fun as the sun goes down, when the action starts and bars crank it up.

Esta playa se extiende al sur hacia Port d'es Torrent y es perfecta si no quieres conducir. No estoy segura de lo limpio que esté el mar en temporada alta debido a los barcos que fondean aquí, ¡pero a mí me parece bastante limpia! Este tramo urbano de arena está repleto todo el día y con la puesta de sol, cuando los bares abren sus puertas, empieza la acción.

EAT, DRINK...
COMER Y BEBER...

1 Rita's Cantina

Paseo Marítimo
Tel: 971.343.387
ritascantina.com

Rita's is like walking into a bar in Cuba. It's in a building with high ceilings and stunning murals. The atmosphere inside is always great. Famous for its breakfasts; I am a fan of their club sandwiches but they also do nachos and crepes!!!

Entrar en Rita's es como entrar en un bar en Cuba, situado en un edificio con techos altos y magníficos murales. El ambiente aquí siempre es muy divertido. Es famoso por sus desayunos; soy fan de su *club sandwich* pero también sirven unos nachos y crepes riquísimos.

2 Villa Mercedes

Paseo del Mar, San Antonio
Tel: 971.348.543
villamercedesibiza.com

It was once an old villa that belonged to one of the island's most important families, this elegant restaurant and lounge bar has a colonial décor and its tables are all candlelit, making it a very romantic spot. They have Mediterranean food and great cocktails, I love the Moroccan themed chill-out area and blankets in case it gets nippy at night. They are open nearly all year long!

Era una antigua finca que pertenecía a una de las familias más importantes de la isla. Este restaurante y sofisticado lounge bar con una decoración colonial y mesas iluminadas por velas, lo convierten en un lugar muy romántico. Tienen cocina mediterránea y magníficos cócteles. Me encanta su zona chill out de temática marroquí.

3 Bar De Tulp
Avda. Dr. Fleming, 16, San Antonio

On prime position on the beach for lounging by day and sunset viewing by night. They have tapas and Spanish food with a Dutch influence, the mismatched furniture inside makes this a fun place to visit.

En primera línea de la playa para tumbarse durante el día y ver la puesta de sol al anochecer. Tienen tapas y comida española con influencia holandesa, su decoración con un mobiliario desigual lo convierten en un lugar divertido.

4 El Chiringuito de's Port
Passeig de la Mar, San Antonio
Tel: 667.650.590

Thanks to friends Tracy and Martin, I now have my new favourite eatery in San Antonio. We had the fried baby squid and a mixed grill which was amazing. They even checked with the fishermen if there was any fresh catch for us. An inexpensive port shack beside the fishing boats. Open all year, lunch and dinner. Love it!

Gracias a amigos Tracy y Martin, ahora tengo mi nuevo lugar favorito en San Antonio. Nos pedímos los chopitos y una parrillada de carne buenissima. Hasta miraron si había alguna captura fresca para servirnos. Un chiringuito de buen precio. Abierto todo el año para almorzar y la cenar. ¡Me encanta!

5 The Jam Shack
Avda. Dr. Fleming, 20, San Antonio
Tel: 636 013 098 - 652 512 705

My friends Nikki and Stevie have just opened a new Jam Shack in San Antonio. A larger version of its predecessor with a boat bar, BBQ and a children's area. Serving the same cocktails and delicious home-made Jamaican food as they did before in Cala Llonga. Good vibes and reggae music all day.

Mis amigos Nikki y Stevie acaban de abrir este nuevo local en San Antonio. Más amplio que su predecesor con un bar-barco, barbacoa y una zona infantil. Sirven los mismos cócteles y comida casera Jamaicana como hacían en Cala Llonga. Buen rollo y música reggae todo el día.

6 Casa Thai
Avda. Isidor Macabich, 8
Tel: 971.343.562

Good value for money and well known by locals. A very basic little place with simple decor, but the service is always good, and the food is tasty. The chicken curry is good and so is the Pad Thai, as well as the spring rolls and chicken satay.

Un establecimiento pequeño y básico con una decoración simple y minimalista, pero el servicio siempre es rápido y la comida está deliciosa y a buén precio. El curry de pollo está buenísimo y el Pad Thai también, además de los rollitos de primavera y el satay de pollo.

TIPS * CONSEJOS

FAMILY SWIM?
NADAR CON LA FAMILIA

ES POUET

A small urban cove on the southern end of San Antonio's promenade and beach. It's perfect for families with kids because the sea is calm and the party crowd tend to prefer being closer to San Antonio town and its louder vibe.

Una pequeña cala urbana en el extremo sur del paseo y playa de San Antonio. Es perfecto para familias con niños porque el mar está tranquilo y la gente de fiesta tienden preferir estar más cerca del centro de San Antonio y su ambiente festero.

SALT D'EN PORTES

This is a small natural rocky cove with a few fishing huts. The water is crystal clear here so it is perfect for snorkeling. Head to Caló des Moro and then walk along the coast a bit.

Una calita rocosa con unas cabañas de pescadores. El agua esta cristalino aquí haciendo que sea perfecto para hacer snorkel. Desde Caló des Moro camina un poco por la costa y llegarás.

SUNSETS!

SUNSET STRIP AND AROUND
PASEO DE LA PUESTA DE SOL Y ALREDEDORES

"click"

People flock from all over the island to witness the sun sinking into the horizon here, which is how this parade of bars and restaurants lining the coast along the northwest of San Antonio got its name. With the clearest view of the spectacle anywhere on the island, the stunning show is greeted with cheers from the crowds that have gathered every evening. A real Ibiza ritual.

La gente viene en masa desde todos los puntos de la isla para presenciar cómo el sol se hunde en el horizonte, que es como este conjunto de bares y restaurantes que bordean la costa del noroeste de San Antonio recibió su nombre. Con la vista más clara de la puesta de sol de toda la isla, esta impresionante espectáculo recibe el aplauso de las multitudes que se reúnen aquí cada atardecer. Un ritual de Ibiza.

...EAT & DRINK...
COMER Y BEBER...

7 Café del Mar

General Balanzat 38,
San Antonio
Tel: 971.348.706
cafedelmaribiza.com

Ibiza's original sunset café. This iconic bar first opened in 1980 making the sunsets of San Antonio world famous, not to mention the chillout music. We used to drive here every weekend and catch that specual moment when there was just a handful of people sitting on the rocks. Now it's packed and a globally recognised brand with its own record label.

El lugar original para ver la puesta de sol. Este emblemático bar fue fundado en 1980 e hizo las puestas de sol de San Antonio famosas en todo el mundo, por no mencionar su música chill out. Solíamos ir cada fin de semana para pillar la puesta cuando sólo había un puñado de personas sentadas en las rocas. Y ahorra se ha convertido en una marca mundialmente reconocida con su propio sello discográfico.

8 Savannah Beach Club

C/ del General Balanzat, 38,
San Antonio
Tel: 971.348.031
savannahibiza.com

On the same strip as Café del Mar and Café Mambo, I always think of Savannah as being for the more laid-back crowd. The daiquiris here are damn tasty, my favourite being the strawberry, and they have a delicious menu, so grab some nosh as the sun dips below the horizon.

En el mismo tramo de Café del Mar y Café Mambo, siempre pienso en Savannah como un lugar para una clientela más tranquila. Los daiquiris aquí están de muerte y tienen una carta riquísima, así que te sugiero que te pidas algo mientras contemplas el sol desaparecer en el horizonte.

9 Mambo Café

C/ de Vara del Rey, San Antonio
Tel: 971.346.638
cafemamboibiza.com

This legendary pre-party bar and sea-fronted restaurant in San Antonio holds events every single night of the summer, and has hosted many famous DJ, while the opening party at the beginning of the season is a sort of official kick-off for all the locals. Owner Javier Anadón opened it almost 20 years ago and these days his sons, Christian and Alan, are in charge. Definitely one of my pre-party spots when I go out on the West side.

Este legendario bar pre-fiesta y restaurante frente al mar en San Antonio celebra eventos todas las noches del verano y ha acogido a todo DJ famoso que puedas imaginar, mientras que la fiesta de apertura al principio del verano es una especie de apertura oficial de la temporada para la gente local. Su propietario, Javier Anadón, lo abrió hace casi 20 años y hoy en día sus hijos Christian y Alan son los encargados. Definitivamente uno de mis locales preferidos para empezar la noche cuando estoy por esta zona.

10 Mint Lounge Bar

Sunset Strip, San Antonio
Tel: 971.595.903.

Javier Anadón created this spot as Café Mambo's little sister bar a few years ago. And with a prime spot on the Sunset strip, it really took off. The menu is Italian-influenced, offering pizzas in funky asymmetrical shapes with gourmet toppings like fig and Gorgonzola,on the menu as well as a selection of homemade pastas. They also have a fantastic cocktail menu - I love the passion fruit caipirinhas!

Javier Anadón abrió este bar como una ramificación de Café Mambo hace unos años. Gracias a su situación privilegiada en este tramo del paseo, su éxito fue inmediato. La carta es de influencia italiana y ofrece pizzas en formas asimétricas con ingredientes gourmet como higo y gorgonzola, además de una selección de pastas caseras. Su carta de cócteles también es fantástica, ¡me encantan las caipiriñas de fruta de la pasión!

11 Golden Buddha

Paseo de Caló des Moro, San Antonio
Tel: 971.345.633

My friends Ramona and Eddy run this gorgeous sun-worshipping spot just a bit further up from the Sunset strip. With Balinese inspired decor and a large sun deck facing the sea, it's a strong competitor to the more famous sunset locations and has a great menu serving tapas and typical Mediterranean dishes as well as delicious curries. Both the prawn and the chicken curry are fantastic and they are famous for their mojitos.

Mis amigos Ramona y Eddy regentan este establecimiento perfecto para adorar al sol un poco al norte del paseo. Con decoración inspirada en Bali y una gran terraza mirando al mar, es un fuerte contendiente para ver la puesta y tiene una carta que incluye tapas y platos típicos mediterráneos además de deliciosos curries. Y son famosos por sus mojitos.

GO SEE * DISFRUTA

GORILLA HIPPY MARKET

Every day from 5pm until midnight there's this fab little hippy market with its stalls by Playa de Pinet. And there are pony rides if you're with kids.

Todos los días de 17:00hrs hasta medianoche hay este mercadillo hippy al lado de Playa de Pinet. Y también hay paseos en pony si vas con niños.

Playa de Pinet
Tel: 971.398.920
gorilahippymarket.es

12 Curry Club

Ctra. San Antonio, 38, San Antonio
Tel: 971.343.604

I love the chicken tikka masala here, which they serve with all the traditional bits on the side. Set in a tropical and beautifully lit garden it's a great spot to start the night. With ample

SHOP * TIENDA
KISS MY FAIRY

DRESS-UP & MAKE-UP
This is the perfect stop-off for those essential party dressing-up pieces, but most importantly they do body painting and make up. Book in advance as on certain nights like the Zoo Project just outside San Antonio requires you to transform yourself into a tiger or any wild animal you can think of. They also sell discounted club tickets.

DISFRÁZATE + MAQUÍLLATE
Este lugar es perfecto para disfraces de fiesta, pero lo más importante es que hacen pintura corporal. Reserva con antelación porque hay noches como The Zoo Project, a las afueras de la ciudad que requiere que te pintes como un tigre u otro animal salvaje que te apetezca. También tienen entradas con descuento para las discotecas.

Avda. Dr Fleming, San Antonio
Tel: 971.803.561 - 674.704.996
kissmyfairy.com

servings and great value for money, this really is an authentic Indian dining experience - in the heart of San Antonio.

Aquí me encanta el Pollo Tikka Masala, que sirven con las guarniciones tradicionales. Está en un precioso jardín tropical y es un lugar genial para empezar la noche. Sirven buenas raciones, y está muy bien de precio; así que es una auténtica experiencia gastronómica india en el corazón de San Antonio.

13 Tijuana Tex-Mex
C/ de Ramón i Cajal, 23
San Antonio
Tel: 971.342.473

I love a good fajita and the atmosphere here is always really lively. Toni the owner has made it fun here with phones on the tables so you can call the table next door, and chalks for kids to colour with.
There's lots of detail in the décor that reminds me of an Indiana Jones set. Authentic Mexican dishes and Mexican beer. Not to mention the tequila!

Me encantan las fajitas y el ambiente de este restaurante es siempre muy animado. El dueño Toni ha creado un lugar muy divertido con teléfonos en cada mesa y tizas de colores para los más pequeños, hay muchos detalles en la decoración que me recuerdan a una cueva tipo Indiana Jones. Platos mexicanos auténticos y cerveza mexicana. ¡Por no mencionar su tequila!

14 The Ship Inn
Plaza de Mercado, San Antonio
Tel: 971.342.130.
theshipibiza.com

A favourite hangout for workers, this is the perfect place to get your face known and have a great start to your stay. They serve hot snacks all day and host late-night pool competitions. There's also a notice board, giving advice on places to stay, jobs and more...so a great stopoff for anyone planning on staying all summer! Open every day from 11 to 6 a.m, yep, these guys are hard-core. They also show live sports every day throughout the year and all the big football matches.

Un favorito entre los trabajadores, éste es el lugar perfecto para darte a conocer y empezar bien tu estancia. Sirven aperitivos calientes todo el día y organizan competiciones de billar por la noche, además hay un tablón de anuncios donde se anuncian apartamentos de alquiler, trabajos y más... ¡ya sabes dónde ir si planeas quedarte todo el verano! Abierto todos los días desde las 11:00 hasta las 6:00, sí, esta gente no duerme. También emiten los eventos deportivos durante todo el año y todos los partidos de fútbol importantes.

15 Ample 32
C/ de la Soletat, 64, San Antonio
Tel: 971.348.132
ample32.com

I have only visited this cosmopolitan bar once

during the Pintxos route in San Antonio in March, and I felt like I could have been in London or Madrid. Tucked far away from the madding crowd of San An, I remember the food looked exquisite and there were wonderful sea views from the terrace and pool area.

Sólo he visitado este bar cosmopolita una vez durante la ruta de Pintxos en San Antonio en marzo, y me sentí como si estuviera en Londres o Madrid. Alejado de la locura de San Antonio, recuerdo que la comida tenía un aspecto exquisito y había magníficas vistas al mar desde su terraza y zona de piscina.

16 Zebra

C/ de la Soletat, San Antonio
Tel: 971.347.867
zebra-ibiza.com

I discovered this bar last year on the corner of a road in San Antonio if your are coming 'round the back from the north side. This little eatery is worth every penny, and has a superb and varied menu at a reasonable price. The oven-roasted chicken is divine and they do pastas, risottos and curries as well.

Situado junto a la carretera de San Antonio si vienes por atrás desde el norte, este pequeño restaurante realmente vale cada céntimo y tiene una carta deliciosa y variada a un precio razonable. El pollo asado es divino y también hacen pastas, risottos y curries.

17 El Sapo

C/ Bisbe Torres, 3, San Antonio
Tel: 971.343.540

The first Peruvian restaurant on the island serving quality food from South America, and while I have yet to visit, I've only had good feedback so I'm happy to recommend it. All my friends say you have to try the chilli mash!

Éste es el primer restaurante peruano en la isla donde sirven comida de calidad de Sudamérica, y aunque todavía no lo haya visitado me han hablado muy bien, así que no me importa recomendarlo. ¡Todos mis amigos dicen que hay que probar el puré con chilis!

18 Menjabé

C/ Progreso, 34, San Antonio
Tel: 636.368.956

You don't have to be a vegetarian to love this place. The falafel in pitta is freshly prepared, and they do a delicious hummus served with a spicy garnish. The food is incredibly good value and I like to buy tubs of hummus to take home to share with my daughter.

No tienes que ser vegetariano para que te guste este local donde no sirven carne. El falafel en pan pitta lo preparan al instante y elaboran un hummus delicioso servido con guarnición picante. La comida tiene un precio increíblemente bueno y me gusta comprar recipientes de hummus para llevarme a casa y compartir con mi hija.

19 Ibiza Rocks Hotel

C/ Cervantes, 27, San Antonio
Tel: 971.340.137
ibizarocks.com

This hotel is the venue for the island's hottest live weekly gigs and Pool Party's from Craig David's to Elrow and We Are Rockstars, showcasing huge names and the world's best DJs. Check the line-up online and get yourself down here for some amazing performances in the mosh pit downstairs.

Este hotel es donde montan conciertos semanales en vivo y Pool Party's, con la fiesta de Craig David, Elrow y We Are Rockstars. Aqui tocan los grandes nombres del momento y los mejores DJs del mundo. Entérate online y vente a disfrutar de actuaciones increíbles en vivo desde la pista de abajo.

20 Restaurante Benítez

C/ Madrid Edificio Reino 1, San Antonio
Tel: 971.345.420

I love the fact they give you a little tapa with each drink here. Serving a variety of typical Spanish dishes, they also offer a set price day menu and cheap breakfasts too!

Me encanta que aquí te den una pequeña tapa con tu bebida. Sirven una variedad de tapas típicas españolas, ¡además ofrecen un menú del día y un desayuno muy baratos!

...EAT + DRINK... COMER Y BEBER...

21 Es Rebost de Can Prats

Calle Cervantes, 4
San Antonio
Tel: 971.346.252

My mum told me about his traditional Ibicencan restaurant. Set in an old town house they serve all the typical Ibicenco dishes such as "Sofrit Pagés" a meat stew with potatoes, garlic and sausage and "Espatlla d'anyell al form", a oven baked leg of lamb. If you prefer fish, the cod with garlic is incredible.

Mi madre me habló de este restaurante ibicenco muy tradicional. Se encuentra en una esquima en una antingua casa de ciudad y sirven todos los platos típicos ibicencos como Sofrit Pagés y cordero al horno.
Si prefieres pescado, el bacalao con alioli esta de miedo.

22 The Skinny Kitchen

Passeig de la mar, 20
Tel: 971.804.644
eatcleanravedirty.com

This is a low carb, super healthy little spot at the far end of San Antonio's marina. You can sit here and enjoy the seaview and watch the boats arrive and leave. They open early and serve homemade meals low in calories, great breakfasts, hangover smoothies, superb detox drinks, protein shakes as well as cocktails. There's a handy car park right infront.

Un sitio que hace comidas caseras bajas en calorías y supersaludables al final del puerto deportivo de San Antonio. Con vistas del mar, puedes ver los yates llegar. Abren temprano y sirven desayunos riquísimos, bebidas detox, batidos para la resaca y también cócteles. Además hay un parking super útil justo enfrente.

23 El Quijote

C/ Ample, 17, San Antonio
Tel: 971.343.681

One of San Antonio's top Tapa Restaurants with a hippy touch to its decor. It's set in a quieter part of town but open til late.

De los mejores restaurantes de tapas en San Antonio con un toque hippy en su decoración. Ubicado en una zona tranquila de la ciudad, pero abierto hasta tarde.

SHOPS...ALGUNAS TIENDAS...

24 Peter The Butcher

C/ de la mar, 24
Tel: 971.342020
peterthebutcheribiza.com

This little butcher opened in 1999 and has been supplying island residents with the finest quality meats prepared the English way ever since. They also stock a fine selection of cheeses. I love the Wensleydale Cheese with Cranberries in it which I love to wat over the Christmas period with Cream Crackers.
You can buy directly from the shop, or online and get it delivered, and their BBQ packs, breakfast boxes and special dinner menus are a genius idea.

Esta pequeña carnicería abrió en 1999 y desde entonces vende carne de gran calidad preparada al estilo inglés a los residentes de la isla. Además ofrece una gran selección de quesos. Puedes comprar directamente de la tienda, online o hacer que te lo lleven a casa, y sus packs para la barbacoa, cajas de desayuno y menús de cena especiales son una idea genial.

Panadería Sa Talaïa

Ctra. Atalaya 3
Tel: 971.800.608

This local bakery sells all sorts of breads and cakes as well as typical flaons made of cheese and mint, however strange it might sound, they are incredible.

Esta panadería tradicional vende todo tipo de panes y pasteles, además de los flaones típicos elaborados con queso y hierbabuena que están increíbles.

...SLEEP...DORMIR

Hotel Puchet

Avda. Doctor Fleming, 51
San Antonio
Tel: 971.390.426
hotelpuchet.com

This modern hotel is very reasonably priced and stylishly decorated throughout. With 212 rooms distributed between four buildings surrounding the pool area, the hotel has its own restaurant, cafe, supermarket,

gym, lounge, and a games room with poole tables and ping pong.
Este hotel moderno tiene precios verdaderamente razonables y su decoración es muy elegante. Alberga 212 habitaciones distribuidas entre cuatro edificios que rodean la zona de piscina, además el hotel tiene su propio restaurante, cafetería, supermercado, gimnasio, salón y una sala de juegos con billares y ping pong.

Ibiza Rocks Hotel At Pikes

Camí de Sa Vorera, San Antonio
Tel: +44.207.952.2919.
ibizarockshouse.com

Wham!'s Club Tropicana video was shot here and Freddie Mercury had his own room - now called the Freddy Mercury Suite. There's a pink tennis court, a dress-up room, a bar right on the pool and of course the infamous Ibiza Rocks After-Parties in the summer. I have the best time every time I find myself here, and the weekly Sunday Roast.
Aquí se filmó el vídeo Club Tropicana de Wham! y Freddie Mercury tenía su propia habitación, ahora llamada Suite Freddie Mercury. ¿Algo más? Hay una pista de tenis rosa, un vestuario para disfrazarse, un bar junto a la piscina y por supuesto las famosas after-parties de Ibiza Rocks durante el verano. Siempre que vengo aquí me lo paso genial, y los domingos hacen asados al estilo británico.

...AN OLD SCHOOL DREAMY SUNSET SPOT
PUESTA DE SOL SOÑADOR

Hostal La Torre

Urb Cap Negret, 25, San Antonio
Tel: 971.342.271
latorreibiza.com

This relatively unknown and "unspoilt by the masses" spot sits perched on the cliffs of Cap Negret north of San Antonio, and has truly unbeatable views of "Sa Conillera" island as well as amazing sunsets – some say the best on the island. The restaurant serves home-made Mediterranean specialties, and I love bagging a spot on the lower patio and sip my drink of choice, and relax with the panoramic sunset as backdrop. Rooms start at 50 euros for a single and go up to 180 for a triple, with breakfast included.
Este establecimiento relativamente desconocido y tranquilo está encaramado en las colinas de Cap Negret al norte de San Antonio, y tiene unas vistas inmejorables del islote de Sa Conillera, además de unas puestas de sol increíbles, algunos dicen que son las mejores de la isla. El restaurante sirve platos mediterráneos caseros, y me encanta sentarme en su terraza y tomarme una copa y relajarme con una de esas puestas como telón de fondo. Las habitaciones cuestan a partir de los 50 euros por una individual hasta los 180 euros por una triple, con desayuno incluido.

DRINKS AND FOOD
COMER Y BEBER

El Reencuentro

Calle del Mar, 5
San Antonio
Tel: 971.346.591
elreencuentroibiza.com

This is a great hang out in San Antonio. It has a cool seating area with old sofas and upstairs it has a great Argentinian steak.
But the main feature here is their live music where local rock bands come and showcase their work. It's a real fun night out so check their event on Facebook.
Un lugar ideal para pasar un buen rato en San Antonio. Cuenta con una zona de estar con sofás viejos y arriba tiene un restaurante asador argentino. Pero lo mejor son las noches de música en vivo, donde las bandas de rock locales vienen a tocar.
Entra en su Facebook para ver sus eventos.

Putumayo

Ctra. Cap Negret 6,
Cala Gracio, San Antonio
Tel: 605.146.531

A colourful funky old school bar and café on the way to Cala Gracioneta with different live music every day. They do delicious soups and food inspired from Surinam, and there's also pool table. It's open all year but quiet in the winter.
Un viejo bar colorido de camino a Cala Gracioneta con música en directo cada día. Ofrecen sopas y comidas ricas inspiradas de Surinam, ¡y hay un billar. Abierto todo el año.

El Chiringuito
CALA GRACIONETA
MEDITERRANEAN CUISINE
CHILL OUT MUSIC
COCKTAILS
ABIERTO TODO EL DÍA - OPEN ALL DAY
info@chiringuitoibiza.com
Tel: 971 348 338
El Chiringuito Cala Gracioneta
CALA GRACIONETA • SAN ANTONIO

THE NORTHWEST COAST (North from San Antonio)
LA COSTA NOROESTE (al norte de Sant Antoni)

If you drive north past San Antonio hugging the coast you will discover the most delightful little coves and beaches including rocky cliffs to swim off. All are perfect sun basking spots and get the sun all day including glorious sunsets, so take a picnic and enjoy your day.

Si conduces hacia el norte pasando San Antonio y tirando por la costa, descubrirás pequeñas calas, playas encantadoras y acantilados donde nadar. Todos son lugares perfectos para tostarse al sol todo el día, y ver unas impresionantes puestas de sol. Llevate un picnic y disfruta de tu día.

Cala Gracio & Cala Gracioneta

Cala Gració is a very popular beach with the locals, and Cala Gracioneta is its baby sister, with a fantastic beach bar. Both have turquoise waters and white sand.

Cala Gració es una playa muy popular entre los residentes y Cala Gracioneta es su pequeña hermana, pero hay un chiringuito magnífico. Ambas tienen aguas turquesas y arena blanca.

El Chiringuito de Cala Gracioneta

Cala Gracioneta, San Antonio
Tel: 971.348.338
chiringuitoibiza.com

Set in a magical little bay, this restaurant at the beach serves up traditional Mediterranean food including fantastic paellas. It is a popular location for weddings as you get the whole bay to yourself, and i've heard that they do great watermelon cocktails!

Situado en una pequeña calita mágica, este restaurante junto a la playa ofrece cocina tradicional mediterránea incluyendo paellas fantásticas. Es un lugar muy popular para celebrar bodas ya que tienes toda la cala para ti, ¡y me cuentan que preparan unos cócteles de sandía riquísimos!

Cala Salada & Cala Saladeta

To get here you take a windy drive north through the forest from San Antonio that ends on a beach with cliffs either side and clear, turquoise waters. It has to be said that a lot of these coves get very full in the high season and are not as idyllic as they are in low season. Cala Saladeta next door is often quieter due to its tricky access by foot. There's a good restaurant on the left side which I've heard does a great seafood paella.

Para llegar, coge la carretera con curvas de San Antonio dirección norte a través del bosque y acaba en esta encantadora playa de arena con acantilados a ambos lados y aguas cristalinas. Tengo que decir que muchas de estas calas se llenan mucho en temporada alta y no son tan idílicas como en temporada baja. Cala Saladeta está al lado y a menudo es más tranquila debido a su complicado acceso a pie. Hay un restaurante a la izquierda que he oído hace una buena paella de marisco.

"click"

Punta Galera

Really popular with the San Antonio night workers, they flock here to soak up the sun and grab some peace before the long hours ahead.
No sand, just flat, smooth rocks that offer a natural tanning bed. Take a picnic and a mask and dive into the deep waters. To get here, take the road to Santa Inés (Santa Agnès) and after about 2km go left and drive to the coast past a residential area. Park and walk down to the rocks that glow red at sunset.

Muy popular entre los trabajadores de San Antonio, que vienen aquí para pillar un poco de paz antes de la larga noche. No hay arena, sólo rocas lisas que ofrecen una cama natural para broncearte. Llévate un picnic y tus gafas para bucear en las aguas profundas y cristalinas. Para llegar aquí coge la carretera a Santa Agnès, después de 2km gira a la izquierda y conduce por la costa pasada una zona residencial. Aparca y baja caminado hasta las rocas, que se vuelven rojas con la puesta de sol.

SANTA INÉS VILLAGE IN THE NORTH WEST
EL PUEBLECITO DE SANTA AGNÈS EN EL NOROESTE

This teeny, tiny village is perhaps best known for its almond blossom, which blooms every February in the light of the full moon. Residents flock to Pla de Corona, the area around, to see this unique spectacle. The little restaurant here serves the best tortilla on the island and there's a little supermarket too. I never tire of the view up to the church from the long straight road you approach along. It's Sign-posted as Santa Agnés.

Este diminuto pueblo es quizá más conocido por la floración de sus almendros, que florecen cada febrero a la luz de la luna llena. Los residentes se dirigen al Pla de Corona para contemplar este espectáculo único y su pequeño restaurante sirve la mejor tortilla de la isla. Hay también un pequeño supermercado y nunca me canso de observar la iglesia desde esta carretera larga y recta que conduce al pueblo.

"click"

EAT + ENJOY... COME Y DISFRUTA...

Can Cosmi

Plaza de la Iglesia, Santa Inés
Tel: 971.805.020

This is where they serve that famous tortilla, which is a mere potato and egg fritata - but boy they do it well! Eat yours on the cute little terrace overlooking the church square with stray cats wandering around under your table, before popping into the great little grocery next door. My advice is to book a table early and then take a walk around the s stunning almond groves.

Aquí es donde sirven la famosa tortilla española, ¡está riquísima! Cómete la tuya en su pequeña terraza con vistas a la iglesia donde los gatos callejeros deambulan y vienen a sentarse bajo tu mesa, antes de ir a comprar tus verduras en la tienda de al lado. Mi consejo es reservar una mesa pronto y luego ir a darte un paseo entre los magníficos campos de almendros.

Las Puertas del Cielo

Santa Inés

A short walk or drive to the left of Can Cosmi and you will reach a little shack near the edge of a cliff with stunning views on clear days of the Mediterranean stretching to Mallorca island. It's very basic so I just grab a drink and take in the fabulous view.

Por un caminito a la izquierda de Can Cosmi está este pequeño kiosko encaramado en lo alto de un acantilado con vistas al Mediterráneo y la isla de Mallorca en dias claros. Es un sitio muy básico, así que normalmente me tomo una bebida y disfruto de sus fabulosas vistas.

Cas Sabater

Plaza Corona, 3, Santa Inés
Tel: 971.805.051
cas-sabater.com

If you love leather and go for the original homemade stuff, don't pass this little

shop without stopping in for a look. With a workshop on site, they've been open since 1988.
Si te gusta el cuero y los artículos de piel artesanales, pásate y entra a echar un vistazo en esta tienda. Tiene un pequeño taller y lleva abierto desde 1988.

SLEEP... DORMIR...

Es Cucons
C/ Camí des Pla de Corona, 110
Tel: 971.805.501
escucons.com

A heavenly restored farmhouse from the sixteenth century, set in the valley near Santa Inés. All the rooms are charmingly decorated and the restaurant offers exquisite Mediterranean food. It's so Ibiza!
Una finca rústica celestial del siglo XVI, situada en el valle cerca de Santa Inés. Todas las habitaciones están decoradas con mucho encanto y el restaurante ofrece exquisita comida mediterránea. ¡Es tan Ibiza!

Casa Datscha
San Antonio > Santa Agnès, Km3
Tel: 971.344.075
casadatscha.net

Friends who stay here tell me that the welcome is friendly and really genuine. It's supposed to be the perfect kind of place to relax away from the madness, and it's only ten minutes from San Antonio town! You can choose from a luxury suite, an apartment, pool suite or a studio.
Mis amigos que se han hospedado aquí me han dicho que la bienvenida es muy cálida, la gente amable y realmente genuina. Es el lugar perfecto para relajarse lejos de la locura, cuando de hecho está a sólo diez minutos de San Antonio. Puedes elegir entre una suite de lujo, un apartamento, suite junto a la piscina o un estudio.

Can Partit
Camino de Talaia
Sta Agnés de Corona
Tel: 971.805.556
canpartit.com

A stunning rural hotel in an old converted farmhouse in the valley of Santa Inés, famous for its almond trees and their blossoms. A handful of gorgeous rooms, a pool and a tree-lined porch all make this place special.
Un precioso hotel rural en una finca antigua reformada en el valle de Santa Inés, famoso por sus almendros. Solo pocas habitaciones, una piscina y un porche arbolado hacen de este lugar especial.

SHOP, EAT + DRINK... COMPRAR, COMER + BEBER...

Can Tixedó
Carretera San Rafae>Sta Inés, Km5
Tel: 971.345.248

Located at the crossroads in the countryside near San Antonio. A great little place to stop and enjoy breakfast or the traditional meals served throughout the day. They make fierce mojitos, caipirinha's and daiquiri's and inside is an art gallery and the store attached sells local craftwork. They host a market selling organic and local products every Saturday from 10 to 4pm.
En un cruce cerca de San Antonio esta este lugar genialoara hacer una parada y disfrutar de un desayuno o probar los platos tradicionales que sirven durante todo el día. También hacen mojitos, caipiriñas y daiquiris que están de muerte. Dentro, hay una galería de arte mientras que la tienda de al lado vende productos de artesanía local. Cada sábado de 10:00 a 16:00. tienen un mercadillo donde vende productos ecológicos y locales.

SAN MATEO SANT MATEU D'ALBARCA

This tiny little village presided over by its gorgeous nineteenth century whitewashed church with a shaded porch is really worth a visit and the village is a lovely quiet spot to stop off and grab some lunch in one of its two (I think) restaurants.

Un pequeño pueblo presidido por su imponente iglesia blanca del siglo XIX y su porche sombreado merece la pena una visita. El pueblo es encantador y perfecto para pararse a comer en uno de sus dos (creo que sólo hay dos) restaurantes locales a dos pasos de la iglesia.

Can Cires

San Mateo
Tel: 629.668.972
cancires.com

If you find yourself in San Mateo with a car full of hungry kids, this place is a great choice for lunch.
A sweet little restaurant set in a 200-year-old finca, the idyllic terrace also has a playground for the smaller ones. Run by Victoria and Francis, they offer a selection of Mediterranean cuisine and traditonal Ibicencan dishes as well as tapas and snacks, so you can eat for a wide range of prices. There's a nice art gallery attached, and you'll find it opposite the church and down the road on the left.
Si te encuentras en San Mateo con un coche lleno de niños hambrientos, este lugar es perfecto para comer. Un restaurante pequeño y agradable situado en una finca de 200 años de antigüedad, una idílica terraza que también tiene un parque para los más pequeños. Los dueños, Victoria y Francis, ofrecen una amplia selección de cocina mediterránea y platos ibicencos además de tapas y aperitivos, puedes comer por una gran variedad de precios. Y además hay una bonita galería de arte al lado. Lo encontrarás frente a la iglesia, bajando por la carretera a la izquierda.

Restaurante Es Camp Vell

Camí de S Pla, 2, San Mateo
Tel: 971.805.036

This restaurant is literally two steps from the church and serves traditional Spanish food. If you are not that hungry and just want a few tapas its the perfect spot, but they do great paellas here and in the evenings they crank up the BBQ.
Closed on Mondays.
Este restaurante está literalmente a dos pasos de la iglesia y sirve cocina española tradicional. Si no tienes mucha hambre y simplemente quieres unas tapas es el lugar perfecto, pero también elaboran paellas deliciosas y por las noches encienden la parrilla. Cerrado los lunes.

5 THINGS YOU SHOULD DO

5 COSAS QUE DEBERÍAS HACER CUANDO ESTÉS AQUÍ

1. Coffee at Café Vista Alegre in San Juan (p.184)
Tomarte un cafe en Café Vista Alegre, San Juan

2. Simple lunch + snorkle at S'illot des Rencli (p.179)
Almuerzo y baño en S'illot des Rencli

3. Afternoon chill at Los Enamorados (p.178)
Pasar la tarde en Los Enamorados

4. Visit On The Beach in Cala San Vicente (p.186)
Pasar un rato en On The Beach en Cala San Vicente

5. Drumming in Benirràs on Sunday (p.176)
Los tambores en Benirràs los domingos

THE NORTH

San Miguel, San Juan & the beaches

El Norte, Sant Miquel, Sant Joan y las playas

THERE ARE MANY IBIZAS, BUT WE ARE ONLY CONCERNED WITH ONE. THE ONE THAT REMAINS DETACHED AND IN ITS DAYDREAM, UNTROUBLED BY FLEETING FRENZY.
Hochi Raad
White and Blue
IBIZA
REAL ESTATE SERVICE
www.whiteandblueibiza.com

...EAT, DRINK...
BEBE, COME.

Can Sulayetas

Venda de Rubió, San Miguel
Tel: 971.334.567
can-sulayetas-ibiza.com

Tete has been running this place for years and it used to be my local when I lived up the hill just next door. They serve all types of sandwiches on local farmer's bread and I particularly like their omelette – made with fresh eggs from their chickens! The last time I was here five of us ate handsomely for 50 euros total. There's a little supermarket stuck to the restaurant and the terrace painted all different colours. They also have free WiFi, and on Sundays the place fills up with loads of island residents who come from all over. It's open all year, which makes it a perfect winter spot.

Hace años que Tete regenta este establecimiento y solía ser mi bar local cuando vivía aquí al lado en las montañas. Sirven todo tipo de bocadillos de pan payés y a mí particularmente me gusta su tortilla, hecha con huevos frescos de sus propias gallinas. La última vez que estuve aquí, éramos cinco y comimos por 50 euros. Hay un pequeño supermercado pegado al restaurante y la terraza está pintada de diferentes colores. También hay WiFi y los domingos se llena de residentes de la isla que vienen de todos los rincones. Está abierto todo el año, haciéndolo un lugar ideal en el invierno.

Es Portitxol

Sometimes I come here in the summer with a picnic and my mask and snorkelling gear. It's an idyllic little bay with fishing huts and slipways, but a bit of a trek if you are not already staying in the North. By car from Sant Miquel town, you head to the Illa Blanca Urbanisation and then park up and take the path on the left. This will take you to Cala des Moltons, the most idyllic little cove, and the views along the way are well worth the walk.

A veces en verano me vengo aquí con unas gafas y snorkel. Es una cala idílica con casetas de pescadores. Está bastante lejos si no te hospedas en el norte. En coche desde San Miguel, ve hacia la urbanización de Illa Blanca y luego aparca y coge el camino a tu izquierda. Esto te llevará a la Cala des Moltons, una calita idílica y las vistas en todo el camino hacen que merezca la pena venir hasta aquí.

SAN MIGUEL SANT MIQUEL DE BALANSAT

I love walking up to the church in the village of San Miguel. It was built between the fourteenth and eighteenth centuries, and stands strong overlooking the land all around. There are a few shops on the way up and on Thursdays there's a craft market in the square before the church, selling only Ibizan products. You can also catch the "ball pagès", a folkloric dance practised by local group at the top in the afternoon. The village below the church has a selection of little bars and restaurants. If you drive down past the road to the church you will eventually reach the Puerto de San Miguel bay which is a nice beach to have lunch and swim.

Me encanta caminar hasta la iglesia en el pueblo de San Miguel. La iglesia fue construida entre los siglos XIV y XVIII, y vigila majestuosamente el campo que la rodea. Hay un par de tiendas en el camino que valen la pena visitar. Los jueves hay un mercado artesanal en la plaza de camino a la iglesia donde sólo venden productos ibicencos y puedes ver el "ball pagès", una danza folclórica que bailan grupos locales por la tarde. El pueblo tiene varios bares y restaurantes, pero si al final del pueblo giras a la derecha justo antes de subir a la iglesia, llegarás al puerto de Puerto de San Miguel que es una playa bonita para comer y nadar.

...DRINK & SNACK ...BEBER Y PICAR...

Estanco Can Xicu

C/ de Missa 7, San Miguel
Tel: 971.334.416

My dad really loved this little Ibicencan bar. It's like time has stood still, in this old post office with its wooden bar and counter painted blue. It's right at the top just before the church. The view is amazing from up here, as is their hierbas liquor.

A mi padre le encantaba este pequeño bar auténtico. Es como si el tiempo se hubiera detenido aquí, en esta antigua oficina de correos con su barra de madera pintada de azul. Lo encontrarás justo antes de la iglesia. Desde aquí arriba la vista es increíble y sus hierbas ibicencas también

...SHOPPING
DE COMPRAS...

Natasha Collis Fine Jewellery

Can Josepet, C/ de Missa 5
Tel: 971.334.654
natashacollis.com

Even the walk to Natasha's shop-slash-studio is a lovely experience and, housed in a 500-year-old building, it's like stepping into a little piece of history. Everything is hand-made here, and so delicately beautiful. She works with 18ct yellow, white and pink gold as well as silver, and her designs are encrusted with diamonds, rubies, emeralds, sapphires and tourmalines. Gorgeous.

Incluso el paseo hasta la tienda-estudio de Natasha es una experiencia encantadora y al estar situado en un edificio de 500 años de antigüedad es como si entraras en la historia. Todo aquí es artesanal, muy bonito y delicado. Trabaja con oro amarillo, blanco y rosado de 18 quilates y sus diseños están incrustados con diamantes, rubíes, esmeraldas, zafiros y turmalinas. Precioso.

Can Planells Art Souvenirs

C/ de Missa, San Miguel
Tel: 971.334.833

A little souvenir shop on the top of the hill right beside the gorgeous church. The lady in here has it all. Gifts, postcards and guidebooks, including this one! If you're in a melancholic mood, you can buy a postcard and then sit opposite at the little bar and write to a friend. That's what I call "a little Ibiza moment".

Una tienda de souvenirs pequeñita en la colina frente a la preciosa iglesia. La mujer que lo lleva tiene aquí de todo: regalos, postales y guías de viaje, ¡incluyendo ésta! Puedes comprar una postal y luego sentarte en la terraza del pequeño bar de enfrente y escribir a un amigo. Es es lo que yo llamaría "un pequeño momento Ibiza".

Dario Bomé

C/ de la Iglesia 10, San Miguel
Tel: 971.334.833

Up the road to the church of San Miguel, this little bazaar-like treasure trove has always been a favourite of my mum's. Her Dutch friend travels all the way from Holland just to visit once a year!
Inside there's a selection of Indian-inspired pieces, lots of leather and accessories and everything feels like a one-off.

Subiendo la carretera hacia la iglesia de San Miguel, está esta pequeña cueva del tesoro estilo bazar que siempre ha sido la favorita de mi madre. Su amiga holandesa viaja desde Holanda especialmente para visitar esta tienda una vez al año. Dentro hay una selección de prendas de inspiración india, montones de cuero y accesorios, todas las piezas parecen ser únicas.

...DINNER TIME...CENAR...

La Luna Nell'orto

Carretera del Puerto, San Miguel
Tel: 971.334.599
lunanellorto.com

A firm favourite with lots of my friends Try and book the table under the fig tree with lamps and candles all around. They do fab home-made pasta and vegetarian crepes, as well as good meat and fish dishes. It's a lovely location for a wedding reception too.

Un firme favorito entre muchos de mis amigos. Reserva la mesa bajo la higuera. Hacen pasta casera y crepes de verdura, además de ricos platos de carne y pescado. Es un lugar encantador para un banquete de boda.

PizzArt Ibiza
C/ Joan Planells y Torres, 1
San Miguel
Tel: 971.334.083

A little Pizza place where most of my northern friends go at least once a week with their hungry kids. Which is hardly surprising as the Pizzas are delicious, probably because there's a Sicilian in the kitchen.
Una Pizzeria donde van muchos amigos mios del norte al menos una vez por semana con sus hijos hambrientos. No me sorprende ya que las Pizzas son deliciosas, probablemente porque hay un siciliano en la cocina.

DOWN IN THE BAY... ABAJO EN LA CALA...

Kiosko Can Tothom
Puerto de San Miguel
Tel: 971.334.128

This restaurant is right is in the middle of the beach and is also open in winter. A perfect pit stop for a cold beer and some lunch. The kids always order chicken nuggets.
Este chiringuito está en medio de la playa y también está abierto en el invierno. Perfecto para parar y pillar una cerveza y picotear algo. Los niños siempre piden los nuggets de pollo.

Utopía Chiringuito
Calo d'es Moltons, San Miguel
Tel: 687.253.491

I love this little cove of Calo d'es Moltons which lies hidden round the left side of the bay of San Miguel. Park your car at the port and then take the little dirt path on far left that runs through the pine forest down to the cove. The restaurant serves seafood and salads all day long. On Friday they do sardines and on sunday Couscous Royal.
Me encanta esta pequeña cala de Caló d'es Moltons que yace oculta por la parte izquierda de la bahía de San Miguel. Para llegar hay que aparcar y andar por el camino de tierra a la izquierda entre los pinos. Hay tumbonas y el restaurante sirve platos de marisco y ensaladas durante el día. Los viernes hacen una sardinada y los domingos couscous royale.

Chiringuito Pascual
Puerto de San Miguel
Tel: 65.679.371

A cute little place in a stunning setting facing the sea which I have heard they serve great tapas as well as good burgers and delicious local dishes. The staff are said to be lovely so it is on my to go list this summer.
Me han hablado tan bien de este chiringuito en un maravilloso entorno frente al mar donde sirven tapas, hamburguesas y deliciosos platos combinados. Esta en mi lista de lugares que tengo que ir a probar este verano.

Port Balanzat
C/ Port San Miguel
Tel: 971.334.527
restauranteportbalansat.com

Well known for its delicious seafood and their top dish the 'bullit de peix', a traditional Ibicenco fish stew with vegetables, served with rice and saffron-infused alioli.
Este es un local muy conocido por sus platos de pescado y marisco, pero su mejor plato es el bullit de peix, un guisado de pescado tradicional ibicenco con patatas, alioli y azafrán y servido con arroz a banda.

ON BY THE ROAD... EN LA CARRETERA...

Aubergine Ibiza
Ctra. de San Miguel km 9.9
Tel: 971.090.055
info@aubergine.com

A quaint farmhouse on the roadside as you drive to or from San Miguel to Santa Gertrudis.
Their dishes are all prepared with freshly picked organic vegetables from their own garden. I love their choice of dips, and salads. The outside gardens are stunning in the summer and their little shop sells all things Ibiza including this guide-book and the wonderful World Family brand.
Una casita payesa reformada en la carretera a San Miguel desde Santa Gertrudis. Sus platos están elaborados con verduras orgánicas de su propio huerto. A mí me encanta la selección de dips riquísimos, y sus deliciosas ensaladas. Los jardines en verano son un puro placer y en la tiendecita venden una selección de cosas de Ibiza incluyendo la gama de World Family y esta guía.

Ca Na Xica

Ctra. de San Miguel km 10.2
Tel: 971.334.409
canaxica.com

My friend Charity told me about this Boutique Hotel near San Miguel that is set in a stunning old farm house with arched balconies overlooking a long swimming pool. The rooms are bright and stylish. It really is the most gorgeous place!

Mi amiga Charity me habló con passión acerca de este Hotel Boutique cerca de San Miguel úbicada en una antigua casa de campo con balcones arqueados y una piscina divina. Las habitaciones son luminosas y elegantes. ¡Es un lugar realmente precioso!

Can Planells

Venda de Rubio, 2, San Miguel
Tel: 971.334.924
canplanells.com

Staying at this converted farmhouse is supposed to be an absolute delight, as I've heard it's just bursting with charm and family history. Set in a garden surrounded by orange groves and almonds, the owners are lovely and with just eight rooms and a heavenly swimming pool it promises a true Ibiza experience.

Hospedarse en esta finca reformada es una verdadera delicia, según me han dicho, está llena de encanto e historia familiar. Rodeado de huertos de naranjos y almendros, la familia Planells, sus propietarios, son muy cordiales y atentos. Sus ocho habitaciones y piscina maravillosa prometen una verdadera experiencia ibicenca.

Hotel Rural Cas Pla

Venda del Rubio, 59, San Miguel
Tel: 971.334.587
caspla-ibiza.com

If you want utter peace and tranquillity in Ibiza, this is where to find it! Set in the rural hills outside San Miguel, a few days here, with its serene suroundings and spacious rooms is the perfect place to recharge your batteries.

Si quieres vacaciones de verdad con paz y tranquilidad, aquí es donde puedes encontrarlas. Situado en las montañas a las afueras de San Miguel, hospedarse aquí con sus tranquilos jardines y habitaciones amplias te ayudarán a cargar las pilas.

Villa Ca'n Maries

Vénda Des Port, 30
Tel: 971.334.566
hotelcanmaries.com

On a hillside just outside Puerto de San Miguel sits this lovely hotel.
Sea views, countryside. a pool,...what more could you want from your holiday!

En una colina a las afueras del Puerto de San Miguel se encuentra este hotel encantador.
Vistas al mar, en pleno campo. una piscina, ... ¿qué más se puede pedir de tus vacaciones?

Hotel Hacienda Na Xamena

Urbanización Na Xamena, San Miguel
Tel: 971.334.500
hotelhacienda-biza.com

Set on the edge of a cliff, you can see for miles, and the waterfalls tumbling down the side of the cliff are incredible. This was the first five-star hotel on the island, and this year it has just had a huge makeover. The rooms all have sea views and a Jacuzzi (except for the singles). Some even have private rooftop pools. The restaurant and pool area is not to be missed.

Está situado sobre un acantilado desde donde puedes ver el mar desde kilómetros y las cascadas suspendidas que bajan por el lado del acantilado lo hacen aún más increíble. Éste fue el primer hotel de cinco estrellas de la isla, y este año le acaban de hacer una buena reforma. Todas las habitaciones tienen vistas al mar y jacuzzi (excepto las individuales). Algunas incluso tienen piscinas privadas en la azotea.
El restaurante y la zona de la piscina es para no perdérselo.

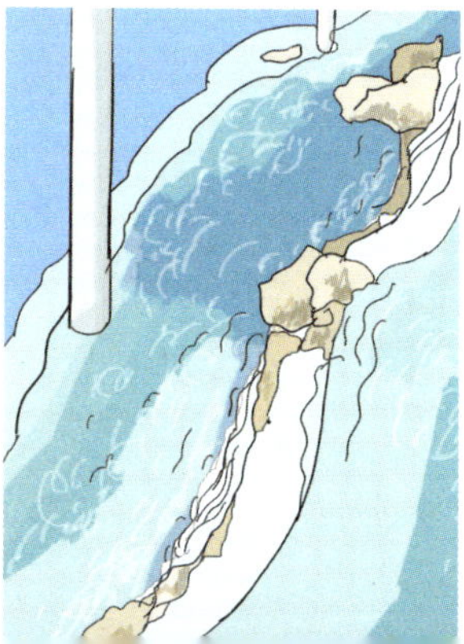

THE NORTH: TOWNS + BEACHES

EL NORTE, LOS PUEBLOS Y LAS PLAYAS

The north of Ibiza reminds me of the Provence region of France. It's greener and more cultivated than the rest of the island, and the Northerners as I like to call them find it hard to leave their local villages and come south. But I suppose that the same thing applies for the Southerners! But the North does have some of the most secluded and beautiful beaches, coves and cliffs, as well as some quaint *pueblos* along the way. The local hippies certainly prefer it, with the main village of San Juan becoming a bit of a long-haired hang out on Sundays when they have the local artisan market.

El norte de Ibiza me recuerda a la región de la Provenza en Francia. Es más verde y más cultivada que el resto de la isla, y para los norteños, como a mí me gusta llamarlos, es difícil abandonar sus pueblos locales y acercarse al sur. Pero supongo que lo mismo les ocurre a los sureños.
El norte tiene calas, playas y acantilados muy aislados y bonitos, además de pueblecitos pintorescos por el camino. Los hippies locales prefieren esta zona, donde su pueblo principal, San Juan, se ha convertido en el centro de reunión los domingos gracias a su mercadillo artesanal.

"click"

BENIRRÀS

DRUMMING HERE EVERY SUNDAY *
TAMBORES CADA DOMINGO

I come to this cove more for the vibe than for the beach itself as I find that the gritty sand here lets it down a bit. The restaurants are good, there's a funky fashion boutique and a great juice bar, so it has everything else covered. And beyond that, Benirràs has a unique atmosphere that's inviting and friendly. The kids like to rent pedalos or kayaks. I myself often grab a lounger, and I always bring a mask in case I decide to take a long swim out to the island of Es Cap Bernat, which stands long and tall in the centre of the bay. It is one of the original hippy beaches and there's a mass exodus here every Sunday when people from all over the island come to listen to, or play the drums at sunset. It's packed in high season.

Voy a esta cala más por su ambiente que por la playa ya que encuentro que su arena sucia decepciona. Pero los restaurantes son buenos, hay una boutique de moda muy funky y un magnífico bar de zumos, así que tiene todos los ángulos cubiertos. Y más aún, Benirràs tiene una atmósfera única muy atractiva y acogedora. Los niños pueden alquilar patines o kayaks. Yo a menudo me cojo una hamaca, y siempre me traigo las gafas y tubo de bucear por si decido nadar hasta la isla de Es Cap Bernat, que es un islote alto en el centro de la bahía. Es una de las playas hippies originales, cada domingo la gente acude en masa desde toda la isla para escuchar a percusionistas tocar a la puesta de sol. Está llena todos los días en temporada alta.

Benirràs 2000

Cala Benirràs
Tel: 971.333.313

This is a relaxed, unassuming restaurant serving traditional Mediterranean food, including a really good paella, of course, which is what I always order. They also do a mean roasted leg of lamb and the service is impeccable. It's always full of Spanish families and very reasonably priced, the kids spend hours on the pool table at the side and they don't mind you getting sand on the floor.

Un restaurante tranquilo y sin pretensiones que sirve cocina tradicional incluyendo una buena paella, que por supuesto es lo que siempre pido aquí. También preparan una pierna de cordero asada riquísima y el servicio es impecable. Siempre está lleno de familias españolas y los precios son muy razonables. Los niños se pasan horas en su mesa de billar y aquí no les importa que el suelo se llene de arena.

Elements

Cala Benirràs
Tel: 971.333.136
elements-ibiza.com

Kiko runs this cool bohemian beach restaurant, and he's a charmer! Us girls like to come here for a catch-up over a glass or two on the terrace in the summer and just soak up the atmosphere, accompanied by sexy deep house tunes. They have a Mediterranean menu and a little pizzería at the end that also does burgers and chips and they are open until late.

Kiko, que dirige este restaurante de playa bohemio, es de lo más encantador. Suelo venir con mis amigas a menudo en verano a charlar y tomarnos unas copas o dos de vino en la terraza y a disfrutar del ambiente, acompañadas de melodías deep house. Tienen un menú mediterráneo y una pequeña pizzería en un extremo que también hace hamburguesas y patatas. Están abiertos hasta tarde.

Sejuiced

Cala Benirràs
sejuiced.eu

Owner Cliff has created a fab little natural juice and smoothie bar within Elements restaurant. I love the "Ibiza Delight," which is like a liquid breakfast made with banana, oats, honey, strawberries…and soya milk, it's soooo good! You can add all sorts of superfood shots, like a dose of spirulina to start the day with energy.

El propietario Cliff ha creado un bar de batidos y zumos naturales dentro del restaurante Elements. Me encanta el "Ibiza Delight", que es como un desayuno líquido con plátano, avena, miel, fresas… y leche de soja, ¡está tan rico! Puedes añadir todo tipo de superalimentos, como una dosis de espirulina para empezar el día con energía.

Rocamar

Cala Benirràs
Tel: 971.333.532

With a prime position on this northern hippy beach, you can actually watch the sun set into the sea from here. The food is good too, but I tend to just order a gin tonic and watch that sun descend across the bay.

Su posición privilegiada en el centro de esta playa hippie, te permite ver una de las mejores puestas de sol de la playa. La comida también es buena, pero suelo pedirme sólo un gin tonic y ver el sol descender.

HIPPY MARKET
MERCADILLO HIPPY

From May to October, there's a great Hippy Market the shade of the trees down by the restaurants facing the beach. You can buy jewelery, clothes and hand crafted objects.

De mayo a octubre, hay mercadillo Hippy a la sombra de los pinos cerca de los restaurantes frente a la playa. Puedes comprar bisuteria, ropa y objetos elaborados a mano.

PORTINATX

"click"

The most Northern beach on the island and a fifteen-minute drive from San Juan which is the nearest village. The sea is translucent here, making it a favourite with snorkellers and scuba divers, and on a clear day you can see all the way to Mallorca.

La playa más al norte de la isla, está a unos 15 minutos en coche de San Juan, el pueblo más cercano. El mar aquí es translúcido, convirtiéndolo en lugar favorito para hacer snorkel y bucear, y en los días claros puedes ver hasta Mallorca.

...AN ORIGINAL PLACE TO STAY
UN LUGAR ESPECIAL DONDE HOSPEDARSE

Los Enamorados

Cala Portinatx
Tel: 971.320.776

Perched on the rocks of a gorgeous little unspoilt cove in the north sits this stunning Bazaar Hotel. Stylish all the way and bursting with good taste. Guests have the chance to experience a true Ibiza setting along with an intimate shopping experience during their stay. All nine rooms are slightly different styled with a surf meets american vintage type influence. Rumour is that their Restaurant and cocktail bar facing the sea is one of the most romantic spots in Ibiza …thus the name. Water activities are available to guests as well as private Yoga classes and heavenly massages by the sea. You won't ever want to leave.

Encaramado en las rocas de una pequeña y preciosa cala en el norte se encuentra este impresionante Bazaar Hotel, elegante y cargado de buen gusto. Los huéspedes tienen la oportunidad de vivir y sentir la verdadera Ibiza, además de poder comprar en el hotel durante su estancia. Cada uno de las nueve habitaciones son diferente, con influencia surfera y vintage. Se rumorea que su restaurante y bar de cócteles frente al mar es uno de los lugares más románticos de Ibiza, de ahí el nombre. Los huéspedes podrán disfrutar de deportes acuáticos, clases privadas de yoga además de masajes. ¡Nunca querrás irte!

El Puerto Restaurante
Playa Puerto de Portinatx
Tel: 971.320.776

I have never eaten here but it's very popular with locals and tourists, and has a great view of the sunset. They do all the basics, a fish stew, paella and grilled meats, as well as lobster and crayfish if you're feeling extravagant.

Nunca he comido aquí pero sé que es una joya junto al mar y muy popular entre los residentes locales y turistas, y tiene vistas magníficas de la puesta de sol. Preparan todos los platos básicos, guisado de pescado, paella, carnes a la parrilla, además de langosta y bogavante.

Hostal La Cigüeña
S'Arenal Petit, 36,
Cala Portinatx
Tel: 971.320.614
laciguenya.com

This cute beachfront hostal is constantly buzzing. You can rent a room or a complete apartment, but get in there at the start of the season because it fills up fast! It also has a small beach bar, La Cigüeña, with a covered terrace, so you can sit in the shade drinking your sangria. They serve snacks in the day and stay open til late – sometimes very late!

Este hostal coqueto en la playa está siempre lleno. Puedes alquilar una habitación o un apartamento completo, pero ve a principios de temporada porque se llena muy rápido. También tiene un pequeño chiringuito en la playa, La Cigüeña, con terraza cubierta, para poder sentarte a la sombra mientras bebes una sangría. Sirven aperitivos durante el día y está abierto hasta tarde, ¡a veces hasta muy tarde!

S'Illot Des Rencli
Carretera Portinatx, km 25.3,
Tel: 971.320.585

This rocky cove with clear turquoise waters is ideal for snorkelling. A little restaurant of the same name serves up delicious fish dishes and has amazing sea views and lovely shaded tables under the pine trees.

La calita rocosa con aguas color turquesa es ideal para el snorkel. Un pequeño restaurante del mismo nombre sirve deliciosos platos de pescado y tiene unas vistas magníficas al mar y mesitas bajo los pinos.

PORTINATX LIGHTHOUSE
"click"

FARO DE ES MOSCARTER

Just after Caló d'en Serra to the left of the beach there is a stunning dirt path that leads to the lighthouse on some austere and dramatic cliffs.

Hay un camino espectacular que llega al faro que está sobre unos acantilados increíbles.

Está justo después del cruce de Calo d'en Serra, a la izquierda de la playa por un camino de tierra.

SWIM * NADAR

ES PAS DE S'ILLA DES BOSC

A tiny strip of sand and rocks that joins the coast to the island opposite the Port of San Miguel, which is what its name states.

Una pequeña lengua de arena y rocas que une la costa con el islote en frente del port de Sant Miquel.

Cala Xuclar

This unspoilt cove at the bottom of a steep, dusty track is surrounded by trees and fisherman's huts, with wooden slipways that are perfect for private sunbathing. Crystal-clear waters and a rocky bottom invite you in for a snorkel, and I like to jump off the rocks with all the kids. It's a great escape, complete with a kiosk-style bar serving fresh fish every day.

Esta calita virgen al final de un camino empinado y polvoriento está rodeada de árboles y casetas de pescadores, con gradas de madera perfectas para tomar el sol en privado. Aguas cristalinas y fondo rocoso que te invitan a bucear, además me gusta saltar desde las rocas con todos los niños. Es un lugar magnífico para escaparse con un chiringuito estilo quiosco que sirve pescado fresco cada día.

Chiringuito Cala Xuclar

Cala Xuclar, Portinatx
Tel: 607.233.019

This beach shack restaurant has been the setting for many a memorable evening with my friends, eating and sipping wine until the moon comes up. The only restaurant here and run by siblings Carlos and Sara, they offer a variety of fresh fish each day as well as great tapas for starters and mixed salads. To make a reservation, you have to send a text message two days in advance! Once here, be warned that there's no cell coverage.

Este chiringuito restaurante ha sido escenario de muchos momentos memorables con mis amigos, comiendo y bebiendo buen vino hasta que saliera la luna. El único restaurante de la playa está regentado por los hermanos Carlos y Sara, quienes ofrecen una variedad de platos de pescado fresco además de magníficas tapas de primero y una variedad de ensaladas.
Para reservar, tienes que enviar un mensaje de texto dos días antes. Una vez aquí, que sepas que no hay cobertura móvil.

Cala Xarraca

You'll find this bay on the way to Portinatx, and despite being considered an insiders' secret, it gets pretty full in the summer. With clear waters it's also perfect for snorkelling and finding shells. There's a good seafood restaurant, and mud baths by the cliffs to the left of the cove.

Encontrarás esta bahía de camino a Portinatx y a pesar de ser considerada un secreto, se llena bastante en verano. Sus aguas cristalinas son perfectas para el snorkel y encontrar conchas. También hay un restaurante de pescado y marisco aquí, y hay baños de barro en el acantilado de la parte izquierda.

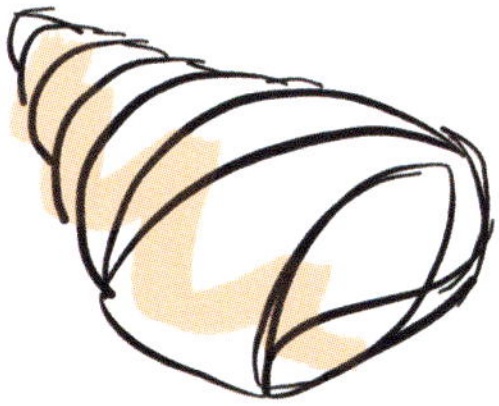

Ses Arcades

Ctra. San Juan, Km 19.3
Tel: 971.333.002

This is a typical roadside Bar and Restaurant and hostel. I have never eaten a meal here but I highly recommend the local toasted bread with tomato and manchego cheese paired with a coffee outside at the round rock table if its available. Theres a chatty parrot in a cage and you will always come across some rugged local reading the paper.
Rooms are 35 euros a night. Of course it's always full.

Se trata de un bar-restaurante en la carretera muy típico que también es hostal. Nunca he comido aquí pero sí recomiendo encarecidamente el pan local tostado con manchego y tomate, con un café al aire libre en la mesa de la roca redonda, si está disponible. Hay un loro enjaulado que no para de cotillear y siempre te encontrarás con algún residente leyendo el periódico. Las habitaciones se alquilan a 35 euros la noche. No es de extrañar que casi siempre esté lleno.

VINTAGE SHOPPING
TIENDA VINTAGE

Mon Chateau en Espagne

Ctra. San Juan, Km 19.3
Tel: 651.034.114

A gorgeous vintage furniture shop on the road to San Juan that is full of divine vintage furniture and objects. Ricard jugs, glass paper weights, art deco lamps and mirors are some of the treasures you will find here. Just writing about it makes me want to go back for a rummage.

Una tienda magnífica de muebles vintage en la carretera a San Juan. Llena de objetos y muebles vintage divinos; jarras Ricard, pisapapeles de cristal, lámparas de estilo art deco y espejos son algunos de los tesoros que encontrarás aquí dentro. Solo hablar de la tienda me da ganas de ir a ojearlo un poco.

...SLEEP AND RELAX
DORMIR Y RELAJARSE...

Can Fuster

Lugar Venda de Ca'S Ripolls, 1
Tel: 971.337.305
hotelruralibizacanfuster.com 5

A charming 150 year old restored farmhouse that you can't miss on the roadside, just before you reach the picturesque village of San Juan. The traditional façade painted in blue and white is like I said, unmissable as you drive past.
The name Fuster comes from a family of carpenters, and they preserve the old tools inside.
The hotel has rooms in and around the house, all with on suite bathrooms. There's a swimming pool and a large shaded garden perfect for reading that book you took with you.

Un agroturismo con mucho encanto que destaca en la carretera cuando estás llegando al precioso pueblo de San Juan con su fachada tradicional Ibicenca pintada de azul y blanco.
Su nombre viene de una familia de carpinteros, del cual conservan las herramientas antiguas dentro.
Con varias habitaciones, dentro y alrededor de la casa con baño propio. Hay una piscina y un amplio jardín con sombra donde puedes disfrutar leyendo ese libro que te trajiste.

SAN JUAN VILLAGE SANT JOAN DE LABRITJA

"click"

This sleepy drive-through village remains pretty much unchanged since the 1960s. One of Ibiza's most unspoilt spots, it's still the meeting point for a lot of the local hippys who gather on Sundays for the authentic little market.

Este pequeño pueblo aletargado permanece intacto desde los años 60. Uno de los lugares mejor conservados de Ibiza, sigue siendo un punto de reunión para muchos de los hippies locales que se reúnen los domingos para un mercadillo auténtico.

...EAT, DRINK & SHOP COMER, BEBER Y COMPRAR...

Vista Alegre

C/ d'Eivissa, 1, San Juan
Tel: 971.333.008

A great place for morning coffee before setting off to a nearby beach, this is the main bar in San Juan village and was a real meeting point in the 1970s for the local hippies. Stop in on a Wednesday to sample their famous "bullit de peix" fish stew.

Un lugar magnífico para el café de la mañana antes de marcharse a una playa cercana, éste es el bar principal de San Juan y era un verdadero punto de reunión para los hippies locales en los años 70. Párate un miércoles para probar su famoso bullit de peix, un delicioso guisado de pescado.

Bar Restaurant San Joan

C/ San Vicente, San Juan
Tel: 971.333.141

A simple Ibicencan bar with no frills whatsoever, this place is always crammed with locals. Grab a coffee and sit outside opposite the beautiful church.

Un bar ibicenco simple sin ningún tipo de florituras, este establecimiento siempre está lleno de gente de Ibiza. Pídete un café y siéntate fuera frente a la preciosa iglesia de San Juan.

Sabores Naturales

C/ Juan Vicent Ferrer, 4, San Juan
Tel: 609.938.475

On your right as you enter the village, this little restaurant only uses vegan products and does great pizzas as well as home-made bread, pastries and cakes using no white sugar. And one of the few places in Ibiza you'll find authentic Chai tea.

A tu derecha cuando entras en el pueblo. Un pequeño restaurante que sólo cocina con productos veganos. Hacen pizzas riquísimas además de panes, hojaldres y pasteles caseros sin usar azucar blanco. También es uno de los pocos sitios donde encontrarás auténtico té Chai.

The Giri Café

Plaza de España 5, San Juan
Tel: 971.333.474
cafe.thegiri.com

Stunning interior design. Think raw stone walls with gorgeous glass details, and all beautifully lit. They open for lunch and dinner and do a modern take on the classic Mediterranean menu. There's a stylish urban bar that does great cocktails. Be warned, it's not cheap.

Un diseño interior precioso; imagina paredes de piedra vista con preciosos detalles de cristal y una iluminación exquisita. Abierto para comer o cenar y sirven una versión moderna de los clásicos mediterráneos. En su barra estilo urbano preparan cócteles deliciosos. Ojo, no es una opción barata.

Lisi Peluquería y estéstica

C/ Ibiza 16, local 2, San Juan
Tel: 971.935 648

My friends in the north and in a radius of 15 km come to this beauty parlour. Hairdresser, waxing, manicures, facials and other beauty treatments, and all reasonably priced.

Mis amigas en el norte y en un radio de 15 km vienen a este salón de belleza. Peluquería, depilación, manicura, tratamientos faciales y más. Todos a un precio razonable.

Peixateria San Juan

Plaza d'Espanya 2, San Juan

For years these local fishermen just supplied most of the restaurants in the area, then David Torres and Javier Ramón Marí decided to open their own store in the village! My very close friend Charity who lives in the neighbourhood says they have the best fish on the island.

Durante años los pescadores locales sólo abastecían a los mejores restaurantes de la zona, entonces David Torres y Javier Ramón Marí decidieron abrir su propia pescadería en el pueblo. Mi intima amiga Charity me dice siempre que tienen el mejor pescado de la isla.

...REST & SLEEP
DESCANSA Y DUERME

Gare du Nord

C/ de Sa Cala, 11
Tel: 673.749.302
garedunordibiza.com

A heavenly bed and breakfast just on the outskirts of San Juan village in the heart of the countryside. It's affordable and cosy and serves heavenly breakfasts. It's perfect for private events as well.

Un pequeño hotelito en el campo al norte cerca del pueblo de San Juan que simplemente divino. Es asequible y acogedor y hacen desayunos celestiales. Perfecto para eventos privados

The Giri Residence

San Juan
Tel: 971.333.345
thegiri.com

A boutique hotel with a fusion of Scandinavian and Balinese design which still manages to respect the 200-year-old property. Just behind the village of Sant Joan, it's the "real Ibiza" – with a touch of luxury. It has a swimming pool and a spa. But not a cheap option.

Este hotel ha sido restaurado con una fusión de diseño escandinavo y balinés pero respetando la finca centenaria. Cerca del pueblo de San Juan, es la verdadera Ibiza, pero con un toque de lujo. Tiene piscina y un spa. No es una opción barata.

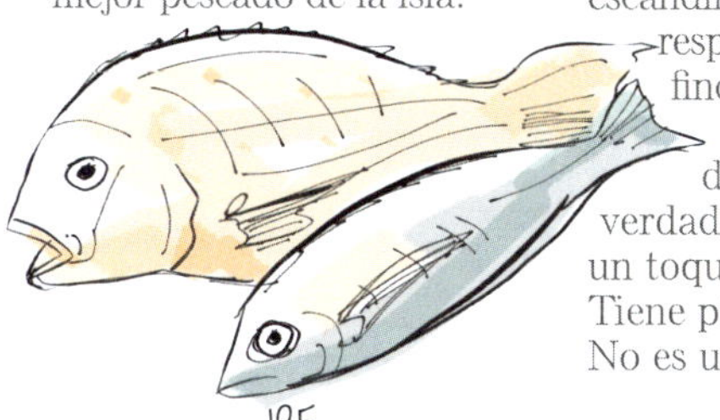

CALA SAN VICENTE SANT VICENT DE SA CALA

This was once the most remote village on the island. You can get here from Sant Juan or from San Carlos. It has a quaint church and nearby is a lovely sandy bay with a few not-so-quaint hotels. There is a Púnic sanctuary up the hill which I've mentioned at the back of the guide and a few nice restaurants and bars down at the beach.

Una vez fue la aldea más remota de la isla. Se puede llegar desde Sant Juan o desde San Carlos. Tiene una pintoresca iglesia y cerca hay una bahía arenosa con algunos hoteles no tan pintorescos. Hay un santuario púnico en la colina que he mencionado en la parte posterior de la guía además de buenos restaurantes y bares en la playa.

On The Beach

Cala San Vicente
Tel: 971.320.115
onthebeachibiza.com

This is a gorgeous chillout slash lounge restaurant on the the beach that hosts great little parties with live gigs and DJs throughout the summer. They also have a yummy kitchen that serves fusion food and vegetarian or, if you prefer, tapas and burgers, as well as juices and cocktails.

Un precioso restaurante y bar chill out en la playa que monta pequeñas fiestas con conciertos en vivo y DJs durante todo el verano. Tienen una cocina deliciosa que sirve comida asiática y vegetariana o, si lo prefieres, tapas y hamburguesas. Además sirven riquísimos zumos y cócteles.

Can Gat

Cala San Vicente
Tel: 971.320.123

Can Gat was the first house ever built on this beach so it has the best sea views. Their lobster paella and fish dishes are out of this world and worth coming all the way for.

Can Gat fue la primera casa construida en esta playa, y tiene vistas privilegiadas. Su paella de langosta, pescado al grill y bullit de peix son excelentes y una buena razón para venir.

Es Cafè casa Pepe

Sant Vicent de Sa Cala
Tel: 971.320.134

A Thai restaurant, located up from the bay in San Vicente village. Go left just after the signs to the Little village of Sant Vicent and left again into a courtyard. They have live music in the evenings.

Un restaurante tailandés situado en el pueblo de San Vicente. Ir a la izquierda justo después de las indicaciones para el pequeño pueblo de Sant Vicent. Tienen música en vivo por las noches.

THE SECRET BEACH
PLAYA SECRETA

SATELLITE BEACH
If you walk, swim and paddle towards the southern end of Aguas Blancas you'll reach this secret cove. It's a fun thing to do and a must for those who love an adventure.
Si caminas y nadas hacia el extremo sur de Aguas Blancas llegarás a esta cala secreta. Es algo divertido y perfecto para los amantes de la aventura.

Aguas Blancas   Aigues Blanques

This Northern beach is a favourite with the island's resident hippies, as well as a few celebs. It's a stunning spot but best to go early as the sun goes behind the cliffs in the early afternoon and the beach becomes fully shaded. Officially a nudist beach, but I keep my kit on! I prefer the southern end, where a tiny shack makes great sandwiches all day on the grill. Be prepared for a tricky walk down from the car.

Esta playa al norte es una favorita entre los hippies de la isla y de algún famoso. Es una playa ideal pero es mejor ir temprano porque el sol se esconde tras el acantilado muy pronto y la playa se queda en la sombra. Es oficialmente nudista, ¡aunque yo no me quito el bañador! Prefiero la zona sur, donde hay un pequeño chiringuito que sirve bocadillos todo el día. Prepárate para caminar un ratito desde el coche.

5 THINGS YOU SHOULD DO
5 COSAS QUE DEBERÍAS HACER CUANDO ESTÉS AQUÍ

---

1. A shot of house Hierbas at Anita's Bar (p.191)
Un chupito de Hierbas en Bar Anita

2. Have fresh fish at Can Colomaret, Cala Nova (p.197)
Comerte pescado fresco en Can Colomaret de Cala Nova

3. Shop at Las Dalias Hippy Night Market (p.202)
Ir de compras al mercadillo hippie de noche de Las Dalias

4. Have a paella at Cala Martina (p.199)
Comerte una paella en Pou d'es Lleó

5. Enjoy dinner and live music at Can Suldat (p.200)
Disfrutar de una cena y música en vivo en Can Suldat

THE EAST
San Carlos, Santa Eulalia & the beaches

El este, Santa Eulària, Sant Carles y las playas

SAN CARLOS SANT CARLES DE PERALTA

A beautifully kept little village, with whitewashed houses and a typical Ibicencan eighteenth-century church, this is the gateway to beaches in the northeast of Ibiza, like Aguas Blancas, Cala Llenya, Cala Mastella and Cala San Vicente, among others. But a few bars and restaurants and a couple of shops mean it's worth parking up for a little wander around.

Un pequeño pueblo bonito con casitas blancas y una iglesia típica ibicenca del siglo XVIII, dando paso a las playas del noreste de Ibiza, como Aguas Blancas, Cala Llenya, Cala Mastella o Cala San Vicente. Pero sus bares, restaurantes y algunas tiendas bonitas hacen que merezca la pena aparcar de camino a la playa y dar un pequeño paseo por el pueblo.

...EAT IN THE VILLAGE
COMER EN EL PUEBLO

Bar Anita (Ca n'Anneta)

Plaza de la Iglesia, San Carlos
Tel: 971.335.090

Facing the stunning church of San Carlos, I've spent many a long lunch in this place which was once famous for serving the "real" absinthe. If you sit outside on the curb you can watch people drive past. Their menu is traditional Spanish at its best. I like the tortilla and the boquerones (marinated fish), all knocked back with a cold beer. The locals still collect their post here.

De cara a la iglesia de San Carlos, he pasado largas sobremesas en este lugar que una vez fue famoso por servir absenta. Si te sientas fuera en la acera puedes observar los coches pasar por delante, y su carta tradicional española es lo mejor. Me gusta la tapa de tortilla española y los boquerones, todo acompañado de una cerveza bien fría. Los que viven aquí ya desde mucho aún recogen su correo en este bar.

Viccio

Edificio Oliveres de Peralta 15, San Carlos
Tel: 971.335.237

This little ice-cream parlour slash cafe opened last year and its owner insists that his is the best ice-cream on the island! Looking at the selection, I have to say I believe him, so when you're feeling worn down by the summer heat and you're headed home after a long day beaching, stop off in the village for a luscious cool down.

Esta pequeña heladería / cafetería es divina y su propietario insiste que su helado artesanal es el mejor de la isla. Mirando la selección, tengo que decir que le creo, así que cuando te sientas agotado por el calor y estés de camino a casa después de un día en la playa, párate en el pueblo para un helado sabroso y refrescante.

Enfarinarte Pizza

Edificio ses Oliveres de Peralta, San Carlos
Tel: 971.335.779

I've been told that this little den makes really great freshly baked pizzas, and is very reasonably priced. You can get a takeaway or eat in on one of their little stools – just call in advance to avoid a long wait.

Me han dicho que en este pequeño local hacen unas pizzas deliciosas y que los precios son muy buenos. Te la puedes llevar o comerla en uno de sus pequeños taburetes; llama con antelación para evitar colas.

...SHOPS TIENDAS

Papillon

Plaza de la Iglesia, San Carlos
Tel: 971.335.237

This little shop is just down from Bar Anita, and if you want traditional Ibiza style in lovely crisp cottons, this is your place. As well as dresses and trousers, they do great bags with pom-poms and some fab metallic sandals, and owner José has everything made in Ibiza and India every year.

Esta tienda pequeñita está a unos pasos del Bar Anita, y si quieres el estilo ibicenco tradicional de algodón tienes que venir aquí. Además de vestidos y pantalones, hacen unos bolsos geniales con pompones y sandalias metálicas fabulosas, el propietario José lo manda hacer todo a mano en Ibiza e India todos los años.

Belinda

Edificio ses Oliveres de Peralta, 4a
Tel: 600.013.943

Belinda stocks up on the exquisite textiles and oriental antiques she sells in this little boutique on her regular journeys through Asia. She also sells clothes. This is a great place to pick up a special gift.

Belinda se abastece de tejidos exquisitos y antigüedades orientales en sus viajes por Asia que después vende en esta boutique. También vende ropa, su tienda es un lugar genial para comprar un regalo especial.

Lottie Bogotie

C/ de la Venda de Peralta, San Carlos
Tels: 971.326.749 - 618.900.128

I never tire of this vintage shop, and year after year I find the best stuff here. Sadly I think the shop is going to close...I love hunting through the jewelwery basket with faux gold charm bracelets, as well as the rails of floral dresses. The prices are really reasonable, and in fact just writing this has made me feel the need to go there for another rummage. If there is no-one in just stick some euros in the post box! I heard a rumour she

might be closing. Hope not!

Nunca me canso de esta tienda vintage, y año tras año encuentro aquí los mejores artículos. Tristemente creo que va a cerrar...
Me encanta rebuscar entre sus collares de coral y brazaletes, además de echar un vistazo en sus percheros de vestidos floreados de segunda mano. Los precios no son disparatados, y tengo que pasarme pronto a echar un vistazo. Si no está la dueña mete el dinero en su buzón. He oido un rumour de que puede que va a cerrar. Espero que no.

Fashion Beauty

Edificio Peralta, local 4B, San Carlos
Tel: 699 05 44 35

Mari Luz is the best manicurist and pedicurist on the whole island as far as I am concerned. She also does massages and facials and other beauty treatments. I live near Ibiza town but still drive all the way here for my appointment. It's worth it, trust me.

En mi opinión, Mari Luz hace la mejor manicura y pedicura en toda la isla. También hace masajes y tratamientos faciales además de tratamientos de belleza. Vivo cerca de Ibiza ciudad, pero conduzco hasta aquí para mi cita. Vale la pena, créeme.

Agroturismo Can Talaias

Carretera Pou d'es Lleó, San Carlos
Tel: 971.335.742
hotelcantalaias.com

This lovely farmhouse used to be the home of the British actor Terry Thomas. His son Cushan now runs the place as a rural hotel alongside his lovely wife Laetti. There's a breathtaking sea view from the terrace and they've created a uniquely Ibizan family-like atmosphere here. It's also a Brit clelebrity hide-out.

Esta encantadora casa payesa fue hogar hace años del actor británico Terry Thomas. Su hijo Cushan es quien ahora lo regenta como un hotel rural junto a Laetti, su encantadora y mujer. Hay unas vistas impresionantes al mar desde la terraza y ambos han creado un ambiente único, ibicenco, familiar y más que relajado.
Es el escondite de las celebridades inglesas.

Hostel Es Alocs

Playa Es Figueral, San Carlos.
Tel: 971.335.079
hostalalocs.com

This is an old-school hostal on the beach of Es Figueral, with views of the sunrise and Tagomago island. A family-run place that's retained that simple Ibiza charm, it sits surrounded by plants and has plenty of shady areas to lie back and relax. The rooms are really affordable - as is their delicious home cooking. There's also live music every Tuesday, and a daily boat to Formentera from the beach in front!

Un hostal en la playa de Es Figueral, con vistas a la salida del sol y a la isla de Tagomago. Un negocio familiar que ha retenido ese encanto simple de Ibiza, está rodeado de plantas y con zonas sombreadas donde tumbarse y relajarse. Las habitaciones son muy asequibles, al igual que su deliciosa cocina casera. También hay música en directo los martes, y un barco a Formentara cada día.

Cala Llenya

I have always liked the laid back vibe on this beach in the north. It's not hard to find but you need to watch the signs from San Carlos. Easy access upon arrival and free parking in the shade under the pine trees.
It's a perfect family beach and you can get the kids to take a windsurfing lesson.
There's a little beach restaurant in the middle of the beach that makes simple inexpensive food.

Siempre me ha gustado el ambiente relajado de esta playa nordica. No es difícil de encontrar pero hay que estar atento a las señales de carretera desde San Carlos .
Tiene fácil acceso y aparcamiento gratuito a la sombra de unos pinos.
Es una playa perfecta para familias y los niños hasta pueden tomar clases de windsurf aqui.
Hay un pequeño restaurante en el centro de la playa que hace que comida sencilla y económica.

Cala Mastella

This is a small cove on the northeastern coast of the island that is known for the little restaurant "El Bigotes" at a little creek perched on its rocky edges. The water is shallow here and it's another great snorkelling spot of mine. To get here you drive from San Carlos and follow the signs to Cala Llenya and then on to Cala Mastella.

Una pequeña cala en la costa noreste de la isla conocida por el pequeño restaurante "El Bigotes" en el pequeño puerto al lado de la cala. El agua es poco profunda y es otro buen lugar para hacer snorkel. Para llegar conduce desde San Carlos y sigue las indicaciones a Cala Llenya y después a Cala Mastella.

El Bigotes

Cala Mastella, San Carlos

This unique little rustic Ibizan spot has been a bit of a secret of locals for years, but the news has spread fast and now everybody loves it. They only serve "bullit de peix" - a fantastic fresh fish dish cooked in saffron with potatoes and "arroz a banda" (rice cooked in fish broth), and it is so rustic here that they still only cook with wood on a fire. For dessert, there's fresh fruit and to make a reservation you have to come here in person!
To get here, take the road to San Carlos and then follow the signs for Cala Llenya, and on to Cala Mastella. The restaurant is on the small fishermens huts to the left of the bay, and it's connected to the shore by a little walkway. You can also park next to the restaurant by driving along the back of the cliff

Este restaurante ibicenco original lleva siendo un secreto de la gente de aquí desde hace años, pero lo malo es que las noticias corren rápido y ahora es el favorito de todos. Sólo sirven bullit de peix: un delicioso guisado de pescado elaborado con azafrán, patatas y arroz a banda. La cocina aquí es tan rústica que todavía cocinan con fuego de leña. De postre sirven fruta fresca. ¡Si quieres hacer una reserva tienes que ir en persona!
Para llegar coge la carretera a San Carlos y sigue las indicaciones a Cala Llenya y Cala Mastella. El restaurante está en el pequeño puerto pesquero a la izquierda de la bahía, y puedes andar por un pequeño sendero a la izquierda o aparcar al lado del restaurante si vas por la parte posterior del acantilado.

Cala Boix

Not far from Pou des Lleó, Cala Boix is Ibiza's only grey sand beach and reached by steep stone steps. The restaurant at the top, Hostal Cala Boix, serves impeccable sea food on a shady terrace, so I'd go for the salt-baked bass while the beach-level chiringuito does a mean cocktail. The sea can be choppy here, so no wimps allowed, plus there's no shade or loungers, so bring factor 50 and a parasol.

No muy lejos de Pou des Lleó, Cala Boix es la única playa de arena gris en Ibiza y para llegar tienes que bajar unos escalones muy empinados. El restaurante Hostal Cala Boix, arriba, sirve pescados frescos en su sombreada terraza, y yo siempre me lo pido a la sal. El chiringuito en la playa hace unos cócteles buenísimos. El mar puede estar revuelto, así que no es para cobardes. No hay sombra ni tumbonas, traete protección y una sombrilla.

Pou des Lleó

Es Canal d'en Martí is actually the name of this picturesque fishermen's cove that is the jetty for the boats that occassionally head over to the island of Tagomago, where you can moor peacefully and enjoy some snorkling.

The cove (Pou des Lleó) next door is lined with ramshackle boatsheds, and around its sides you'll find the most stunning little rocky swimming spots. And just before both coves is the popular Hostal Restaurante Pou des Lleó, where the paellas and stews are popular with the locals.

Es Canal d'en Martí es el verdadero nombre de esta calita. En esta calita pintoresca está el embarcadero desde donde salen algunos barcos a Tagomago, la islita de enfrente donde puedes tirar el ancla y bucear tranquilamente disfrutando de estar practicamente solos. La cala de (Pou des Lleó) de al lado está flanqueada por casetas de pescadores y por sus acantilados encontrarás zonas preciosas para nadar. Al llegar encontrarás el Hostal Restaurante Pou des Lleó, donde las paellas y guisados son famosos entre los isleños.

Restaurante Pou des Lleó

Pou des Lleó
Tel: 971.335.274

This is one of my summer Sunday favourites, and is the best for typical Ibicencan food. They serve the best paellas and "bullit" fish stews in the northeast of the island, and their selection of seafood starters is really good as well. But be careful not to fill up too much before the main course arrives like I always do! Great value for money too.

Éste es uno de mis favoritos los domingos en verano y es el mejor para comida típica ibicenca. Sirven las mejores paellas y bullit de peix del norte de la isla, Éste es uno de mis favoritos los domingos en verano y es el mejor para comida típica ibicenca y su selección de primeros de marisco también es muy buena. Pero ten cuidado y no comas demasiado antes de que llegue tu segundo plato como siempre hago yo. Los precios también son muy buenos.

Cala Nova

Just a kilometre or two north of Es Cana, this long sandy beach has clear turquoise waters. It's a family beach and great for kids as it generally has small waves that are perfect or them to play in. There's also a selection of great restaurants and a strategically-placed watch tower to make sure everyone stays safe!

Justo a un kilómetro o dos al norte de Es Canàr, esta playa alargada tiene aguas turquesas. Es una playa familiar y perfecta para los niños ya que suele tener pequeñas olas para que jueguen. También hay una buena selección de restaurantes y una torre de vigía estratégicamente situada para asegurar que todo el mundo está a salvo.

Can Colomaret

Cala Nova, Es Canar
Tel: 627.358.197

This is a really simple Ibizan-style beach shack on the sand (think wood slats and a palm roof), where you can also grab a lounger outside and set up camp for the day. A family-run place, the Can Colomaret family from Sant Carles are always friendly and it's priceless watching mum boss her two sons around. I love the sardines here, and they also do great hamburgers, omelettes and salads. They are only open in summer.

Un chiringuito muy simple en la arena al puro estilo ibicenco (imagínate listones de madera y techos de palmera). Puedes cogerte una hamaca en la arena y pasarte un día entero al sol. Es un negocio familiar donde la familia Colomaret de San Carlos siempre son muy amables. Ver a la dueña dando órdenes y a sus dos hijos mientras trabajan no tiene precio. Me encantan las sardinas y hacen unas hamburguesas, tortillas y ensaladas riquísimas. Sólo abren en verano.

Es Restaurant de Atzaró ♡ ♡

Cala Nova, Es Canar
Tel: 971.078.228
atzaro.com

This recently renovated seafood restaurant perched high on the far side of Cala Nova beach really has the best location in the area. It's all done out in modern bleached wood, blue tones, and has an endless sea breeze cooling it down all day. I think it's just the perfect place to enjoy a romantic dinner or a cocktail at sundown. Think music, cocktails, waves, stars...

Este increíble restaurante de pescado recientemente renovado está en la punta más alta de la playa de Cala Nova y la verdad es que tiene la mejor ubicación de la zona.

Con su decorado de madera decolorada, tonos azules y sus espacios grandes goza de una eterna y refrescante brisa marina todo el día. En mi opinion es el lugar perfecto para una cena romántica o un cóctel al anochecer. Piensa en música, cócteles, olas, estrellas...

CAMPING ON IBIZA

Camping en Ibiza

You can pitch a tent, park your camper van, hire a static mobile home or a bungalow.
Prices range depending on the accommodation and the month.
They have all the usual amenities of a camping site, but with a bit of an ibiza touch.
Some of the sites have pools and all of them are by the sea.

Puedes montar una tienda de campaña, estacionar tu caravana, alquilar una casa móvil o un bungaló. Los precios varían dependiendo del alojamiento y el mes.
Tienen todas las comodidades habituales de un camping, pero con un toque ibicenco.
Algunos de los sitios tienen piscina y todos ellos están al lado del mar.

Bell Tent Ibiza
Mark: 687123216
Ayelen: 630.225.174
belltentibiza.com

Camping La Playa
Cala Martina
Tel: 971.338.525
campingibizalaplaya.com

Camping Es Cana
Av. D'es Canar, 68
Tel: 971.332.117
campingescana.com

Camping Cala Nova
Playa de Cala Nova, Es Canar
Tel: 971.331.774
campingcalanova.com

Camping Cala Bassa
Cala Bassa, San José
Tel: 971.344.599
+
Carrer 19, Port des Torrent - San Antonio
Tel: 971.347.469
campingsonline.com

Camping San Antonio Ibiza
San Anonio
Tel: 633.527.181
camping-sanantonio.com

* *Book ahead of time to ensure you get a place. These sites get full pretty fast.*
Reserva con antelación para asegurarte una plaza. Se suelen llenar rápido.

Restaurante Cala Martina

Playa Cala Martina, Es Canar
Tel: 971.338.745

A favourite of mine and of many residents because they serve good food at affordable prices, and it is open all year, and nothing beats lunch on the beach in winter, They do a great paella, the fish is always delicious and the setting is perfect. It's best at the beginning or end of the summer though, when the beach is less packed.

Uno de mis favoritos y de muchos residentes porque la comida es buena, a buen precio, está abierto todo el año y no hay nada mejor que comer en la playa en invierno. Hacen una paella muy rica y el pescado está delicioso, además el entorno es perfecto. Es mejor ir al principio o final del verano, cuando la playa está menos llena.

Chirincana Beach Bar

Playa Cala Martina, Punta Arabi Es Canar
Tel: 971.338.525
chirincana.com

This hippy Argentinian camping bar-slash-restaurant sits up from the beach between the shade of a little pine forest and the camping site of Es Canar. They serve tapas, vegetarian food, pizzas and salads. Sundays seems to be popular here and wednesdays they do live music at sunset.

Este colorido restaurante-bar camping a lo hippy está enclavado en un extremo de la playa entre un pequeño bosque y el camping de Es Canar, con el mercadillo a un paso. Sirven comida vegetariana, pizzas y ensaladas. Los domingos tiene un ambiente genial por la noche y los miércoles música en directo al anochecer.

Cala Martina

This heavenly strip of sand lies north of Santa Eulalia to the right of the Road to Es Canar. With a few decent restaurants and a sailing, windsurf and diving school as well, it's a great family beach. You can see the islands of Illa Redona and Illa Santa from here, which are fun to windsurf out to, and it's also good for a swim after you've visited the huge Hippy Market held in Es Canar every Wednesday. (p.219)

Este tramo de arena al norte de Santa Eulalia y a la derecha en la carretera a Es Canar es divino. Con un par de restaurants decentes y una escuela de vela, windsurfing y buceo es una opción perfecta para familias. Puedes ver las islas de Illa Redona e Illa Santa desde aquí, es genial hacer windsurfing hasta ellas, y también está muy bien para darse un baño después de visitar el gigantesco mercadillo hippy de Es Canar los miércoles. (pág.219)

ON THE ROAD TO SANTA EULALIA TOWARDS SAN CARLOS
EN LA CARRETERA A SAN CARLOS DESDE SANTA EULALIA

Cas Pagés

Ctra. San Carles, Santa Eulalia
Tel: 971.319.029

A favourite of mine when I'm up in the northeast, this place is run by sisters Carmen and Lucia who have created one of the best traditional restaurants in Ibiza in the basement of their own home. In winter, they have a fire blazing away inside and in the summer the little shaded terrace at the back is just heavenly. Famous for their BBQ, this place is a meateaters must. I love the "Sobrasada," which is a roasted local sausage. Like all good old-school Ibiza eateries, they don't take credit cards nor can you reserve in advance. Just get here early if you want a good table. Only cash.

Uno de mis favoritos cuando voy al norte, este establecimiento lo llevan las hermanas Carmen y Lucía, que han creado uno de los mejores restaurantes tradicionales de Ibiza en el sótano de su propio hogar. En invierno, hay una chimenea con un fuego dentro y en verano su pequeña terraza a la sombra es simplemente divina. Es famoso por sus carnes a la parrilla, un esencial para los amantes de la carne. A mí personalmente me encanta la sobrasada. Como todo buen restaurante ibicenco clásico no aceptan tarjetas de crédito ni puedes reservar con antelación. Simplemente

ON THE ROAD TO ES CANAR FROM SANTA EULALIA...
EN LA CARRETERA A ES CANAR DESDE SANTA EULALIA

Babylon Beach

Punta Es Farallo, Es Canar
Tel: 971.332.181
babylonbeachbar.com

This restaurant-slash-beach bar really has it all, and looks gorgeous. Think Ibizan driftwood chic, with original little details in every corner. It's become one of the most popular hangouts in the northeast of the island, and you can either come for lunch with the whole gang (there's a great kids play area at the back) or dinner, with the tables out front looking right out to sea. There are also loungers or bean bags for enjoying the sun, and a beach-shack-style bar for drinks. To get there take the road to Es Canar from Santa Eulalia and look for the sign on the right.

Este restaurante – chiringuito realmente lo tiene todo y además es precioso con su madera reciclada y pequeños detalles originales en cada esquina. Se ha convertido en un punto de reunión muy popular entre la gente del noreste, y puedes venir para comer con todos tus colegas (ya que hay una zona para niños atrás) o cenar, con mesas mirando directamente al mar. También hay tumbonas o pufs para relajarse al sol y una barra estilo cabaña para tus copas. Para llegar hasta aquí coge la carretera de Es Canar desde Santa Eulalia y busca la señal a la derecha.

Can Suldat

Ctra. Es Canar, KM5, Santa Eulalia
Tel: 635.228.582

I love this place, they do goulash and a great sirloin steak, but the cheese fondue is what this place is famous for. In this little overgrown rustic finca, a meal feels a bit like dining with friends at home. They have a live guitarist on the weekend and Peter, the owner, makes a superb limoncello served in a big ice bowl.

Aquí hacen goulash además de un solomillo riquísimo, pero es famoso por su fondue de queso. Comer en esta finca rústica es como comer con amigos en casa. También tienen música de guitarra y Peter el dueño, sirve un limoncello riquísimo.

Sansara

Santa Eulalia>San Carlos
Tel: 971.807.231 - 657.877.363
sansaraibiza.com

This is a lovely restaurant that is out in the countryside just off the road from Santa Eulalia to San Carlos. It's a refreshing change from the usual Ibiza places as it hosts laid-back music events and has really good food. I always have a Thai curry, and the kids go for the pizzas. If you are into your puddings don't leave without trying the tarte flambée. Check their webpage for the music agenda.

Un acogedor restaurante en el campo, cerca de la carretera de Santa Eulalia camino a San Carlos. Es un sitio diferente a los lugares habituales de Ibiza, tiene un entorno hippy y relajado, con buena comida y música en vivo. Siempre pido curry tailandés, y los niños prefieren las pizzas. Si te gustan los postres prueba la tarta flambeada. Busca el calendario músical en su web.

ZZZZZZZ... SLEEP NEAR ES CANAR

DORMIR POR ES CANAR...

Hostal Mar y Huerta

Avda. Es Canar, 118, Santa Eulalia
Tel: 971.330.787
hostalmaryhuerta.com

A great little sleeping option if you want to be in this area. It's affordable and clean and near everything you need to have a great holiday.

Una opción genial para dormir si quieres hospedarte por esta zona. Es asequible y limpio y está cerca de todo lo que necesites para unas vacaciones fantásticas.

Hostal Flamingo

C/ Font d'Atzaro, 25, Es Canar
Tel: 971.330.717
hostalflamingoibiza.com

The Ferrer family built this family-friendly hotel in 1968 and like to make you feel at home. It's located in a quiet area near the beach, that's surrounded by fields set back from the bay, and it's all decorated in authentic Spanish style and spotlessly clean. It has a bar and a pool and rooms range from 30-90 euros with breakfast included, so it's a really good budget option. Open all summer.

La familia Ferrer construyó este hotel para familias en 1968 y les gusta hacer que te sientas como en casa. Está situado en una zona tranquila cerca de la playa, rodeada de campo y decorada con auténtico estilo español, y está impecablemente limpio. Tiene bar y piscina y las habitaciones cuestan entre 30-90 euros con desayuno incluido, es una opción buena y económica. Abierto todo el verano.

Las Arenas Hostal

Avenida d'Es Canar, 138, Santa Eulalia
Tel: 971.330.790

This simple, family-run hotel is a budget option with bags of local charm. The sunrise from the rooms here is just unreal if you get up early enough, and they have a great little restaurant at street level.

Este hotel simple y familiar es económico y derrocha encanto local. El amanecer desde las habitaciones es estupendo si te levantas lo suficientemente pronto y tienen un magnífico restaurante a nivel de calle.

LOOK OUT FOR THE SIGNATURE RED EARTH IN THIS PART OF THE ISLAND...

FÍJATE EN LA TIERRA ROJIZA QUE ES COMÚN POR ESTA ZONA DE LA ISLA...

THE HIPPY MARKETS Los mercadillos

LAS DALIAS

This Hippy Market is just before San Carlos village and has become legendary on Ibiza. I love going here for a bit of boho retail. The lovely owner Juanito has done an amazing job with the place which began as a live music venue, hosting artists like the Rolling Stones, or so they say... It's now a crafts market where islanders sell their creations. In the summer it gets really packed and also very hot, so I tend to visit the night market which takes place on Sunday and Monday evenings. There's a restaurant too, and a few little places to snack and have fresh juices.

El mercadillo hippy de San Carlos se ha convertido en una leyenda en Ibiza y me encanta visitarlo para comprar ropa y accesorios bohemios. Juanito, su encantador propietario, ha hecho un trabajo increíble con lo que empezó siendo un local de música en directo, acogiendo a artistas como los Rolling Stones, o eso dicen... Ahora es un mercado de artesanos y diseñadores donde los isleños venden sus creaciones. En verano se llena mucho y también hace muchísimo calor, así que suelo visitar el mercadillo nocturno que tiene lugar los domingos y lunes. También hay un restaurante y algún que otro sitio para comerse un aperitivo y tomarse un zumo natural.

San Carlos. Sat / Sáb: 10 - 18 hrs. Mon + tues / lun + mar: 17-24 hrs.
Only sundays in August/solo domingos en agosto 17-24 hrs.
Tel: 971.326.825 - lasdalias.es

CALA LLENYA MARKET

This is a must on a Sunday in Ibiza. Drive north towards San Carlos, pass Las Dalias and turn right round the back of the village of San Carlos and follow the windy road until you reach a crossraods where you drive straight over and you will see the market.
It's messy and loud and full of locals selling their bits. Everything is second hand here. I love my coffee at the bar and always bump into someone I know. The Paella here is good and cheap but it sells out fast so you need to get in the queu at the bar to order.
The rock band screams out as you wander around in search of something you don't really need. When you're done and hot from walking around, you can head down to the beach which is 5 minutes away.

Un plan genial para el domingo.
Para ir, conduce hacia el norte en direcci'on a San Carlos, deja atrás el mercadillo de Las Dalias y gira a la derecha por detrás del pueblo de San Carlos. Sigue la carretera hasta llegar a un cruce y sigue de frente y llegarás al mercadillo. Es caótico y ruidoso, y está lleno de gente vendiendo sus cosas, de segunda mano. Me encanta tomarme un café en el bar y siempre me cruzo con alguien que conozco. La paella es barata y bastante buena, pero ponte a la fila ya que se agota rápido. Llama la atención la banda de rock mientras paseas alrededor en busca de algo que en realidad no te hace falta. Cuando acabas, siempre puedes bajar a la playa, que está a sólo 5 minutos para refrescarte.

Cala Llenya. Sundays/domingos, 9 - 15 hrs.

PUNTA ARABÍ

When I was little this was the only hippy market on the island. It was very small and set in a field around pine trees with a small bar up the hill called The Hobbit, and all the island hippies gathered here to sell their hand made products. Times have changed since then and this hippy market has become the largest of many scattered around the island. It's only open on Wednesdays in the summer, so avoid heading northeast, on this day unless you're actually heading to the market because the traffic is hell. Tourists and locals come from all over the island. There is a restaurant, a shaded tent in the centre and lots of stalls. If you fancy cooling off when you're done shopping, there's a gorgeous beach nearby called Cala Martina.

Cuando era pequeña éste era el único mercadillo hippy de la isla. Era muy pequeño y básico, situado en un campo rodeado de pinos con un pequeño bar llamado The Hobbit. Todos los hippies de la isla se reunían aquí para ofrecer productos artesanales. Los tiempos han cambiado desde que este mercadillo se ha convertido en el más grande de los que se organizan por toda la isla. Sólo abierto los miércoles durante el verano, así que evita ir hacia el noroeste este día a menos que quieras venir aquí, porque el tráfico es un infierno. Los turistas y gente local vienen de toda la isla. Hay restaurantes y una tienda a la sombra en el centro. Si cuando te marches quieres refrescarte en el mar, hay una playa preciosa muy cerca llamada Cala Martina.

Punta Arabí, Es Canar. Wednesdays/miércoles, 10 - 18 hrs.
Tel: 971.330.650 - hippymarket.info

SANTA EULALIA THE + EAST
SANTA EULÀRIA DES RIU Y EL ESTE

The Eastern part of Ibiza comprises a varied selection of coves and beaches, as well as the main town of Santa Eulalia, which is unique in that it has the only river in the Balearics running through it. The church of Santa Eulalia, Es Puig de Missa, sits perched on top of the hill, and was declared a site of scenic beauty by the Ministry of Culture in 1952 and a historical monument in 2002. This town has fabulous restaurants and a gorgeous beach with a wide promenade. It has a residential vibe off-season, being home to so many of the island's expat residents, and really comes alive in the summer.

La parte este de Ibiza comprende una selección variada de calitas y playas, además del pueblo de Santa Eulalia que es único porque tiene un río que lo atraviesa. La iglesia de Santa Eulalia, Es Puig de Missa, se encara perfectamente en lo alto de la colina y fue declarado paraje pintoresco por el Ministerio de Cultura en 1952 y monumento histórico en 2002. Este pueblo tiene restaurantes fabulosos y una playa preciosa con un amplio paseo que realmente cobra vida en verano. Tiene un ambiente más vacacional, siendo el hogar de muchos extranjeros que residen en la isla.

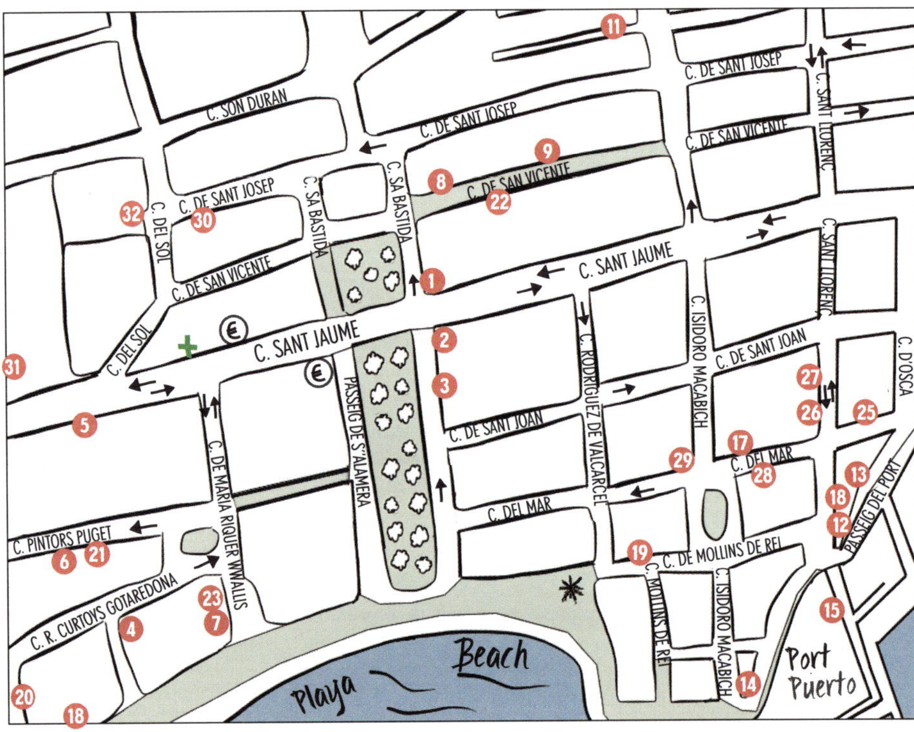

...EAT & DRINK

COMER Y BEBER

1 Royalty

C/ San Jaime, 51, Santa Eulalia
Tel: 971.331.819

My parents used to sit here when they first visited the island and found themselves in Santa Eulalia to meet friends. Around since the 1930s, they have proper old-school Spanish waiters and a selection of really good value tapas.

Mis padres solían sentarse aquí cuando visitaban la isla y quedaban en Santa Eulalia para ver a sus amigos. Abierto desde los años 30, ofrece un servicio clásico y una magnífica selección de tapas a muy buen precio.

2 Can Cosmi

C/ San Jaime 44, Santa Eulalia
Tel: 971.807.315

One of the three oldest cafés in this town,and said to be the first place on the island to make the famous toasted bread with tomato, garlic rubbed in, plus parsley. A family business since 1948, they serve traditional tapas all day and you can get a beer and a Pincho for €1,80.

Una de las cafeterías más antiguas del pueblo, éste fue el primer lugar de la isla en hacer la famosa tostada de pan con tomate, ajo y perejil. Un negocio familiar abierto desde 1948, sirven tapas tradicionales todo el día y puedes pedirte una caña y un pincho por 1,80€.

3 Croissant Show

Paseo de Salamera, Santa Eulalia
Tel: 971.319.610

The truth is, they do the best coffee in Santa Eulalia. I nearly always have mine here, along with a butter rich croissant. It reminds me of a patisserie in Paris with its showcase of French pastries.

La verdad es que, ¡hacen el mejor café de Santa Eulalia! Suelo tomarme el mío aquí junto a un croissant de mantequilla. Me recuerda a una pastelería en París con su gran mostrador de pasteles franceses.

4 Sa Vida Sana

C/ Ricardo Curtoys Gotarredona, 3, bajo 2 - Santa Eulalia
Tel: 971.338.536

My brother introduced me to this delicatessen-slash-café a few years ago, and I always come here when I'm in the neighbourhood. It's the perfect place for a healthy home-made lunch, with its salad bar and great set meñu. I love the roast beef and the couscous salad – but it's all scrummy!

Mi hermano me trajo a este delicatessen-cafetería hace unos años, y siempre vengo cuando estoy en el barrio. Es el lugar perfecto para una comida casera sana, con su mostrador de ensaladas y un magnífico menú del día. Me encanta la ternera asada con ensalada de couscous, ¡todo está riquísimo!

5 Taco Paco

C/ San Jaime, 1, Santa Eulalia
Tel: 971.807.556

A great Mexican restaurant that's been charmingly decorated in a sort of mish-mash style. Old leather sofas are mixed up with recycled chairs and lanterns, and fairy lights outside create a lovely atmosphere. You can't leave without trying the nachos with guacamole, melted cheese and crème fraîche.

Un restaurante mexicano genial que ha sido decorado con mucho gusto en una especie de batiburrillo de estilos. Viejos sofás de piel mezclados con sillas recicladas y farolillos, las lamparillas fuera crean un ambiente encantador. No puedes marcharte sin probar los nachos con guacamole, queso fundido y crème fraîche.

6 Samos Deli

C/ Pintores Puget, Santa Eulalia
Tel: 971.338.863
samos-group.com

This little German bakery is famous for its yummy breads, but they also do all sorts of cheeses, sausages and pretzels too. You can also grab a pastry and coffee to have on the spot.

Esta pastelería alemana es famosa por sus deliciosos panes, pero también tiene una selección de quesos, salchichas y pretzels. Puedes comprar una pasta y un café y tomártelo aquí mismo.

7 Restaurante Cana Suni

C/ Mariano Riquer 6, Santa Eulalia
Tel: 971.319.177

One of the best value places in town, and the lovely couple who own this place do amazing home-cooked, typically Spanish food. Its popular with the locals, which is a good sign. They really serve something for everyone, a set menu, normal menu, and delicious specials written on a board. Afterwards you can take a nice stroll down the promenade by the sea.

Uno de los sitios más económicos del pueblo, y la encantadora pareja que lleva este local hace una comida casera española muy rica. Es muy popular entre los lugareños, lo que es una buena señal. Aquí realmente sirven para todos los gustos, un menú del día, un menú normal, y luego una pizarra con deliciosas especialidades. Y después de comer puedes darte un agradable paseo por el paseo marítimo.

8 Chiang Mai

C/ San Vicente, 25, Santa Eulalia
Tel: 971.331.307

This authentic Thai restaurant is on a walking street which runs sideways from the Town Hall and is definitely worth visiting. I order the selection of starters and a green chicken curry to follow. Plus it's very reasonably priced and there's a takeaway option too.

Este restaurante tailandés está en una calle peatonal cerca del ayuntamiento, es un restaurante preferido mío y vale la pena probarlo. Siempre me pido una selección de primeros seguido de un curry verde de segundo. Delicioso. Además los precios son razonables y puedes pedírtelo para llevar.

9 Kathmandu

C/ San Vicente, 49, Santa Eulalia
Tel: 971.339.635
kathmanduibiza.com

If you like your Indian food like I do, then this place on the "restaurant street" is for you. They do great kormas, tikkas and biryanis, all served with heaps of naan bread. My favourite is their luscious, creamy chicken tikka masala, and they have a very reasonably priced set menu that allows you to choose from ten different starters, main dishes and desserts.

Si te gusta la comida india como a mí, entonces este establecimiento en la calle de restaurantes es para ti. Hacen deliciosos kormas, tikkas y biryanis, todo servido con montones de pan naan. Mi favorito es su pollo tikka masala deliciosamente cremoso, y tienen un menú a precio muy razonable que te permite elegir entre diez primeros, segundos y postres.

10 Kokoro Sushi Lounge

C/ San Juan 38, Santa Eulalia
Tel: 971.332.089

This restaurant in the marina opened last summer but has already got an outstanding reputation for serving the best Japanese fusion food in Santa Eulalia. The décor is lovely and it's really worth a visit. The fish dishes are also amazing.

Este restaurante en la marina que abrió el verano pasado ya se ha ganado una reputación excelente por servir la mejor cocina de fusión japonesa del pueblo. También sirven unos platos de pescado riquísimos.

11 Vegi

C/. Historiador Clapés, 12
Santa Eulalia
Tel: 971.592.063
vegi-eulalia.info

My brother Thor works in Santa Eulalia and is a vegetarian and he took me here one lunchtime and everything I tried was delicious. This Little place has vegan, vegetarian and gluten-free home-made dishes. They do take away and have a home delivery service.

Mi hermano trabaja aqui y es vegetariano, yme trajo aquí para comer y todo lo que probé era delicioso. Este pequeño lugar tiene una selección de comida casera vegana, vegetariana y sin gluten. También tienen un servicio de entrega a domicilio.

12 El Puntal

C/ San Lorenzo, 21,
Santa Eulalia.
Tel: 971.807.523.

My dear friend Danny Bussard first took me here one afternoon for some tapas, and they have a great wine list as well. But I've since discovered their big English breakfasts, which are a great way to start to the day! Find it just before the entrance of the Marina.

Mi amigo Danny Bussard me trajo aquí por primera vez una tarde de tapas, y además tienen una carta de vinos muy buena. Desde entonces, he descubierto que preparan un buen desayuno inglés, que es una forma magnífica de empezar el día. Encuéntralo a la entrada de la marina.

13 Ring o' Bells

C/ del Mar, 14, Santa Eulalia
Tel: 971.331.943

Hayden and Yvette run this great British pub at the entrance to the Marina, and are so friendly and welcoming. You can grab a pint for just €2,50, in which case they have Carling as well as Estrella. Or in my case make it a Bloody Mary and a game of darts or pool, thank you very much! There's also Wifi and a multi-screen TV, so you can sit back and watch the sports. Snacks are available and they have authentic Mr Whippy ice-cream for the kids.

Hayden e Yvette regentan este pub inglés a la entrada de la marina y son muy simpáticos y amables. Puedes beberte una pinta por 2,50€, tanto de Carling como de Estrella. Para mí, un Bloody Mary y una partida de dardos o billar, ¡gracias! También hay WiFi y TV multi-pantalla, para que puedas relajarte y ver el deporte. Hay aperitivos disponibles y tienen el auténtico helado Mr Whippy para los niños.

14 El Bacaro

C/ Isidoro Macabich, 35
Santa Eulalia
Tel: 971.331.943

This Italian restaurant does delicious pizzas, pasta dishes, Venetian dishes and salads. It is in a lovely position facing the sea.
The waiters are friendly and work fast and in the summer it's best to book if you want to sit outside on the terrace.

Este restaurante italiano frente al mar hace pizzas buenísimas, pastas, platos típicos de Venecia y ensaladas. Los camareros son muy atentos y rápidos, y en verano lo mejor es reservar porque la terraza de fuera se llena.

15 Guaraná

Puerto Deportivo, 8,
Santa Eulalia
Tel: 971.395.444
guaranaibiza.com

This is the only nightclub in "Santa" (as us locals call the town). They host live music events and have DJs playing, and the terrace is perfect for sipping a long drink on a summer's evening while watching everyone stroll past along the Marina.

Ésta es la única disco de "Santa" (como la llamamos nosotros los isleños). Presentan música en vivo y DJs, y la terraza es perfecta para tomarse una copa por la noche en verano mientras observas a la gente pasear por la marina.

16 Bollywood

Puerto Deportivo local 16, zona 4
Santa Eulalia
Tel: 971.331.253

This is my mum's absolute undisputed favourite Indian on the island, and one of mine too. The owners are super friendly and attentive and the food is really aromatic and fresh. I always have the chicken tikka masala while my daughter prefers the korma, and you just *have* to get a side order of cheese naan, you won't regret it! It's down in the port area with views of the boats. They also do takeaway.s here.

Este sitio es de los favoritos de mi madre, y a mí también me chifla. Los propietarios son encantadores y la comida es aromática y fresca Suelo comer pollo tikka masala y mi hija prefiere el korma, y tienes que pedirte naan de queso, ¡no te arrepentirás! Está en el puerto deportivo y tiene vistas estupendas a los barcos. También hacen comida para llevar.

17 Cafetería Alberto's

C/ del Mar, 17, Santa Eulalia
Tel: 971.332.064

This breakfast and tapas bar has been around for 40 years or so and is a great option for that morning hunger. It has cute little tables just at the entrance looking onto the street.

Un bar de desayunos y tapas que lleva abierto unos 40 años y es una opción magnífica para saciar el hambre matutino. Tiene mesitas en la calle muy monas.

18 Passion

Paseo Maritimo, Santa Eulalia
Tel: 971.807.323
passion-ibiza.com

Lana recently opened this addition to her Passion family on the Santa Eulalia promenade. It is a prime position with sea views and a sea breeze too ! Heavenly decor that reminds me of health cafes in Australia serving her renown nutrient rammed menus for all the health-conscious in the east.

Lana recientemente abrió esta nueva adición a su familia Passion en el paseo marítimo de Santa Eulalia. Tiene una ubicación privilegiada, vistas al mar y también puedes disfrutar de la brisa del mar. Una decoración divina que me recuerda a los cafés saludables de Australia y que sirve menús llenos de nutrientes para todos los que se cuidan en el este de la isla.

...SHOPPING DE COMPRAS...

19 Herbolario Pranathy Corner Shop

C/ Mollins de Rei, 1, Santa Eulalia
Tel: 971.334.627

Two lovely ladies have this Eco Shop that has absolutely everything you could possibly need that is health giving. Osteopathy, healing, massage, supplements, weight control management and so on. Go visit them if you are in need of advice or if you just feel like getting healthier. They are the best.

Dos simpáticas mujeres llevan esta tienda Eco que tiene absolutamente todo lo saludable que puedas necesitar. La osteopatía, curación, masages, suplementos, gestión y de control de peso y más. Si estás necesitas asesoramiento o si simplemente ttienes ganas de vivir una vida más saludable. Ellos son los mejores.

20 White Island Corner Shop

C/ Juan Tur Tur, Santa Eulalia
Tel: 971.338.832

A little piece of Britain in Spain, this is where I get my little treats over the winter, from Richmond sausages and pork pies to Wensleydale cheese, crumpets and Monster Munch crisps. The owners are sweet and friendly and always up for a little chat.

Un pedazo del Reino Unido en España, aquí es donde vengo a comprar pequeños caprichos en invierno, desde salchichas Richmond a empanadas de cerdo, queso Wensleydale, Crumpets y patatas Monster Munch. Los propietarios son muy dulces y amables y les va mucho la charla.

21 Arroz y Bambú

C/ Pintores Puget, Santa Eulalia
Tel: 971.336.621
arroz-y-bambu.com

If you need ingredients for a curry or other Asian meals, then this place will have everything you're after. All reasonably priced, they offer spices and other specialities from Thailand, Indonesia,

the Philippines, India, Mexico, Ecuador...
Si necesitas ingredientes para un curry u otro plato oriental, ésta es la tienda donde encontrarás todo lo necesario. Todo a buen precio, ofrecen especias y otras especialidades de Tailandia, Indonesia, Filipinas, India, México, Ecuador...

22 Mari Bodega

C/ San Vicente, 24, Santa Eulalia
Tel: 971.330.665

This is a great store owned by lovely Margarita who sells a wide selection of food and drink and all the island products. You can´t miss the red doors!
Una tienda en Santa Eulalia que regenta la encantadora Margarita y donde encontrarás una amplia selección de comida y bebida de la isla. ¡Fácil de encontrar por sus puertas rojas!

23 Queens & Kings of Joy Fashion

C/ Mariano Riquer Wallis s/n, Santa Eulalia
Tel: 971.807.878

This is where you can find all the trendy Ibiza brands in one shop. They get new items every week, and you can shop your entire new beach look here, from flip-flops to a straw hat, and everything in between. Owner Irma always welcomes you with a smile.
Aquí es donde puedes encontrar todas las marcas de moda de Ibiza en una sola tienda. Reciben prendas nuevas cada semana, y puedes comprar tu look entero de playa, desde chanclas a sombreros de paja. Su propietaria Irma siempre te recibe con una gran sonrisa.

25 Sugar Chic Ibiza

C/ del Mar, 19, Santa Eulalia
Tel: 971.330.014

This place is cupcake heaven! And owners Isabel and Antonio have also created a store that looks good enough to eat – it feels like the walls are made of icing, and the chairs and tables of candy. You can sit here and have a cup of tea and cake, buy a selection to take home or even take classes on making them yourself.
¡Este sitio es un paraíso de las magdalenas! Y los propietarios Isabel y Antonio han creado una tienda tan bonita que está para comérsela, parece que las paredes están hechas de cobertura de azúcar y las sillas y mesas de caramelo.
Puedes sentarte y tomarte un té y un trozo de pastel, comprar una porción para llevarte a casa o incluso apuntarte a las clases para hacerlos tú mismo.

26 Octopus Shop

C/ San Lorenzo, 22, Santa Eulalia
Tel: 971.807.492
octopusshop.puzl.com

I check this little quirky shop out every time I go into Santa, as it has such original things for kids and grownups alike. Fantastic for stocking fillers, they sell everything from fun games to colourful lamps and cardboard build-it-yourself insects. It's toyshop heaven.
Cada vez que voy a Santa Eulalia echo un vistazo a esta tienda ya que tiene objetos muy interesantes para niños y mayores. Es fantástico para llenar los calcetines de pequeños regalos en Navidad, venden de todo, desde juegos divertidos a lámparas coloridas e insectos que tienes que construir tú mismo. ¡Un paraíso de juguetes!

27 Polen

C/ San Lorenzo, 14, Santa Eulalia
Tel: 634.843.374

Alice opened this sweet little health shop last summer and stocked it with an amazing selection of quality products. Think bio/eco food and drinks, and healthy snacks for the kids.
Alice abrió esta pequeña tienda sana el verano pasado y la llenó de una increíble selección de productos de calidad como bebidas y comida bio/eco y picoteos sanos para los niños.

28 Marc & Dani Soluciones Informáticas

Calle Del mar, 12, Santa Eulalia
Tel: 971.338.079
markydani.com

Need service on your laptop? A new hard drive? These guys can solve any computer

related problem you have.
¿Necesitas reparar tu portátil? ¿Necesitas un disco duro? Estos chicos pueden solucionar cualquier problema informático que te pueda surgir.

29 El Ramo De Flores

C/ I. Macabich, 22, Santa Eulalia
Tel: 971.330.186 – 659.830.882
ramodeflores.com

This little corner florist is open all year, including holidays and Sunday mornings. Whatever the occasion, they have an incredible selection of fresh cut flowers and always arrange them beautifully.
Esta tiendecita en la esquina frente a la plaza del cañón está abierta todo el año, incluyendo días festivos y domingos.Independientemente de la ocasión, siempre tienen una gran selección de flores recién cortadas y hacen unos ramos preciosos.

30 Vintage Icons & Echoes

C/ De la Iglesia, 20, Santa Eulalia
Tel: 971.336.820

A fab shop full of colourful, funky hats and shoes, retro glasses, mad clothes and uniforms, and accessories. It is at the back of town near to the market and the new parking. Perfect for dressing up.
Una tienda alegre y colorida, llena de sombreros y zapatos funky, gafas retro, uniformes y accesorios. Está en la parte trasera de la ciudad, cerca del mercado y el nuevo aparcamiento. Perfecta para disfrazarse.

...SLEEP DORMIR

31 Buenavista

Avda. Padre Guasch, 9, Santa Eulalia
Tel: 971.330.003
ibizabuenavista.com

This hotel is up a little lane on the hill that leads to the church of Puig de Missa as you drive into Santa Eulalia town. It's classically Spanish in style with a lot of stately charm, and was the first hotel built in Santa Eulalia. Set in spectacular gardens and with incredible panoramic sea views, it's a family run business, and has a regular clientele. It also has its own restaurant, a swimming pool and a sun deck.
Este hotel está en la colina de camino a la iglesia de Puig de Missa a la entrada de Santa Eulalia. Tiene un estilo clásico español con mucho encanto y fue uno de los primeros hoteles construidos en Santa Eulalia.

ES MERCAT
FOOD MARKET/MERCADO

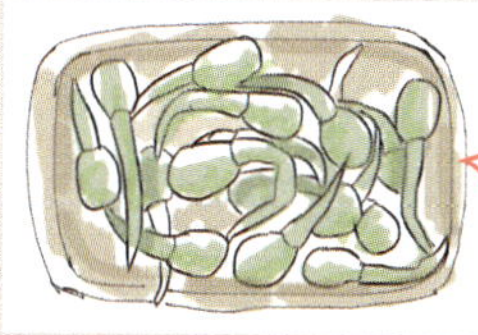

I ♡ THE OLIVES STUFFED WITH CHILLIS
ME ENCANTAN LAS GUINDILLAS

I love this busy market, which generally gets overlooked by visitors because it's hidden at the back of Santa Eulalia town. It offers a range of high quality vegetables and local produce, and has a butcher, a store selling German specialities, a hardware store, a seamstress and even a guy who fixes shoes. So it's a must!
Me encanta este mercado tan concurrido, generalmente los visitantes lo pasan por alto porque está escondido en la parte trasera de Santa Eulalia. Ofrece una variedad de verduras y productos locales de gran calidad y tiene carnicerías, una tienda que vende especialidades alemanas, una ferretería, una costurera e incluso un reparador de calzado. ¡Un esencial!

C/del Sol o Carrer Son Duran.
Open: 07:00 - 14:00

Situado entre unos jardines espectaculares y unas vistas panorámicas al mar, es un negocio familiar y tiene una clientela habitual. Además tiene su propio restaurante, piscina y solárium.

32 Ca's Catalá

C/ del Sol, Santa Eulària
Tel: 971.338.649 - 662.311.094
cascatala.com

My friends Lulu and Mathew run this sweet boutique hotel that looks small from the outside but surprises you when you go inside with its large living room, its pool and terrace and its lovely rooms all decorated with lots of taste. It's very reasonably priced.

Mis amigos Lulu y Mathew llevan este hotel con mucho encanto en el pueblo, que parece pequeño desde afuera, pero que sorprende cuando entras, con grán salón, su terraza amplia alrededor de la piscina y sus habitaciones todas decoradas con un montón de estilo.

* Insotel Fenicia Prestige Suites

C/ Narcisos, Santa Eulalia.
Tel: 971.807.000
insotelhotelgroup.com

On the outskirts of Santa Eulalia in the Siesta complex and in prime position where the river meets the sea. This five star hotel has a magnificent entrance and reception area, a stunning pool and a spa on the ground floor. Perfect for families or couples, and has all the facilities for large receptions and corporate gatherings.

A la salida de Santa Eulalia en el barrio de Siesta. Este hotel de cinco estrellas tiene una entrada y recepción majestuosas, su zona de piscina es impresionante y además presume de uno de los mejores spas de la isla. Es perfecto para familias y parejas y tiene todas las instalaciones necesarias para grandes banquetes y reuniones empresariales.

TEATRO ESPAÑA
THE CINEMA EL CINE

Driving through Santa Eulalia you can't miss this old cinema, built in 1929 and recently restored to its former glory. It is like an real old theatre inside with stunning curved balconies. It screens a mixture of films including some in English with subtitles. Just check the posters or website for info.

Al cruzar por el centro de Santa Eulalia no puedes pasar por alto este viejo cine. Fue construido en 1929 y ha sido restaurado recientemente devolviéndolo a su antigua gloria. Dentro es como un viejo teatro con elegantes balcones curvados. Emiten una mezcla de películas incluyendo algunas en inglés con subtítulos. Echa un vistazo a su cartelera fuera o la web.

C/ San Juame, 81, Santa Eulalia
Tel: 971.331.943
santaeulariadesriu.com

Aguas de Ibiza Lifestyle & Spa

Salvador Carnacho, 9, Santa Eulalia
Tel: 971.319.991
aguasdeibiza.com

This five-star resort is run by one of Ibiza's oldest families. The rooms have stunning sea views, there are three indoor and three outdoor swimming pools plus an amazing spa. To top it off, they serve a really great breakfast on the rooftop terrace.

Este complejo de cinco estrellas está dirigido por una de las familias más antiguas de Ibiza. Las habitaciones tienen vistas increíbles al mar, tienen tres piscinas interiores y otras tres exteriores y un spa. Además, sirven el mejor desayuno en la terraza de la azotea.

A DIFFERENTE SUPERMARKET

AS YOU HEAD OUT OF TOWN
AL SALIR DEL CENTRO

Supermercado Diferente

C/. Cesar Puget Riquer, 7
Santa Eulalia
Tel: 971.338.836
supermercadodiferente.com

All my dutch friends are raving about this new shop that opened in Santa Eulalia. They say it has a great choice of Dutch food so they can finally get all the yummy dutch things they miss like Coffee Japp cake, sausage roll, Filet American, buttermilk and much more...
Oh, and they are open ALL day. No SIESTA for them!

Todos mis amigos holandeses están encantados con esta nueva tienda que abrió en Santa Eulalia. Dicen que tiene una selección increibe de comida holandesa asi que finalmente pueden tener todas las cosas deliciosas que añoran de holanda como el pastel de café Japp, la salchicha, filete Americain, suero de leche y mucho más...Están abiertos todo el día, ¡sin siesta!

...EAT ...COMER

Can Xarc

C/ Des Riu 17, Santa Eulalia
Tel: 971.093.093

A restaurant on the sea front and right at the river mouth of the Santa Eulalia river. It is a perfect spot to spend the day with family and also great for any event as it has some very cosy spaces inside as well as great chill out spots and a lot of seating options. Last but not least they specializes in authentic Ibizan style grilled meat and fish.

Un restaurante en primera línea de mar y justo en la desembocadura del río de Santa Eulalia. Es un lugar perfecto para pasar el día con la familia y para celebrar cualquier evento, ya que cuenta con un interior muy acogedor y un chill out. Están especializados en pescados y carnes a la brasa al auténtico estilo ibicenco.

Seventeen

Los Lirios, 17, Siesta
Tel: 971.330.930
seventeen-ibiza.com

I tried this restaurant last summer with friends that were staying at the summer complex next door and it was such a pleasant surprise. Good affordable italian food. And a log oven for pizzas.

Cené en este restaurante el verano pasado con amigos que se alojaban en el complejo de al lado y fue muy agradable. Comida italiana buena y muy asequible, y horno de leña para pizzas.

ON THE ROAD
EN LA CARRETERA

CAN GUASCH FRUIT MARKET
TIENDA DE COMESTIBLES

A great roadside grocery store on the way to Santa Eulalia from Ibiza, that is open every day. They have amazing bread and a vast vegetable stand with all sorts of exotic fruit.

Una tienda de comestibles en la carretera de Santa Eulalia a Ibiza. Abierto todos los días. Tienen pan delicioso y verduras con montones de frutas exóticas.

Carretera Ibiza > Santa Eulalia
Tel: 871.330.860
supercanguasch.com

URGENT REMINDER - RECORDATORIO URGENTE

WATERLESS IBIZA

IBIZA HAS HARDLY ANY WATER SO PLEASE BE AWARE

IBIZA SIN AGUA

IBIZA TIENE POCA AGUA. PORFAVOR PRESTAD ATENCIÓN

• •

HELP TO SAVE WATER - AYUDA A AHORRAR AGUA

1. TURN OFF TAPS WHEN BRUSHING TEETH
2. WATER GARDEN THE MINIMUN
3. DON'T PULL TOILET CHAIN FREQUENTLY
4. TAKE SHORT SHOWERS

1. APAGAR GRIFOS MIENTRAS CEPILLAS DIENTES
2. REGAR LO MÍNIMO
3. TIRAR POCO CADENA VÁTER
4. TOMAR DUCHAS CORTAS

THANKYOU
GRACIAS

Cala Olivera

A sandy little cove surrounded by rocks and pine trees that remains totally unspoilt and wild.
It's a long way down a dusty dirt track, but the little shack at the end serving home-made specials is worth the drive. Be prepared to fight for a spot on the beach though, as it's only 30 metres in length. If the beach is too full climb up onto the rocks on the right and dive into the crystal-clear sea.
Esta pequeña calita de arena rodeada de rocas y pinos permanece totalmente virgen y salvaje. El camino es largo y polvoriento, pero el pequeño chiringuito al final sirve cocina casera que merece la pena el trayecto. Prepárate a luchar por tu sitio en la playa, ya que sólo tiene 30 metros de largo. Si la playa está llena, sube por las rocas a la derecha y zambúllete en su mar de aguas cristalinas.

Chiringuito de Cala Olivera

Cala Olivera, Roca Llisa
Tel: 619.617.556
I don't know who they are but the people running this shack set back from the beach have created a heavenly little eatery for people who want to hide away from the masses. I come here for the omelettes, and the fresh fish of the day is always good. I think I had some incredibly good sardines last time I came.
No sé quien lleva este bar pero han conseguido crear un pequeño restaurante para aquellos que quieren alejarse de las aglomeraciones. Vengo aquí por sus tortillas y pescado fresco del día, que siempre está muy rico. Creo que una vez comí aquí unas sardinas increíblemente buenas.

Casa Piedra

Ctra. Cala Llonga, Polígono 18,
Tel: 971.196.558
restaurante-casapiedra-ibiza.com
You will find this little restaurant on a bend just before you turn to Cala Llonga as you come from the Golf Club. It is a favourite amongst the locals, and sits overlooking a lemon grove.
Encontrarás este pequeño restaurante en una curva en la carretera justo antes de jirar al pueblo de Cala Llonga. Es un favorito entre la gente local, y está situado mirando hacia un huerto de limoneros

Cala Llonga

A deep bay with a wide sandy beach that gets rather ruined in the summer due to the overflow from its large hotels. Still, it's great if you have kids because it has a little park at the back beneath the shade of the pines and a selection of restaurants on the beach front and others set back in the urbanization.
Una bahía profunda con una playa ancha de arena que en verano se estropea debido a la gran cantidad de turistas que emanan de sus grandes hoteles. Aún así, es perfecta para niños porque hay un pequeño parque detrás, bajo la sombra de los pinos, y varios restaurantes en la playa y en a la entrada a la urbanización.

...EAT & DRINK...
COMER Y BEBER...

El Deseo

Ctra. Cala Llonga 143
Cala Llonga
Tel: 971.196.154
eldeseoibiza.com
Really good Mexican food in a lovely spot. They do Mexican tapas and my favourite being the Ceviche, as well as Mexican platter, fajitas, wraps, quesadillas,

enchilladas, burgers and salads. Oh and they also do mexican breakfasts and full english or continental.
Muy buena comida mexicana en un lugar encantador. Hacen tapas mexicanas y mi favorita es el ceviche. Tienen platos mexicanos, fajitas, wraps, quesadillas, enchilladas, hamburguesas y ensaladas. Ah, y también hacen desayunos mexicanos, ingleses y continentales.

The Terrace

C/ Cala Llonga, 68
Tel: 657.556.457

This little British-run roadside restaurant on the way down to Cala Llonga Beach is perfect for hungry kids. They do tapas, excellent main dishes and the sangria is great. I love the "patatas bravas"– fried chunky chips with hot sauce, and they do some great puddings too.
Este pequeño restaurante de carretera en el camino a la playa de Cala Llonga es perfecto para niños hambrientos. Hacen tapas, excelentes platos principales y la sangría aquí está muy rica. Me encantan las patatas bravas y también hacen postres deliciosos.

Cafetería Los Albatros

C/ Cala Llonga

My Spanish friend Pepito runs this place. It's great for going to watch the football as they have a huge TV screen and the food's classically Spanish.
There's a kids menu and Pepito is a fan of never letting you go thirsty.
Mi amigo Pepito, que siempre va a cien, dirige este local. Es genial para ir a ver el fútbol, ya que tienen una gran pantallapara ver los partidos desde la terraza y la comida es tradicional y buena.

...EAT, DRINK, & PARTY
COMER, BEBER Y GOZA...

Amante

Sol d'en Serra, Cala Llonga
Tel: 971.196.176
amanteibiza.com

This cool hangout in between Cala Llonga and the Golf Club has amazing sea views and is perfect for romantic dining, weddings and other big get-togethers. Full moon dining seems to be a "thing" here, and they also show outdoor movies so check what's coming on: limeinthecoconut.es
Este precioso restaurante entre Cala Llonga y el Club de Golf tiene unas vistas impresionantes al mar y es perfecto para bodas y otros grandes eventos. Las noches de luna llena son muy populares aquí y además ponen películas al aire libre. Echa un vistazo a sus estrenos en: limeinthecoconut.es

...SLEEP & REST
DORMIR Y DESCANSAR...

Can Pere

C/ Jesús-Cala Llonga,
Roca Lisa, Jesús
Tel: 971.196.600

This elegantly restored finca hotel has stone walls and beamed ceilings, as well as impressive views from a stunning hilltop location. Each of the four suites has a modern bathroom with Jacuzzi,Wifi and Balinese daybeds with curtains that blow in the breeze surrounding the swimming pool, life doesn't get much better than this.
Esta encantadora finca reconvertida tiene muros de piedra y techos de sabina, además de unas vistas impresionantes desde su situación privilegiada en lo alto de la montaña. Sus cuatro suites tiene un baño moderno con jacuzzi y WiFi. Y con camas balinesas con cortinas que vuelan con la brisa alrededor de la piscina, la vida no podría ser mejor.

Can Domo

Ctra. Cala Llonga, km 7.6,
Tel: 971.331.059 - 618.550.897
candomo.com

This chic little paradise run by a Pau and alexandra that sits in a secluded 17th-century farmhouse on a hilltop near Roca Llisa's Golf Course. Come and experience their quaint little restaurant, charming bedrooms with white washed beams and a pool with hammocks and gardens and olive trees surrounding it.
Este paraíso pequeño y chic creado por Pau y Alexandra, se encuentra en una finca del siglo XVII situada en. El matrimonio entre David y alto de una colina cerca de Roca Llisa. Ven y disfruta de su restaurante pequeño y pintoresco, sus habitaciones con encanto de vigas encaladas y una piscina con hamacas rodeada de jardines y olivos.

The secret place
54
Hjordis Fogelberg

5 THINGS YOU SHOULD DO

5 COSAS QUE DEBERÍAS HACER CUANDO ESTÉS AQUÍ

---

1. Tapas at Bar Costa in Santa Gertrudis (p.225)
   Tapas en Bar Costa en Santa Gertrudis

2. Shop a bit of Boho at World Family (p.247)
   Comprar hasta saciarte en la Galería Elefante

3. Sushi + cocktails at Nagai (p.237)
   Sushi y cocteles en Nagai

4. Have a healthy lunch at La Paloma Café (p.242)
   Comerte un almuerzo sano en La Paloma Café

5. Dine a meaty grill at Can Balafia (p.242)
   Cena de carne al grill en Can Balafia

INLAND
Santa Gertrudis San Lorenzo, on the roads & San Rafael

El interior, Santa Gertrudis Sant Llorenç, por las carreteras y Sant Rafel

SANTA GERTRUDIS + INLAND

SANTA GERTRUDIS DE FRUITERA Y EL INTERIOR DE LA ISLA

"click"

There are a few little villages inland with divine little places to eat and shops on the roads leading in and out, and lots of off-the-beaten-track hotels. This section covers the ones in the heart of the island that are worth a visit, neither north or south but still very reachable. One of these is Santa Gertrudis which is perfect for a visit any time of day. Over the last years it has expanded rapidly with all sorts of chic shops and restaurants, but thankfully the lovely town houses have all stayed true to their original style. There are a few banks, supermarkets, a gym and an indoor swimming pool at the back of the village.

Hay algunos pueblecitos en el interior de la isla en cuyas carreteras puedes encontrar magníficos restaurantes y tiendas, además de diversos hoteles que se salen de la ruta habitual. Esta sección cubre los que se encuentran en el corazón de la isla y que son de fácil acceso. Uno de ellos es Santa Gertrudis, perfecto para una visita a cualquier hora del día. Se ha expandido rápidamente en los últimos años con todo tipo de tiendas chic y restaurantes, pero afortunadamente sus preciosas casas adosadas han conservado su estilo original. También hay bancos, supermercados e incluso un gimnasio y una piscina cubierta al fondo del pueblo.

CAN YOU FIND THE FAKE PIGEON SOMEWHERE IN THE SQUARE?

PUEDES ENCONTRAR LA PALOMA FALSA? ESTA POR LA PLAZA

...TO EAT AND SNACK
PARA COMER Y TAPEAR

Bar Costa

Plaza de la Iglesia,
Santa Gertrudis
Tel: 971.197.021

This place only serves sandwiches and cold cuts or cheese boards, and is an absolute classic with the locals. Hanging hams line the ceiling as you enter, and the walls are covered with art by local artists. A firm winter favourite with an open fire roaring inside, and it's really good value.

Aunque este bar sólo sirva bocadillos y platos de fiambres y quesos, es un clásico absoluto entre los ibicencos. Los jamones cuelgan del techo a la entrada, y las paredes están cubiertas de cuadros de artistas locales. Un firme favorito para invierno con su gran chimenea, además es muy barato.

Bar Restaurant Ulivans

Plaza de la Iglesia,
Santa Gertrudis
Tel: 971.197.176

Directly facing the church on the square, this restaurant is great to go to with a big group as it's very reasonably priced. It's perfect to perch up and just watch the world go by. They have a good selection of tapas and main dishes.

En la plaza, frente a la iglesia, este restaurante es un lugar perfecto para ir en familia o en grupo ya que sus precios son muy razonables. Es un lugar magnífico para sentarse y ver la gente pasar. Tienen una buena selección de tapas y platos principales.

Restaurante Santa Gertrudis

Plaza de la Iglesia,
Santa Gertrudis
Tel: 971.197.057

The sisters Cati and María run this family restaurant that has been here for almost 40 years. The locals call it "the paella place", because as well as their traditional menu, on Sundays they serve large trays with paella that they make on a wood stove.

Las hermanas Cati y María llevan este local familiar que abrió hace casi 40 años. Se conoce entre los lugareños como "el de las paellas" ya que además de su menú tradicional, los domingos sirven bandejas de paella hechas en su fuego de leña.

La Fromagerie

C/ Venda de Parada, 12
Santa Gertrudis
Tel: 686.678.794

This is a luscious, exclusive cheese-smelling shop...sorry I meant selling! The cheeses are imported from many different regions of France, and they also do foie gras and a selection of wines to enjoy with your tasting.

Una tienda exclusiva de quesos deliciosos. Éstos son importados de múltiples regiones de Francia y también venden foie gras y una selección de vinos que puedes disfrutar con tu degustación de quesos.

Bistro Plaza

Plaza de la Iglesia,
Santa Gertrudis
Tel: 971.197.075
bistroplaza.es

Fabrice and Charlie run this bistro-style restaurant, and I tell you these Belgians really know how to make a good onion soup! I come here often for a glass of wine with friends. Try the steak tartare.

Fabrice y Charlie dirigen este encantador restaurante bistro y te puedo decir que estos belgas saben cómo hacer una buena sopa de cebolla. Yo me tomo aqui copitas con amigas a menudo. No te vayas sin probar su steak tartare.

Es Cantó

Plaza de la Iglesia,
Santa Gertrudis
Tel: 971.197.060

Always bustling with locals, this is a great little place to have a coffee or grab a quick tapa or my preferred steak and chips. It is the nearest café to the church and one of my preferred daytime meeting points.

Siempre lleno de gente local, es un pequeño bar perfecto para un café, una tapa o el bistek con patatas. Es la cafetería más cercana a la iglesia y de mis puntos de encuentro preferidos.

Musset

Santa Gertrudis
Tel: 971.197.671

A charming meeting point just opposite the playground, making it very handy for parents. An all

IBIZA
Aurobelle
NEW
ANANDA
IBIZA
www.balibohogirl.com
everyone needs a little Ibiza in their life
Aurobelle®
IBIZA
peace
LIFE IS BETTER AT THE BEACH
Today I will Choose JOY
LOVE

day café and restaurant, they have the best carrot cake in town. The waitresses are really sweet and always have my wine waiting...
Un simpático lugar de encuentro y está frente a un parque infantil, perfecto para los padres. Cafetería y restaurante abierto todo el día, tienen el mejor pastel de zanahoria del pueblo. Las camareras son simpatiquísimas y siempre tienen el vino blanco preparado.

Estanco de Santa Gertrudis

Plaza de la Iglesia,
Santa Gertrudis
Tel: 971.197.058

Run by the Can Pep Roig family since 1943, this authentic little grocery store with its Tabacos sign above the door hasn't changed a bit in the last century – except for the fact that the peseta is now obsolete!
Propiedad de la familia Can Pep Roig desde 1943, esta tienda auténtica de verduras con su cartel de Tabacos sobre la puerta no ha cambiado nada en el último siglo, ¡excepto por el hecho de que la peseta se ha quedado obsoleta!

Macao Café

C/ Venda des Poble, 8,
Santa Gertrudis
Tel: 971.197.835
macaocafesg@gmail.com

A popular Italian restaurant on the island. Many of the island residents like myself have been enjoying its food since it first opened. The food is top class and I always have the "Milanesa", breaded veal with a tomato and rocketsalad. The outside terrace is always rammed so booking is essential.
Un restaurante italiano muy popular en la isla. Muchos residentes como yo, llevamos disfrutando de su cocina desde que abrió por primera vez en el puerto de Ibiza. La cocina es de primera y siempre me pido la Milanesa con ensalada de rúcula y tomate. La terraza de fuera siempre está llena, así que reservar con antelación es esencial.

Vivo

C/ Venda des Poble s/n
Santa Gertrudis
Tel: 647.053.518
vivoibiza.com

A new Mediterranean restaurant that brings you the taste of Sicily with a Peruvian and international influence. Rich on seasonings at the hand of their amazing chef Francesco Scarpulla who will make your taste buds go crazy. There is a charming outdoor garden that is perfect to sit and enjoy a cocktail or your dinner in the summer.
Un restaurante nuevo mediterráneo que te ofrece platos elaborados con influencias Sicilianas, peruanas e internacionales. Rico en condimentos a la mano de su increíble chef Francesco Scarpulla. Con una preciosa zona exterior ajardinada donde puedes disfrutar cenando o tomandote un coctel en verano.

Plaisir

C/ Venda de Fruitera
Santa Gertrudis
Tel: 971.197.722
plaisir.es

A super sweet place that seems small but stretches out to a fab patio at the back with a Ping Pong table! The décor is great with so many cool details. It's kid friendly and has games and books for kids inside. The food is heavenly and really fresh and also not over priced and they do brunches to die for with Bloody Marys!!!
Un lugar superdulce que parece pequeño desde fuera, pero se extiende a un patio en la parte trasera con una mesa de ping-pong. La decoración es original con detalles interesantes y tiene juegos y libros para los niños. La comida es deliciosa y muy fresca, y no es caro, además hacen unas comidas con Bloody Marys para morirse.

Wild Beets

C/ Venda de Llatzer, 9
Santa Gertrudis
Tel: 971.197.870
wildbeets.com

The healthiest restaurant here. Creator Cliff only uses organic and ecological ingredients. There's a fridge full of cold pressed juices for cleanses and detox's, perfect for those of you rushing.
El restaurante más saludable del pueblo. Cliff el creador sólo utiliza ingredientes orgánicos y ecológicos. Hay una nevera de zumos para aquellos que tienen prisa.

My Way

C/ Venda de Früiteria
Santa Gertrudis
Tel: 971.932.536

Very good hamburgers but they also have a great system here that allows you to choose the ingredients you want in your burger by filling in a list.

Muy buena hamburguesería que además tienen un sistema genial para los pedidos: te dan una lista y eliges los ingredientes que quieres en tu hamburguesa.

...DIVINE SHOPS ..TIENDAS DIVINAS

Aurobelle Shop

C/ Vénda de Parada, 1
Santa Gertrudis
Tel: 654.209.798
aurobelle.com

Almost everything in the shop is designed and sourced carefully by Jane the owner in cooperation with small fair trade communities in India.
The clothes are beautiful and here you can find stunning embroidered shirts and dresses, sarongs, scarfs and accessories.
They have another shop in San José.

Casi todo en la tienda está cuidadosamente diseñado por Jane, la propietaria, en cooperación con pequeñas comunidades en la India.
La ropa es divina y puedes encontrar camisas y vestidos bordados, pareos, bufandas y accesorios. Tienen otra tienda en San José.

The Rose

C/ Venda de Fruitera 2,
Santa Gertrudis
Tel: 971.197.935 - 680.955.615

A heavenly shop and gallery run by Claudina and Aldo, who are the sweetest couple and have the most incredible taste when it comes to clothes and interiors. The last time I passed by I was given a gin and tonic and could hardly get back up from their divine sofas! Check out their kaftans, I've got my eyes on a tie-dyed one.

Los simpáticos Claudina y Aldo tienen esta preciosa tienda de ropa y diseño de interiores, y es que gusto no les falta. La última vez que me paré me invitaron a un gin tonic y casi no me pude levantar de su divino sofá. Pruébate una de sus túnicas, yo le tengo el ojo echado a una desteñida.

The Plenty

C/ Venda de Fruiterá 2,
Santa Gertrudis
Tel: 971.197.725

My friend Alonso who loves the flea markets first thing on a Saturday morning, decided to open this gorgeous Shop/Restaurant with his friends from The Rose. The concept is that "everything you see is for sale". Vintage meets new.

Mi amigo Alonso que ama a los mercados de pulgas lo primero que un sábado por la mañana, decidió abrir esta tienda/restaurante precioso con sus amigos de la rosa.
El concepto es que "todo lo que ves está a la venta". Vintage y nuevo.

Baron

C/ Venda de Fruitera 5,
Santa Gertrudis
Tel: 971.197.273
baron-ibiza.com

This is a really stylish clothes and accessory shop for men. They sell brands that are all about quality. I love their linen shirts. You must pass by if you are in the village.

Esta es una tienda de ropa elegante para hombres. Buenas marcas y sobretodo calidad. Me encantan sus camisas de lino. Debes pasarte si estás en el pueblo.

Es Cucons Tienda

Plaza de la Iglesia
Santa Gertrudis
Tel: 971.197.756

A pretty little shop set in an authentic farmhouse in centre of the village. They sell household items, textiles, accessories and clothes. I find it impossible to go by without going in and I always buy something!

Una tiendecita ubicada en una auténtica casa payesa en el pueblo. Vende cosas para el hogar, textiles, complementos y también ropa. A mí me cuesta mucho pasar por aquí sin entrar a mirar, y siempre me compro algo.

Nino D'agata

Plaza de la Iglesiá, 6,
Santa Gertrudis
Tel: 971.197.225
ninodagata.com

Nino and Barbara's jewellery shop is a true treasure trove. This lovely italian couple have lived on the island for years and are experts in

HOW TO MAKE GAZPACHO

COMO HACER GAZPACHO

by Bel Fogelberg (my mum)

15 minutes - 15 minutos

You will need:
Electric mixer
Big jug

Ingredients:
8 tomatoes (1,2kg)
1 green pepper
1 cucumber
1 garlic clove
250ml Olive oil
50ml vinegar
Dried bread
Salt + pepper
Add water if too thick

Method:
Chop everything up and chuck it in the mixer, wizz, add liquids, and crumble up a handfull of dried bread. Season to taste.

Necesitarás:
Batidora
Jarra grande

Ingredientes:
8 tomates
1 pimiento verde
1 pepino
1 diente ajo
250ml Aceite de oliva,
50ml Vinagre
Pan seco
Sal y pimienta
Agua si esta muy espeso

Método:
Picar todo y poner en la batidora, batir y añadir líquidos, un puñado de pan seco, sal y pimienta.

* CHILL BEFORE SERVING

ENFRIAR ANTES DE SERVIR

fine jewellery, so come here if you're looking to invest in a truly unique piece.
La joyería de Nino y Bárbara es una cueva del tesoro. Llevan viviendo en la isla muchos años y son maestros artesanos de la joyería fina, echa un vistazo aquí si quieres invertir en una pieza realmente única.

Libro Azul Ibiza

Sa Nova Gertrudis, Santa Gertrudis.
Tel: 971.197.454
libro-azul-ibiza.com

Everyone needs a good book and here you can pick up the perfect read in English or German. They also do a great selection of coffee table books if you're looking for a stylish gift.
Todo el mundo necesita un buen libro y aquí puedes escoger la lectura perfecta en inglés o alemán. También tienen una gran selección de libros de mesa si buscas un regalo elegante.

Libreria Serreta

Can Serreta, Santa Gertrudis
Tel: 971.932.529

This is a really handy little Book Shop and News Agent which is just on the roadside as you leave the village on your way north. It is a family run business and perfect for grabbing the papers, buying stationary or a gift.
Una pequeña librería muy práctica justo al salir del pueblo en dirección al norte. Es un negocio familiar perfecto para comprar la prensa o un regalo.

...DELICATESSEN TAKE AWAY
PARA LLEVAR

Picadeli

Can Serreta, Local 1
Santa Gertrudis
Tel: 971.197.121
picadeli-ibiza.com

This is a roadside takeaway with the added twist of having a spot to park in front and a comfy sofa outside. They make the yummiest healthiest food using the best ingredients. I can't stop buying their Babaganush.
Un lugar de comida para llevar en la carretera, pero con la diferencia de tener un sitio para aparcar en frente y un sofá afuera. Hacen una comida deliciosa con los mejores ingredientes. No paro de comprar su babaganush.

Can Escandell

Ctra. Sant Miquel
Tel: 971.197.798

I love this roadside supermarket. It really does stock everything you need, and they have a great selection of organic and healthy food at the back, including gluten free options. As you enter check out the ceiling with all the baskets hanging - the real Ibiza!
Me encanta este supermercado junto a la carretera. Realmente vende todo lo que necesitas y tienen una gran selección de comida orgánica y sana en la parte trasera, incluyendo alimentos sin gluten. Cuando entres echa un vistazo al techo del que cuelgan montones de cestos, ¡la verdadera Ibiza!

Las Cicadas

Santa Gertrudis
Tel: 671.805.764
lascicadas.com

This hotel offers you a true ibizan experience. It is set in a 500 year-old Finca in the countryside near Santa Gertrudis and surrounded by olive trees and nature. It has that feel of staying at a friends bohemian country home with stylish and intimate touches everywhere, in a very rustic environment. There's a large pool and the rooms are all uniquely styled in that divine Ibiza way.

Este hotel te ofrecerá una verdadera experiencia ibicenca. Se encuentra en una finca de 500 años en pleno campo cerca de Santa Gertrudis y rodeada de olivos y naturaleza. Tendrás la sensación de estar en una gran casa de campo bohemia de algún amigo con un ambiente elegante y rústico. Hay una gran piscina y todas las habitaciones tienen ese estilo ibicenco único.

Galeria Elefante

Ctra. San Miguel, 3.2km, Santa Gertrudis
Tel: 971.197.017

This old converted finca is an absolute labyrinth of delights, that my dearest friend Victoria has created alongside her business partner Sharon. Stocking goodies from all corners of the globe, you'll find everything from furniture and clothes to artwork and books, making it perfect for gifts with an extra-special touch.

Esta vieja finca ha sido convertida en un pequeño laberinto de delicias que mi querida amiga Victoria ha creado junto a su socia Sharon. Venden objetos de todos los rincones del mundo, encontrarás desde mobiliario a ropa, arte y libros. Perfecto para un regalo con un toque extra especial.

...TO EAT ON THE ROAD
COMER POR LA CARRETERA

Restaurante Can Pau

Ctra. Santa Gertrudis
Tel: 971.197.007

I first came to this family-run farmhouse restaurant as a baby! It still serves traditional Catalan cuisine like it always did. A family business that has been passed down from generation to generation. I love dining outside in their pretty covered porch in the gardin.

¡La primera vez que vine a este restaurante de la familia Pau era un bebé! Siguen sirviendo la misma cocina tradicional catalana de siempre. Es un negocio familiar que ha pasado de generación en generación. Me encanta cenar con amigos en la terraza cubierta en el jardin.

Can Caus

Ctra. Santa Gertrudis Km 3.5,
Tel: 971.197.516
cancaus-ibiza.com

With its large open grill, this rustic place is a meat eater's dream, but they do also offer choices for vegetarians. There's also a great little supermarket-type shop next

SLUIZ
THE CONCEPT STORE

A warehouse-style shop on the road as you head to Santa Gertrudis.
The Dutch owners have heaps of creativity and good taste making this warehouse-style store a show case of everything you wish you could have in your home. A vast selection of custom-made home accessories, recycled type furnishings and bohemian and basic clothes for women and men that you just want to buy all.
You can also take a break from your shopping and grab a coffee or have lunch with friends.

Una tienda estilo almacén en la carretera de Ibiza a Santa Gertrudis.
Los propietarios son holandeses y tienen un montón de creatividad y buen gusto creando un escaparate de todo lo que deseas para tu hogar y para tí Tienen una amplia selección de accesorios hechos a medida para el hogar, muebles tipo reciclados y ropa bohemia para mujeres y básicos para hombres.
También puedes cojerte un pequeño descanso y tomarte un café o hasta almorzar aquí con tus amigas.

Santa Gertrudis.
Tel: 971.931.206
sluizibiza.com

door which has a great meat counter, so perfect for that weekend BBQ you planned. I love their "Sobrasada", Ibicencan matured red sausage, which they sell as well as serve in the restaurant.

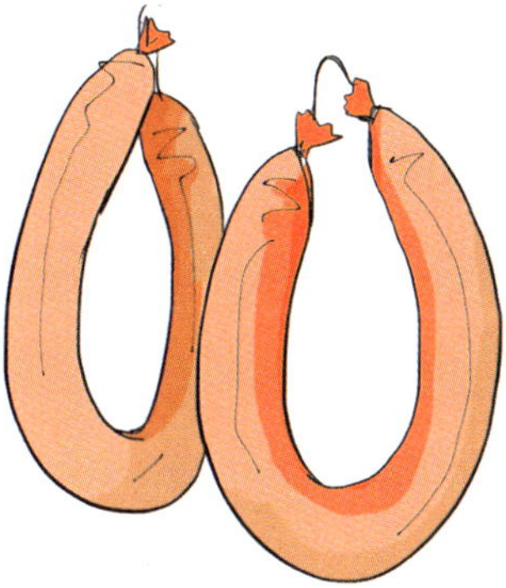

Con su gran parrilla, este restaurante rústico es el sueño de los amantes de la carne pero también ofrecen platos vegetarianos. Además hay un supermercado magnífico al lado con una gran selección de carnes, perfecto para esa barbacoa de fin de semana que tienes planeada.
Me encanta la sobrasada de aqui que venden y sirven.

..CA NA NEGRETA...
TAPAS

Sa Barda

Ctra. San Juan Km 4,2
Ca na Negreta
Tel: 971.315.204.

These guys are on the road to Santa Eulalia about 4km out of Ibiza, and specialise in homemade open sandwiches with a huge array of toppings, as well as tapas. The locals all stop for their morning coffee or coñac here - or rather, coffee in a coñac! It's also got a lovely terrace and very reasonable prices.
Estos chicos en la carretera de Santa Eulalia a unos 4km de Ibiza se especializan en montaditos caseros con una gran variedad de ingredientes, además de una selección de tapas. La gente de aquí se para a tomar el café de la mañana o para un coñac, ¡o un carajillo de coñac! También tiene una agradable terraza y precios razonables.

Sa Cafeteria

Ctra. Ibiza a Santa Eulalia, Km 6
Ca Na Negreta

A firm favourite of mine on the Santa Eulalia road right beside the Go Karts. I stop here for a coffee and a "Bikini" cheese and ham sandwich and sit at my cosy spot by their log fire in the winter.
This sweet family run place also has WiFi.
Uno de mis favoritos en la carretera de Santa Eulalia, pegado a los Go Karts. Suelo parar aquí a tomarme mi café con leche y un sándwich mixto, y en invierno siempre me siento junto a la chimenea.
Este lugar tan acogedor también tiene wifi.

Can Toni

Ctra. Eivissa-Sant Joan, Km 4
Ca na Negreta, Santa Gertrudis
Tel: 971.190.973

This is one of my roadside favourites on the way out of Ibiza Town heading

LA CHOZA
THE VEG SHACK
FRUTAS Y VERDURAS

A great roadside vegetable stand that is a bit larger than most of its kind, and with a great array of local and organic produce. The Spanish TV blazes inside as you search for that perfect lettuce, and they also stock bread, nuts, oils and a little section out the front of over-ripe goods at a fraction of their original price.
Un puesto de verduras que es un poco más grande de lo habitual, con una gran variedad de productos locales y ecológicos. La TV española está a todo volumen mientras buscas la lechuga perfecta; también venden pan, frutos secos, aceites y una selección de productos muy maduros a una fracción de su precio original.

Carretera San Miguel,
San Miguel
Tel: 971.310.228
lamasiadensort.com

towards Santa Eulalia. It's a proper trucker's and worker's bar, grease and all, with a supermarket attached. The tapas are really good and I normally have the "Ensaladilla rusa" - which is a potato-and-mayo salad - and the fried squid rings. The staff are also lovely and it's open all day.

Desde Ibiza a Santa Eulalia está uno de mis establecimientos de carretera favoritos. Es un bar de camioneros y trabajadores, con un supermercado al lado. Las tapas están muy buenas, yo suelo pedirme la ensaladilla rusa y los calamares a la romana. El personal es muy atento y está abierto todo el día.

SHOPPING...

COCOQ

Ctra. Ibiza a Santa Eulalia, km 6.2
Tel: 971.090.186
cocoqibiza.com

A huge warehouse of a home store on the road to Santa Eulalia/San Juan. Big brands come together here. Furniture, home ware, wine, clothes, art and more. The great thing is that you can park up right outside!

Una tienda en una nave enorme en la carretera de Santa Eulalia - San Juan. Aquí se juntan las grandes marcas y se venden muebles, artículos de hogar, ropa, arte y hasta vinos. ¡Puedes aparcar justo al lado de la entrada!

Ibiza Troc

Ctra. San Miguel, Santa Gertrudis
Tel: 620.452.086

On the road to Santa Gertrudis coming from Ibiza town, you'll see a warehouse on the left with furniture spilling out onto the street where they buy and sell anything from a piano to a tennis racquet. I love this place and have had my eye on the pinball machines in the back for ages! It's an amazing find for first time residents too, who want to furnish theirnew place with a bit of vintage.

En la carretera de Santa Gertrudis, encontrarás este gran almacén a la izquierda con mobiliario desbordándose hacia la calle. Compran y venden de todo desde un piano a una raqueta de tenis. Me encanta este sito y tenía el ojo puesto en una maquina de Pin Ball. Es un hallazgo fantástico para residentes recién llegados que quieran amueblar su nuevo hogar con algo un poco vintage.

ON THE ROAD
EN LA CARRETERA

CAN CASTELLÓ
DECO + ART

A decoration shop that you will see from the road. It sells all types of furniture ranging from shabby chic to classic vintage pieces. They have a lot of Eastern objects and sculptures as well as oriental doorways, sculptures, tiling and art. There's a huge open-air warehouse at the back so it's worth a good walk about.

Una tienda de decoración divina que verás desde la carretera. Vende todo tipo de muebles desde estilo rustico chic a piezas clásicas.
Tienen muchos objetos y esculturas orientales, así como puertas, azulejos y arte. Hay un almacén enorme al aire libre en la parte trasera por lo que merece un largo paseo por alrededor.

Ctra Ibiza > Santa Eulalia
Tel: 971 31 65 46

A Peace of Ibiza
A Peace of Ibiza
facebook.com/apeaceofibiza

Bambuddha Grove

Ctra. San Juan,
Tel: 971.197.510
bambuddha.com

I love this place! It stands apart from the bling which sometimes feels like it's going to engulf the whole island, and with its Eastern inspired interior that has recently been redesigned, transports you straight back to a restaurant in the Balinese jungle of Ubud. Buddha watches on as you tuck into the most delicious pan-Asian cuisine. My favourite dishes are the green chicken curry and the crispy duck. It also tends to turn into a little party as the clock strikes midnight.

¡Me encanta este sitio en verano! Se aleja del lujo que a veces parece que va a engullir la isla entera, y con una re-decoración interior inspirada en Oriente te transporta directamente a un restaurante en Ubud de la jungla balinesa. Buda te observa mientras degustas la cocina pan-asiática más deliciosa, y mi plato favorito es el Curry Verde.

Nagai

Ctra. San Juan, Km 9.5
Tel: 971.807.308
nagairestaurant.com

I sometimes just go here for a cocktail! My favourite is the Moscow Mule which has finely chopped ginger in the mix to give it a real kick. But the real winner in this restaurant is the incredible fusion sushi menu! All set in a renovated finca offering a cute and cosy interior with open fires in the colder months and a starlit outdoor setting in the summer.

¡A veces vengo aquí sólo para un cóctel! Mi favorito es el Moscow Mule que tiene jengibre en la mezcla para darle un toque picante. Pero lo mejor del restaurante es la increíble carta de sushi y de fusión. Todo en el marco de una finca renovada con un interior acogedor y coqueto con chimeneas para los fríos meses de invierno y una terraza iluminada por las estrellas para el verano.

Restaurante Ses Escoles (Oleoteca)

Ctra. San Juan, Km 9,2
Tel: 871.870.229

This divine family run restaurant and shop selling island products, just opened and although I have only tried a few tapas, I plan to return very soon as the menu looks amazing.

Este precioso restaurante familiar y tienda que vende productos de la isla abrió recientemente sus puertas y aunque solo he probado unas cuantas tapas, he ojeado el menú y planeo volver muy pronto.

Cicale

Ctra. San Juan,
Tel: 971.325.151
cicaleibiza.com

I go here when I want to treat myself to superb Italian food. It's not cheap but totally worth it and all set in a 250 year old finca. They use produce plucked from their onsite veggie patch offering pastas and risottos as well as meats and fish.

Vengo aquí para comer comida italiana excelente a pesar del precio. Esta casa de 250 años de antigüedad utiliza productos locales recogidos de su huerto. Su carta ofrece pastas y rissotos además de carnes y pescado.

Juanito's

Ctra. San Juan, Km.15.4
Tel: 971.325.082

A traditional roadside eatery that's been serving up rustic Ibicencan grilled meats for over 40 years. There's a kind of dingy bar area at the entrance, but the best spot is out back in view of the grill so you can watch your food being cooked. No frills here, just simple vegetables alongside your meat and a good shot of hierbas when you finish.
I also love their cheese on peasant bread with a coffee in the morning.

Un restaurante tradicional ibicenco junto a la carretera que sirve carnes a la parrilla desde hace más de 40 años. Hay una especie de bar deslucido a la entrada, pero el mejor sitio es atrás, con vistas a la parrilla, así puedes ver cómo se prepara tu comida. Aquí no hay florituras, simplemente verduras con tu carne y un buen chupito de hierbas para acabar. También me gusta su pan payés con queso con un café por la mañana. Cerrado los lunes.

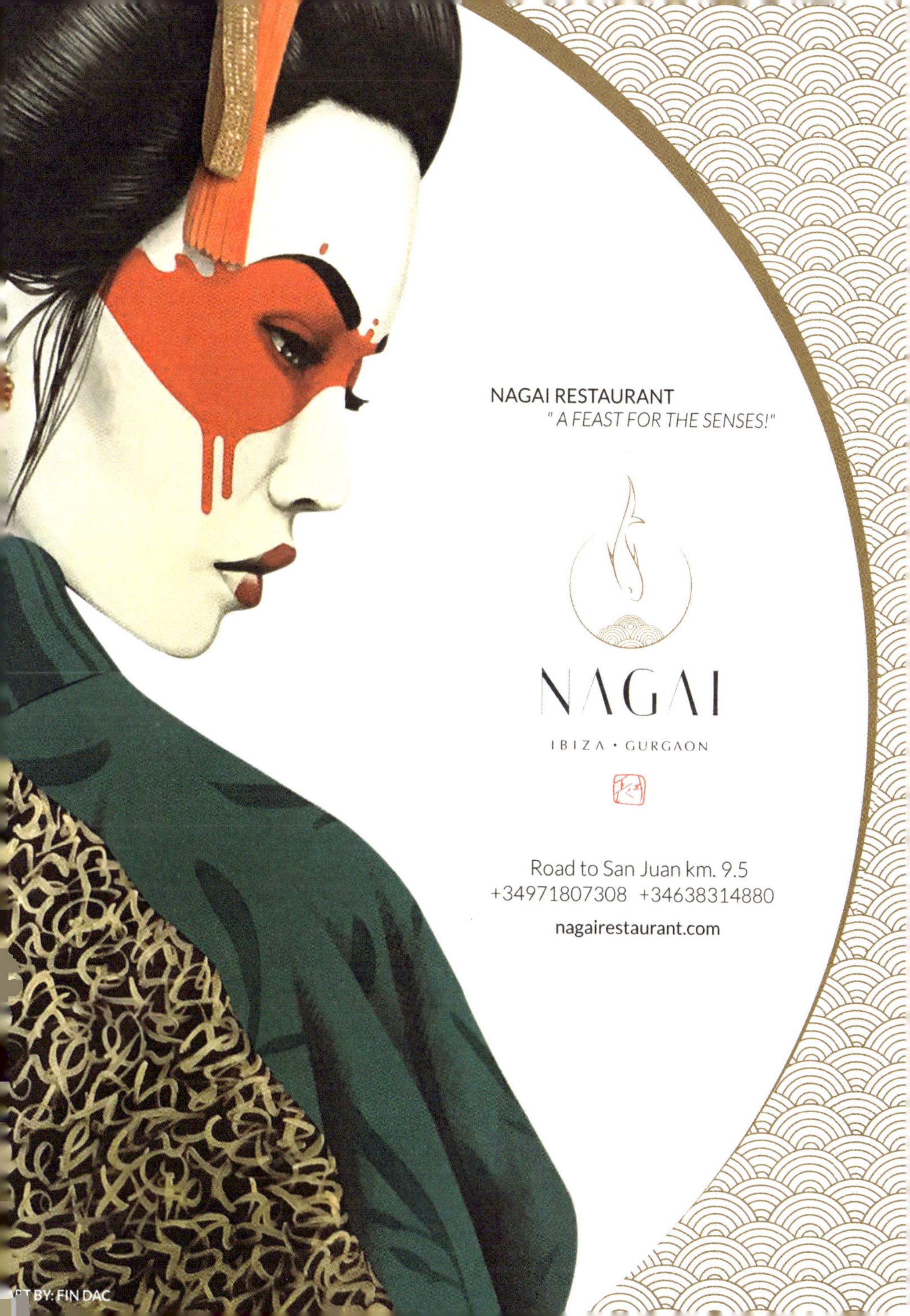
NAGAI RESTAURANT
" A FEAST FOR THE SENSES!"
NAGAI
IBIZA • GURGAON
Road to San Juan km. 9.5
+34971807308 +34638314880
nagairestaurant.com
BY: FIN DAC

SAN LORENZO SANT LLORENC DE BALAFIA

This delightful little village with its 18 century church perched on a little hill surrounded by fertile fields, has remained intact despite the passing of the years. Beside the church is a great picnic area where you can barbecue safely in a beautiful pine forest.
The tiny whitewashed village of Balàfia with its majestic old towers and the spring (where a popular dance is held in August) sits a kilometre or so from the church.

Este es un pequeño pueblo encantador cuya iglesia del siglo XVIII se alza sobre la colina rodeada de campo, y se ha mantenido intacta con el paso de los años. Cerca de la iglesia hay una zona de picnic donde se pueden hacer barbacoas en un bosque entre pinos naturales.
El pequeño pueblo de Balàfia, con sus majestuosas torres de piedra y su fuente (donde tiene lugar el baile popular en agosto) se encuentra a un kilometro mas o menos de la iglesia.

...IN SAN LORENZO VILLAGE
EN EL PUEBLO DE SAN LORENZO...

La Paloma

C/ Can Pou, 4, San Lorenzo
Tel: 971.325.543
palomaibiza.com

I absolutely adore this place - and the owners for making it! It's one of the most loved restaurants on the island and very popular in the summer with celebrities and stylish locals, but always super laid-back. The food here is prepared with care and tastes utterly homemade every time, and I always have the baked aubergine parmigiana and La Paloma salad, but if you're a meat eater the steak is out of this world. The décor and cute wall paintings add to the whole enchanting atmosphere, and during the day 'Paloma Café' takes over from the restaurant serving lovely healthy breakfasts, salads and focaccias in the shady garden terrace. In addition there´s a guy playing the accordion in the garden, which brings even more magic to the place.

Adoro este lugar, ¡y a los propietarios por haberlo creado! Es uno de los restaurantes más admirados de la isla y muy popular en verano entre las celebridades y gente elegante, pero es muy relajado. La comida aquí está preparada con mucho cariño y esmero y siempre tiene un sabor totalmente casero. Siempre me pido las berenjenas a la parmigiana y la ensalada La Paloma, pero si te gusta la carne, el solomillo está de muerte. La decoración y sus preciosos murales añaden encanto al ambiente, y durante el día 'La Paloma Café' toma el relevo del restaurante y prepara desayunos sanos, ensaladas y focaccias a la sombra de su jardín. A menudo hay un acordeón sonando en el jardín que aporta aún más magia al lugar.

Can Balàfia

Ctra. San Juan, km 15,4
Tel: 971.325.019

I love this place and don't get here enough. Their chicken and lamb chops are just crispy perfection and served with the best thinly-cut chips, not to mention the tomato and onion salad that never tastes as good when I make it at home. In the summer, their garden is one of the simplest, most Ibizary places you can possibly eat. They only accept cash.

Adoro este sitio y no vengo lo suficiente. El pollo y las chuletas de cordero crujientes vienen servidos con las mejores patatas fritas, por no mencionar la ensalada de tomate y cebolla que nunca sabe igual de bien cuando la preparo en casa. En verano, el jardín es uno de los más simples, pero su entorno no podría ser más ibicenco. No aceptan tarjeta de credito.

...ON THE ROAD...
POR LA CARRETERA...

Es Pins

Ctra. San Juan, Km 14
Tel: 971.325.034

I find myself here a lot, as it's simple, tasty and cheap. They have the best "Alioli" on the island and make their own bread with cumin seeds that I sometimes buy and take home, along with a little pot of the famous garlicky mayonnaise alioli). Serving grilled meats, seafood casseroles and paellas, try their peasant "crosta" salad if you like tomatoes and garlic, and their lamb chops are great. Wednesdays closed.

Siempre acabo viniendo aquí, ya que sirven comida simple, buena y barata. Tienen el mejor alioli de la isla y preparan su propio pan con semillas de comino, que a veces compro y me llevo a casa junto a un bote de alioli. Sirven carnes a la parrilla, cacerolas de marisco y paellas. Prueba su ensalada de crostas si te gusta el tomate y el ajo, sus chuletas de cordero están riquísimas. Cerrado los miércoles.

IT'S TIME FOR VITAMIN SEA

OFFICIAL STORE
The Store
SAL de IBIZA®
SAL de IBIZA®
Cristal de la Vida
IBIZA
...Fashion Brands, Gastronomy, Music, Books ...
SANTA EULALIA - CARRETERA SANTA EULALIA KM.3,4
SAN JOSÉ - CARRETERA IBIZA - SAN JOSÉ KM.6,5
SAL de IBIZA®
Cristal de la Vida
IBIZA
Unique on The Store

Ca na Pepeta

Ctra. San Juan
Tel: 971.325.023

The classic whitewashed facade of this place, with its blue painted doors is as cute as a postcard and a landmark on the San Juan road. I don't go here that often but by the looks of it most of the island locals do, as its lovely shaded terrace is consistently packed throughout the week. Closed Tuesdays.

La fachada blanca de este lugar con sus puertas pintadas de azul es de postal y un punto de referencia en la carretera de San Juan. No vengo aquí pero parece que gran parte de la isla sí, ya que su terraza a la sombra siempre está a tope toda la semana. Cerrado los martes.

Can Guimó Tabac

Ctra. San Juan,
Tel: 971.325.116

This delightful little place stuck to the San Juan road is run by sweet Esteban and Carolina and is a favourite lunch spot of mine when in the area. They make the tastiest meals, that are all organic and fresh. I love the warm "Pan de yuca", which is a small, round cheese bread of cassava flour from Ecuador. It has a tobacco shop stuck to it as well with P.O. boxes.

Este coqueto restaurante pegado a la carretera de San Juan regentado por Esteban y Carolina es uno de mis lugares favoritos para almorzar si estoy en la zona. Todo aquí esta recién hecho y es ecológico. Prueba el "Pan de Yuca" que son bollitos de queso y harina de cassava de Ecuador. Tiene un estanco al lado y apartados de correos.

Can Curuné

Ctra. San Juan, Km 17,5
Tel: 971.333.054

A roadside restaurant, bar and shop that nourishes the surrounding countryside community with its restaurant and organic-focused supermarket. I love having a morning coffee here, a lunch with friends or a dinner after the beach. The owners are lovely, and if you just need to do a quick shop and don't fancy bumping into anyone, go in the back way from the car park! They serve Moroccan food with the obligatory mint tea every Saturday. Closed Sunday.

Este restaurante, bar y tienda alimenta a la comunidad rural de la zona con su restaurante y supermercado esencialmente ecológico, me gusta tomarme un café por las mañanas aquí, comer con amigos o cenar después de la playa. ¡Me encanta! Los propietarios son muy simpáticos, y si necesitas hacer una compra rápida y no te apetece encontrarte con nadie, entra por la parte trasera desde el aparcamiento. Sirven comida marroquí con el obligatorio té de menta cada sábado. Domingo cerrado.

HANDCRAFTED
WORLD FAMILY
IBIZA
WITH LOVE
Ibiza
In The Campo
Crta.San Joan Km17-500
07810 Sant Joan de Labritja
(Next to Can Curuné)
Info +34 971 333 201
Barcelona
Bulevard Rosa
Paseo de Gracia n° 55,
tienda n°40
08007 Barcelona
Info +34 932 721 082
www.worldfamilyibiza.com

..SHOPS ON THE ROAD

TIENDAS POR LA CARRETERA..

World Family Ibiza

Ctra. San Juan, Km 17,5
Tel: 646.757.827
worldfamilyibiza.com

Merel and Alok have created a colourful boho empire here. Think tassels and beads. They started out with a store in Las Dalias market and now have shops worldwide and an online store. Most of their pieces are one-offs and they've even been featured in Vogue. I dare you to go and leave empty-handed!

Merel y Alok han creado aquí un imperio boho lleno de color, Piensa en flecos y cuentas. Empezaron con una tienda en Las Dalias, y ahora tienen tiendas por todo el mundo y una tienda online. La mayoría de las piezas son únicas e incluso han salido en la revista Vogue. ¡Te reto a ir y salir con las manos vacías!

Sal de Ibiza

Ctra. Ibiza > Santa Eulalia km 3.4, Santa Eulalia

A shop selling a superb line of products made with 100% natural salt. Salt collected exclusively in the Natural Reserve of Ses Salines does not contain any additives or preservatives and has not undergone any refining. Simply sun-dried and ground in ancient stone, and high in minerals that are vital for our health. I love the hibiscus salt!

Una tienda que vende una línea de productos hechos con sal 100% natural. La sal es recogida exclusivamente en la Reserva Natural de "Ses Salines" y no contiene ningún tipo de aditivos ni conservantes además no se ha sometido a ningún tipo de refinación. Simplemente se ha secado al sol y molido. Es rica en minerales que son vitales para la salud. Me encanta la sal de la flor de hibisco!

..SLEEP INLAND

DORMIR EN EL CAMPO..

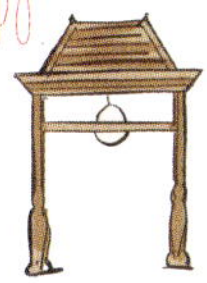

Atzaró

Ctra. Sant Juan, km 15
Tel: 971.338.838
atzaro.com

The Guasch family have made this family estate the most popular country hotel on the island. An oasis with ponds and orange groves. Its annual opening party marks the arrival of the summer for us locals. You don't have to be a guest to enjoy everything it has on offer. There's an amazing spa where you can book yourself in for a beauty treatment or a massage, and I love sweating it out in the Hammam steam room followed by a refreshing dip in the long freshwater pool.
The Veranda restaurant has a great day menu which makes this place perfect in every way.

La familia Guasch ha convertido su propiedad familiar en el hotel rural más popular de la isla. Un oasis de jardines y huertos de naranjos. Su fiesta de apertura anual marca la llegada del verano para los isleños. Y no tienes que ser huésped del hotel para disfrutar de todo lo que ofrecen aqui. Hay un spa magnífico donde puedes reservar tratamientos de belleza o un masaje, me encanta sudar en su hammam seguido de un refrescante baño en su larga piscina de agua natural.
El restaurante Veranda ofrece un menú del día haciendo que este lugar sea realmente perfecto.

Can Martí

Ctra. Ibiza>San Juan
Tel: 971.333.500
canmarti.com

This renovated Ibicencan farmhouse is also an ecologically-aware oasis. You can rent a cosy, rustic apartment with antique Indian furniture, whitewashed walls and your own kitchen, and there's even a grocery store selling organic produce grown on the on-site farm. The water in the natural pool is filtered through a system of gravel and plants, so it doesn't require salt or chemicals, and there's a scented hammam where you can get a massage.

Esta renovada finca ibicenca también es un oasis ecológico. Puedes alquilar un apartamento acogedor y rústico con mobiliario indio antiguo, paredes encaladas y tu propia cocina. Incluso hay una tienda de verduras que vende productos ecológicos en el mismo complejo de la finca. El agua de la piscina natural se filtra a través de un sistema de grava y plan-

Super ca'n Guasch

THE STORY OF CAN GUASCH

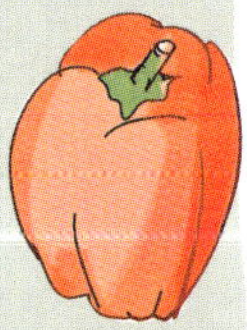

The story of "supermarket" Can Guasch started 30 years ago, when times were different and we're talking about the last century! Things have changed so much since then... People would buy anything that they could not grow or make at home. Every time a new product came to Can Guasch it was a an event. Neighbors and friends came running to the store to be the first to see. Every afternoon, before closing, they would all got together in Can Guasch to make "xerradeta" and tell the stories of the day. In those days, of course, Internet and mobile phones were yet to be invented. Today Can Guasch offers a wide range of fruits and vegetables from the island and outside, as well as a variety of health products, cereals, nuts and other delicacies from around the world. Although the years have passed, Can Guasch remains a corner to find that bit of history and the true essence of Ibiza.

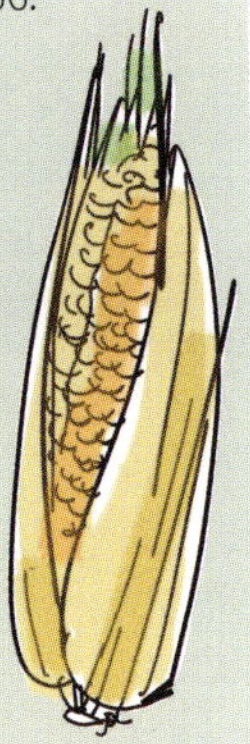

LA HISTORIA DE CAN GUASCH

La historia del "supermercado" Can Guasch empezó hace ya 30 años, cuando los tiempos eran otros - ¡y es que estamos hablando del siglo pasado! Las cosas han cambiado tanto desde entonces... La gente iba a comprar todo aquello que no se podía cultivar o elaborar en casa.

Cada vez que llegaba un producto nuevo a Can Guasch era todo un acontecimiento. Vecinos y amigos se acercaban corriendo a la tienda para ser los primeros en verlo y probarlo.

Todas las tardes, antes de cerrar, nos juntábamos en Can Guasch para hacer la xerradeta y contarnos las anécdotas del día.

En esos días, claro está, Internet y los móviles estaban aún por inventar. Hoy en día Can Guasch ofrece un amplio surtido de frutas y verduras de la isla y de fuera, gran variedad de productos para la salud, cereales, frutos secos y otros manjares provenientes de todo el mundo.

tas y por eso no requiere sal o químicos para su mantenimiento. Hay un hamman aromatizado donde puedes darte también un masaje

Agroturismo Can Gall

Ctra. San Juan, km 17,2
Tel: 971.337.031
agrocangall.com

When friends stayed here last summer I went to visit for the first time, and fell in love with it. It's set in a beautiful old farmhouse with little chill out areas and lots of bougainvillea, and all exquisitely done. Rustic luxe to the max, there are 11 rooms and a gorgeous pool surrounded by a pretty patio.

Cuando unos amigos míos se hospedaron aquí el año pasado fui a visitarlos por primera vez y me enamoré al instante. Está situado en una vieja finca con pequeñas zonas de chill out y muchas buganvillas, y todo decorado de forma exquisita. Lujo rústico al máximo, 11 habitaciones y una piscina rodeada de un patio encantador.

Casa Naya

Ctra. San Juan, km 16.5
Tel: 971 325.264
casanaya.com

I have never been to this hotel but friends tell me that they loved it. A true get a way in the north with gorgeous rooms and a heavenly swimming pool. There is also a jacuzzi and a tennis court if you fancy a game. The team here is very friendly and always happy to help you. Not more than 20 minutes away from the beach.

Nunca he estado en este hotel pero amigos me dicen que les encantó. Escondido en el campo en el norte con habitaciones preciosas y una piscina celestial. También hay un jacuzzi y una pista de tenis, si te apetece un partido. El equipo aquí es muy amable y siempre dispuesto a ayudarte. A no más de 20 minutos en coche de la playa..

Can Marquet

Ctra. San Lorenzo > San Juan
Tel: 971.197.558
canmarquet.com

People rave about this traditional farmhouse hotel which is over 100 years old. Located on top of a hill surrounded by gardens, fruit trees and vines, it has panoramic views over the countryside all the way to Santa Gertrudis and a lovely swimming pool to lounge by.

Sólo oigo cosas buenas de este hotel tradicional en una finca centenaria Está en lo alto de una montaña rodeado de jardines, árboles frutales y viñedos, con vistas panorámicas desde el campo hasta Santa Gertrudis y hay una piscina donde relajarse.

Casa Colonial

Ctra. Santa Eulalia, Km 2
Tel: 971.338.001
casa-colonial-ibiza.com

Admittedly I have not been here for a while but was pleasantly surprised the last time I went.
It is a gorgeous restaurant set in an old colonial style farm house. They do a lot of big events here but it is also a very romantic spot, so it is perfect for a cosy dinner for 2.

La verdad es que hace tiempo que no vengo aquí pero cuando fui me sorprendió gratamente. Es un precioso restaurante en una antigua casa de campo de estilo colonial. Hacen grandes eventos, pero también es un lugar muy romántico y perfecto para una cena íntima para 2.

Les Terrasses

Ctra. Santa Eulalia, Km 1
Tel: 971.332.643
lesterrasses.net

French elegance meets boho chic in this cosy hotel. With twelve elegantly whitewashed casitas and a shaded swimming pool set into a lush walled garden, this place is so charming, quirky and romantic. They do Moroccan Nights and Provençale cooking the rest of the time.

Elegancia francesa mezclada con boho chic en este acogedor hotel rural. Con doce casitas blancas y una piscina a la sombra en un exuberante jardín amurallado. Este lugar es tan encantador, extravagante y romántico. Hacen noches Marroquíes y el resto del tiempo ofrecen cocina provenzal.

SAN RAFAEL SANT RAFEL

This is a little drive through village on the way to or from San Antonio. From its church you have a stunning view of Ibiza Town. Hosting a lovely selection of restaurants and a handy gas station at the back as you head to San Antonio. It's like the quiet before the storm in summer!

Éste es un pueblo pequeño de camino a San Antonio. Desde su iglesia tienes impresionantes vistas de la ciudad de Ibiza. Tiene una selección de restaurantes buenos y una gasolinera muy útil en la salida hacia San Antonio. ¡En verano es como la calma antes de la tormenta!

..EAT ..COMER

Es Furnell

Pintor Narcís Puget, 2, San Rafael
Tel: 971.198.975

This little roadside takeaway place does heavenly home-made food. The blackboard outside has all their day specials up, which range from rabbit stews to Basque fish dishes. Every day they do a different menu but on Sundays there's always paella.

La comida casera para llevar de este pequeño establecimiento está deliciosa. La pizarra de fuera anuncia los platos del día, con una variedad que incluye desde estofado de conejo a platos de pescado vascos. Cada día cambian el menú pero los domingos siempre hay paella.

Can Pilot

Carretera Eivissa, San Rafael
Tel: 971.198.293
asadorcanpilot.com

This place is a favourite with island residents, as the food is simple and really good and all at a reasonable price. I love the "entraña" which is a tender strip of meat grilled with masses of sea salt to make it soooo damn juicy. They also have lamb chops, chicken and a giant T-Bone, which is part-cooked on a charcoal BBQ and then brought to your table on a mini-grill. All accompanied with roast peppers, tomatoes or potatoes. It's great for lunch on a Sunday and always packed with Ibicenco families. As you can't book here and it gets very busy, get here early.

Este sitio es un favorito entre los residentes de la isla, ya que la comida es simple pero muy buena y a un precio muy razonable. Me encanta la entraña a la parrilla con montones de sal gruesa que la hace tan jugosa. También tienen chuletas de cordero, pollo y un chuletón gigantesco, que lo cocinan parcialmente en la parrilla y luego lo traen a tu mesa en un mini-grill. Todo acompañado de pimientos, patatas y tomates asados. Es magnífico para comer los domingos y siempre está lleno de familias ibicencas. Como no puedes reservar y se llena rápido, lo mejor es llegar pronto.

CERAMICS CAN KINOTO

A little roadside ceramic workshop here since the 1970s, and if you are after traditional Ibicenco plates, jugs and figurines you have to stop and look.

Un taller de cerámica en la carretera que lleva aquí desde 1970. Si te gustan platos, jarras y figuras tradicionales ibicencos, tienes que pararte a ver.

Av. S R Isidor Macabich Av. D, 44, San Rafael,
Tel: 971 19 82 62
cankinoto.com

Es Tancó

Avenida Isidor Macabich, 9
San Rafael
Tel: 971.198.599

This unpretentious roadside eatery is great for their rice dishes, and every Tuesday and Thursday they do a "NON STOP PIZZA" night. They also do great cheese boards to stave of the hunger pangs while you wait for your meal.

Este restaurante sin pretensiones es magnífico por sus platos de arroz y cada martes y jueves también hacen una pizza tras otra toda la noche. También preparan una riquísima tabla de quesos para calmar el hambre mientras esperas tu comida.

Can Fresco

Avda. Isidor Macabich, 11
San Rafael
Tel: 680.374.653

This is a great little drive by eatery beside Es Tanco. It serves homemade food all day long, and from May to October it is open 24 hours.

Un pequeño restaurante para llevar comida casera a casa y que está abierto todo el día. De mayo a octubre está abierto las 24 horas del día.

A DRINK ON THE OUTSKIRTS...
DE COPAS POR LAS AFUERAS...

Ibiza Underground

Ctra. Ibiza > San Antonio
Tel: 971.198.015
ibizaunderground.com

The ultimate insider's secret, Underground's flyers insist 'it's not for everyone.' An Ibiza clubbing experience with a twist, this large renovated finca in San Ráfael plays host to the islands hottest unknown talent, so you'll be mingling with the local cool-cats.

Como un secreto muy bien guardado, los flyers del Underground dicen 'no es para todos los públicos'. Es un toque diferente a la experiencia normal del clubbing en Ibiza. En esta enorme finca en San Rafael es donde se reúnen talentos de la isla y la gente más enrollada de la zona y de los alrededores.

DINING ON THE OUTSKIRTS...
COMER A LAS AFUERAS...

Las Dos Lunas

Ctra. Ibiza > San Antonio, Km5
Tel: 971.198.102
lasdoslunas.com

The food is delicious and the wine list is really good. This classic restaurant has been here forever with gorgeous staff serving heavenly food in a beautiful setting of enclosed gardens on the side on the big road just after Amnesia nightclub. There's also a little shop selling great dresses and tops that'll makes you want to get changed again half way through the night.

La comida es deliciosa y la carta de vinos es muy buena. Este restaurante clásico lleva aquí toda la vida con un servicio muy amable que sirve comida deliciosa en un entorno precioso de un jardin encerrado. También hay una pequeña tienda que vende bonitos vestidos y tops y hará que quieras cambiarte de modelito a media noche.

LA BELLE IBIZA

in the centre of San Rafael village is this gorgeous place made up of different bohemian spaces all with a Balearic touch. The perfect place for a cocktail at one of their Bars after which you can choose to dine inside or outside on their beautiful flowered terrace under the stars. They offer a fusion of Spanish and French cuisine with Asian influences, and touches of Nikkei, Check their website for events all summer. Their is also a fab shop. Closed mondays.

Un lugar precioso con espacios bohemios en el centro de Sant Rafel. El lugar perfecto para tomarte un cóctel en uno de sus bares y luego cenar dentro o fuera en su hermosa terraza floreada bajo las estrellas. Ofrecen cocina española y francesa con influencias asiáticas y toques de Nikkei. visita su pagina web para ver los eventos durante el verano. También hay una tienda divina. Cerrado los lunes.

Avda. Isidor Macabich 6,
San Rafael,
Tel: 971.198.335
labelleibiza.com

5 THINGS YOU SHOULD DO
5 COSAS QUE DEBERÍAS HACER CUANDO ESTÉS AQUÍ

1. Hire a Mehari (p.256)
Alquilar un Mehari

2. Swim across the divide to Espalmador island
Nada por el entre-agua a la isla de Espalmador

3. Go riding on the beach with Es Boixets (p.304)
Montar a caballo en la playa con Es Boixets

4. Pizza + Pannacota at Macondo, Sant Ferrán (p.273)
Pizza y Pannacota en Macondo, Sant Ferrán

5. Watch the sunset from Punta Rasa, Cala Saona
Ver la puesta de sol desde Punta Rasa, Cala Saona

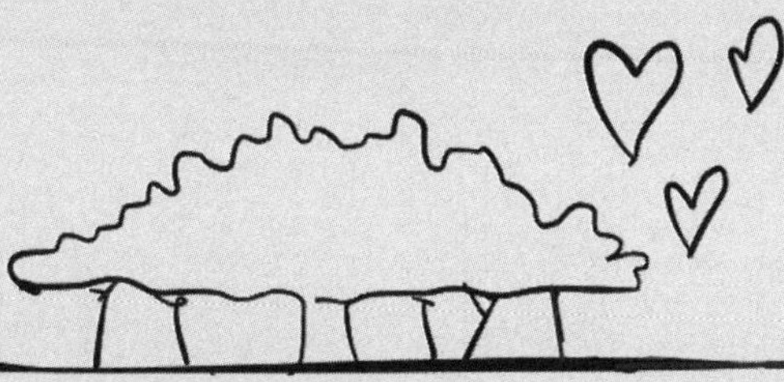

FORMENTERA

La Savina
San Francisco
San Fernando
Es Pujols, Es Caló,
La Mola & beaches

La Savina, Sant Francesc,
San Ferrán, Es Pujols, Es Caló,
La Mola y las playas

AGENDA

POPULAR PARTIES, EVENTS AND MARKETS ON FORMENTERA
FIESTAS POPULARES, EVENTOS Y MERCADILLOS

Things that are worth going to. Cosas que merecen la pena hacer.

Check websites for exact dates/Ver info web para fechas exactas
formenteranatural.comAgenda ,*formenteranatural.com, formenterajazzfestival.com*

MAY-MAYO

- **Fiestas de San Ferrán**. End of May/final de mayo.
- **VIII Edición NB Formentera 8km.** Info: formenteratorun.com
- **Walk Formentera/Vuelta a pie.** Info: amicsdeformentera.cat
- **Market/Mercadillo, la Savina**. Every day/todos los dias.
- **Market/Mercadillo, La Mola.** Wednesdays + Sundays/miercoles y domingos. 17 - 22 h.
- **Market/Mercadillo,Sant Ferran.** Thurs, Fridays + Saturdays/Jueves, viernes y sab. 21 - 24 h.
- **Market/Mercadillo, Sant Francesc**. Mondays to Saturdays/Lunes a Sabado. 10 - 14 h
- **Market/Mercadillo, Es Pujols**. Every day/todos los dias. 20 a 24 hs

JUNE-JUNIO

- **Summer Solstice/Fiestas de San Juan, 23-24.**
- **Formentera Jazz Festival:** Friday + Saturday/viernes y sabado. Info: formenterajazzfestival.com
- **Regata XXVIII Trofeo Peñon De Ifach.** Info: trofeopeñondeifach.es
- **Formentera Flower de Sant Joan, La Mola.** Info: formenteranatural.comAgenda
- **Live music/musica en vivo, Es Pujols.** Thursdays/jueves.
- **Live Rock/musica rock, Sant Ferran.** Fridays/viernes.
- **Live Jazz/musica jazz en vivo, Sant Francesc.** Saturdays/sabados.
- **Market/Mercadillo, la Savina**. Every day/todos los dias.
- **Market/Mercadillo, La Mola.** Wednesdays + Sundays/miercoles y domingos. 17 - 22 h.
- **Market/Mercadillo,Sant Ferran.** Thurs, Fridays + Saturdays/Jueves, viernes y sab. 21 - 24 h.
- **Market/Mercadillo, Sant Francesc**. Mondays to Saturdays/Lunes a Sabado. 10 - 14 h
- **Market/Mercadillo, Es Pujols**. Every day/todos los dias. 20 a 24 hs

JULY-JULIO

- **Open Air Cinema in O.V/Cine al aire libre V.O., Sant Francesc.** Tuesdays/martes
- **Open Air Cinema in O.V/Cine al aire libre V.O., Sant Ferran.** Thursdays/jueves.
- **Fiestas del Carmen, La Savina.** Info: formenteranatural.comAgenda
- **Formentera Flower Beach/playa, Es Pujols.** Info: formenteranatural.comAgenda
- **Formentera Flower San Jaume, Sant Francesc.** Info: formenteranatural.comAgenda
- **Live music/musica en vivo, Es Pujols.** Thursdays/jueves.

JULY-JULIO (CONT)

- **Live Rock/musica rock, Sant Ferran.** Fridays/viernes.
- **Live Jazz/musica jazz en vivo, Sant Francesc.** Saturdays/sabados.
- **Market/Mercadillo, la Savina**. Every day/todos los dias.
- **Market/Mercadillo, La Mola.** Wednesdays + Sundays/miercoles y domingos. 17 - 22 h.
- **Market/Mercadillo,Sant Ferran.** Thurs, Fridays + Saturdays/Jueves, viernes y sab. 21 - 24 h.
- **Market/Mercadillo, Sant Francesc**. Mondays to Saturdays/Lunes a Sabado. 10 - 14 h
- **Market/Mercadillo, Es Pujols**. Every day/todos los dias. 20 a 24 hs

AUGUST-AGOSTO

- **Open Air Cinema in O.V/Cine al aire libre V.O., Sant Francesc.** Tuesdays/martes
- **Open Air Cinema in O.V/Cine al aire libre V.O., Sant Ferran.** Thursdays/jueves.
- **Fiestas, Es Calo.** Info: formenteranatural.comAgenda
- **Live music/musica en vivo, Es Pujols.** Thursdays/jueves.
- **Live Rock/musica rock, Sant Ferran.** Fridays/viernes.
- **Live Jazz/musica jazz en vivo, Sant Francesc.** Saturdays/sabados.
- **Market/Mercadillo, la Savina**. Every day/todos los dias.
- **Market/Mercadillo, La Mola.** Wednesdays + Sundays/miercoles y domingos. 17 - 22 h.
- **Market/Mercadillo,Sant Ferran.** Thurs, Fridays + Saturdays/Jueves, viernes y sab. 21 - 24 h.
- **Market/Mercadillo, Sant Francesc**. Mondays to Saturdays/Lunes a Sabado. 10 - 14 h
- **Market/Mercadillo, Es Pujols**. Every day/todos los dias. 20 a 24 hs

SEPTEMBER-SEPTIEMBRE

- **Open Air Cinema in O.V/Cine al aire libre V.O., Sant Francesc.** Tuesdays/martes
- **Open Air Cinema in O.V/Cine al aire libre V.O., Sant Ferran.** Thursdays/jueves.
- **Live music/musica en vivo, Es Pujols.** Thursdays/jueves.
- **Live Rock/musica rock, Sant Ferran.** Fridays/viernes.
- **Live Jazz/musica jazz en vivo, Sant Francesc.** Saturdays/sabados.
- **Market/Mercadillo, la Savina**. Every day/todos los dias.
- **Market/Mercadillo, La Mola.** Wednesdays + Sundays/miercoles y domingos. 17 - 22 h.
- **Market/Mercadillo,Sant Ferran.** Thurs, Fridays + Saturdays/Jueves, viernes y sab. 21 - 24 h.
- **Market/Mercadillo, Sant Francesc**. Mondays to Saturdays/Lunes a Sabado. 10 - 14 h
- **Market/Mercadillo, Es Pujols**. Every day/todos los dias. 20 a 24 hs

OCTOBER-OCTUBRE

- **Fiestas del Pilar, La Mola** Info: formenteranatural.comAgenda
- **Live music/musica en vivo, Es Pujols.** Thursdays/jueves.
- **Live Rock/musica rock, Sant Ferran.** Fridays/viernes.
- **Live Jazz/musica jazz en vivo, Sant Francesc.** Saturdays/sabados.
- **Market/Mercadillo, la Savina**. Every day/todos los dias.
- **Market/Mercadillo, La Mola.** Wednesdays + Sundays/miercoles y domingos. 17 - 22 h.
- **Market/Mercadillo,Sant Ferran.** Thurs, Fridays + Saturdays/Jueves, viernes y sab. 21 - 24 h.
- **Market/Mercadillo, Sant Francesc**. Mondays to Saturdays/Lunes a Sabado. 10 - 14 h
- **Market/Mercadillo, Es Pujols**. Every day/todos los dias. 20 a 24 hs

LA PRIMERA EMPRESA EN FORMENTERA DE ALQUILER DE MEHARIS
THE FIRST MEHARI RENTAL COMPANY IN FORMENTERA
FORMENTERA MEHARIS
Vive tus vacaciones con un coche diferente
Enjoy your holiday with an original car
DISPONEMOS DE ASISTENCIA 24 HORAS CON MEHARIS DE SUSTITUCIÓN
WE HAVE A 24 HOUR BREAKDOWN SERVICE WITH MEHARI REPLACEMENTS
www.formenterameharis.com
info@formenterameharis.com

FORMENTERA

It can be easy to forget that you don't have to travel to the other side of the world to find outstandingly beautiful places, and Formentera always reminds me of this. Ibiza's little sister island is one of my favourite spots on earth, and whenever I come here I feel blessed that it remains so unspoilt despite the tourism. I know it sounds mad, but I come here on holiday from Ibiza!

Puede ser fácil olvidarse de que no tienes que viajar al otro lado del mundo para encontrar lugares de verdadera belleza, y Formentera siempre me recuerda esto. La hermana pequeña de Ibiza es uno de mis lugares favoritos de la tierra y siempre que vengo aquí me siento bendecida porque continúa intacta a pesar del turismo. Sé que suena a locura pero vengo aquí de vacaciones desde Ibiza.

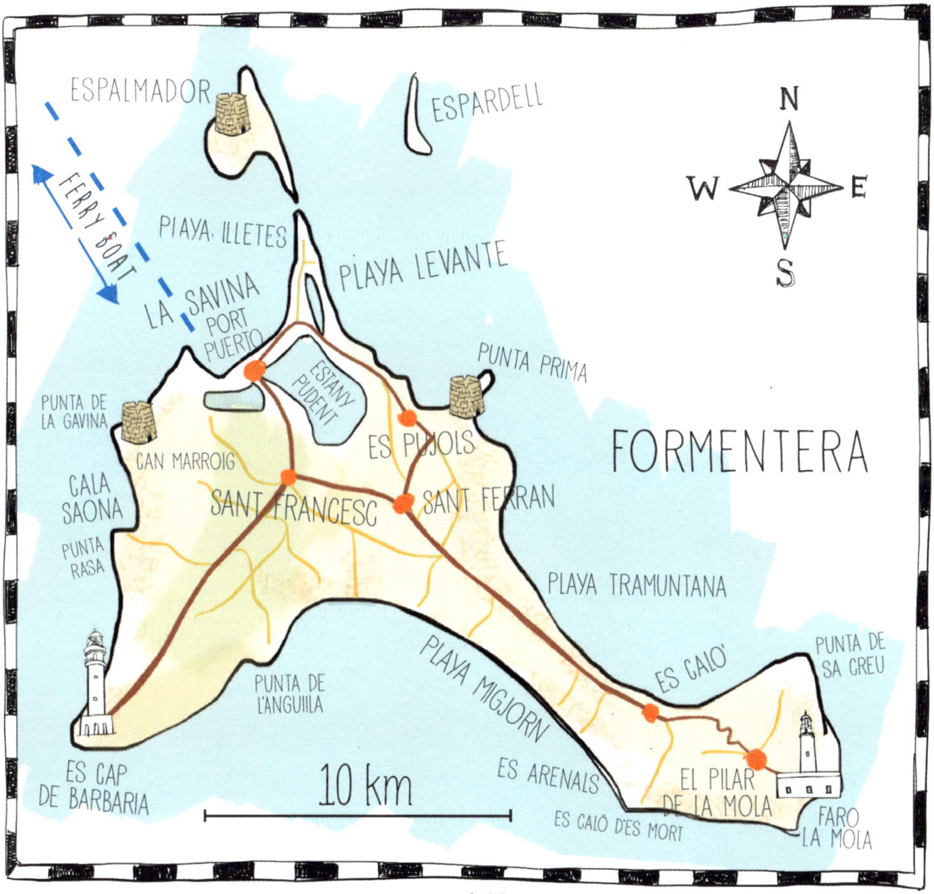

LA SAVINA PORT - PUERTO

"click"

This little fishing port is where you arrive on the ferry from Ibiza, and immediately the world slows down to half the pace. The gateway for the whole island, the little town here has a great choice of car and bike rentals (opposite page) just up from the dock and a selection of hotels, bars and shops dotted all around. If you're short on cash, rent a bicycle and cycle to Illetes beach, which is directly on the left as you leave the village. In the evenings there's a little hippy market.

Este pequeño puerto pesquero es donde llegas en ferry desde Ibiza, e inmediatamente el mundo parece disminuir su paso al menos a la mitad. Es el punto de salida para toda la isla y por ello este pequeño pueblo tiene una gran selección de alquileres de coche y motos junto al muelle y una selección de hoteles, bares y tiendas esparcidos por todas partes. Si tienes poco presupuesto, alquila una bicicleta y pedalea hasta la playa de Illetas, que está a la izquierda al salir del pueblo. Por las noches hay un pequeño mercadillo hippy.

..EAT, DRINK + SLEEP
...COMER, BEBER + DORMIR

Luna
La Savina
Tel: 971 321 585

Some friends were on a loved-up weekend and decided to try this place as it looked intimate and sort of romantic. I'm happy to recommend it as they said the staff were delightful and helpful when it came to the menu, and it was all delicious. I plan to try it for myself next time I'm in the port.

Unos amigos estuvieron de fin de semana romántico y decidieron probar este lugar ya que parecía muy íntimo y romántico. Me alegra recomendarlo ya que me dijeron que el servicio era encantador y amable y la comida estaba deliciosa. Planeo probarlo la próxima vez que esté en el puerto.

Amarre 32
Marina Deportiva de Formentera
La Savina

I only know about this café because my daughter says that they have the best potato omelette in the world! It is right beside her diving school and a great little spot for a coffee and a omelette.

Conozco esta cafetería porque mi hija dice que tienen la mejor tortilla de patatas del mundo. Está justo al lado

de la escuela de buceo y es un lugar perfecto para tomarte un café y una tortilla.

Gastro...mania

C/ Almadrava, 67
La Savina
Tel: 971.323.311

A Little spot on the roadside in the main port of La Savina. They do food all day and take-away as well. You can also grab your picnic here if you are off on a boat for the day.

Un pequeño local a la llegada al puerto de la Savina. Hacen comida todo el día; además, si vas a pasar un día en barco también tienen servicio para llevar.

Formentera Bakery

C/ Mare de deu del Carme, 1
La Savina
Tel: 722.266.925
formenterabakery.com

This is a charming little café slash bakery. It's a perfect place to stop for a coffee and breakfast after arriving on the ferry from Ibiza like we did. They make homemade cakes and breads. We sat outside on their sweet little terrace and ordered freshly baked croissants.

Una lugar encantador que es cafetería y panadería a la vez. Perfecto para tomarse un café y desayunar después de llegar en el ferry desde Ibiza, como hicimos nosotros. Nos sentamos en su coqueta terraza y pedimos croissants recién horneados con los cafés. Además hacen tartas caseras y pan.

Café del Lago

Ed. Sabina Playa,
Avenida del Mediterráneo, 20
La Savina/Estany de Peix
Tel: 971.323.187
cafedellago.es

Set on the edge of the salty lake with stunning views just as you leave the port and head towards Illetas. They serve classic italian dishes using fresh produce from the island.

Ubicado justo a la salida del puerto en dirección Illetas y con impresionantes vistas al lago. Sirven platos italianos clásicos elaborados con productos frescos de la isla.

Can Carlitos

C/ Almadrava, s/n, La Savina
Tel: 971.322.570
cancarlitosformentera.com

This gorgeous restaurant opened last year and has become an immediate success due to its delicious tapas, seafood and rice dishes. The place is always full so book in advance.

Este restaurante abrió el año pasado y se ha convertido en un éxito inmediato debido a sus exquisitas tapas, mariscos y paellas. Está siempre lleno así que reserva con antelación.

CAR OR BIKE RENTAL

Motorbikes, scooters, bicycles and, yes, cars, but unless you have a lot of luggage or kids, get a motorbike as it's much more fun.

Motos, scooters, bicis y, coches, pero a menos que lleves mucho equipaje o niños, alquilar una moto que es lo más divertido.

MOTORENT MITGORN
Puerto de La Savina
Tel: 971.322.787
motorentmigjorn.com

LA MOLA RENT
Puerto de La Savina
Tel: 971.323.554
M: 679.493.790
lamolarent.com

diving center

VELLMARI

OPEN WATER DIVER - DIVE MASTER - DISCOVER SCUBA - SNORKELLING

UNA EXPERIENCIA INOLVIDABLE PARA TODAS LAS EDADES

ESPECIALISTAS EN EXCURSIÓNES DE SCUBA Y SNORKEL

EL EQUIPO DE VELLMARI TE ACOMPAÑARA EN TU AVENTURA

FORMENTERA DIVE CAMP

AN UNFORGETTABLE EXPERIENCE FOR ALL AGES.

WE SPECIALIZE IN SCUBA AND SNORKELING EXCURSIONS

THE VELLMARI TEAM WILL TAKE YOU ON AN ADVENTURE

"My daughter loves the Formentera Dive Camp every summer"
"A mi hija la encanta el Formentera Cive Camp de cada verano"

HJORDIS FOGELBERG, MY IBIZA & FORMENTERA

Marina de Formentera, 14 - 07870 La Savina, Formentera (Spain)

Info + reservas: +34.971.32.105

www.vellmari.com • formentera@vellmari.com

DESCUENTO EN TODAS LAS ACTIVIDADES
DISCOUNT ON ALL ACTIVITIES
-15%

.. SLEEP...DORMIR

Hostal La Savina

Avda. Mediterranea, 22-40
La Savina
Tel: 971.322.279
hostal-lasavina.com

Friends of mine rave about this place, and if you like to stay near the port it's perfect. With a friendly atmosphere and really nice décor, they serve fabulous breakfasts, but it's great for dinner too.
There's a DJ playing ambient music on the terrace almost every day as the sun sets in the little lagoon "Estany des Peix" behind the hotel. Book a room with a sea view and you'll be in heaven.
Mis amigos sólo me hablan maravillas de este sitio y si quieres hospedarte cerca del puerto es perfecto.
Con una atmósfera cordial y una decoración muy bonita, sirven desayunos fabulosos y también es magnífico para cenar. Hay un DJ pinchando música ambiente en la terraza casi cada anochecer en la pequeña bahía "Estany des Peix" detrás del hotel. Reserva una habitación con vistas al mar y estarás en la gloria.

Hotel Lago Dorado

Camí de Can Marroig
Tel: 971.321.261

Ideal if you want a taste of the raw side of Formentera but still near the main port. There's no sandy beach but a stunning alternative sunset view over the saltwater lake. With a vintage touch, this is a no-frills option but has a great pool and restaurant with a sunset terrace.
El sitio ideal si quieres probar la Formentera más virgen pero necesitas estar cerca del puerto. No hay playa de arena pero es una alternativa preciosa para contemplar la puesta sobre las salineras. Con un toque vintage, es una opción sencilla pero con piscina, un restaurante magnífico y una terraza con vistas.

El Sueño

Porto Saler
Tel: 971.323.213
elsueño.com

I came across this little place once after leaving La Savina Port and just deciding to take a road on the right that I did not know at all.
I love doing that!
They serve simple tasty food and drinks everyday except Sundays. A great Little pitt stop where you can sip a glass of wine after the beach.
Tropecé con este bar restaurante mientras conducía por una carretera a la derecha después de salir del puerto de La Savina. Me apeteció cojer una carretera que no conocía. ¡Me encanta hacer eso!
Sirven una comida sabrosa y sencilla todos los días excepto los domingos. Parada perfecta para disfrutar de una copa de vino después de la playa.

SAN FRANCISCO SANT FRANCESC XAVIER

"click"

I call it the capital town of Formentera because it somehow seems the largest, although I am not sure it actually is. The church square here is like something out of a movie and scattered all around are lovely little shops and bars that are very inviting in the heat of the day. Parking is best at the back of the church. To get there, drive to the right as you enter the town and go up Carrer de Sant Joan until you see the parking.

Lo llamo la capital de Formentera porque de alguna forma parece ser la más grande, aunque no estoy segura de si lo es. La plaza de la iglesia es como sacada de una película y a su alrededor hay encantadoras tiendas y bares que vienen muy bien cuando el sol pega fuerte. Es mejor aparcar detrás de la iglesia. Para llegar aquí, gira a la derecha al entrar al pueblo y sube por Carrer de Sant Joan hasta que veas el parking.

* This parish church was built as a fortress in the early eighteenth century, to shelter from the numerous raids by pirates who invaded the island.

* Esta iglesia parroquial fué construida como una fortaleza a principios del siglo XVIII, para protegerse de las numerosas incursiones de piratas que invadían la isla.

..EAT, DRINK + SLEEP
..COMER, BEBER + DORMIR

Bar & Hostal Centro

Plaça Constitució, 3,
Sant Francesc
Tel: 971.322.063

One of the oldest Bars and Hostals in San Francisco Right in the middle of the main square facing the church, it originally opened in 1933 and is still run by the same family. You can stay in a simple room for under 40 euros a night and if you are lucky you'll even get a view of the beautiful church from your room. This little bar is always full of locals and sits right opposite the church in prime people-watching position. One of the oldest bars / guesthouses on the island, it used to be where the only radio telephone was located in the 1970s and has been run by the same family for over 40 years. Open all day.

Uno de los bares y hostales más antiguos de Sant Francesc. Ubicado justo en el centro de la plaza con la iglesia de frente, este lugar se inauguró en 1933 y todavía está a cargo de la misma familia. Puedes alquilar una habitación sencilla por menos de 40 euros la noche, y si tienes suerte podrás ver la hermosa iglesia desde tu habitación. Este pequeño bar siempre está lleno de gente local y se sitúa justo en frente de la iglesia en primera línea para contemplar a la gente pasar. Es uno de los bares / casa de huéspedes más antiguos de la isla y solía tener el único teléfono por radio en los años 70. Lleva en manos de la misma familia más de 40 años. Abierto todo el día.

Fonda Platé

C/ Jaume I, Sant Francesc
Tel: 971.322.313

Bang in the centre of San Francesc, this sprawling café bar is always packed with locals and tourists, and I always feel nostalgic when I sit here. It's like time stopped while the rest of the world continued on. Serving fresh juices and great salads alongside tasty bocadillos and they have live music too.

Justo en pleno centro de San Francesc este bar cafetería siempre está lleno de gente local y turistas sentados fuera, y no sé porqué pero me siento muy nostálgica cuando vengo aquí. Es como si el tiempo se detuviera mientras el resto del mundo continúa. Sirven zumos naturales y ensaladas magníficas además de bocadillos muy ricos. También tienen música en directo.

Café Matinal

C/ De Arxiduc Lluis Salvador, 18
Sant Francesc
Tel: 971.322.547

Hidden on a little side street just across from Bar Platé in the centre of town, this place is famous for its large and varied breakfasts and exquisite brunches. I love their home-made yogurt and muesli but they also do a large choice of pastries and juices. It's a lively little place.

Escondido en una de las calles traseras frente al Bar Platé en el centro del pueblo, este local es famoso por su gran variedad de desayunos y almuerzos exquisitos. Me encanta su yogur con muesli casero pero también hay una gran selección de bollería y zumos.

Sa Panxa

Avda. Castelló Guasch, 48
Sant Francesc
Tel: 971.329.106

My friend Sophie who is an enormous fan of Formentera and escapes over to the island whenever she can, came acros this little eatery on one of her last visits and raved about the pizzas. Something about caramelized onions on top. They have live music on certain eveninga so it sounds like a little hotspot to me.

Mi amiga Sophie, que es una enorme fan de Formentera y se escapa a la isla cada vez que puede, encontró este pequeño restaurante en una de sus últimas visitas y me hablo maravillas de las pizzas. Algo sobre cebolla caramelizada....Ponen music en vivo en ciertas noches por lo que me suena como gran opcion un dia de estos.

DON'T MISS IN JULY
EN JULIO NO TE PIERDAS

FLOWER POWER PARTY
visitformentera.com/agenda

Ca Na Pepa

Plaça de sa Constitució, 5, Sant Francesc
Tel: 971.321.091
canapepa.com

I got quite overexcited when I first discovered this quaint Italian cafe. The breakfasts here are heavenly. Try their Eggs Benedict or their American-style pancakes, and they also do great lunches and tapas. So relaxed and rustic-chic, with that faded wood vibe throughout, I always find it hard to leave.

Me alegré un montón cuando descubrí esta pequeña cafetería italiana, ya que los desayunos aquí son divinos. Prueba sus Huevos Benedict o sus tortas al estilo americano, y también preparan comidas y tapas deliciosas. Es relajado, chic y con un diseño interior en madera desteñida por todo el local, siempre me cuesta marcharme de aquí.

Giovale

Santa Maria, 59, Sant Francesc
Tel: 971.322.758

We always head here for breakfast when we're doing a shop in this area. It's easy to find as it sits perched by the roundabout at the entrance of San Francesc, and with its whitewashed beachy terrace covered with a climbing grapevine, is easy to spot from the road. The breakfast menu features the names of all the beaches of the island, and they serve good coffee and juices.

Siempre desayunamos aquí cuando venimos a hacer la compra. Es fácil de encontrar ya que está al lado de la rotonda en la entrada de San Francesc, y con su terraza blanca cubierta de viñas es fácil reconocerlo desde la carretera.
La carta de desayunos presenta nombres de las playas de la isla, y sirven muy buen café y zumos.

Cafeteria Es Glop

Afueras, 5 s/n, Edif. sa Sanieta, Sant Francesc
Tel: 971.322.966

This restaurant-slash-bar gets overlooked, but I once came in here on a rainy day and liked it a lot. My friend Karyn and I had a large eggy breakfast and juices that left us feeling completely replenished! They have a little free-for-all swap-shop, so grab a second-hand parasol and get on that beach already!

Este restaurante bar suele ser pasado por alto, pero una vez vine aquí un día de lluvia y me encantó el ambiente y su servicio. Está a las afueras de San Francesc. Mi amiga Karyn y yo nos tomámos un gran desayuno con huevos y zumos que nos dejó totalmente llenas. Tienen una tienda de intercambio, así que píllate una sombrilla de segunda mano y vete directo a la playa.

..EAT, DRINK + ENJOY THE DAY,
YOU ARE ON THE BEST PLACE IN THE WORLD!
...COME, BEBE + DISFRUTA DE TU DÍA, ¡ESTÁS EN EL MEJOR LUGAR DEL MUNDO!

Nautilus Cafeteria

Avda. 8 d'Agost
Sant Francesc
Tel: 673.083.050

A café on the corner of the street facing the supermarket. It is perfect for a tapa and a beer when you've just been shopping and need a little something. It is always packed with locals and it does italian style tapas too.

Esta cafetería situada en la esquina frente al supermercado hace ricas tapas al estilo italiano. Es perfecta para tomarte una caña y una tapa después de hacer compras. Siempre está llena de vecinos.

Es Marès Cafetería

C/ de Santa Maria,15
Sant Francesc
Tel: 971.323.216
hotelesmares.com

Attached to the Es Marès Hotel and always bustling with life, they serve lovely breakfasts on the white-washed shady terrace here. With home-made cakes and a selection of teas, there's also a lovely view of the quaint little street to enjoy.

Pegado al Hotel Es Marès y siempre rebosante de gente, sirven deliciosos desayunos en su blanqueada terraza. Con pasteles caseros y una selección de tés, también puedes disfrutar de una encantadora vista a las pequeñas callejuelas del pueblo.

Bollicine

Avda. Pla del Rey 77, Sant Francesc
Tel: 971.321.244
bollicine.es

A small cozy restaurant that offers excellent food at a good price. The staff here are friendly and everything tastes homemade. Sadly they don't have a great outside space as its right ion the sidewalk. But really worth a visit!

Un restaurante pequeño y acogedor que ofrece excelente comida a un buen precio. El personal es amable y todo sabe muy casero. No tienen mucho espacio exterior por estar justo en la acera, pero realmente vale la pena visitarlo.

Ca Na Joana

C/ de Berenguer Renart, 2
Sant Francesc
Tel: 971.323.160
canajoanaformentera.com

This is a stunning restaurant in the center of San Francisco. Set in an old town house with raw Stone walls.
It has such a romantic feel about it. The food is good but the setting is somehow better… I will return.

Un precioso restaurante en el centro de Sant Francesc ubicado en una casa antigua con paredes de piedra. Tiene un ambiente muy romántico y la comida es buena, pero el entorno es mejor... Volveré.

Ca Nova

C/ Eivissa, 14
Sant Francesc
Tel: 971.321.646

Giorgio, George and Vincent have this sweet place on the walking street serving amazing blend coffees, cocktails, tapas and salads. They also have a Little shop.

Giorgio, George y Vincent regentan este lugar muy agradable en la calle peatonal que sirve cafés, especiales, cócteles, tapas y ensaladas. También tienen una pequeña tienda.

Big Store

C/ d'Isidor Macabich, 2
Sant Francesc
Tel: 971.322.154

A surfer-style vintage bar with sweet, colourful chairs on the terrace and a collection of mismatched leather couches and chairs inside. This is a great place to start your day on a positive note, what with all that colour and their freshly squeezed natural juices. The local Italians love this spot.

Un bar estilo surfero con coquetas sillas de color en la terraza y una colección de sofás de piel y sillas desiguales. Es un lugar fantástico para empezar el día de forma positiva, con todo ese color y sus zumos recién exprimidos. A los italianos de la isla les encanta este sitio.

SHOPPING... FRESH PASTA?
PASTA FRESCA?

Il Pirata del Tortello

Sant Francesc
Tel: 687.091.745

A fabulous fresh pasta shop on the outskirts of town, they do the best raviolis here with some really fancy fillings. I love the eggplant and scamorza!
Closed Mondays.

Una tienda fabulosa de pasta fresca en las afueras del pueblo, hacen los mejores raviolis frescos con rellenos muy originales. Me encantan los de berenjena con scamorza.
Cerrado los lunes.

Pepi

C/ des Pla del Rei,
Sant Francesc
Tel: 971.322.314

I have a look in this shop every time I'm in Formentera. Selling vintage things, jewellery, accessories and bags, I bought a great skull ring here and always have my eye on a suede leather tassel bag. Find it on the main non-pedestrian street that goes through San Francesc to Cap des Barbaria.

Siempre que voy a Formentera echo un vistazo a esta tienda. Venden artículos vintage, joyería, accesorios y bolsos. Compré una anillo de calavera muy chulo y tengo echado el ojo a un bolso de ante con flecos. La encontrarás en la calle principal que va de Sant Francesc a Cap de Barbaria.

Las Brisas

Can Toni Guillerm, Sant Francesc
Tel: 971.322.815

I always find it impossible to not take a look inside this shop with its blue doors and rickety cane porch located just to the left of the church in the main square. They sell aged leather bags to die for and clothes for men and women. It's not cheap but still worth a look inside...

Me cuesta no entrar a echar un vistazo dentro de esta tienda con sus puertas azules y su desgastado porche de bambú justo a la izquierda de la iglesia en la plaza principal de Sant Francesc. Venden preciosos bolsos de piel y ropa para hombre y mujer. No es barato pero merece la pena mirar por si te apetece darte un capricho.

Balàfia

Sant Francesc
Tel: 659.397.181

I love this shop for its raw materials and ethnic, eco-chic. With masses of colours and textures, you'll find it off the square near the church of Sant Francesc. They also have great hats, necklaces and scarves.

Me encanta esta tienda de materias primas y eco-chic étnico. Con montones de colores y texturas, la encontrarás junto a la plaza cerca de la iglesia de Sant Francesc. También tienen magníficos sombreros, collares y pañuelos.

Vintage

C/ de Santa Maria 3, Plaza de La Iglesia, Sant Francesc
Tel: 971.321.984
vintageformentera.com

This boutique sits directly opposite Bar Platé at the top of Carrer Jaume I and Av. Vuit d'Agost. Full of gorgeous things and perfect for gifts, a little bracelet or a necklace to give your outfit a more Formentera vibe! They sell light and cool clothing and have tons of accessories displayed in cute baskets on top of the central table as you come in.

Esta encantadora boutique está justo enfrente del Bar Platé al final del Carrer Jaume I y la Avda. Vuit d'Agost. Tiene cosas preciosas y es perfecta para regalos. Suelo pararme para comprar algún brazalete o collar para darle a mi vestido un toque más formenterense. Venden prendas ligeras y frescas y tienen montones de accesorios distribuidos en bonitos cestos sobre una mesa central en la entrada.

Perfumeria Centrale

Can Toni Guillerm, Sant Francesc
Tel: 636.235.015

Right beside Las Brisas they sell a selection of scents made with the island aromas of salt and sea, lemon, resin or juniper. Just divine!

Justo al lado de Las Brisas venden una selección de aromas hechos de sal y mar, limón, resina, arena o madera de sabina... ¡Es divina!

Full Moon

C/ de Eivissa, 6,
Sant Francesc
Tel: 9713.22.376

A vintage bike guards the entrance to this cute, white-washed shop, which must have been photographed many a time. Dresses, tops, hats, bags, kaftans, sarongs and bikinis...

Una bici antigua guarda la entrada de esta tienda monísima y blanca, que debe haber sido fotografiada un millón de veces. Vestidos, tops, sombreros, bolsos, túnicas, pareos y bikinis...

Rhei

C/ Ibiza, 15
Sant Francesc
Tel: 971.322.804

If you feel the need to do a bit of retail therapy this little shop sells nice Womanswear, shoes, accessories, bags, home wear and it also has as a little art space.

Si sientes la necesidad de hacer compras, esta pequeña tienda vende cosas muy bonitas para mujer, además de zapatos, accesorios, bolsas o ropa de casa. También tiene un pequeño espacio de arte.

Acacia

Santa María, 8
Sant Francesc
Tel: 971.321.206
acaciaformentera.com

If you feel the need to do a bit of retail therapy this little shop sells nice Womanswear, shoes, accessories, bags, home wear a little art space.

Si sientes la necesidad de hacer compras, esta pequeña tienda vende cosas muy bonitas para mujer, además de zapatos, accesorios, bolsas o ropa de casa. También tiene un pequeño espacio de arte.

Ca Teua

Avda. Pla del Rey, 7
Sant Francesc
Tel: 971.321.078
cateua.com

A decoration shop at the round-a-bout into San Francesc that I always visit everytime I'm on the island. Three friends all island lovers, who love art, architecture and crafts decided to open this wonder. All objects and furniture in here have been made with materials from the island. Recycling and restoring. It is a treasure trove of island delights.

Una tienda de decoración justo antes de la rotonda a San Francesc que visito cada vez que estoy en la isla. Tres amigos, todos amantes de la isla, del arte, de la arquitectura y de la artesanía decidieron abrirla juntos. Los muebles y objetos estan elaborados con materiales propios de la isla, reciclando y restauradolos.

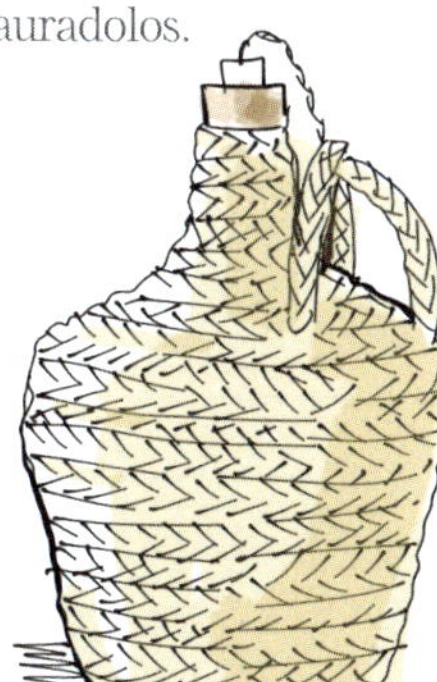

EAT + ENJOY
COMER Y DISFRUTAR

Can Gavinu

Ctra. de Sant Francesc, km 3,3
Tel: 971.322.421

A restaurant that has a definate Italian vibe to it. You can't miss it on the roadside as you drive from Sant Francesc to Sant Ferran. They serve great pasta dishes and home made raviolis which I love. The setting is divine with a terrace at the back of the old house.

Restaurante con un aire italiano que está perfectamente a la vista en la carretera que va desde Sant Francesc a Sant Ferran. Sirven ricos platos de pasta y raviolis caseros que a mí me encantan. La terraza en la parte de atrás de la finca es divina.

Can Carlos

Sant Francesc
Tel: 971.322.874
cancarlos.com

I make sure I go here once a summer, as it's certainly not cheap but the food is exceptional. If you take the kids give them a sandwich at home beforehand! They do delicious homemade pastas, meats, fish dishes and salads, and the dessert menu is absolutely mouth-watering. Tables are set in a delightful garden with fairy lights and soft music, making this the perfect place for a romantic evening after a long day beaching. Easy to find, just drive straight through

San Francesc towards the Barbaria lighthouse and it's there on your right just outside town.
Me aseguro de venir aquí al menos una vez en verano, ya que no es barato pero la comida es excepcional. Si traes a los niños dales un bocata en casa antes de venir. Hacen deliciosas pastas caseras, carnes, pescado y ensaladas y la carta de postres te hará la boca agua. Las mesas están distribuidas en un precioso jardín con lamparillas y música suave, convirtiéndolo en el restaurante perfecto para una cena romántica después de un largo día en la playa. Fácil de encontrar, atraviesa San Francesc hacia el faro y está a tu derecha justo a las afueras del pueblo.

Restaurante Es Cap

Ctra. Cap de Barbaria, Cruce de Cala Saona
Tel: 971.322.104

Sitting at the crossroads to Cala Saona bay and the Cap de Barbaria on the road from Sant Francesc, with tables set on a simple little terrace under a canopy of vines. I always go here when I come back from the Lighthouse sunset as it's really reasonably priced. The chef makes a great fish soup, which my daughter devours in seconds, while my favourite dish is the meat cooked on hot stones at your table, served with vegetables and potatoes.
Un restaurante simple, justo en el cruce de Cala Saona con

Cap de Barbaria en la carretera de Sant Francesc. Disfruta en su terraza pequeña y pintoresca protegida por un manto de viñas. Solemos venir despues de ver la puesta desde Cala Saona.
El chef prepara una deliciosa sopa de pescado que mi hija devora en segundos, mientras que mi plato favorito es el de carne asada sobre una piedra caliente, servido con verduras y patatas.

A MI Manera

Ctra.de Cala Saona
Tel: 871.322.903
amimaneraformentera.com

A unique restaurant set in the beautiful fields surrounded by wild nature. Lovely Chill out areas and shady patios is their look and feel. They specialise in seafood here and it really is the perfect place for a private event or a wedding reception.
Un restaurante único con zonas chill out y rincones de sombra situado en los hermosos campos salvajes de la isla. Son especialistas en mariscos y es un lugar per fecto para celebrar un evento privado o una boda.

Sud

Ctra. de Cala Saona, Cap de Barbaria
Tel: 971.322.903
sudformentera.com

Quite hidden away which is what I like. It's far from the tourist trail, inland and with views of the countryside. Set in an old Formentera farm house with a delightfiul outside terrace with tables among the trees and gardens. Simple mediterranean food.
Me gusta que esta escondido en el interior apartado del turismo y con vistas al campo . Úbicado en una antigua casa de campo Formenterense con una terraza exterior y mesas entre los árboles y jardines.
Cocina mediterranea.

..SLEEP AND ENJOY
...DUERME Y DISFRUTA

Es Marès

C/ de Santa María, Sant Francesc
Tel: 971.323.216
hotelesmares.com

This place sits bang in the centre of Sant Francesc. A boutique-style hotel with pale interiors and signature Formentera driftwood touches, rooms are sun-soaked and extremely comfortable. It also has spa treatments and is a great winter option as it`s open all year.
En el centro de Sant Francesc está este hotel boutique de interiores pálidos y toques de madera desteñida. Con habitaciones bañadas por el sol, es extremadamente cómodo. También ofrecen

tratamientos de spa así que es una buena opción para el invierno porque está abierto todo el año.

Casa Ariadna

Cami Vell de Sant Francesc a Cala Saona
casaariadnaformentera@gmail.com

This divine B&B in an old country house is exquisitely decorated. The rooms are all large but don't offer much privacy as the family live in the house as well. Located in Cala Saona, bougainvillea decorates terraces that overlook the ocean, and it's a great choice if you want a homey feeling. Surrounded by bougainvillea-draped porches overlooking the ocean, the breakfast buffet is legendary.

There's also very little phone coverage, but that can be a plus if you want to really disconnect. The Wifi does work though!

Esta divina casa de huéspedes en una vieja casa de campo ha sido decorada con exquisito encanto. Las habitaciones son grandes pero no ofrecen mucha privacidad ya que la familia también vive en la casa. Situada en Cala Saona, la buganvilla decora las terrazas que miran al mar, y es una opción magnífica si quieres un ambiente familiar. Hay muy poca cobertura móvil, pero eso puede ser algo bueno si realmente quieres desconectar. Aunque el Wifi funciona bien.

Hotel Cala Saona

Playa Cala Saona
Tel: 971.322.030
hotelcalasaona.com

In the most stunning location, and actually considered one of the most beautiful bays on the island. The sunset here is mid-blowing and on a clear day you can see Es Vedrà Island in Ibiza.

The hotel was recently refurbished and it has had a serious facelift, now becoming a 4 star Spa Hotel with a top restaurant, a boutique, a spa, a Gym and a luxurious swimming pool. The bedrooms are large and have gorgeous sea views or forest views and the suites have their own private terraces with jacuzzis. It is not a bohemian experience but perfect if you want to feel like royalty.

Este hotel se encuentra en una de las bahías más hermosas de la isla. Tiene una puesta de sol alucinante y en un día claro se puede apreciar la isla Es Vedrà en Ibiza. El hotel fue recientemente reformado, convirtiéndose en un hotel de 4 estrellas con un restaurante, una boutique, un spa, un gimnasio y una piscina de lujo. Las habitaciones son espaciosas y cuentan con magníficas vistas al mar o al bosque, además las suites tienen sus propias terrazas privadas con jacuzzis. Aunque no es una experiencia bohemia, es perfecta si quieres sentirte como un rey.

FORMENTERA CHIC

BOHO SLEEPING

DURMIENDO AL ESTILO BOHEMIO

A boutique online agency offering bijou apartments and studios across the island, this place will help bring out your inner boho babe! Think hammocks, lots of pale, driftwood furniture and cicadas chirping nearby. My favourite is the sea-view studio in La Savina.

Una agencia online que ofrece pequeños apartamentos y estudios por toda la isla, aquí te ayudarán a sacar tu boho interior: hamacas, montones de mobiliario de madera desteñida y en las cigarras chirriando cerca. Mi favorito es el estudio con vistas al mar en La Savina.

Av. Mediterráneo, 2, La Savina
Tels: 611.279.474 -602.650.734
formenterachic.com

Ses Eufabietes

Playa de Migjorn
Tel: 971. 322.595
seseufabietes.com

A 10 minute drive from the back of San Francesc-Ca Mari way. In the thick of a pine tree forest is Ses Eufabietes. Its kind of perfect for a romantic getaway or for those in search of peace and quiet. The apartments are all kitted out really nicely and there is a comunal pool and bar that serves food and drinks all day. The beach is a fun five minute walk through the forest.

Ses Eufabietes se encuentra en medio de un bosque de pinos. El lugar perfecto para una escapada romántica o para una familia en busca de paz y tranquilidad. Los apartamentos están muy bien y hay una piscina comunitaria y un bar que sirve comida y bebidas durante todo el día. La playa está a cinco minutos divertidos a pie a través del bosque.

Bungalows Es Pins

Ctra. De Ca Mari , Ca Mari
Playa de Migjorn
Tel: 971.328.291
espins.es

Bungalows set in a pine tree forest just a few metres from Migjorn Beach near the quiet area of Es Ca Marí. The complex has been here since the 70's and consists of apartments and rooms built in the Formentera style in small blocks of 4 and 8 units surrounded by pine trees and gardens overlooking the main restaurant and bar that has a pool and a nice terrace.

Unos bungalows situados en un bosque de pinos a pocos metros de la playa de Migjorn, cerca de la zona de Es Ca Marí. El complejo lleva aquí desde los años 70 y tiene apartamentos y habitaciones construidas al estilo de Formentera, en pequeños bloques de 4 y 8 unidades rodeados de pinos y jardines y con vistas al restaurante principal y al bar. Cuentan con una piscina y una bonita terraza.

..EAT AND ENJOY...
COME Y DISFRUTA

Restaurante Marlaca

Urb. Paraíso de los Pinos
Es Mal Pas
Tel: 971.321.670
marlaca.es

A Little oasis of a spot. tucked away at the end of a dusty track that is a bit hard to find but totally worth it. It is part of a holiday complex called Paraíso de los Pinos so you can follow the signs after crossing through Sant Francesc village. A relaxing atmosphere and delicious food. The beef tartar starter is great and then the cod brandade or the sirloin steak for seconds.

Un pequeño oasis escondido al final de un camino polvoriento algo difícil de encontrar, pero merece la pena. Es parte de un complejo turístico llamado Paraíso de los Pinos, así que sigue las indicaciones después de cruzar el pueblo de Sant Francesc. Tiene un ambiente relajado y una comida deliciosa.
El tartar de ternera está muy bueno y la brandada de bacalao o el bistec de solomillo están deliciosos.

Restaurante Pelayo

Playa de Migjorn
Tel: 984.835.946

I discovered this simple shack like restaurant two years ago with friends. It has a surfy vibe and they do a Paella on Sundays. The food is simple but ok and it's 2 steps from the sea and the beach is wild with no sunloungers so its pretty.

Hace dos años descubrí este sencillo restaurante tipo cabaña. Tiene un ambiente surfero y los domingos hacen paella. La comida es sencilla pero buena y está a 2 pasos del mar; además la playa es salvaje y no tiene tumbonas ni casi gente.

SAN FERNANDO SANT FERRAN DE SES ROQUES

One of my favourite villages in Formentera, you actually drive through it from Sant Francesc and Es Pujols. The church square is set back from the main road and there's a selection of old school bars and restaurants, as well as a little craft and handmade – only hippy market most evenings up by the church.

Uno de mis pueblos favoritos en Formentera, de hecho lo pasas conduciendo desde Sant Francesc ó Es Pujols. La plaza de la iglesia está detrás de la carretera principal y hay una selección de bares y restaurantes antiguos, además de un mercadillo hippy de productos artesanos, hechos a mano casi todas las noches junto a la iglesia.

..EAT IN THE SQUARE... COME EN LA PLAZA

Macondo

C/ Mayor 1, Sant Ferran.

My favourite restaurant in the whole world! I personally am not a big pizza person, but the pizzas here are out of this world. I also love their large salads and the mussels are also exquisite. For pudding try the Pannacotta, it's unbelievable! This wooden-benched place is set in the charming main walking street just down from Sant Ferrán church, and while you wait for your order you can take it in turns to walk up to the church through the little hippy market. You also have to try the Limoncello - made by the owner's mama, or so he says!

¡Mi restaurante favorito en todo el mundo! No suele gustarme la pizza, pero las que hacen aquí son fuera de serie. Sus ensaladas y sus mejillones, son exquisitos. No te vayas sin probar la Pannacotta con chocolate. Este local de bancos de madera está situado en la calle peatonal de Sant Ferrán, y mientras esperas tu pedido puedes tomar turnos para caminar hasta la iglesia recorriendo el pequeño mercadillo hippie. Me encanta sentarme y ver la gente local prepararse para la noche, y además tienes que probar el limoncello, está hecho por la mamá del dueño, ¡o eso dice!

Quartieri Spagnoli

C/. de La Cala En Baster, 10
Sant Ferran
Tel: 609.415.350

At the back of San Ferran village, to the far side of the Church is this house with a great Italian restaurant and cocktail Bar. I have never tried it but I have heard from friends that the pizzas are great and they do take away as well.

En la parte posterior del pueblo de Sant Ferran se encuentra esta casa con un restaurante italiano y un bar de cócteles. No lo he probado aún, pero mis amigos me han contado que las pizzas están muy ricas y que tienen servicio de comidas para llevar.

SLEEP, EAT...
COME, DUERME...

Fonda Pepe

C/ Mayor, Sant Ferran
Tel: 971.328.033

Just past the church of Sant Ferrán is one of the most mythical places in Formentera. Bob Dylan is said to have played chess here and Pink Floyd were linked to it in the 1960s, when they composed the music for the film "More" and spent time on the island. Attracting a colourful collection of locals, glam hippy wannabes and tourists, this restaurant has a dark, sombre interior and nothing much has changed with the decor since the 1970s. Good, cheap food and you can't book, so get here early and queue outside.

Justo pasado la iglesia de Sant Ferrán encontrarás uno de los lugares más míticos de Formentera. Se dice que Bob Dylan se sentaba aquí y jugaba al ajedrez y la banda Pink Floyd lo frecuentaba en los años 60, cuando compuso la música para la película More y pasó un tiempo en la isla. Atrae a un grupo variopinto de gente local, hippies glamurosos y turistas, y su interior oscuro y sombrío no ha cambiado mucho desde los años 70. La comida es buena y barata pero no puedes reservar, así que ve pronto y haz cola fuera con todos.

Hostal Illes Pitiüses

Avda. de Juan Castelló Guasch, 48
Sant Ferrán
Tel: 971.328.189

A hostal located on on the main road at the crossroads to Es Pujols and la Mola in Sant Ferran that is perfect to stay in, reasonably priced and comfy. The rooms facing the road can be a little noisy, especially with all the motorcycle traffic, although at night after the sun has set the traffic becomes minimal. It's ten minutes by car from most of the beaches, and I often come here to plug in my laptop as they have Wifi access and great breakfasts.

Un hostal sencillo situado en al borde del pueblo en la carretera principal a La Mola. Es un lugar perfecto para dormir a un precio razonable. Las habitaciones que dan a la carretera pueden ser un poco ruidosas, especialmente con el tráfico de motos de la isla, aunque por las noches después de la puesta de sol, el tráfico es mínimo. Está a diez minutos en coche de la mayoría de las playas y a menudo vengo aquí a enchufar mi ordenador porque tienen acceso wifi y un buen desayuno.

THE ISLAND WITH FISH IN THE TREES

PEIX SEC

A VARIETY OF LOCAL FISH, DRIED TRADITIONAL STYLE
IN THE SUN AND WIND, ON A JUNIPER TREE BRANCH.

VARIEDAD DE PESCADO LOCAL, SECADO AL SOL Y VIENTO,
AL ESTILO TRADICIONAL EN UNA SABINA, ÁRBOL LOCAL.

THE FLYING GURNARD, (Dactyopterus volitans)

This is a fish found in Formentera waters that looks normal when calm. When excited, it spreads its "wings", that are semi-transparent but tipped with a beautiful phosphorescent bright blue coloration to scare away predators.

PEZ GOLONDRINA (Dactylopterus volitans)

Este pez se encuentra en aguas de Formentera y parece normal cuando esta tranquilo. Pero cuando se excita, extiende sus "alas", que son semi-transparentes, pero con puntas de un hermoso color azul fosforescente para ahuyentar a los depredadores.

ES PUJOLS

This is the most touristy town on the island, but I have to admit it has a really pretty beach, some great restaurants, the best little ice-cream parlour and a little hippy market on the promenade. There is also an array of street bars at the back of the promenade so it's great for a silly night out, all with a strong Italian influence.

Éste es el pueblo más turístico de la isla pero tengo que admitir que tiene muy buenos restaurantes, la mejor heladería y un mercadillo hippie en el paseo que me encanta. También hay una variedad de bares en las callejuelas cerca del paseo así que es genial para una noche loca, y todo con un toque muy italiano.

EAT + ENJOY...
COME Y DISFRUTA

Kiosko Bartolo
Playa Es Pujols

A real Old-school Formentera lunch shack. I actually almost decided not to put it in the guide but then I need to share places like this with my readers and I also want to support the owners. They have simple salads and do the most amazing grilled prawns. It is down the little wooden walkway towards Chez Gherdi and a

cheaper option as well.

Un chiringuito de lo más auténtico para almorzar. En realidad casi decidi no ponerlo en la guía pero luego pensé que tengo que compartir lugares como este con mis lectores y también quiero apoyar a los propietarios. Tienen ensaladas y unas gambas a la plancha para morirse. Se llega por una pequeña pasarela de madera que también va a Chez Gherdi y es una opción más barata.

Chezz Gerdi
Es Pujols
Tels: 971.328.603 - 648.020.106

An Italian gourmet restaurant which you can walk to from Es Pujols if you take a right along the wooden seafront promenade. With lovely beachy decor, it's perfect if you are feeling a bit extravagant. Serving grilled meats, seafood and pasta as well as pizzas, I love the clam spaghetti.

Un restaurante gourmet italiano al que puedes llegar caminando desde Es Pujols si vas hacia la derecha por el paseo de madera junto al mar. Tiene una decoración preciosa y es perfecto si tienes ganas de darte un capricho, Sirven carnes al grill, pescado y pasta además de unas pizzas. Me encantan sus espaguetis con almejas.

Can Loca
Paseo Marítimo, Es Pujols
Tel: 971.321.883

Mediteranean food on a sweet driftwood style terrace. A romatic setting and a top spot for people watching and sea views.

Comida mediterránea en una terraza con mucho estilo decorada con madera blanqueada por el mar. Tiene un entorno romántico con vistas al mar y es un lugar perfecto para ver la gente.

Maritim
Paseo Marítimo, Es Pujols,
Tel: 971.328.259

Pepe runs this popular traditional Formenteran restaurant that serves rice dishes and seafood as well as pizzas. A bunch of my Ibiza friends love to take the boat over, moor up in the bay in front and eat here. It's open til late every day.

Pepe lleva este popular restaurante de cocina tradicional de Formentera, con un menú variado de arroces

y pescado además de pizzas. A mis amigos de Ibiza les gusta venir en barco, atracarlo en la cala de enfrente y comer aquí. Abierto hasta tarde cada día.

Bé Va Bé

C/ Espardell, Es Pujols
Tel: 971.328.554

This is a great little ice-cream parlour that is kind of hidden down one of the backstreets that leads off from the seafront. Absolutely the best on the island, my favourite flavour is the Nutella!

Una super heladería pequeñita escondida en una de las calles traseras si te alejas del mar. Sin duda el mejor helado de la isla, ¡mi sabor favorito es el de Nutella!

Integral

Avda. Miramar, Es Pujols
Tel: 971.323.561

A little vegetarian place I discovered by chance with my friend Karyn, and we were both delighted as the service was lovely and attentive, and the food yummy and affordable and their little terrace is super cute. Try their falafel and hummus.

Un pequeño vegetariano que descubrí por casualidad con mi amiga Karyn y ambas nos quedamos encantadas ya que el servicio es encantador y atento, y la comida está realmente rica y es asequible y su terracita mola mucho. Prueba su falafel y hummus.

People

S'Escull des Corsaris, Playa Es Pujols.

This stylish wooden beach bar just a five minute walk along the beach from Es Pujols has held onto its simple Formenteran charm although it's been modernised a bit now as befoe it was really just a wooden shack... and I liked it like that... We always walk across from our summer house on Playa de Levante and grab some cold Coronitas chased with a shot of tequila.

Este chiringuito monissimo de madera en la playa está a cinco minutos andando de Es Pujols por la playa y ha logrado mantener el encanto de Formentera aunque lo renovaron hace poco y a mi me gustaba más su simpleza anterior... Siempre vamos caminando desde nuestra casa de verano en la Playa de Levante y nos tomamos unas Coronitas bien frescas y un chupito de tequila.

La Casa Della Piadina

Avda. Miramar, 65, Es Pujols
Tel: 971.329.154
thebeachformentera.com

This is a tiny place on the road as you exit Es Pujols towards Illetas. My Italian friends say it's like being back home with all the Italian newspapers. Open from early morning til late at night, they do great breakfast and very tasty burritos, all made with lovely fresh ingredients and there´s free Wifi,

Un lugar pequeño en la carretera saliendo de Es Pujols de camino a Illetas. Mis amigos italianos dicen que es como volver a casa ya que siempre tienen toda la prensa italiana. Abierto desde temprano por la mañana hasta tarde por la noche, hacen deliciosos desayunos y unos burritos muy sabrosos, todo hecho con ingredientes frescos. WiFi gratis.

Casanita

C/des Fonoll Marí, 101
Es Pujols
Tel: 971.321.968

A cantina type place located on the edge of Es Pujols as you head towards Illetas that serves delicious food. Very seafood based and freshly prepared. A cosy interior with great attention to detail. Seafood risotto, mussels, crab pasta and yummy deserts are what you can expect here.

Un lugar tipo cantina ubicado a las afueras de Es Pujols, en dirección a Illetas, que sirve una comida riquísima a base de marisco fresco. Tiene un interior muy acogedor y lleno de detalles. Prueba el risotto de marisco, los mejillones, la pasta con cangrejo y sus deliciosos postres.

Cincpedres

C/ Punta Prima 5, Es Pujols
Tel: 971.321.940
cinqpedres.com

This is a great spot for a healthy breakfast to start your day. However it is open all day.
They do brunch, lunch and great pasta dishes,. They also have a Little shop.

Aunque está abierto todo el día, es el lugar perfecto en el que tomarte un desayuno saludable para arrancar por la mañana. Preparan el brunch, almuerzos y platos de pasta. También tienen una pequeña tienda.

TAKE AWAY...
PARA LLEVAR

Don Pollo

Avda. Miramar, Es Pujols
Tel: 971.328.076

When we can't face cooking we just whizz down to this place on the roadside in Es Pujols to grab a yummy rotary roast chicken. Don't forget to ask for an extra splash of the delicious cooking juices.

Cuando no nos apetece cocinar nos acercamos a este pequeño lugar en Es Pujols y compramos un pollo a l'ast. No te olvides de pedir extra de caldo.

"click"

DON'T MISS IT, ON THE BEACH!
¡NO TE LO PIERDAS, EN LA PLAYA!
FLOWER POWER PARTY
VISITFORMENTERA.COM/AGENDA

..SHOP A BIKINI
CÓMPRATE UN BIKINI...

Janne Ibiza
C/Punta Prima, Es Pujols
Tel: 971.328.963
janneibiza.es

This is a great little swimwear shop. The designs were first created for a beach stall on Salinas Beach in Ibiza many years ago and became so popular that this delightful shop was then opened in Formentera. Try on a tanga (thong) – if you dare!

Una tienda fantástica de bañadores. Los diseños fueron creados por primera vez para un puesto en la playa de Salinas en Ibiza hace años y se hizo tan popular que posteriormente abrió esta encantadora tienda en Formentera. ¡Si te atreves pruébate el tanga!

..SLEEP + RELAX
DORMIR Y RELAJARSE...

Sa Vinya
C/Punta Prima, 37, Es Pujols
Tel: 971.328.347

I often stay here when I come for a short trip when friends are in Es Pujols with their boat. Just outside the mad zone it's quieter here, the staff are friendly and you can book a standard room or a little bungalow. There's also a pool which the kids love. Prices are very reasonable with breakfast included and served on a lovely shaded porch.

Suelo hospedarme aquí si vengo para una estancia corta y tengo amigos en Es Pujols con su barco. Alejado de la locura, es bonito y tranquilo, el personal es muy amable y puedes reservar una habitación estándar o un bungaló. También tienen piscina que a los niños les encanta. Los precios son razonables y con desayuno incluido, servido en su encantador porche a la sombra.

Sa Volta
C/ Miramar 94, Es Pujols
Tel: 971.323.160
savolta.com

A good hotel right on the main Street down to the sea. Opened in the early 70's but has since been refurbished, It does not have sea views but its 2 minutes walk from the beach. I stayed here when a gang of us came for the Flower Power Party that happens in Es Pujols in the summer and as the hotel is in the heart of Es Pujols its perfect. It has a conference room, a chill out cocktail bar and a pool.

Un buen hotel en la calle principal en dirección al mar, inaugurado a principios de los 70 pero que ha sido reformado. No tiene vistas al mar, pero tardas 2 minutos andando a la playa. Me alojé aquí cuando unas amigas y yo vinimos a la fiesta Flower Power que se celebra cada verano aquí en Es Pujols, y ya que el hotel está en el corazón de Es Pujols, es el lugar perfecto. Cuenta con una sala de conferencias, un chill-out, un bar de cócteles y una piscina.

..DRINKS + DANCE
DE COPAS Y JUERGA...

Bananas Bar & Co
C/de Roca Plana, Es Pujols
Tel: 619.143.277
bananasformentera.com

I used to go here a lot years back, and it always reminds me of a raucous après-ski lounge bar - but on a hot Spanish island! The crowd is mainly Italian, so brush up on the lingo and prepare to flirt and mingle. They have a very popular happy hour.

Hace años solía venir aquí y siempre me recordaba a las salas après ski, pero en una calurosa isla española. La clientela es principalmente italiana, así que ponte al día de la jerga y prepárate a flirtear y mezclarte con ellos. También tienen una happy hour muy popular.

Tipic
Avda. Miramar, 164, Es Pujols
Tel: 676.885.452
clubtipic.com

Unlike Ibiza, there really isn't a lot of choice regarding the nightlife, so if you fancy an all-nighter this is the only place to go. As legend has it, they opened with a Pink Floyd gig in 1971 and these days Sven Väth's Cocoon hosts a pop-up party in the summer, so keep your eyes on the posters outside for dates. If you're staying in Ibiza, you can actually get the last boat over and the first one back the next morning, or just grab a room in Es Pujols which is walking distance. So go get your rave

on, Formentera style!
A diferencia de Ibiza, realmente no hay muchas opciones en cuanto a discotecas, así que si te apetece salir toda la noche éste es el único lugar. Como cuenta la leyenda, abrieron con un concierto de Pink Floyd en 1971 y hoy en día se celebran fiestas *pop-up* de Cocoon durante todo el verano así que mantente atento a los posters para más detalles. Si te hospedas en Ibiza, puedes coger el último barco y luego coger el primero de la mañana para volver a Ibiza, o simplemente alquílate una habitación Es Pujols. Así que ve a darte una buena fiesta, ¡al estilo de Formentera!

..ROADSIDE EATERIES
COMER POR LA CARRETERA

Restaurante La Tortuga
Crta. de La Savina a la Mola
Tel: 971.328.967
restaurantlatortuga.com
A charming little roadside option with a cosy terrace. I've been past it countless times without stopping, but my friend Karyn says that they have a good Mediterranean menu. She asked me to recommend it!
Un pintoresco restaurante junto a la carretera con una terraza acogedora perfecta para una cena informal. Lo he pasado innumerables veces sin pararme, pero mi amiga Karyn dice que es una delicia y tenen una deliciosa carta mediterránea, ¡me pidió que lo recomendara!

Can Dani
Ctra. de La Mola, Km 8,5
Tel: 971.328.505
candaniformentera.com
A great gourmet restaurant serving traditional dishes that have been adapted to become more sophisticated, but still maintaining the island's traditional style of cooking. The emphasis is on local ingredients and they do great wines.
Un restaurante gourmet que sirve platos tradicionales que han sido adaptados a platos más sofisticados, pero que mantienen el estilo de la cocina tradicional. El énfasis está en los ingredientes locales y además tienen unos vinos riquísimos.

Caminito
Ctra. de La Savina, Es Calò
Tel: 971.328.106
caminitoformentera.es
Unmissable as it stands tall on the side of the road as you leave Es Pujols is Formentera's answer to an Argentinian steakhouse. They have a really nice gang working here with great service. The meat is delicious and it is an ideal spot for a large group of people. A lovely setting by the pool which is lit at night.
No puedes pasar deapercibido este asador estilo argentino en Formentera .
Tienen un gran servicio, y una selección de carne al grill deliciosa. Es un lugar ideal para un grupo grande de personas. En un entorno precioso con vistas y su zona de mesas alrededor de la piscina iluminada por la noche.

SUPERMARKET OFIUSA SPAR

Supermarkets are expensive on the island, there's no disputing it. Out of all the supermarkets here, and not mentioning the huge ones.This one is on the road to La Mola just after Sant Ferrán. It has the widest range of products and a nice section of fresh goods to the right with a butcher, bakery and a choice of vegetables and fruit.

I ♥ THAT SUPERMARKETS IN FORMENTERA USE ONION SKIN BAGS NOT PLASTIC.

Los supermercados son caros en la isla , no hay que disputar . De todos los supermercados aquí, y no mencionar el enorme ones.This uno está en la carretera de La Mola justo después de Sant Ferrán . Cuenta con la más amplia gama de productos y una buena sección de productos frescos a la derecha con una carnicería , una panadería y una selección de verduras y frutas.

ES CALÓ DE SANT AGUSTÍ

"click"

This is a stunning little place on the sea, just before the road starts to go up the hill to La Mola. There's a small fishing port and some gorgeous beaches, including Ses Platgetes which are absolutely heavenly.

Este precioso lugar está frente al mar, justo antes de que la carretera empiece a subir a La Mola. Hay un pequeño pueblo pesquero y algunas preciosas calas, incluyendo Ses Platgetes, que son un verdadero paraíso.

Restaurante Can Rafalet

Venda des Carnatge, 1-11, Es Caló
Tel: 971.327.077

I celebrated a birthday here once, as I love this little fishing village with its "Le Grand Bleu" views. There were about 15 of us and we shared a paella and some starters, and it was delicious and affordable, considering that Formentera is generally 20% more expensive than Ibiza. They specialise in rice dishes and seafood, but you should reserve in advance as it usually gets full - especially on the weekends, as it's popular with the locals.

Celebré un cumpleaños aquí hace unos años, ya que me encanta este precioso pueblecito pesquero y sus vistas al "Gran Azul". Éramos unos 15 y compartimos una paella y algunos primeros y estaba todo delicioso y a muy buen precio, considerando que Formentera suele ser un 20% más caro que Ibiza. Se especializan en platos de arroz y pescado, y tienes que reservar con antelación ya que siempre se llena, especialmente los fines de semana, porque es muy popular entre la gente de aquí.

Restaurante Es Caló

C/ Vicari Joan Marí, 14, Es Caló
Tel: 971.327.311

Located in the little fishing village of Es Caló just before you wind up to La Mola, the views of the cliffs and deep blue sea from here are stunning. And with its open-air setting and chic wooden furniture, this place just exudes fine dining.

Situado en el pequeño pueblo pesquero de Es Caló, justo antes de subir hacia La Mola, las vistas de los acantilados y el mar azul profundo desde aquí son impresionantes. Y con su terraza al aire libre y su mobiliario chic de madera, este lugar proporciona comidas sofisticadas.

Restaurante Pascual

Es Caló de Sant Agustí
Tel: 971.327.014

A great seafood eatery. They do a delicious seafood grill here. The family that runs it is charming and the prices are reasonable and the new terrace is a plus especially in the evening for dinner when it is all lit up.

Un buen restaurante de marisco con unos propietarios encantadores. Hacen una deliciosa parrillada de pescado y los precios son muy razonables. La nueva terraza es un verdadero placer, especialmente para cenar por la noche cuando está todo iluminado.

Es Cupinà

Playa d'Escupinà
Tel: 971.327.221
restauranteescupina.com

A stunning restaurant perched on the dunes with stunning seaviews and serving Mediterranean food. They specialise in Paellas and seafood but also have amazing starters and salads.

Un impresionante restaurante en las dunas con unas vistas fascinantes al mar que sirve comida mediterránea. Son especialistas en paellas y mariscos, pero también tienen unos entrantes y unas ensaladas deliciosas.

EL PILAR DE LA MOLA

Drive up here to experience the most amazing clifftop views from the lighthouse. The little village also hosts a hippy market every Wednesday and Sunday from 4 to 9.30pm. If you're feeling fit you can cycle here, but be warned – it's a hell of a ride up.

Conduce hasta aquí para experimentar las vistas más alucinantes desde el acantilado junto al faro. Este pequeño pueblo también tiene un mercadillo hippy cada miércoles y domingo de 16:00 a 21:30h. Si te sientes en forma puedes subir en bicicleta, pero estás advertido, no es nada fácil.

DON'T MISS IN JUNE
EN JUNIO NO TE PIERDAS
FLOWER POWER PARTY
IN THE SQUARE!
¡EN LA PLAZA!
visitformentera.com/agenda

..EAT, DRINK, ENJOY...
COMER, BEBER, DISFRUTAR...

Can Toni

Plaça del Pilar, 1 y 2
Tel: 971.327.377
cantoniformentera.com

This was always my pitstop years ago after cycling up to La Mola. On Sundays you'd find all the men in one room playing cards while the women peeled oranges outside. 15 years ago there were hardly any bars in this village, so this was like a little peasant meeting spot. The bar is over 100 years old now and has a new restaurant specializing in Catalan cuisine, at reasonable prices.

Aquí solía ser donde me paraba después de subir en bicicleta a la Mola. Recuerdo que los domingos te encontrabas a los hombres en una sala jugando a las cartas mientras las mujeres pelaban naranjas fuera. Hace 15 años casi no había bares en este pueblo, así que éste era el punto de encuentro de los payeses. El bar ya ha cumplido los 100 años y tiene un nuevo restaurante que se especializa en cocina catalana a precios razonables.

Codice Luna

Faro de la Mola
Tel: 675.636.725
codiceluna.com

Claudio runs this pretty Bar/ Café at the end of

HIPPY MARKET
MERCADILLO HIPPY
FIRA DE LA MOLA

This artisan hippy market is held up in Pilar de la Mola, which is the little village in La Mola on the way to the lighthouse. You can find a wide range of items here, mainly leather shoes, belts, jewellery and clothing, and all made by local artisans, many of whom settled in Formentera in the 1960s. There's also live music and it's best to visit at the end of the day when the heat is more bearable.

Este mercadillo artesanal está en el pequeño pueblo del Pilar de La Mola de camino al faro de La Mola. Puedes encontrar una variedad de artículos como calzado y cinturones de piel, joyería y ropa, todo hecho por artesanos locales, la mayoría de los cuales se asentaron en Formentera en los años 60. También hay música en directo y es mejor ir a visitarlo al final del día cuando no hace tanto calor.

Wednesday + Sunday
Miércoles + domingo
16.00-21:00 hrs

the road of La Mola, facing the lighthouse. It's an amazing location apart from the bus loads of tourists wandering around near the cliffs.
I enjoyed a couple Alhambra beers here last time with friends but just wish the girls working here were a bit more friendly. Cash only by the way.
Claudio regenta este increíble bar-cafetería al final de la carretera de La Mola, frente al faro. Cuenta con una fantástica ubicación y hasta allí llegan autobuses llenos de turistas para ver el faro y los acantilados. La última vez que fui allí disfruté de unas cervezas Alhambra con mis amigos, aunque las chicas que trabajan aquí podrían ser un poco más simpáticas.
No aceptan tarjetas.

SHOPPING, DECO + JEWELS...
DECO Y JOYAS...

Can Xicu
Avda. de La Mola, 27
Tel: 650.003.308 - canxicu.es

I for one love driftwood, so when I first stumbled across this rustic farmhouse that's been transformed into a gorgeous interiors shop I almost fainted. The emphasis is on craftsmanship, creating a very unique Mediterranean feel, and while they specialize in furniture made from reclaimed objects, you'll also find beautiful photographs, paintings and kitchenware.
Como me suele gustar la madera desgastada cuando me encontré por primera vez con esta finca rústica que ha sido transformada en una preciosa tienda de decoración, casi me desmayo. El énfasis está en los artículos artesanales que crean un sentimiento mediterráneo único, y mientras que se especializan en mobiliario hecho de materiales reciclados, también encontrarás fotografías, pinturas y utensilios de cocina preciosos.

Majoral
Avda. La Mola, 0, El Pilar
Carrer de Jaume I, 29,
Sant Francesc
Tel: 971.321.148
majoral.com

This Spanish-run family jewellery business is headed by Enric Majoral, who creates an authentic and ever-changing collection inspired by the Formentera landscape. His workshop is here too, so you can watch him in action.
This summer they are opening another store in Ibiza for those of you who don't get a chance while visiting Formentera.
Esta joyería perteneciente a una familia española está encabezada por Enric Majoral, que crea una colección auténtica y cambiante de joyas inspiradas en el paisaje de Formentera. Su taller también está aquí, así que puedes verlo en plena acción. Este verano abren otra tienda en Ibiza para aquellos que no tienen la oportunidad de ver la tienda en Formentera.

Playa Migjorn

I think this beach is the longest on the island. I tried to swim the length of it once and ended up walking half way in my bikini and getting really burnt! The water is blue through and though, and the dunes are protected and well looked after with wooden walkways weaving along the sand. The little twisted trees and bushes create a stunning and wild backdrop. You'll find a variety of bars ranging in prices and style dotted along the beach, the following being my favourites.

Creo que ésta es la playa más larga de la isla. Intenté nadarla de lado a lado una vez y acabé caminando a mitad de camino en bikini y me quemé enterita. El agua es totalmente azul, y las dunas están protegidas y muy cuidadas con pasarelas de madera que serpentean por toda la arena. Los pequeños árboles retorcidos y su vegetación crean un fondo impresionante y silvestre. Encontrarás una variedad de bares con distintos precios y estilos esparcidos a lo largo de la playa, los siguientes son mis favoritos.

..TO EAT & DRINK...
COMER Y BEBER...

Voga Marí

Playa de Migjorn
Tel: 971.329.053
vogamari.es

Sensational seafood, a candlelit walkway and secluded seating for two on the beach, this place has romance written all over it. Inspired by the small sea urchin after which it's named, the décor is monochrome and pretty swanky.

Pescado y marisco sensacional, una pasarela iluminada por velitas y mesitas aisladas en la playa, este lugar es la encarnación del puro romanticismo. Inspirado en el pequeño erizo de mar del que ha adoptado su nombre, la decoración es monocroma y muy elegante.

Blue Bar

Playa de Migjorn Km 7.9
Tel: 666.758.190
bluebarformentera.com

This place is a must for all Formentera visitors. It is so different and out there, and will make you smile at your inner trance kid! The inside is like a planetarium on acid, and all really blue. They also serve luscious cocktails and delicious food, and even though the sun goes down a bit sooner here due to the headland it is still one of the most popular sunset spots on the island.

Ask them when the Alien is due to arrive, and make a date to meet it!
Este lugar es esencial para todo visitante de Formentera. Es tan diferente y hará sonreír al niño que llevas dentro. El interior es como un planetarium de lo más psicodélico y todo es realmente azul. Además sirven cócteles y comida deliciosa y aunque la puesta aquí es un poco más pronto sigue siendo uno de los lugares más populares para contemplarla. Pregúntales cuándo está previsto que lleguen los alienígenas, ¡pide una cita para conocerlos!

Lucky Bar
Playa de Migjorn

Another great little shack right on the beach oozing that laid-back summer atmosphere that I so love. I adore sitting on their wooden benches with my feet in the warm sand eating a salad and listening to the chilled-out music. The last time I came I swam in from a boat for a cold beer and ended up staying hours.
Otro pequeño chiringuito justo en la playa que encarna el ambiente relajado de verano que tanto me gusta. Adoro comerme una ensalada sentada en sus bancos de madera con mis pies metidos en la arena, escuchando música chill out. La última vez que vine nadé hasta aquí desde un barco para tomarme una caña fresca y acabé quedándome horas.

Kiosco Bartolo
Playa de Migjorn

This cute shack stands on wooden stilts looking out to sea, a bit like something out of Robinson Crusoe. Located at the end of Migjorn beach, nearer to La Mola, it has tables in the shack and then scattered around. The nearest bay is Es Caló des Mort, which is my favourite for snorkelling. Known for their hamburgers, you can have yours with a fried egg.
Este gracioso chiringuito situado sobre palos de madera mirando al mar parece sacado de Robinson Crusoe. Situado al final de la playa de Migjorn, cerca de La Mola, tiene mesitas dentro y a su alrededor. La bahía más cercana es Es Caló des Mort, que es mi favorita para el snorkel. Conocido por sus hamburguesas, puedes pedirte la tuya con un huevo frito.

10.7
Playa de Migjorn, Km 10.7
Tel: 660.985.248
10punto7.com

A perfect place if you want a sunset party vibe, where everyone piles up onto the roof to get the last glimpse of the sun going down behind the headland. The cool Italian crowd come here, so be warned for some seriously styled booties! They also host weddings down on the beach, and their restaurant has great salmon sashimi on the menu as well as other dishes.
Este sitio tiene ambiente de fiesta con la puesta de sol, donde todo el mundo se apelotona en su azotea para ver los últimos rayos del sol hundirse detrás del cabo. Aquí su clientela está compuesta de italianos sofisticados, así que vístete con tus mejores trapitos. También celebran bodas en la playa

y la carta del restaurante incluye delicioso sashimi de salmón y otros platos del mismo estilo.

Flipper & Chiller

Playa de Migjorn, Km 11
Tel: 971.187.596

I often come to this colourful beach spot for a cocktail, but they also have a great menu, good music and are right by the beach. They stay open after sundown too, so it's a classic place to dance the evening away under the stars.

A menudo vengo a esta playa variopinta para tomarme un cóctel, pero también tienen una carta deliciosa, buena música y está junto a la playa. Tienen abierto después de la puesta y es un lugar clásico para bailar toda la noche bajo las estrellas.

Piratabus

Migjorn, km 11
piratabus.com

I love this place, and always come here when I am in the area. It used to actually be a shack stuck to an old red bus years ago and now still just a simple wooden shack with a pirate flag flying up above. It's ideal for a tapa of marinated fish and a sunset drink and gets pretty rammed in high season. The view is stunning as the sun sets behind the headland of Cap des Barbaria.

Me encanta este lugar y siempre que estoy por la zona paso por aquí. Hace años era una cabaña unida a un viejo autobús rojo, ahora es una cabaña de madera con una bandera pirata ondeando que se llena de gente en temporada alta. Ideal para una tapa de boquerones en vinagre y una copa, viendo cómo se pone el sol detrás de la punta de Cap des Barbaria... impresionante.

Sol y Luna

Playa de Migjorn
Tel: 629.040.265

A no-frills place that sits back from the beach at the western end of the of Migjorn, with a simple and very authentic feel about it. It's great for an affordable lunch with friends, and we always end up emptying the hierbas bottle that sits on the table after lunch. Order the seafood paella. To get here, follow the old road to La Mola from Sant Francesc, it should be signposted.

Este local sencillo está situado a unos metros de la playa de Migjorn y tiene un ambiente simple y auténtico. Es magnífico para una comida con amigos por un buen precio y siempre acabamos bebiéndonos toda la botella de hierbas que dejan en nuestra mesa después de comer. Pidete la paella de marisco. Para llegar desde Sant Francesc, sigue el viejo camino de La Mola, debería esta señalado.

Sa Platjeta

Playa de Migjorn
Tel: 971.187.614

If you want a change from the crowded and more expensive beach restaurants on Illetes, this is a perfect choice. A lovely little restaurant just two steps from the beach and tucked away in the shade of the pine trees, they do fabulous fish stews, fried lobster and grilled sardines, as well as a killer sangria. Great value for money it's perfect for a long, lazy lunch. To get here, turn right off the second roundabout after Sant Francesc and take the old La Mola road. It's the third on the right towards the sea.

Si quieres alejarte de los chiringuitos más caros y concurridos del sur y buscas algo diferente, este sitio del oeste es perfecto. Un restaurante pequeño y encantador a dos pasos de la playa y

escondido a la sombra de los pinos. Preparan deliciosos guisos de pescado, langosta, y sardinas al grill, además de una sangría de muerte. Ya que sus precios son buenos es perfecto para una sobremesa larga. Para llegar, gira a la derecha en la segunda rotonda después de Sant Francesc y coge la vieja carretera a La Mola. La tercera salida a la derecha dirección al mar.

Kiosko 62

Camino de Can Simonet, I
Playa de Migjorn
Tel: 697 84 07 95

A little wooden shack at the end of Migjorn beach that is open all year. I hardly want anyone to know about it, but they deserve the business... Go at sunset for a real Formentera experience with your mojito in hand. See if you can find it!!

Un pequeño kiosko de madera al final de la playa de Migjorn que esta abierto todo el año. Casi no quería que nadie lo supiera, pero merecen negocio... Una verdadera experiencia de Formentera con tu mojito en la mano. ¡Suerte encontrándolo!

..SLEEP + RELAX...
DORMIR Y RELAJARSE...

Es Pas

Playa de Migjorn
Tel: 687.807.819

This Agroturismo is a brand new option at the smarter end of the scale. I like the upstairs rooms – they're light and breezy and have balconies overlooking the pool deck or the surrounding countryside, and it's just a short stroll to either the beach or the village of Es Caló.

Este agroturismo es una nueva opción al sector más sofisticado. A mí me gustan las habitaciones del piso superior, son luminosas y aireadas y tienen balcones con vistas a la piscina o al campo. Además está situado a un pequeño paseo de la playa o del pueblo de Es Caló.

Astbury Formentera

Passeig Marítim 52, La Savina
Tel: 971.323.505
formenteravillas.es

They have a choice of places dotted all over the island. You can chose from little private bungalows near the sea, to larger villas with shared pools. Some are set back in the pine trees and hava a more rough and tumble vibe and others are more modern.
Tienen una a selection de lugares maravillosos por toda la isla. Puedes elegir entre pequeños bungalows privados cerca del mar, a villas más grandes con piscinas. Algunos situadas entre pinares que son más rudos y otros más modernos.

Gecko Beach Club

Playa de Migjorn, Ca Mari
Tel: 971.328.024
geckobeachclub.com

This is a boutique hotel located at the end of Migjorn beach that is less of my favorite boho style but they do do yoga courses and guests can borrow electric bikes to explore the island courtesy of the hotel.
Este es un hotel boutique al final de la playa de Migjorn que no es del estilo bohemio que a mi me gusta pero ofrecen clases de yoga y los huéspedes pueden tomar prestadas las bicicletas para explorar la isla.

Casa Serena

Playa de Migjorn, Km. 8,9
Tel: 618.104.170
casaserenaformentera.com

Thanks to Yolanda Torres from Hotel Atzaró, I heard about this gorgeous place a week before this guide went to print. It has five gorgeously unique rooms, all with their own chillout areas.
I can't wait to go and stay. It' sounds so divine!!
Gracias a Yolanda Torres del Hotel Atzaró, descubrí este precioso lugar una semana antes de que esta guía se imprimiera. Consta de cinco habitaciones, todas decoradas de forma única y todas con su propia zona chill out.

Las Dunas Playa

Playa de Migjorn, Km. 11
Tel: 971.328.041
dunasplaya.com

After years of camping out on the dunes or grabbing a cheap hostal inland, I discovered this place with private stand-alone apartments set among the pines and dunes. There's a little bar with a pool table and a sandy area for the kids. But it's the infinity pool with a view of the deep turquoise sea that makes this place a winner. It's affordable, and just a short walk down to the beach.
Después de años acampando y en las dunas u hospedándome en hostales baratos, descubrí este sitio con bungalós privados y aislados entre los pinos y las dunas. Tiene un pequeño bar con billar y zona para los niños. Pero es la piscina con vistas al mar turquesa lo que hacen que este sitio sea de mis favoritos. Es asequible y sólo a un paseo corto hasta la playa.

Apartamentos Pueblo Balear

Playa de Migjorn
Tel: 610 07 23 68
pueblobalear-formentera.com

Apartments perfect for two, four or six people right on the beach of Migjorn and next to the Blue Bar. Try to book one on the first floor with a terrace and sea views. I think the owners are Italian, but I am not sure as I have never stayed here, but friends say they were delightful.
Una selección de apartamentos de dos, cuatro o seis personas a pie de playa en Migjorn y justo al lado del Blue Bar. Si puedes, intenta reservar uno en el primer piso con terraza y vistas al mar. Creo que los dueños son italianos, yo no he estado nunca pero me dicen amigos que se han hospedado aqui que son muy simpaticos los que lo llevan.

(+one last) THING YOU SHOULD DO.

(la última) COSA QUE DEBERÍAS HACER CUANDO ESTÉS AQUÍ.

Swim naked in the sea.

Have no care in the world, be free and remember that when you get home you might wish that you had done it...

Nada desnudo en el mar.

No tengas ninguna preocupación en el mundo, sé libre y recuerda que cuando vuelvas a casa es posible que desees haberlo hecho...

THE NORTH: BEACH RESTAURANTS + BARS
EL NORTE: CHIRINGUITOS Y RESTAURANTES DE PLAYA (PLATJA)

Playa/Platja Levante

One of my favourite beaches on this island, I first came here when I was eight and it's still almost as untouched as it was then. More isolated than its neighbours, it's a real oasis of white sand and turquoise waters - not even the Caribbean can compare! Lined by dunes, it's always less crowded due to its length and wilder seas.

Una de mis playas favoritas de la isla, vine aquí por primera vez cuando tenía ocho años y sigue siendo tan virgen como lo era antes. Más aislada que sus playas vecinas, es un verdadero oasis de arenas blancas y aguas turquesas, ¡ni el Caribe podría compararse a esto! Alineada con dunas, siempre hay menos gente debido a que el mar suele estar más revuelto.

...TO EAT... PARA COMER...

Tanga
Playa de Levante
Tel: 971.187.905
restaurantetanga.com

This large beach restaurant serves really top-notch food. The roof here is held up by an enormous piece of drift-wood that the sea brought in years ago, and its shady and cool in the extreme summer heat. I love the baked cod in a little clay pot that comes out all creamy and lush. They also do fantastic rice dishes, fresh fish and lobster. Don't forget to get some chupitos in at the end of your meal with the owner Rafa.

Este chiringuito grande sirve comida de alta calidad. Su techo se apoya en un gigantesco trozo de madera que el mar trajo hasta aquí hace años, aportando sombra en los días de calor extremo. Me chifla su bacalao al horno en un pequeño cuenco de barro, es cremoso y suave, también preparan fantásticos platos de arroz, pescado fresco y langosta. No te olvides de tomarte el chupito de rigor con Rafa, el dueño, al acabar de comer.

Kiosco Levante
Playa de Levante

Drive towards Illetas but then vear off right to Levante beach to simple wooden beach shack is set up a bit in the dunes of Levante Beach. The prices here are really reasonable, and it's known for its omelettes, salads and burgers. A perfect place to go with kids.

Conduce a Illetas pero gira a la derecha a este sencillo chiringuito de madera está situado en las dunas de la playa de Levante. Precios muy razonables y es popular por sus tortillas, ensaladas y hamburguesas. Un sitio ideal para ir con los niños.

...SLEEP... DORMIR...

Hostal Sa Roqueta
Playa de Sa Roqueta, Levante
Tel: 971.328.506

The amazing sea view really makes this place, and it has a gorgeous little beach right beside it. The rooms are very basic so try and get a sea view. Breakfast is heaven by the sea. It's perfect if you're on a budget and looking for some peace and quiet. The nearest town is Es Pujols if you want a bit of action.

Las increíbles vistas al mar hacen que este sitio sea realmente especial y también el hecho de que hay una playa al lado. Las habitaciones son básicas y merece la pena reservar con vistas al mar. Desayunar aquí es ideal con el mar al lado. Perfecto si tu presupuesto es bajo y buscas tranquilidad. El pueblo más cercano es Es Pujols, por si te apetece un poco de acción.

Illetes (Playa/platja)

A stunning, narrow strip of sand with the sea on both sides. Often quite choppy on the eastern side, it's mostly calm on to the northwest, where yachts anchor in their droves. The sand is heavenly white and fine, but I myself get overwhelmed with the amount of people that seek out this little strip of paradise in the summer. I generally park as far to the end as I can and then walk from there to the little beachy inlets to enjoy the view of the island of Espalmador.

Un impresionante tramo de arena estrecho con mar a ambos lados. A menudo el mar está revuelto en la parte este, pero está mucho más calmado en el noroeste, donde los barcos echan el ancla en masa. La arena es increíblemente blanca y fina, pero a mí me agobian las multitudes que buscan este pequeño pedazo de paraíso en pleno verano. Generalmente aparco al final del todo y camino hasta las pequeñas calitas de arena para disfrutar de las vistas a la isla de Espalmador.

El Pirata

Playa de Illetes
Tel: 971.324.064

I like to go here by boat with friends then swim in for lunch at one of its shady long tables. Hugely popular with locals and tourists as well as loads of Ibiza residents, it sits right at the start of Illetes beach. The kids love their pizza and I always go for the seafood paella, which never fails to impress. Less expensive than some of its beach neighbours it's also less full of the high-maintenance glam crowd, which I generally try and avoid!

Me gusta venir aquí en barco con amigos y luego nadar hasta el restaurante y comer en una de sus cómodas mesas. Es muy popular entre la gente local y turistas además de residentes de

Ibiza, está justo al principio de la playa de Illetes. A los niños les encanta su pizza pero yo siempre me pido la paella de marisco, que nunca deja de sorprenderme. Menos caro que sus vecinos y además hay menos clientela glamurosa y exigente, ¡lo que generalmente intento evitar!

Juan y Andrea

Playa de Illetes
Tel: 630.258.144
juanyandrea.com

This is one of the most famous beach bars in Formentera, as celebrities and the uber rich descend from their yachts to eat here all summer long. Known for their exorbitant prices, the food is really good. Specializing in fresh fish and lobster paella that you can enjoy with your feet in the sand.

Éste es uno de los chiringuitos más famosos de Formentera, ya que las celebridades y los ricachones descienden aquí desde sus yates para comer durante todo el verano. Conocido por sus precios desorbitados, la comida es muy buena. Especialistas en pescados fresco y paellas de langosta, hay muchos otros platos que puedes disfrutar con los pies en la arena.

Es Molí de Sal

C/ Afores, Playa de Illetes.
Tel: 971.187.491
esmolidesal.es

This old salt grinding windmill hosts one of the island's most iconic restaurants. Offering Mediterranean fare and a huge selection of quality wines, I haven't eaten here for a while but I know that King Juan Carlos of Spain and interior designer Phillippe Starck are regulars! Sunsets here include the stunning views to Es Vedrà, so it's definitely worth a visit.

Este viejo molino de sal alberga uno de los restaurantes más icónicos de la isla. Ofrece cocina mediterránea y una gran selección de vinos de calidad, hace tiempo que no como aquí pero sé que el Rey Juan Carlos y el diseñador Phillippe Starck son habituales. Las puestas de sol incluyen preciosas vistas al islote de Es Vedrà, realmente merece la pena una visita.

El Tiburón

Playa de Illetes
Tel: 659.638.945
tiburon-formentera.com

I love sharks – including the huge one they have on their roof! This place really fills up in the high season, so we just grab mojitos from the bar and sit in front watching the sun go down. It always turns into a little party here at sunset, and if you can get a table, remember they do a really good lobster salad and a mean T-bone steak, as well as mini burgers to die for.

Me encantan los tiburones, incluyendo el ejemplar enorme que tienen en el tejado. Este lugar realmente se llena en temporada alta, por eso nosotros solemos pedirnos un mojito del chiringuito y sentarnos en frente para ver la puesta de sol con la música de fondo. Siempre acaba en una pequeña fiesta después de la puesta y si consigues una mesa, recuerda que preparan una ensalada de langosta y un chuletón riquísimos, las mini hamburguesas también están de muerte.

Beso Beach

Playa de Cavall d'en Borràs
Tel: 622.222.113
besobeach.com

I just adore this beach restaurant that sits tucked within the dunes and juniper trees on this stunning beach which is the nearest to the port. I love its shaded shack-like design that's just perfect for a long lazy lunch with its roof fans. After lunch, I like to sip cocktails until it's time to get the boat back to Ibiza. If you're lucky enough to be sleeping on Formentera, you can enjoy the place a bit longer and watch the sun set into the sea.

Me encanta este lugar metido entre las dunas y los enebros que destaca en esta playa cercana al puerto. Su restaurante tipo cabaña es preciosa y aqui puedes disfrutar de una deliciosa comida con una larga sobremesa con sus ventiladores de techo. Después de comer, yo suelo tomarme unos cocteles hasta la hora de coger el barco de vuelta a Ibiza. Si tienes la suerte de dormir en Formentera, puedes quedarte aqui y ver la puesta de sol.

"THE FIXERS"
"LOS MANITAS"

✱ PLUMBER–FONTANERO
Diego
625.463.380

DRIFTWOODL CARPENTRY
Roger
652.584.174

MECHANIC–MECÁNICO (IBIZA)
Luciano
665.354.088

MECHANIC/MECÁNICO
(SAN ANTONIO)
Tino
607.950.385

✱ HOUSE MAINTENANCE
MANTENIMIENTO CASAS
Charity
680.612.469

APPLE TECHNICIAN
Rafa
670.226.118

GARDENERS–JARDINEROS
Max 606.771.819
Marcus 685.486.470

MECHANIC–MECÁNICO
(SAN ANTONIO)
Faustino
971.341.869

W. MACHINE–LAVADORA
A Nice Man (Forgot name)
902.929.591

INTERNET–SATELLITE ✱
Roel
636.000.747

INTERNET–MULTIMEDIA
Tom
606.831.347

---

24 HR
ELECTRICIAN–ELECTRICISTA
600.495.972
676.214.067

THINGS TO DO

Cultural, Family, Sport, Adventure & more...

COSAS PARA HACER
Cultura, famila, deporte, aventura y más...

THINGS TO DO AND KNOW
COSAS PARA HACER Y SABER

Ancient tombs, caves, museums, historical buildings, extreme sports, adventure parks, courses, eco dwellings, walks and bike rides, all at your reach.
Antiguas tumbas, cuevas, museos, edificios históricos, deportes extremos, parques de aventura, viviendas ecológicas, caminatas y paseos en bicicleta, todo a tu alcance.

HISTORICAL-CULTURAL STUFF CULTURA E HISTORIA

COVA D'ES CULLERAM, CALA SAN VICENTE (NORTH) **Cala de San Vicente**

If you're a bit of a frustrated archaeologist and love a cave and a fossil or anything remotely similar, up a hill in the northeast of the island near Cala San Vicent there's a cave that was a place of pilgrimage in the Punic period (around the C5th BC). These rites ensured safe passage to the after-life for loved ones, and over 600 miniature effigies of the Carthaginian goddess Tanit were found here, along with evidence of ritual sacrifice and a stone altar. Items discovered are on display in the Necropolis Puig des Mollins in Ibiza Town.

Si eres un arqueólogo frustrado y te encantan las cuevas, los fósiles o cualquier cosa parecida, al noreste de la isla, cerca de Cala Sant Vicent hay una cueva extraordinaria que era donde se hacían ritos funerarios en la era Púnica (alrededor del siglo V a.C.). Estos ritos aseguraban un pasaje seguro a la otra vida y aquí se hallaron más de 600 esfinges de la diosa cartaginesa Tanit, junto a restos de sacrificios rituales y un altar de piedra. Los restos descubiertos se exhiben en la Necrópolis de Puig des Molins en Ibiza Ciudad.

NECRÓPOLIS PUIG DES MOLINS IBIZA **Vía Romana, 31, Ibiza**

Tel: 971.301.771 • Tues-Sat/mar-sáb: 10- 14h + 18:30 - 21h Sun/dom: 10 - 14h. 2,40 € maef.es

My childhood school was right next to this museum and as kids we played in the tunnels not realising that this hill was in fact an ancient burial ground dating back to the 7th century BC. Phoenician tombs and more than 3000 burial chambers were discovered here. Now this honeycombed hill is all fenced off as a UNESCO World Heritage site. A trip through the museum provides you with a sharp insight into the lives and deaths of the Phoenicians.

Mi colegio estaba junto a este museo y de niña jugaba con mis amigos en los túneles sin ser conscientes de que esta colina era un cementerio antiguo que se remonta al siglo XVII a.C. Aquí se descubrieron más de 3000 tumbas fenicias. Ahora esta colina está vallada y es Patrimonio Histórico de la Humanidad de la UNESCO. Una visita al museo te proporcionará una buena idea de la vida y muerte de los fenicios.

MUSEU PUGET IBIZA

C/ Major, 18, Ibiza, Tel: 971.392.137 • May - Jul: 10 - 14h + 17 - 20h - Sat + Sun/sáb + Dom: 10 - 14h

This museum is hidden down a small street just before the Cathedral on the way up to Dalt Vila. Entry is free and they have a permanent and a temporary collection. It's well worth the stroll up here to visit it.

Este museo se encuentra escondido en una pequeña calle justo antes de la catedral en Dalt Vila. La entrada es gratis y tienen una colección permanente y otra temporal. Realmente merece la pena subir a visitarlo.

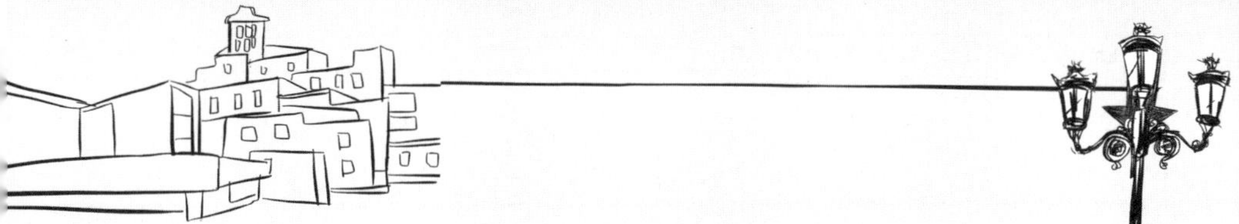

MUSEU D'ART CONTEMPORANI D'EIVISSA (MACE) IBIZA

Ronda Narcís Puget s/n. Dalt Vila, Ibiza. Tel: 971.302.723 Tue-Sat/mar-sáb: 10 - 13:30 + 17 - 20

If you walk up Carrer Avicenna to Dalt Vila which is the road behind Plaza de Parque that runs alongside the town walls, go through the tunnel, you will come out beside the MACE, Museum which exhibits both established artists and younger names. It's all housed in a historical arsenal made modern by military engineer Simon Poulet, the original bunker that stored the weapons of Dalt Vila's ancient fortress.
Free entry.

Si subes por el Carrer Avicenna a Dalt Vila, que es la carretera detrás de la Plaza del Parque y que transcurre junto a las murallas de la catedral, pasarás un túnel y saldrás junto al MACE (Museo de Arte Contemporáneo de Eivissa) que exhibe obras de artistas conocidos y artistas emergentes más jóvenes. Está situado en un edificio histórico diseñado por el ingeniero militar Simon Poulet, utilizando un viejo búnker donde se guardaban las armas de la fortaleza antigua de Dalt Vila. La entrada es gratis.

MUSEO DE ETNOGRAFÍA SANTA EULALIA (EAST)

Can Ros des Puig de Missa, Santa Eulària des Riu. Tel: 971.332.845 - 971.338.154
Mon-Sat/lun-sáb: 10:00 - 14 + 17:30 - 20 • Sun/dom: 11 - 13:30.

Located up on the hill by the stunning church of the Puig de Missa in Santa Eulalia, Can Ros is an old Ibizan farmhouse that has been reborn as an ethnography museum. A permanent exhibition of rural Ibicencan household objects, utensils, instruments, weapons, clothes and personal items, they also hold workshops where traditional craftsmen show how to create musical instruments, clothing, shoes, toys and objects made from natural fibre. It's a lovely walk up too, and the view at the top is worth every step.

En la colina al lado de la impresionante iglesia de Puig de Missa en Santa Eulalia se encuentra Can Ros, una antigua casa de campo ibicenca que se ha mantenido como museo etnográfico. Es una exposición permanente de la vida rural ibicenca, la arquitectura, los objetos del hogar, utensilios, instrumentos, armas, ropas y artículos personales, y aquí también realizan talleres donde los artesanos tradicionales muestran cómo crean instrumentos, ropa, zapatos, juguetes y objetos hechos de fibras naturales. Es un bonito paseo y la vista vale la pena.

LA COVA DE CAN MARÇÀ (NORTH)

covadecanmarsa.com

Puerto de San Miguel. Tel: 971.334.776
Open every day/abierto cada día.

The cave is located in the north of the island near the bay of San Miguel.
The formations in the caves are stunning and there are lakes with added special effects with light and sound.
Smugglers used the cave to store their goods years ago. The cave is open every day to the public and is fun to visit with the family.

La cueva está situada en el norte de la isla cerca de la bahía de San Miguel.
Las formaciones de las cuevas son impresionantes y hay lagos con efectos especiales añadidos con luz y sonido. Los contrabandistas utilizaban la cueva para depositar sus mercancías hace años. La cueva está abierta todos los días al público y es un buen plan para ir con la familia.

A NICE WALK AND A DAY OUT UN BONITO PASEO Y UN DÍA AL AIRE LIBRE

ES BROLL (NORTH)

Santa Inés

This is one of my favourite walks in Ibiza, especially at the start of the summer when it's not too hot. Taking you through a little oasis of green made up of a complex valley-wide irrigation system originally installed by Moorish settlers in the 10th century. The legend goes that years ago a pig dug up the earth with its snout and discovered the natural stream. It keeps the valley lush all year round and makes it a magical place for a walk. Take the road from San Rafael to Santa Inés and go right at Bar Can Tixedó, at the signpost for Pou de Escarabata. Or come from San Mateo towards Santa Inés and you will see the signs.

Éste es uno de mis paseos favoritos en Ibiza, especialmente al principio del verano cuando no hace tanto calor. Es un pequeño oasis de vegetación compuesto por un sistema de irrigación por acequias construido por los moros en el siglo X. Cuenta la leyenda que hace unos años un cerdo excavó la tierra con su hocico y descubrió el arroyo natural. El agua mantiene el valle frondoso todo el año y lo convierte en un lugar mágico para dar un paseo. Coge la carretera de San Rafael a Santa Inés, gira a la derecha por el Bar Can Tixedó y luego coge el camino indicado como Pou des Escarbat.

AQUARIUM CAP BLANC

Ctra. de Cala Gració, San Antonio
Tel: 663.945.475
aquariumcapblanc.com • 10 - 22h

This place is a perfect day out for the family. The Aquarium is a natural cave with five sea water inlets which allow constant circulation and renovation of the water, therefore allowing sea life to live freely and naturally here. It's great for kids to see the marine life up close, and the installations are used by the "CREM", the Marine Recuperation Centre, so there are often sea animals like turtles recovering here. On an average day you can see octopus, starfish, lobsters, crabs, varieties of fish, eels and rays, and apart from the living animals you can also see shark eggs, sea sponges, gastropods and other sea invertebrates.
There's a small bar looking out to sea connected to the aquarium that serves grilled sardines, salad and entrance to the aquarium, all for €12.50.
Call for a reservation.

Este sitio es perfecto para un día en familia. El acuario es una cueva natural con cinco entradas de mar que permite constante circulación y renovación del agua, permitiendo que la vida marina viva de forma libre y natural. Es magnífico para que los niños vean la vida marina de cerca, y las instalaciones son utilizadas por "CREM", El Centro de Recuperación Marina, así que a menudo encuentras animales marinos, como tortugas, recuperándose aquí. Un día normal puedes ver pulpos, estrellas de mar, langostas, cangrejos, variedades de peces, anguilas y rayas, y aparte de animales puedes ver huevas de tiburón, esponjas de mar, gasterópodos y otros invertebrados marinos. Hay un pequeño bar con vistas al mar conectado al acuario que por 12,50€ incluye entrada al acuario, parrillada de sardinas y ensalada. Llama para reservar.

SURF LOUNGE IBIZA (WEST)

Camí des Molí, 10, San Antonio, Ibiza. Tel: 902.051.959 surfloungeibiza.com

My daughter loves this place and goes a lot in the summer with friends. It boasts the with the only Flowrider, an artificial wave machine, on the island. The wave can accommodate up to 20 riders at a time. All ages can enjoy it as no experience is necessary. And there's a cafe for you to sit and wait in.

A mi hija la encanta este lugar y va mucho en el verano con amigos. Cuenta con la única Flowrider en la isla, una máquina de olas artificiales. La ola puede acomodar hasta 20 personas a la vez. Todas las edades pueden disfrutar de esta actividad. Y hay un café para sentarse y esperar a los suyos.

IBIZA AIR ZONE (WEST)

Cami des Molí No.3, Cala de Bou. Tel: 678.832.418
Open every day from 11/abierto todos los días desde las 11h. Adults/adultos: 26.5 €. Kids/niños: 13.5 €

Ibiza is the home of Spain's first Air Zone Park, where you get strapped into a giant inflatable ball and rolled down a hill! The Vortex Orb is big enough to fit two people inside, which makes me laugh at the very thought. If you're looking for a challenge in balance, you have to try the Amphibios, where you "walk" across water in a ball without getting wet. And if you're in for a game with friends, you can get into a bumper fight - where you run around like crazy in the bumper field. Bring comfortable clothes and swimming costumes. Its located just southwest of San Antonio.

Ibiza es el hogar del primer Parque Air Zone de España, donde te atan a una bola hinchable gigante y ¡te empujan rodando por una cuesta! La Vortex Orb es lo suficientemente grande para que quepan dos personas, lo que me hace reír sólo de pensarlo. Si buscas un desafío, tienes que probar la Amphibios, con la que puedes caminar por el agua sin mojarte. Y si quieres jugar a algo divertido con tus amigos, prueba el "bumper", que puedas luchar con tus amigos y correr como un loco en un campo de unos 100m^2. Trae ropa cómoda y bañador. Está situado al suroeste de San Antonio.

ACROBOSC IBIZA (WEST)

Avda. s'Argamassa, 82, Santa Eulalia del Río. Tel: 649.667.071 acroboscibiza.com

Just recently opened, this unique course offers a fun outdoor option and is all the rage with kids and young teens. Set in an area of pine trees just 100m from Cala Pada beach, there are two circuits you can follow, according to your height and age. There are instructors watching all the time, and after a little trial it's up to you to get around. Insurance is included in the price, and special rates are available for groups so it's great for birthday parties.

Recientemente abierto, esta pista americana es una buena opción de ocio al aire libre y tanto a niños como a adolescentes les encanta. Situado en una zona de pinos a 100 metros de Cala Pada, hay dos circuitos, según estatura y edad. Hay instructores vigilando todo el tiempo y después de una pequeña prueba el resto es cosa tuya. El seguro está incluido en el precio y tienen tarifas especiales para grupos así que es perfecto para cumpleaños.

SUP BOAT IBIZA (WEST)

Tel: 666.255.803 + 625.410.746 supboatibiza.com

Many of my friends have invested in these stand-up paddle boards, and I am definitely joining the craze this year! As you paddle you feel like an Amazon warrior…all while discovering the coastline of the island from the sea. Oh, and it's great for getting rid of a few extra pounds around the waist.

Muchos de mis amigos tienen estas tablas de paddle surf y yo definitivamente me voy a unir a la moda este año. Mientras remas te sientes como una guerrera del Amazonas, al mismo tiempo que descubres el litoral de la isla desde el mar. ¡Ah! Y es magnífico para deshacerte de esos kilos que te sobran en la cintura.

MOUNTAIN BIKE TOURS

Tel: 616.129.929 ibizamtb.com

Cycling is among the best ways to discover the island from the inside, as this way you get to see places that are unreachable by car. The guys that run the tours have been riding around the island for 20 years, and will take you to the most authentic and unexplored parts of the island. They offer a choice of options, all along routes that take you to fabulous beaches, through the breathtaking countryside and past historic monuments. If you decide you want to explore the island by yourself, they also have bicycles you can hire.

El ciclismo es la mejor forma de descubrir la isla desde dentro, ya que así puedes ver muchos lugares a los que no puedes llegar en coche. Los chicos al mando de estas rutas llevan recorriendo la isla 20 años, y te llevarán a las partes más auténticas e inexploradas de la isla. Ofrecen una variedad de opciones, las rutas pueden llevarte a playas fabulosas, a través de paisajes rurales impresionantes y pasar por monumentos históricos. Si decides que quieres explorar la isla por ti mismo, también tienen bicis de alquiler.

ANFIBIOS IBIZA (SOUTH)

Edificio Acapulco, Carretera de Playa D'en Bossa. Tel: 971.303.915 anfibios.com

They started offering windsurfing lessons in 1979, and in 1983 they introduced sailing with sailboats and catamaran lessons. Another decade later they started a scuba diving centre, and this year they've added Stand-up paddle and kayak to this endless list of activities! Whether you fancy a kayak or paddle tour to see the Posidonia fields, or taking a catamaran over to Formentera, this is the place to make it happen. Keep those kids active and off their iPads, I say!

Empezaron ofreciendo clases de windsurfing en 1979 y en 1983 introdujeron las clases de vela y catamarán. Una década más tarde empezaron con las clases de buceo y este año han añadido el Paddle Surf y Kayak a su interminable lista de actividades. Tanto si te apetece ir a una excursión en kayak o paddle surf para ver las praderas de Posidonia, o coger un catamarán a Formentera, éste es el lugar perfecto. ¡Y mantendrás a los niños activos y alejados de sus iPads!

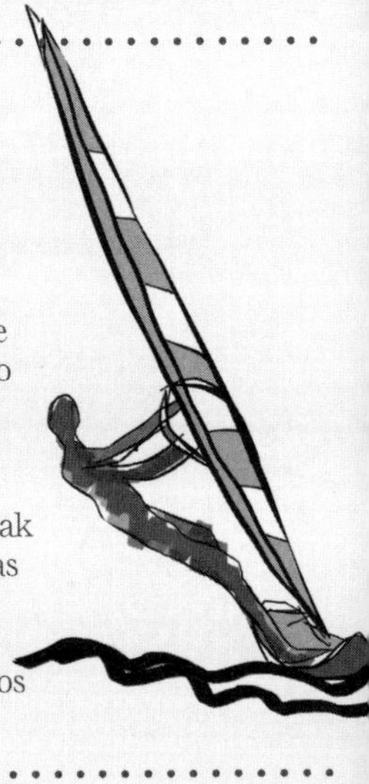

✳ CLUB NÁUTICO SAILING SCHOOL (IBIZA)

Avda. de Santa Eulària del Río, Ibiza. Tel: 971.313.363.

This sailing school is run by lovely Sebastián Vidal, who offers morning courses every summer for beginners in Optimist boats, and refresher courses to sailors that have already had lessons. You need to reserve your spot before the summer season as spaces and courses are limited.

Sebastián Vidal es el director de esta escuela de vela que ofrece cursos matutinos cada verano para principiantes en barcos Optimist, y cursos de reciclaje para los que ya hayan recibido clases. Necesitas reservar tu plaza antes del verano porque en la temporada estival las plazas y cursillos están muy limitados.

✳ WALKING IBIZA (IBIZA/FORMENTERA)

Toby Clarke. Tel: 608.692.901 walkingIbiza.com

No matter how fit you are, walking is something everyone can enjoy.
If you want to take a walk with someone who really knows his way on this island call Toby and he will guide you. His walks are through stunning wild places on the island and he advises you to take good walking shoes, a stick, suncream and water.

No importa cuál sea tu forma física, todo el mundo puede distrutar de un buen paseo. Si quieres ir de paseo con alguien que sabe y conoce la isla a fondo, llama a Toby y él te guiará por sus caminos.
Sus paseos son por lugares salvajes en la isla y te aconseja que vengas con buen calzado, un palo, protección solar y agua.

✳ IBIZA MULTISPORT KITESURF

Cervantes 7, San Antonio. Tel: 661.979.924

Kite-surfing has become very popular in both Ibiza and Formentera, and they offer different courses here depending on your level. The most popular beaches for it are Cala Martina (Es Canàr), Playa Pinet (San Antonio Bay) and Playa d'en Bossa.

El kite-surfing se ha vuelto muy popular en Ibiza y Formentera y aquí ofrecen cursos dependiendo de tu nivel. Las playas más populares para este deporte son Cala Martina (Es Canàr), Playa Pinet (San Antonio) y Playa d'en Bossa.

✳ CESAR'S WATERSPORTS (EAST)

Platja de s'Argamassa, Es Canar. Tel: 670.629.961 watersportscesars.com

My lovely friend Rachel from Atzaró Hotel took me here years ago and not only did I have the best beach day, we also sampled the delish paella that Cesar himself makes at the restaurant under the pines overlooking the sea. Work up an appetite trying out an array of nautical sports at the beach, from jet skis to parachute sailing, banana rides and water skiing. Special paella days are Sunday and Wednesday.

Mi amiga Rachel del Hotel Atzaró me trajo aquí hace unos años y no sólo fue el mejor día de playa, también probamos una deliciosa paella que el mismo César prepara en el restaurante bajo los pinos mirando al mar. Abre apetito probando una serie de deportes acuáticos en la playa, desde motos acuáticas a parasailing, banana y esquí acuático. Los días especiales de paella son los domingos y miércoles.

RUTAS ES BOIXETS. HORSE RIDING (FORMENTERA)

Formentera. Tel: 669.572.896 • vicent_juan@hotmail.com • rutasesboixets.com

This is such a great option if you are staying in Formentera or visiting for a few days. They offer horse trecking rides all over the island of Formentera, inland rides, coastal rides and then most specially the beach rides using Minorcan race horses.
Apart from riding they also offer the horses for any events on the island: weddings, photo reportages. and they have elegant carriage rides or for weddings!
Prices:
1h: 35 euros, 2h: 60 euros
Beach route: 2:30h, 80euros.

Una gran opción si estas alojado en Formentera o de visita a la isla durante unos días. Ofrecen rutas a caballo por toda la isla de Formentera, rutas de interior, rutas por costa y luego más especialmente las rutas por la playa Trabajan con caballos de raza menorquina.
Aparte de montar, también ofrecen los caballos para cualquier evento en la isla: bodas, reportajes fotográficos y tienen paseos en carruajes elegantes o para las bodas!
Precios:
1h: 35 euros, 2h: 60 euros
Ruta playa: 2:30h: 80 euros.

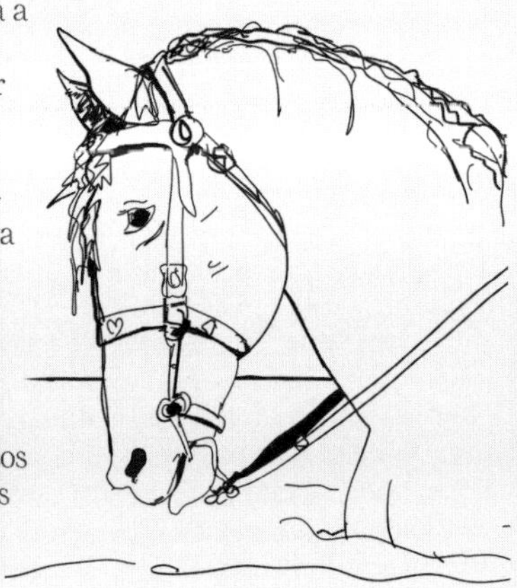

HORSE RIDING (SANTA GERTRUDIS)

Cami des Cas Ramons, Santa Gertrudis. Tel: 616.533.691

If you want to have riding lessons, go out on a hike or do a moonlight ride contact Vicente at these stables just outside Santa Gertrudis as you head towards San Miguel.
The horses are well trained and they speak English and Spanish here, and on Saturdays you can leave your kids for the day to learn the basics of horse riding

Si quieres clases de equitación, salir de excursión a caballo o hacer un paseo a la luz de la luna llena, ponte en contacto con Vicente en estos establos a las afueras del pueblo de Santa Gertrudis en dirección a San Miguel. Los caballos están bien entrenados y aquí hablan inglés y español. Los sábados puedes dejar a tus hijos para aprender lo básico de la equitación.

IBIZA HORSE VALLEY (SAN JUAN)

Cami des Cas Ramons, Santa Gertrudis. Tel: 680.624.911. ibizahorsevalley.com

This stunning plot of donated land started as a shelter for maltreated and abandoned horses and developed into a riding stables that offer treks through the beautiful hills, and to the seaside on trained, healthy rehabilitated horses that live in the best of habitats. They greatly appreciate donations and / or sponsorship.

Esta impresionante parcela de tierra donada comenzó como un refugio para caballos maltratados y abandonados y se ha convertido en un centro ecuestre que ofrece recorridos por las hermosas colinas hasta la orilla del mar en caballos adiestrados y rehabilitados que viven en el mejor de los hábitats. Se aprecian mucho las donaciones y/o los patrocinios.

ALTERNATIVE FITNESS DEPORTE ALTERNATIVO

✳ IBIZA CLIFF DIVING (EVERYWHERE)

Tel: 607.038.837 or + 638.780.885 ibizacliffdiving@gmail.com • cliffdivingibiza.com • FB: Ibiza Cliff Diving

If you like a little adrenalin rush this is a perfect way to get it as well as enjoying the stunning lanscape the island offers.
Ismael and Daan will be at your side all the way. They will take you to beautiful, hidden spots on the Ibiza and get you to overcome your fears and jump off cliffs into the sea. It's not just the physical feeling, but above all a mentally invigorating one.
Your first jump is hard to describe in words. You feel full of life, energy, courage and strength, as well as refreshed.
My first jump was unbelievable and I had the strong desire to do it all again!

Si quieres una inyección de adrenalina, ésta es la mejor manera de conseguirla mientras disfrutas del paisaje que ofrece la isla. Ismael y Daan estarán a tu lado saltando. Te llevarán a los rincones más escondidos y bonitos de Ibiza y te ayudarán a superar tus miedos y a dar ese salto desde los alcantilados al mar. No se trata sólo de eso, sino de toda una experiencia mentalmente revitalizante.
La sensación después de tu primer salto es difícil de describir. ¡Te sientes lleno de vida, energía, corajey fuerza.
Mi primer salto fue increíble y tuve el deseo fuerte de volver a repetirlo.

✳ THE WORKOUT CLUB IBIZA (ON THE BEACH)

Tel: 677.045.023 twc-ibiza.com FB: The Workout Club Ibiza

Marisa & Virgil started this workout club a few years ago with the aim to help improve your quality of life by providing training and nutrition programs.
Their methods are fun and very effective and for men and women of all fitness levels offering physically and mentally challenging programs that are also fun and motivating. The classes take place outdoors on different beaches around the island. I am addicted, specially to sprinting barefoot down the beach, but I hate the press-ups!!

Marisa & Virgil abrieron este club hace unos años con el objetivo de ayudar a mejorar tu calidad de vida a través de programas de entrenamiento y nutrición.
Sus métodos son divertidos y muy eficaces, y para hombres y mujeres de cualquier estado físico y mental, con programas estimulantes, divertidos y motivadores. Las clases tienen lugar al aire libre en diferentes playas de la isla. Yo soy adicta, especialmente a las carreras de velocidad descalza por la playa, ¡pero odio las flexiones!

RETREATS + YOGA

✳ IBIZA RETREATS RETREATS, YOGA, WELLNESS AND HEALING EVENTS

Santa Eulalia Del Río. Tels: 662.093.499 - 670.348.292 • ibizaretreats.com

Run by Susie and Larah, Ibiza Retreats is a heart-based organizaion that devotes itself to offering its clients yoga and wellness holidays for deep healing and transformation on the island.

Dirigido por Susie y Larah, Ibiza Retreats es una organizaion que se dedica a ofrecer a sus clientes unas vacaciones de yoga y de bienestar para una curación profunda y transformación en la isla.

BEAUTY & MASAGE BELLEZA Y MASAJE

✳ PURE BALANCE REFLEXOLOGY, CLINICAL REFLEXOLOGY, NATURAL LIFT FACE MASSAGE

Ctra. de San Juan, km 8.5, Santa Eulalia Del Río. Tels: 671.430.531 • purebalancereflexology.com

Virginia uses reflexology to relieve you of stress, back pain, migranes, arthritis, insomnia and also does an amazing natural lift face mask by boosting your circulation and stimulating your nervous system, using facial reflexology, Japanese face masage all combined with an Indian head masage.

Virginia usa la reflexología para aliviar la tensión, el dolor de espalda, la artritis o el insomnio. Hace rejuvenecimiento facial con una mascarilla, aumentando la circulación y estimulando el sistema nervioso, usando reflexología facial y un masaje japonés combinado con un masaje indio de cabeza.

✳ AMANDA TIZZARD (MASSAGE)

Morna Valley. 60€/h in studio - 90€/h mobile (to your home). Tel: 639.152.912 • amandatizard@hotmail.com

Lovely Amanda Tizzard is an experienced massage and craniosacral therapist. She blends an interesting mix of massage and deep relaxation techniques to suit each client. An expert in releasing physical and emotional blockages. Deep tissue massage, cranio sacral or both. After her treatments you will feel renewed. She specialises in back, neck and shoulder pain.

Amanda Tizard es una masajista y terapeuta craneosacral con mucha experiencia. Combina una interesante mezcla de masajes con relajación profunda que se adaptan a cada cliente. Experta en la liberación de bloqueos físicos y emocionales. Masajes de tejido profundo, craneales. Después de sus tratamientos te sientes renovada. Especializa en espalda, cuello y dolores de hombro.

✳ SPIRITOFIBIZA **Tel: 664 383 872 • www.spiritofibiza.net**

A fab mobile wellbeing service on the island. From Yoga and Massage to palm readings. I had an amazing deep tissue massage with them which I would highly recommend. If you want they also do facials and teeth whitening!!

Un servicio fantástico de bienestar móvil en la isla. Yoga, masaje lecturas de la mano. Tuve un masaje increíble y profundo con ellos que recomiendo. Si quieres también puedes hacerte faciales y hasta blanquearte los dientes!

CUPCAKES, CAKES, MACARONS, COOKIES, WOOPIE PIES...

✳ SUGAR RUSH IBIZA BY NILO (BAKING FOR PRIVATE EVENTS, PARTIES...)

Tel: 671.436.125

Deliciously baked goodies for special occasions, where the possibilities in design and flavouring are endless and the only limit is your imagination. It's the best way to add a personal touch to a special moment or to indulge into a piece of heavenly sweetness on a regular day.

Pasteles, galletas, cupcakes horneados para ocasiones especiales, donde las posibilidades de diseño y gusto son infinitas y el único límite es tu imaginación. Es la mejor manera de añadir un toque personal a un momento especial o para disfrutar de dulzura celestial en un día normal.

GET YOURSELF A STICKER!!

¡PÍLLATE UNA PEGATINA!!

✳ LA CASITA VERDE (INLAND) **San José, Tel: 971.187.353**

chris@greenheart.info • casitaverde.com Sun/dom: 14 - 19h + 17 - 20h

Earth friendly Chris Dews started this thriving eco place years ago. Their doors are open to the public every Sunday throughout the year, when the team at Casita Verde serve up healthy, vegetarian (and cheap) lunches from 2pm, made almost entirely from local produce. Following lunch, at around 4.30pm, a tour of the property takes place where you can visit a network of unique eco-dwellings including a tree-house, Gaia centre, bottle house and a magic cave. It's an eye opener for the kids and there's also activities and a playground to keep the little ones entertained.

Chris Dews, amante de la naturaleza, fundó este lugar ecológico hace años. Sus puertas están abiertas al público los domingos durante todo el año, y el equipo de Casita Verde sirve comidas sanas y vegetarianas desde las 14:00, todo hecho con productos locales. Después del almuerzo, a las 16:30, dan un paseo por la finca, donde visitarás viviendas ecológicas incluyendo una casita en un árbol, un hogar en un horno de cal, el centro Gaia, una casa hecha de botellas y una cueva mágica. Es educativo y divertido para los niños, hay actividades y un parque para mantener a los más pequeños entretenidos.

BE GREEN IN IBIZA AND FORMENTERA

by Chris Dews (Casita Verde)

Whether you're a resident or a visiting tourist, the islands need a careful and conscious population to keep them in good condition. So, how can we be more eco-friendly here?

• Start by ensuring not to leave any litter behind when out for a picnic or a beach visit. Take a plastic bag with you and pick up litter dropped by others, or join in with beach cleaning events. Ibizalimpia.com

• Recycle waste.

• Use a minimum of fuel.

• Use your own shopping bag to buy groceries.

• Switch off the lights when not in use.

• Reduce water consumption.

For any home remedies ask Chris Dews at Casita Verde. Tels: 971.187.353- 608.838.190

SER ECOLÓGICO EN IBIZA Y FORMENTERA

por Chris Dews (Casita Verde)

Tanto si eres residente como un turista de visita, las islas necesitan una población consciente para mantenerlas en buen estado.

¿cómo podemos ser más ecológicos aquí?

• Empieza por asegurarte de no dejar basura atrás cuando salgas de picnic o visites la playa. Llévate una bolsa de plástico y recoge basura depositada por otros y la tuya, y únete a eventos de limpieza de playas. Ibizalimpia.com

• Recicla tu basura.

• Usa el mínimo de gasolina.

• Usa una cesta para tu compra.

• Apaga las luces cuando no las utilices.

• Reduce el consumo de agua.

Para remedios locales pregunta a Chris Dews en Casita Verde. Tels: 971.187.353 - 608.838.190

ART CLASES CLASES DE ARTE

✳ ART CLASES WITH JOEL (SAN JUAN)

San Juan. Tel: 699.296.169 • joelricedesign@gmail.com

Joel offers art classes designed to spark creativity and imagination in children and adults in the garden of his Bohemian artist house. Private classes can be arranged.

He also instructs students working for their GCSE and A level art exams. All levels of experience welcome.

Joel ofrece clases de arte para despertar la creatividad y la imaginación en niños y adultos en el jardín de su casa bohemia.

Tambien ofrece clases privadas.

Ayuda extra con examenes de Arte GCSE y A Level británico para estudiantes.

Todos los niveles son bienvenidos.

IBIZA

EAT/DRINK
COMER/BEBER

Bar 1805 (Bistro)
C/ Santa Lucía, 7,
Sa Penya,
Tel: 651.625.972
bar1805ibiza.com

Bar Los Amigos
C/ de Felip II, s/n,
Tel: 971.313.818

Bar Maravillas
C/ de Manuel Sorà, 6
Tel: 634.234.543

Bella Napoli
Av. Sta. Eulària des Riu, 9,
Tel: 971.310.105

Bistrot El Jardín
Plaça de la Constitució, 11,
(Mercado Viejo)
Tel: 669.606.565

Café Madagascar
Plaça del Parc, 4,
Tel: 971.555.555

Can Alfredo
Paseeig de Vara de Rey, 16,
Tel: 971.311.274

Can Gourmet
C/ de Montgri, 18b,
Tel: 611.395.994

Can Terra
Av. d'Ignasi Wallis, 14,
Tel: 971.310.064

Can Pou Bar
C/ Lluis Tur i Palau, 19,
Tel: 971.310.875

Can Vadell
C/ d'Annibál, 13
Tel: 971.310.728

Comidas Bar San Juan
C/ Montgri 8,
Tel: 971.311.603

Cositas Ricas
C/ de Pere Francès, 21,
Tel: 871.518.806

Chill Café
Via Púnica, 49,
Tel: 971.399.736

Dôme
C / d'Alfons XII, 5,
Sa Penya,
Tel: 971.317.456

El Zaguán
Av. Bartomeu de
Roselló, 15,
Tel: 971.192.882

Es Baladre
C/ de Vicente Cuervo, 19,
Tel: 971.311.967

El Portalon
Plaça dels Desamparats, 1,
Dalt Vila,
Tel: 871.110.925
elportaloneivissa.com

El Pirata
C/ Cipriano Garijo, 10,
Puerto de Ibiza
Tel: 971.192.630

El Rincón del Puerto
C/ Enmig, 50, Sa Penya
Tel: 971.314.665
rincondelpuertoibiza.com

Es Tap Nou
C/ de Madrid, 18,
Tel: 971.399.841
estapnou.es

Gelato Ibiza
Passeig de Vara de Rey, 12,
Tel: 971.931.133

Hostal Parque
Plaça del Parc, 4,
Tel: 971.301.358.
hostalparque.com

Il Pavone
C/ d'Enmig, 22, Sa Penya
Tel: 971.315.555

La Bodega
C/ Bisbe Torres Mayans, 2,
Tel: 971.192.740

La Bufalina
Passeig de Vara de Rey, 13,
Tel: 971.302.894

La Cava
Passeig de Vara de Rey, 4,
Tel: 971.316.074
lacavaibiza.com

La Dispensa
C/ la Santa Creu, 10,
Dalt Vila
Tel: 971.124.365

La Oliva
C/ la Santa Creu, Dalt
Vila, Ibiza
Tel: 971.305.752

La Tagliatella
Av. Sta. Eulària des Riu, 15,
Tel: 971.194.136
latagliatella.es

La Tana
C/ del Passadis, 3,
Sa Penya,
Tel: 630.258.984

La Virgen
C/ de La Mare de Déu, 75,
Sa Penya
Tel: 665.594.705

Las Libertinas
C/ Ses Pasadis, 10,
Tel: 648.169.535

Locals Only
Plaça del Parc, 5,
Tel: 971.301.997
localsonlyibiza.com

Los Pasajeros Puerto
C/ Vicente Soler, 6, 1º,
Tel: 653.350.961

L'Oriental
C/ de Castella, 7,
Tel: 634.036.334.

Mar A Vila
Av. d'Ignasi Wallis, 16,
Tel: 971.314.778
maravilaibiza.com

Osteria Il Gatto e La Volpe
C/ del Passadis, 28,
Sa Penya,
Tel: 871.700.738

Out of Time People
C/ Jaume, 2,
Tel: 971.392.321

Paradise lost
C/ del passidis, 14,
Sa Penya,
Tel: 627589205
paradiselostibiza.com

Pastis
C/ Avicena, 2, Ibiza
Tel: 971.391.999
pastisibiza.com

Restaurante Pinocho
C/ d'Enmig, 18,
Sa Penya
Tel: 971.310.176

Savianda
C/ Bartolomé Vicente
Ramón, 27
Tel: 971.314.719

S'Escalinata
C/ Portal Nou, 10,
Dalt Vila,
Tel: 653.371.356
sescalinata.es

Sunrise
C/ de La Mare de Déu, 44,
Sa Penya
Tel: 677.489.827

Sushiya Aoyama
Plaça de sa Drassaneta, 13,
Sa Penya
Tel: 627.861.566

Sushi and Love
C/ Carles III, 19
Tel: 971.318.013

Teatro Pereyra
C/ del Comte Rosselló, 3,
Tel: 971.304.432
teatropereyra.com

Taller de Sa Penya
C/ Alt, 7, Sa Penya,
Tel: 971.312.190
borisbuono.com

Thai'd Up
Plaza de Sa Riba,
Tel: 971.191.668

The Rock Bar
C/ Cipriano Garijo,
Tel: 971.310.129

Va Bene Disco Burger
Av. Bartomeu de Roselló, 14,
Tel: 971.194.180

White Buddha
C/ Cipriano Garijo,
Tel: 625.529.406
whitebuddhaibiza.com

SLEEP/DORMIR

Casa Huéspedes
Passeig de Vara de Rey, 7,
Tel: 971.301.376
hibiza.com

El Mirador
Plaça d'Espanya, 4,
Dalt Vila
Tel: 971.303.045
hotelmiradoribiza.com

Hostal La Marina
C/ Barcelona, 7
Tel: 971.310.172
hostal-lamarina.com

Hostal Juanita
C/ de Joan d' Austria, 17,
Tel: 971.314.828
hostaljuanita.com

La Ventana
C/ de sa Carrossa, 13,
Dalt Vila,
Tel: 971.390.857
laventanaibiza.com

Torre del Canónigo
C/ Mayor, 8, Dalt Vila
Tel: 971.303.884
latorredelcanonigo.com

Urban Spaces Hotel
Via Púnica, 32,
Tel: 871.517.174

SHOP/TIENDAS

Angels
Passeig de Vara de Rey, 10,
Tel: 971.310.775
angelsshopibiza.com

Bagus
C/ de Pere Sala, 1,
Tel: 971.301.373
ibizabagus.es

Cachirulo Balloon Shop
Via Punica, 11,
Tels: 971. 391.846
666. 108.624
cachiruloysusamigos.com

Campos de Ibiza
C/.de Vicente Cuervo, 20,
Tel: 971.806.886
camposdeibiza.com

Can Murenu
Passeig Vara de Rey, 5.
Tel: 971.301.930

Cerrafer
Via Púnica, 53
Tel: 971.307.520

Croissant Show
Plaça de la Constitució,
Tel: 971.317.665
croissant-show-ibiza.com

Delta Disco
Av. d'Espanya, 7
Tel: 971.306.721
discosdeltaibiza.com

Don Kroquet
C/ de Catalunya, 10
Tel: 661.628.996

El Rápido
C/ Aragón, 69,
Tels: 971.391.037
M: 647.802.148

Farmacia Juan Tur Viñas
C/. d'Antoni Palau, 1
Tel: 971.310.015

Ferretería Ibiza
C/ de Joan d'Austria, 17,
Tel: 971.315.823

Ho-La-La Vintage
Plaça de la Constitució 12,
(Mercado Viejo)
Tel: 971.316.537
holala-ibiza.com

Inkadelic
Plaça de la Constitució 10,
(Mercado Viejo)
Tel: 676.168.122
inkadelictattooing.com

La Boutik
C/. de Sa Creu, 12,
Tel: 971.199.740

La Cucaña
C/ d'Aragó, 107
Tel: 971.303.880

Le Studio
C/ de Manuel Sora, 25,
Tel: 658.216.746
lestudioibiza.com

Lovy Ibiza by The Sandal Shop
Passeig de Vara de Rey, 12,
Tel: 971.317.602

Mathiss Ibiza
Via Púnica, 18, Ibiza
Tel: 971. 393.489
mathissibiza.com

Mercería Luis Valero Sala
C/ de Sa Xeringa, 8
Tel: 971.310.187

Moms & Babies
Av. d'Espanya, 17
Tel: 971.307.766
momsandbabies.es

Natural
Via Púnica, 40
Tel: 971.302.075

Mayurka
Passeig de Vara de Rey,10, +
Av. d'Ignasi Wallis, 11
Tel: 971.398.362

Purnima
C/ del Bisbe Azara, 5,
Tel: 971.302.772

Religion
C/ del Comte de Roselló,14,
Tel: 626.392.720
religionclothing.com

ReVolver
C/ del Bisbe Azara, 1,
Tel: 971.318.939
revolveribiza.com

Petit Salon de Té
C/ d'Antoni Guasch Juan, 2,
Tel: 971. 307.102

Sa Majesté
C/ de La Mare de Déu, 67,
Sa Penya
samajeste.com

Sid Shanti's Take Away Food Service
C/ Abad i Lasierra,
Tel: 971.578.518
sidshanti.com

Sombrerería Bonet
C/ del Comte Rosselló, 6,
Tel: 971.310.668

The Barber Ibiza
C/ Menorca, 8,
Tel: 971.312.877

Vadepelo
Passeig de Vara Rey, 7, 2º,
Tel: 971.393.469

Vincente Ganesha
C/ de Guillem de Montgri,14,
Tel: 971.193.605

LA MARINA BOTAFOCH

EAT/DRINK COMER/BEBER

A Son de Mar
C/ Ponent, 118,
Marina Botafoch
Tel: 971.313.151
restauranteasondemar.com

Bar Barlovento
Port Deportivo Marina
Botafoch
Tel: 971.317.717

Box 7
Passeig Joan Carles I, 39
Tel. 971.199.880
box7ibiza.com

Club Náutico Ibiza
Av. de Santa Eulària des
Riu, 1006
Tel: 971.314.023

Downtown Ibiza
Ibiza Gran Hotel,
Passeig Joan Carles I, 17
Tel: 971.599.050
cipriani.com/locations/ibiza

Il Giardinetto
Passeig de Joan Carles I
Marina Botafoch
Tel: 971.314.929

Just Fish Ibiza
Marina Botafoch,
Local 105b
Tel: 971.508.761

Keeper
Paseo Juan Carlos I, s/n
Tel: 971.310.509
keeperibiza.com

La Terrasse Botafoch
Marina Botafoch, Local 114
Tel: 971.316.654

Los Pasajeros Botafoch
Marina Botafoch
Tel: 971.317.828

Passion Botafoch
Passeig Juan Carles I, 23,
Edificio Mediteraneo
Tel: 971.305.130
passion-ibiza.com

Prince Bakery
Paseo Juan Carlos I, Local 3
Tel: 871.718.361

Sa Calma
Marina Ibiza
Tel: 971.595.595

Sa Nansa
Av. 8 d'Agost, 27
Tel: 971.318.750
restaurantesanansa.com

Sushi Point
Marina Botafoch, Local 205
Tel: 971.318.153
sushipointibiza.com

Temakinho Ibiza
Marina Botafoch, Local 113
Tel: 971.199.944

Trattoria del Mar
Marina Botafoch
Tel: 971.193.934
trattoriadelmaribiza.com

SLEEP/DORMIR

El Hotel (Pacha)
Paseo Juan Carlos I
Tel: 971.806.806

Hotel Argos
Playa de Talamanca
Tel: 971.312.162
hotelargos-ibiza.com

Ibiza Gran Hotel
Paseo Juan Carlos I
Tel: 971.806.806

INDEX-INDICE

Ocean Drive
Marina Botafoch
Tel: 971.318.112

✳ ✳ ✳ ✳

TALAMANCA

EAT/DRINK
COMER/BEBER

Bar Alegría
C/ de Talamanca
Talamanca
Tel: 971.313.574

Bar Flotante
C/ de Talamanca,
Talamanca
Tel: 971.190.466

El Pulpo Restaurante
C/ de Talamanca,
Talamanca
Tel: 971.191.530

Hostal Talamanca
C/ de Talamanca,
Talamanca
Tel: 971.312.463
hostaltalamanca.com

La Bodega Talamanca
C/ Ses Figueres, 18,
Talamanca
Tel: 672.494.847
labodegaibiza.es

Restaurante Bellamar
C/ de Talamanca,
Talamanca
Tel: 971.191.335

Sa Punta
C/ Calandria, Sa Punta
Tel: 971.193.424

Talamanca Club
C/ de Ses Feixes
Talamanca
Tel: 971.313.574

The Fish Shack
C/ Calandria, Sa Punta,
Talamanca

The Harbour Club
C/ de Talamanca,
Talamanca
Tel: 971.193.380
theharbourclub.com

✳ ✳ ✳ ✳

HOTELS

Destino Pacha Ibiza Resort
C/ Pettirojo, 18 Cap Martinet
Tel: 971.317.411
destinoibiza.com

Hostal Talamanca
C/ de Talamanca,
Talamanca
Tel: 971.312.463
hostaltalamanca.com

Hotel Simbad
C/ Ses Figueres, 22,
Talamanca
Tel: 971.311.862
hotelsimbad.es

Lux Isla
C/ Josep Pla, 1, Talamanca
Tel: 971.313.469
luxisla.com

✳ ✳ ✳ ✳

JESUS

EAT/DRINK

Ascua
C/ Faisán, 8, Jesús
Tel: 971.194.881
ascua.es

Bon LLoc
Ctra. a Cala Llonga, Jesús
Tel: 971.311.813

Canadian
C/ des Cap Martinet, 8,
Jesús
Tel: 971.194.881
canadiancoffeeculture.co

Carnicería JR Can Español
C/ des Cap Martinet
Tel: 971.300.269

Carpe Diem
C/ des Cap Martinet, 54,
Jesús
Tel: 971.314.520

El Deseo Jesús
C/ des Cap Martinet, 7,
Tel: 971.194.635
eldeseoibiza.com

Kodo
C/ des Cap Martinet,
Esq Llinquer, Jesús
Tel: 971.193.319
kodoibiza.com

La Vinería
C/ des Cap Martinet, 3,
Tel: 971.191.827
lavineriaibiza.com

Marc's Restaurante
Ctra. Cala Llonga Km 0,6,
Tel: 971.316.245
restaurante-marcs-ibiza.com

Ses Torres
C/ de Jesús > Cap Martinet
Tel: 971.318.932

✳ ✳ ✳ ✳

SHOP/TIENDAS

Rita Savor
C/ des Cap Martinet,
Edif. Balcón de Jesús,II
Tel: 971.190.305

Comestibles + Papelería Can Pascual
Ctra. Cala Llonga, Jesús
Tel: 971.310.528

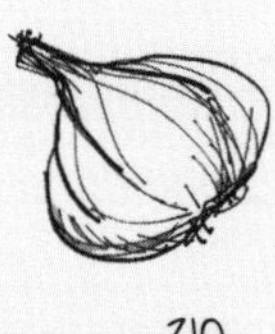

Ferretería Clapés Guasch
Local 3, Jesús
Tel: 971.313.276

Clínica Veterinaria Jesús
C/ Faisán, 4, Jesús
Tel: 971.312.929
Emergency
Tel: 649.984.777

✳ ✳ ✳ ✳

PUIG D'EN VALLS

EAT/DRINK
COMER/BEBER

Es Cami Vell
C/ Vicente Marí Mayans, s/n
Puig d'en Valls, Ibiza
Tel: 971.316.665

Oli Tapas
C/Mar Mediterràni, 34,
Puig d'en Valls
Tel: 971.315.951

✳ ✳ ✳ ✳

SHOP/TIENDAS

Box 3
Polig. Sa Blanca Dona S. 1,
Nave 3 - Puig d'en Valls,
Tel: 971.199.731
box3ibiza.com

Decathlon
Finca Sa Olivera, 3,
Tel: 971.318.088
decathlon.es

Fita
Av. de Sant Joan de Labritja, 25-33
Tel: 971.313.062
fitaibicentro.com

✳ ✳ ✳ ✳

FITNESS

BFIT Ibiza Sports Club
C/ Metge Domingo Nicolau
Balançat, 4, Ibiza
Tel: 971.806.885
bfitibiza.com

OUTSKIRTS

EAT/DRINK
COMER/BEBER

Bar Astro
C/ Portinatx, 1,
Av. Sant Josep
Tel: 971.302.338

Eat is Life
Av. la Pau, Ibiza,
Tel: 971.312.201
eatislife.es

Charlotte Cafe-Ibiza
C/ de Canaries, 36,
Tel: 971.315.405
charlotteibiza.com

Miss Saigon
Av.d'Espanya, 59
Tel: 871.021.769

Kathmandu Ibiza
C/ de Canaries, 28, B8
Tel: 971.931.506
kathmandu2ibiza.com

Kebab La Paz
C/ de Balears - C/ Agapit Llobet

202 Hamburger & Delicious
C/del Bisbe Abad y Lasierra, 34,
Tel: 971.313.919

✳ ✳ ✳ ✳

SHOP/TIENDAS

Bicicletas Juan Ferrer
C/ d'Atzarò, 14,
Casas Baratas
Tel: 971.391.401
bicicletasjferrer.com

Cinema Complex Multicines
C/ des Cubells,
Tel: 971.315.211

Confort
Av. Sant Josep de sa Talaia, 18,
Tel: 971.306.831
confort-electro.com

Pinturas Martínez
C/ d'Atzarò, 15,
Tel: 971.301.081
martinezpinturas.com

Pinturas Rubio
Riu Guadiana, 17,
Carretera San José
Tel: 971. 303.683
pinturasrubio.es

Vila Parc Bowling
C/ des Cubells, 32, Ibiza
Tel: 971.199.540
bowlingvilaparc.com

Wash and Drink
Av. d'Espanya, 53,
Tel. 971.306.379

FIGUERETES

EAT/DRINK

All Café Bistro
Passeig Ses Pitiusas, 28
Figueretes
Tel: 971. 301.925

Casa 13 Piadina
C/ Periodista Francesc Escanellas, 13, Figueretes
Tel: 971.306.154

Restaurante Soleado
Passeig Ses Pitiusas, s/n,
Figueretas
Tel: 971.394.811
soleadoibiza.com

Retro Gusto
C/ Del País Basc, 6,
Figueretes

The Boo
Av. Pedro Matutes Noguera, 43, Figueretes
Tel: 661.690.434

SLEEP/DORMIR

Hostal Pitiusa
C/ de Galicia, 29,
Figueretes
Tel: 971.301.905
hostalpitiusa.com

Hotel Cenit
Archiduque Luis Salvador,
Los Molinos, Figueretes
Tel: 971.30.40.93
hotelcenit.com

Es Vivé
C/ de Carles Roman Ferrer, Figueretes
Tel: 971.301.902

THE SOUTH + BEACHES

EAT/DRINK COMER/BEBER

Beachouse
C/ de Platja d'en Bossa, 2
Playa den Bossa
Tel: 971 39 68 58
beachouseibiza.com

El Chiringuito
Es Cavallet
Tel: 971.395.485
elchiringuitoibiza.com

Forty Fives Bistro Bar
Carrer de La Punta,
Playa d'en Bossa
forty-fives.com

La Escollera
Es Cavallet
Tel: 971.396.572
laescolleraibiza.com

Lips Reartes Ibiza
Porreres, 1,
Playa d'en Bossa
Tel: 971.300.415

Passion d'en Bossa
Edificio Bossamar
C/ de Platja d'en Bossa
Tel: 971.305.130

SLEEP/DORMIR

Hotel Garbi
C/de la Murtra, 5,
Playa d'en Bossa.
Tel: 971.300.007
hotelgarbi-ibiza.com

Santos Ibiza Coast Suites
C/ Bruc, 3,
Playa d'en Bossa
Tel: 971.301.023
santosibizacoastsuites.com

Santos Dorado Suites
C/ Bruc, 3,
Playa d'en Bossa
Tel: 971.393.268
santosibizacoastsuites.com

Tropicana Coast Suites
Deessa Tanit, 10/12
Playa d'en Bossa
Tel: 971.393.268
tropicanaibizacoastsuites.com

SANT JORDI

EAT/DRINK COMER/BEBER

Vinyl Burger
Ctra. del'Aeropuerto 31,
Sant Jordi
Tel: 971.395.935
vinylburgeribiza.com

Rasca Lobos
Av. Vicente Serra, 25.
Sant Jordi
Tel: 971.395.860

S'Hortet Verd
C/ dels Pirineus, 11,
San Jordi
Tel: 971.308.030
shortetverd.info

Pinzimonio
Carrer de Montblanc, 23,
Sant Jordi
Tel: 971.932.971

SHOP/TIENDAS

Ferretería FSJ St Jordi
Ctra. Aeropuerto Km 3, 9
Tel: 971.395.646

Tabac St Jordi
Ctra. Aeropuerto 61 B,
Sant Jordi
Tel: 971.396.589

Heladería St Jordi
Ctra Aeropuerto, Edificio Las Olas
Tel: 971.599.566

SALINAS

EAT/DRINK COMER/BEBER

Coricancha
Ctra. de Ses Salines,
San Francisco
Tel: 971.074.226
coricanchaibiza.com

Experimental Beach
Playa d'es Codolar,
Playa de Las Salinas
Tel: 664.331.269

Jockey Club
Playa de Las Salinas
Tel: 971.395.788
jockeyclubibiza.com

San Francisco Bar
Ctra. de Ses Salines,
San Francisco
Tel: 971.940.174

Sa Trinxa
Playa de Las Salinas
Tel: 637.826.183
satrinxa.com

SHOP/TIENDAS

Echoamano
Ctra. Sa Canal,
Las Salinas
Tel: 971.932.032
hostalsalinas.com

Super Can Pep Tixedó
Ctra. de Las Salinas
supercanpeptixedo.com

SLEEP/DORMIR

Boutique Hostal Salinas
Ctra. Sa Canal,
Las Salinas
Tel: 971.308.899
hostalsalinas.com

EAT/DRINK COMER/BEBER

Can Salinas
Ctra. de Las Salinas,
Km3.7
Tel: 971.396.563

La Ponderosa
Ctra. del Aeropuerto, km 7
Tel: 673.453.940

SA CALETA

EAT/DRINK COMER/BEBER

Restaurante Sa Caleta
Playa d'es Bol Nou,
Sa Caleta
Tel: 971.187.095

Rincon de Es Codolar
Ctra. Sa Caleta,
Es Codolar
Tel: 971.396.011

Soul Beach Café
Playa Es Codolar
Tel: 672.883.583
soulbeachcafe.com

SLEEP/DORMIR

Es Raco
Ctra Sa Caleta,
Es Codolar
Tel: 971.591.541
esraco.eu

Cosmos Grand Hostal
Ctra. Sa Caleta,
Es Codolar
Tel: 971.308.077 -
646.062.595
cosmosibiza.com

SOUTHWEST

EAT/DRINK
COMER/BEBER

Bar Restaurante Llumbi
Es Cubells
Tel: 971.802.128

Blue Marlin
Cala Jondal
Tel: 971.410.117
bluemarlinibiza.com

Ca Na Vergara
Cala d'Hort
Tel: 971.935.036

Es Boldadó
Camí de Cala d'Hort, s/n
Cala d'Hort
Tel: 626.494.537
restauranteboldado.net

El Carmen
Cala d'Hort
Tel: 971.187.449

Es Savina
Cala Jondal
Tel: 971.802.766 -
674.404.645

Es Xarcú
Es Porroig
Tel: 971.187.867

Ses Boques
Playa de Ses Boques,
Es Cubells
Tel: 606.081.570

Km5
Ctra. Ibiza > San José
Tel: 971.396.349
km5-lounge.com

La Gourmandise
Ctra. San José >
San Jordi
Tel: 627.681.930

Mo
Ctra. de Es Cubells, km 5,5
Cala de Bou
Tel: 971.802.150
restaurantemoibiza.com

Ostería La Taverna
Ctra. San José, km 1 >
San Jordi
Tel: 971.303.221

Tropicana
Cala Jondal
Tel: 971.187.520
tropicanaibiza.com

Vino & Co
Ctra. San José >
San Jordi
Tel: 971.305.324
vinoyco.com

Yemanja
Cala Jondal
Tel: 971.187.481
yemanjaibiza.com

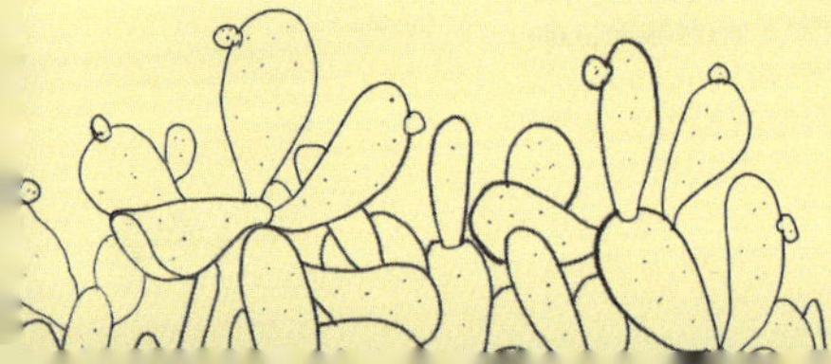

THE WEST, BEACHES + SAN ANTONIO

EAT/DRINK
COMER/BEBER

Ample 32
C/ de la Soletat, 64,
San Antonio
Tel: 971.348.132
ample32.com

Casa Thai
Avda. Isidor Macabich, 8
Tel: 971.343.562

Café del Mar
General Balanzat 38,
San Antonio
Tel: 971.348.706
cafedelmaribiza.com

Curry Club
Ctra. San Antonio, 38,
San Antonio
Tel: 971.343.604

El Quijote
C/ Ample, 17,
San Antonio
Tel: 971.343.681

El Sapo
C/ Bisbe Torres, 3,
San Antonio
Tel: 971.343.540

Es Rebost de Can Prats
Calle Cervantes, 4
San Antonio
Tel: 971.346.252

Golden Buddha
Paseo de Caló des Moro,
San Antonio
Tel: 971.345.633

Ibiza Rocks Hotel
C/ Cervantes, 27,
San Antonio
Tel: 971.340.137
ibizarocks.com

Kama Sushi
General Balanzat, 43,
San Antonio.
Tel: 687.280.376

Mambo Café
C/ de Vara del Rey,
San Antonio
Tel: 971 346.638
cafemamboibiza.com

Menjabé
C/ Progreso, 34,
San Antonio
Tel: 636.368.956

Mint Lounge Bar
Sunset Strip, San Antonio
Tel: 971.595.903.
sugarseaibiza.com

Rita's Cantina
Paseo Marítimo
Tel: 971.343.387
ritascantina.com

Restaurante Benítez
C/ Madrid Edificio Reino 1,
San Antonio
Tel: 971.345.420

Savannah Beach Club
C/ del General Balanzat, 38,
San Antonio
Tel: 971.348.031
savannahibiza.com

The Ship Inn
Plaza de Mercado,
San Antonio
Tel: 971.342.130.
theshipibiza.com

Tijuana Tex-Mex
C/ de Ramón i Cajal, 23
San Antonio
Tel: 971.342.473

El Tiburón
Passeig de la Mar, 20
San Antonio
Tel: 971.340.803

Villa Mercedes
Paseo del Mar, San Antonio
Tel: 971.348.543
villamercedesibiza.com

Zebra
C/ de la Soletat,
San Antonio
Tel: 971.347.867
zebra-ibiza.com

SHOP/TIENDAS

Peter The Butcher
C/ de la mar, 24
Tel: 971.342020
peterthebutcheribiza.com

Panadería Sa Talaïa
Ctra. Atalaya 3
Tel: 971.800.608

SLEEP/DORMIR

Hostal La Torre
Urb Cap Negret, 25,
San Antonio
Tel: 971.342.271
latorreibiza.com

Hotel Puchet
Avda. Doctor Fleming, 51
San Antonio
Tel: 971.390.426
hotelpuchet.com

Ibiza Rocks Hotel at Pikes
Camí de Sa Vorera,
San Antonio
Tel: +44.207.952.2919.
ibizarockshouse.com

EAT/DRINK

El Reencuentro
Calle del Mar, 5
San Antonio
Tel: 971.346.591
elreencuentroibiza.com

Putumayo
Ctra. Cap Negret 6,
Cala Gracio, San Antonio
Tel: 605.146.531

INDEX-INDICE

PORT DE'S TORRENT

* * * *

EAT/DRINK
COMER/BEBER

C'an Pujol
C/ des Caló,
Port d'es Torrent
Tel: 971.341.407

Kumharas
C/ de Lugo, 2,
Port d'es Torrent
Tel: 971.85.740
kumharas.org

Pom
Av. San Agustí, 73/75,
Cala de Bou
Tel: 971.078.182

Relish Ibiza
C/ d'es Caló,
Port d'es Torrent
Tel: 971.808.809
relishibiza.com

The Olive Tree
C/ Cantabria 40,
Port d'es Torrent
Tel: 971.340.907

* * * *

SAN JOSE

EAT/DRINK
COMER/BEBER

Bar Ca'n Bernat Vinya
C/ de Pere Escanelles,
San José
Tel: 971.800.703

Café Can Llorenç
C/ Can Pou, 2, San José
Tel: 971.801.601

Can Limo
Ctra. S.José, km 5,
Tel: 971 .800.550
canlimoibiza.com

Destino
Plaza de la Iglesia,
San José
Tel: 971.800.703

Es Galliner
C/ de l'Ajuntament, 2,
San José
Tel: 971.803.554

Es Vergé
Ctra. Sant Josep
Tel: 971.800.041
esverge.com

La Focacheria
C/ Bernat Toni, 10
San José
Tel: 971.801.130

La Movida Café
C/ de Pere Escanelles,
San José
Tel: 971.800.002

No Te Olvides De Acordarte
C/ de Cas Vildo, San José
Tel: 678.962.434

Passion San José
C/ de Pere Escanelles,
San José
Tel: 971.801.085
passion-ibiza.com

Pizzico di Pepe
C/ Can Bernat Toni, 10
Tel: 971.801.139

Racó Verd
Ctra.Port d'es Torrent,
San José. Tel: 971.341.407

* * * *

SHOP/TIENDAS

Aurobelle
C/ Bernad Toniet, 5,
San José
Tel: 971.800.920
aurobelle.com

Carnisseria Can Toni
C/ de Can Cantó, 3,
San José
Tel: 971.800.707

El Palio
C/ de Pere Escanellas, 32
San José
Tel: 971.800.047

Pescadería Oliver
C/ de Can Cantó, 3,
San José
Tel: 971.800.420

Silk Ibiza
C/ Pere Escanellas, 19,
San José
Tel: 971.801.698
silkibiza.es

* * * *

SLEEP/DORMIR

Villa Toscana
Vedra y Vedranells,
San José
Tel: 646.184.112

Les Jardins de Palerm
Can Pujol d'en Cardona,
San José. Tel: 971.800.318
jardinsdepalerm.com

Can Xuxu
Es Porroig, San José
Tel: 971.187.867

Ses Pitreras
C/ Valladolid, 1-3,
San Agustín
Tel: 971.345.000
sespitreras.com

* * * *

EAT/DRINK
COMER/BEBER

Chimi Churri
Ctra. Cala Conta, San José
Tel: 971 80 42 15
esverge.com

Bar Stop
Crta. Cala Conta + Cala Tarida
Tel: 971.346.985

Falsonueve
C/. Sant Josep km 11,5,
San José
Tel: 971.800.111
falsonueve.com

Botiga Can Jordi
Ctra. Ibiza >San José
Tel: 971.800.182

Can Domingo
Ctra. Ibiza >San José,
Km. 9.8
Tel: 971.800.184
candomingoibiza.com

Sluiz
Ctra. Ibiza >San José,
Km 8
Tel: 981.800.005

Can Berri Vell
Plaza Major, San Agustín
Tel: 971.344.321

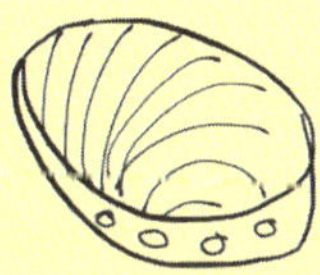

* * * *

BEACHES

Aisea Terraza-Bar Hotel Club Cala Tarida
Cala Tarida,
Tel: 971.806.167
aiseaibiza.com

Can Jaume Beach Bar
C/ Castelldefels, 5,
Cala Vadella,
Tel: 971.808.127
canjaume.com

Can Vicente
Cala Carbó,
Tel: 971.808.155

Cana Sofia
C/ Castelldefels, 10 , Cala Vedella
Tel: 971.808.273
canasofia.com

Chiringuito Cala Tarida
Cala Tarida,
Tel: 971.090.160
chiringuitocalatarida.com

El Balneario
Cala Carbó
Tel: 971.808.251

El Chiringuito de Cala Gracioneta
Cala Gracioneta,
Tel: 971.348.338
chiringuitoibiza.com

Ses Eufabies
Cala Tarida,
Tel: 971.806.328
eufabies.com

María Luisa
Cala Vadella,
Tel: 971.808.012

S'Illa Des Bosc
Cala Conta
Tel: 971.806.161
sillladesbosc.com

Sunset Ashram
Cala Conta,
Tel: 661.347.222

* * * *

SANTA INÉS

EAT/DRINK
COMER/BEBER

Can Cosmi
Plaza de la Iglesia,
Santa Inés
Tel: 971.805.020

SHOP/TIENDAS

Cas Sabater
Plaza Corona, 3,
Santa Inés
Tel: 971.805.051
cas-sabater.com

SLEEP/DORMIR

Es Cucons
C/ Camí des Pla de Corona, 110
Tel: 971.805.501
escucons.com

* * * *

SHOP/TIENDAS

Can Tixedó
Carretera San Rafae>Sta Inés, Km5
Tel: 971.345.248

Can Partit
Camino de Talaia
Sta Agnés de Corona
Tel: 971.805.556
canpartit.com

Casa Datscha
San Antonio > Santa Agnès, Km3
Tel: 971.344.075
casadatscha.net

* * * *

SAN MATEO

EAT/DRINK
COMER/BEBER

Can Cires
San Mateo
Tel: 629.668.972
cancires.com

Can Sulayetas
Venda de Rubió, San Miguel
Tel: 971.334.567
can-sulayetas-ibiza.com
Tel: 971.805.036

Restaurante
Es Camp Vell
Camí de S Pla, 2, San Mateo

THE NORTH SAN MIGUEL

* * * *

EAT/DRINK

Estanco Can Xicu
C/ de Missa 7, San Miguel
Tel: 971.334.416

* * *

SHOP/TIENDA

Can Planells
Art Souvenirs
C/ de Missa, San Miguel
Tel: 971.334.833

Dario Bomé
C/ de la Iglesia 10, San Miguel
Tel: 971.334.833

Natasha Collis Fine Jewellery
Can Josepet,
C/ de Missa 5
Tel: 971.334.654
natashacollis.com

* * * *

EAT/DRINK
COMER/BEBER

Aubergine Ibiza
Ctra. de San Miguel km 9.9
Tel: 971.090.055
info@aubergine.com

Kiosko Can Tothom
Puerto de San Miguel
Tel: 971.334.128

La Luna Nell'orto
Carretera del Puerto, San Miguel
Tel: 971.334.599
lunanellorto.com

Port Balanzat
C/ Port San Miguel
Tel: 971.334.527
restauranteportbalansat.com

Utopía Chiringuito
Calo d'es Moltons, San Miguel
Tel: 687.253.491

* * * *

SLEEP/DORMIR

Can Planells
Venda de Rubio, 2, San Miguel
Tel: 971.334.924
canplanells.com

Hotel Hacienda Na Xamena
Urbanización Na Xamena, San Miguel
Tel: 971.334.500
hotelhacienda-ibiza.com

Hotel Rural Cas Pla
Venda del Rubio, 59, San Miguel
Tel: 971.334.587
caspla-ibiza.com

Villa Ca'n Maries
Vénda Des Port, 30
Tel: 971.334.566
hotelcanmaries.com

* * * *

BENIRRAS

EAT/DRINK
COMER/BEBER

Benirràs 2000
Cala Benirràs
Tel: 971.333.313

Elements
Cala Benirràs
Tel: 971.333.136
elements-ibiza.com

Sejuiced
Cala Benirràs
sejuiced.eu

Rocamar
Cala Benirràs
Tel: 971.333.532

PORTINATX

SLEEP/DORMIR

Hostal La Cigüeña
S'Arenal Petit, 36, Cala Portinatx
Tel: 971.320.614
laciguenya.com

Los Enamorados
Cala Portinatx
Tel: 971.320.776

* * * *

EAT/DRINK
COMER/BEBER

Bar Restaurant San Joan
C/ San Vicente, San Juan
Tel: 971.333.141

Chiringuito Cala Xuclar
Cala Xuclar, Portinatx
Tel: 607.233.019

El Puerto Restaurante
Playa Puerto de Portinatx
Tel: 971.320.776

S'Illot Des Renclí
Ctra. Portinatx, km 25.3,
Tel: 971.320.585

* * * *

SAN JUAN

EAT/DRINK
COMER/BEBER

Ses Arcades
Ctra. San Juan, Km 19.3
Tel: 971.333.002

Sabores Naturales
C/ Juan Vicent Ferrer, 4, San Juan
Tel: 609.938.475

The Giri Café
Plaza de España 5, San Juan
Tel: 971.333.474
cafe.thegiri.com

Vista Alegre
C/ d'Eivissa, 1, San Juan
Tel: 971.333.008

* * * *

SHOP/TIENDAS

Lisi Peluquería
C/ Ibiza 16, local 2, San Juan
Tel: 971.935 648

* * * *

SLEEP/DORMIR

Can Fuster
Venda de Cas Ripolls 1,
Tel: 971.337.305
hotelruralibizacanfuster.com

Gare du Nord
C/ de Sa Cala, 11
Tel: 673.749.302
garedunordibiza.com

The Giri Residence
San Juan
Tel: 971.333.345
thegiri.com

* * * *

SAN VICENTE

EAT/DRINK
COMER/BEBER

Es Cafè casa Pepe
Sant Vicent de Sa Cala
Tel: 971.320.134

Can Gat
Cala San Vicente
Tel: 971.320.123

On The Beach
Cala San Vicente
Tel: 971.320.115
onthebeachibiza.com

Bambuddha Grove
Carretera San Juan,
Tel: 971.197.510
bambuddha.com

Can Balàfia
Ctra. San Juan, km 15,4
Tel: 971.325.019

Can Caus
Ctra. Sta Gertrudis,
Km 3.5,
Tel: 971.197.516
cancaus-ibiza.com

Can Curuné
Ctra. San Juan, Km 17,5
Tel: 971.333.054

Can Guimó Tabac
Ctra. San Juan,
Tel: 971.325.116

Can Toni
Ctra. Eivissa-Sant Joan, Km 4
Ca Na Negreta,
Santa Gertrudis
Tel: 971.190.973

Ca na Pepeta
Ctra. San Juan
Tel: 971.325.023

Cicale
Carretera San Juan,
Tel: 971.325.151
cicaleibiza.com

Es Pins
Ctra. San Juan, Km 14
Tel: 971.325.034

Juanito's
Ctra. San Juan, Km.15.4
Tel: 971.325.082

La Paloma
C/ Can Pou, 4,
San Lorenzo
Tels: 971.300.657
Tel: 971.325.543
palomaibiza.com

Nagai
Carretera San Juan,
Km 9.5
Tel: 971.807.308
nagairestaurant.com

Restaurante
Ses Escoles (Oleoteca)
Carretera San Juan,
Km 9,2
Tel: 871.870.229

Sa Barda
Ctra. San Juan Km 4,2
Ca na Negreta
Tel: 971.315.204.

SHOP/TIENDA

La Choza
Carretera San Miguel,
San Miguel
Tel: 971.310.228
lamasiadensort.com

Cocoq
Ctra. Santa Eulalia, km 6.2
Tel: 971.090.186
cocoqibiza.com

Ibiza Troc
Ctra. San Miguel,
Santa Gertrudis
Tel: 620.452.086

World Family Ibiza
Tel: 646.757.827
worldfamilyibiza.com

Sal de Ibiza Store
Ctra. Santa Eulalia km 3.4,
Santa Eulalia
Tel: 637.079.249

SLEEP/DORMIR

Atzaró
Ctra. Sant Juan, km 15
Tel: 971.338.838
atzaro.com

Can Gall
Ctra. San Juan, km 17,2
Tel: 971.337.031
agrocangall.com

Can Martí
Ctra. Ibiza>San Juan
Tel: 971.333.500
canmarti.com

Can Marquet
Ctra. San Lorenzo
Tel: 971.197.558
canmarquet.com

Casa Colonial
Ctra. Santa Eulalia, Km 2
Tel: 971.338.001
casa-colonial-ibiza.com

Les Terrasses
Ctra. Santa Eulalia, Km 1
Tel: 971.332.643
lesterrasses.net

SAN RAFAEL

EAT/DRINK
COMER/BEBER

Es Furnell
Pintor Narcís Puget, 2,
San Rafael
Tel: 971.198.975

Can Pilot
Carretera Eivissa,
San Rafael
Tel: 971.198.293

Es Tancó
Av. Isidor Macabich, 9
San Rafael
Tel: 971.198.599

Can Fresco
Avda. Isidor Macabich, 11
San Rafael
Tel: 680.374.653

Ibiza Underground
Ctra. Ibiza >San Antonio
Tel: 971.198.015
ibizaunderground.com

Las Dos Lunas
Ctra. Ibiza >San Antonio,
Km5
Tel: 971.198.102
lasdoslunas.com

La Belle
Av. Isidor Macabich,
San Rafael,
Tel: 971.198.335
labelleibiza.com

FORMENTERA

LA SAVINA

Motorent Migjorn
Puerto de La Savina
Tel: 971.321.111
motorentmigjorn.com

La Mola Rent
Puerto de La Savina
Tel: 971.323.554
Tel: 971.327.022
lamolarent.com

EAT/DRINK
COMER/BEBER

Amarre 32
Marina Deportiva de
Formentera
La Savina

Café del Lago
Ed. Sabina Playa,
Av. del Mediterráneo, 20
La Savina/Estany de Peix
Tel: 971.323.187
cafedellago.es

El Sueño
Porto Saler
Tel: 971.323.213
elsueño.com

Formentera Bakery
C/ Mare de deu del
Carme, 1
La Savina
Tel: 722.266.925
formenterabakery.com

Gastro...mania
C/ Almadrava, 67
La Savina
Tel: 971.323.311

Luna
La Savina
Tel: 971 321 585

SANT FRANCESC

EAT/DRINK
COMER/BEBER

Bar & Hostal Centro
Plaça Constitució, 3,
Sant Francesc
Tel: 971.322.063

Big Store
C/ d'Isidor Macabich, 2
Sant Francesc
Tel: 971.322.154

Bollicine
Avda. Pla del Rey 77,
Sant Francesc
Tel: 971.321.244
bollicine.es

Café Matinal
C/ De Arxiduc Lluis Salvador, 18, Sant Francesc
Tel: 971.322.547

Cafetería Es Glop
Afueras, 5 s/n, Edif. Sa
Sanieta, Sant Francesc
Tel: 971.322.966

Ca Na Joana
C/ de Berenguer, Renart, 2
Sant Francesc
Tel: 971.323.160
canajoanaformentera.com

Ca Na Pepa
Plaça de sa Constituciò, 5,
Sant Francesc
Tel: 971.321.091
canapepa.com

Ca Nova
C/ Eivissa, 14
Sant Francesc
Tel: 971.321.646

Can Carlos
Sant Francesc
Tel: 971.322.874
cancarlos.com

INDEX-INDICE

Can Gavinu
Ctra. de Sant Francesc, km 3,3
Tel: 971.322.421

Es Marès Cafetería
C/ de Santa Maria,15
Sant Francesc
Tel: 971.323.216
hotelesmares.com

Fonda Platé
C/ Jaume I,
Sant Francesc
Tel: 971.322.313

Giovale
Santa Maria, 59,
Sant Francesc
Tel: 971.322.758

Sa Panxa
Av. Castelló Guasch, 48
Sant Francesc
Tel: 971.329.106

Il Pirata del Tortello
Sant Francesc
Tel: 687.091.745

Nautilus Cafeteria
Avda. 8 d'Agost
Sant Francesc
Tel: 673.083.050

SHOP/TIENDA

Acacia
Santa María, 8
Sant Francesc
Tel: 971.321.206
acaciaformentera.com

Balàfia
Sant Francesc
Tel: 659.397.181

Ca Teua
Avda. Pla del Rey, 7
Sant Francesc
Tel: 971.321.078
cateua.com

Full Moon
C/ de Eivissa, 6,
Sant Francesc
Tel: 9713.22.376

Las Brisas
Can Toni Guillerm,
Sant Francesc
Tel: 971.322.815

Pepi
C/ des Pla del Rei,
Sant Francesc
Tel: 971.322.314

Perfumeria Centrale
Can Toni Guillerm,
Sant Francesc
Tel: 636.235.015

Rhei
C/ Ibiza, 15
Sant Frances
Tel: 971.322.804

Vintage
C/ de Santa Maria 3,
Plaza de La Iglesia,
Sant Francesc
Tel: 971.321.984
vintageformentera.com

CALA SAONA

EAT/DRINK
COMER/BEBER

A MI Manera
Ctra. de Cala Saona
Tel: 871.322.903
amimaneraformentera.com

Restaurante Es Cap
Ctra. Cap de Barbaria,
Cruce de Cala Saona
Tel: 971.322.104

Restaurante Marlaca
Urb. Paraíso de los Pinos
Es Mal Pas
Tel: 971.321.670
marlaca.es

Sud
Ctra. de Cala Saona,
Cap de Barbaria
Tel: 971.322.903
sudformentera.com

SAN FERRÁN

EAT/DRINK
COMER/BEBER

Fonda Pepe
C/. Mayor, Sant Ferran
Tel: 971.328.033

Hostal Illes Pitiüses
Avda. de Juan Castelló
Guasch, 48, Sant Ferrán
Tel: 971.328.189

Quartieri Spagnoli
C/. de La Cala En
Baster, 10
San Ferran
Tel: 609.415.350

ES PUJOLS

EAT/DRINK
COMER/BEBER

Bananas Bar & Co
C/ de Roca Plana,
Es Pujols
Tel: 619.143.277
bananasformentera.com

Bé Va Bé
C/ Espardell, Es Pujols
Tel: 971.328.554

Caminito
Ctra. de La Savina,
Es Calò
Tel: 971.328.106
caminitoformentera.es

Can Loca
Paseo Marítimo, Es Pujols
Tel: 971.321.883

Casanita
C/ Des Fonoll Marí, 101
Es Pujols
Tel: 971.321.968

Chezz Gerdi
Es Pujols
Tels: 971.328.603 - 648.020.106

Cincpedres
C/ Punta Prima 5,
Es Pujols
Tel: 971.321.940
cinqpedres.com

Don Pollo
Avda. Miramar,
Es Pujols
Tel: 971.328.076

Maritim
Paseo Marítimo,
Es Pujols,
Tel: 971.328.259

Integral
Avda. Miramar,
Es Pujols
Tel: 971.323.561

La Casa Della Piadina
Avda. Miramar, 65,
Es Pujols
Tel: 971.329.154
thebeachformentera.com

Restaurante La Tortuga
Crta. de La Savina a la Mola
Tel: 971.328.967
restaurantlatortuga.com

Sa Volta
C/ Miramar 94, Es Pujols
Tel: 971.323.160
savolta.com

Tipic
Avda. Miramar, 164,
Es Pujols
Tel: 676.885.452
clubtipic.com

SHOP/TIENDA

Janne Ibiza
C/Punta Prima, Es Pujols
Tel: 971.328.963
janneibiza.es

CTRA. LA MOLA

Can Dani
Ctra. de La Mola, Km 8,5
Tel: 971.328.505
candaniformentera.com

ES CALÓ

EAT/DRINK
COMER/BEBER

Es Cupinà
Playa d'Escupinà
Tel: 971.327.221
restauranteescupina.com

Restaurante Can Rafalet
Venda des Carnatge, 1-11,
Es Caló
Tel: 971.327.077

Restaurante Es Caló
C/ Vicari Joan Marí, 14,
Es Caló
Tel: 971.327.311

Restaurante Pascual
Es Caló de Sant Agustí
Tel: 971.327.014

INDEX-INDICE

LA MOLA

EAT/DRINK
COMER/BEBER

Can Toni
Plaça del Pilar, 1 y 2
Tel: 971.327.377
cantoniformentera.com

Codice Luna
Faro de la Mola
Tel: 675.636.725
codiceluna.com

SHOP/TIENDA

Can Xicu
Avda. de La Mola, 27
Tel: 650.003.308
canxicu.es

Majoral
Avda. La Mola, 0, El Pilar
Carrer de Jaume I, 29,
Sant Francesc
Tel: 971.321.148
majoral.com

BEACH BARS
CHIRINGUITOS

Beso Beach
Playa de Cavall d'en
Borràs
Tel: 622.222.113
besobeach.com

Blue Bar
Playa de Migjorn Km 7.9
Tel: 666.758.190
bluebarformentera.com

Flipper & Chiller
Playa de Migjorn, Km 11
Tel: 971.187.596

El Pirata
Playa de Illetes
Tel: 971.324.064

Es Molí de Sal
C/ Afores,
Platja de Illetes.
Tel: 971.187.491
esmolidesal.es

El Tiburón
Playa de Illetes
Tel: 659.638.945
tiburon-formentera.com

Juan y Andrea
Playa de Illetes
Tel: 630.258.144
juanyandrea.com

10.7
Playa de Migjorn, Km 10.7
Tel: 660.985.248
10punto7.com

Piratabus
Migjorn, km 11
piratabus.com

Restaurante Pelayo
Playa de Migjorn
Tel: 984.835.946

Sa Platjeta
Playa de Migjorn
Tel: 971.187.614

Sol Y Luna
Playa de Migjorn
Tel: 629.040.265

Tanga
Playa de Levante
Tel: 971.187.905
restaurantetanga.com

Voga Marí
Playa de Migjorn
Tel: 971.329.053
vogamari.es

SLEEP/DORMIR

Apartamentos Pueblo Balear
Playa de Migjorn
Tel: 610 07 23 68

Bungalows Es Pins
Ctra. De Ca Mari,
Playa de Migjorn
Tel: 971.328.291
espins.es

Casa Serena
Playa de Migjorn, Km. 8,9
Tel: 618.104.170
casaserenaformentera.com

Es Pas
Playa de Migjorn
Tel: 687.807.819

Es Marès
C/. de Santa María,
Sant Francesc
Tel: 971.323.216
hotelesmares.com

Formentera Chic
Avda. Mediterráneo, 2,
La Savina
Tels: 611.279.474
formenterachic.com

Gecko Beach Club
Playa de Migjorn,
Ca Mari
Tel: 971.328.024
geckobeachclub.com

Hostal La Savina
Av. Mediterranea, 22-40
La Savina
Tel: 971.322.279
hostal-lasavina.com

Hostal Sa Roqueta
Playa de Sa Roqueta,
Levante
Tel: 971.328.506

Hotel Cala Saona
Playa Cala Saona
Tel: 971.322.030
hotelcalasaona.com

Hotel Lago Dorado
Camí de Can Marroig
Tel: 971.321.261

Las Banderas
Playa de Migjorn, Km 18,7
Tel: 971.321.896

Las Dunas Playa
Playa dc Migjorn, Km. 11
Tel: 971.328.041
dunasplaya.com

Sa Vinya
C/Punta Prima, 37,
Es Pujols
Tel: 971.328.347

Ses Eufabietes
Playa de Migjorn
Tel: 971. 322.595
seseufabietes.com

CAMPING

Bell Tent Ibiza
Mark: 687123216
Ayelen: 630.225.174
belltentibiza.com

Camping La Playa
Cala Martina
Tel: 971.338.525
campingibizalaplaya.com

Camping Es Cana
Avda. D'es Canar, 68
Tel: 971.332.117
campingescana.com

Camping Cala Bassa
Cala Bassa, San José
Tel: 971.344.599
+
Carrer 19, Port des
Torrent - San Antonio
Tel: 971.347.469
campingsonline.com

Camping Cala Nova
Playa de Cala Nova,
Es Canar
Tel: 971.331.774
campingcalanova.com

Camping San Antonio
San Antonio
Tel: 633.527.181
camping-sanantonio.com

CULTURE

Aquarium Cap Blanc
Ctra. de Cala Gració,
San Antonio
Tel: 663.945.475
aquariumcapblanc.com

La Cova de Can Marçà
Puerto de San Miguel.
Tel: 971.334.776
covadecanmarsa.com

Museu d'Art Contemporani d'Eivissa (MACE)
Ronda Narcís Puget s/n.
Dalt Vila, Ibiza.
Tel: 971.302.723

Museo de Etnografía
Santa Eulalia
Can Ros des Puig de
Missa,
Santa Eulària des Riu.
Tel: 971.332.845 -
971.338.154

Museu Puget Ibiza
C/ Major, 18, Ibiza,
Tel: 971.392.137

Necrópolis Puig Des Molins Ibiza
Vía Romana, 31, Ibiza
Tel: 971.301.771

NOTES